THE GREATEST WORKS OF
HAL LINDSEY

•

THE LATE GREAT PLANET EARTH

•

SATAN IS ALIVE AND WELL ON PLANET EARTH

THE GREATEST WORKS OF
HAL LINDSEY

•

THE LATE GREAT PLANET EARTH

•

SATAN IS ALIVE AND WELL ON PLANET EARTH

Published in 1994 by

Inspirational Press
A division of Budget Book Service, Inc.
386 Park Avenue South
New York, NY 10016

Inspirational Press is a registered trademark of Budget Book Service, Inc.

Published by arrangement with Zondervan Publishing House.

Library of Congress Catalog Card Number: 94-77189

ISBN: 0-88486-104-X

Printed in the United States of America.

CONTENTS

THE
LATE GREAT
PLANET EARTH   1

SATAN IS
ALIVE & WELL
ON PLANET EARTH   159

THE
LATE GREAT
PLANET EARTH

O O O o o o O O O O

CONTENTS

Introduction   5

1   Future Tense   7

2   When Is a Prophet a Prophet?   13

3   Do We Really Live and Learn?   19

4   Israel, O Israel   31

5   Russia Is a Gog   45

6   Sheik to Sheik   57

7   The Yellow Peril   65

8   Rome on the Revival Road   71

9   The Future Fuehrer   79

10   Revival of Mystery Babylon   93

11   The Ultimate Trip   109

12   World War III   119

13   The Main Event   137

14   Polishing the Crystal Ball   147

Notes   155

ACKNOWLEDGMENTS

Grateful appreciation is extended to the following for permission to quote from their copyrighted materials:

LIFE Magazine: From *Reminiscences*, by General Douglas MacArthur, *Life* Magazine, © 1964 Time Inc.

THE LOCKMAN FOUNDATION. For Scriptures from *The New American Standard Bible, New Testament.* © 1960, 1962, 1963 by The Lockman Foundation.

NATIONAL COUNCIL OF THE CHURCHES OF CHRIST. For Scriptures from *The Revised Standard Version of the Bible.* © 1952, 1956 by The Division of Christian Education, National Council of Churches of Christ in the United States of America.

SIMON & SCHUSTER, INC. For quote from *Has Man a Future?* by Bertrand Russell. © 1962 by Simon & Schuster, Inc.

VAN NOSTRAND REINHOLD CO. For quotes from *China: Emerging World Power* by Victor Petrov. © 1967 by Litton Educational Publishing, Inc., by permission of Van Nostrand Reinhold Co.

ZONDERVAN PUBLISHING HOUSE. For Scriptures from *The Amplified Bible: The Amplified Old Testament* © 1962, 1964 by Zondervan Publishing House. *The Amplified New Testament* © 1958 by The Lockman Foundation.

INTRODUCTION

THIS IS A book about prophecy—Bible prophecy. If you have no interest in the future, this isn't for you. If you have no curiosity about a subject that some consider controversial, you might as well stop now.

For the past thirteen years I have been giving messages on Bible prophecy throughout the United States, Canada and Mexico. The interest in this aspect of Bible study has been amazing, particularly in the past few years. People who are confronted with the state of the world today are eager to learn what the Best Seller has to say about the future. As a traveling speaker for Campus Crusade for Christ I had the opportunity to give messages on prophecy to thousands of people. These messages have consistently proven to be popular with every age group.

This is not a complex theological treatise, but a direct account of the most thrilling, optimistic view of what the future could hold for any individual. I make no claim of knowing exactly when the world is going to end. In fact, I have never taken to the hills with my possessions and loved ones to await Doomsday. I believe in a hope for the future.

We have been described as the "searching generation." We need so many answers—answers to the larger problems of the world, answers to the conditions in our nation, and most of all, answers for ourselves.

How do we know in what direction we should go? How can we separate truth from opinion? In whom can we trust?

On one side we hear that the answer to our dilemma is education. Build bigger and better schools, hire more teachers, develop a smarter generation. Has the academic community found the answers? There are many students who are dissatisfied with being told that the sole purpose of education is to develop inquiring minds. They want to find some of the answers to their questions—solid answers, a certain direction.

What do the politicians say? "We have the solutions to the problems. Elect us and we'll prove it to you."

I am not downgrading the importance of electing honest, intelligent men to positions of leadership. This is important, terribly important, but are they able to provide the answers to the basic and visceral questions of man?

Throughout history we have seen impressive strides taken by men who were stepping ahead of their time. We have seen reforms advanced from ideas generated by men of vision. And yet governments change, men falter and fall, great ideas are sometimes rejected by the shortsightedness of other men. Are we able to say that the answer is in the realm of political action?

There are other places men search for answers: philosophy, meditation, changing environment, science. Please don't misunderstand me, all of these are good if used properly. However, if we are to be absolutely honest, if we are to use our intellectual integrity, let's give God a chance to present His views.

In this book I am attempting to step aside and let the prophets speak. If my readers care to listen, they are given the freedom to accept or reject the conclusions.

Hal Lindsey

1 ∘ Future Tense

We believe whatever we want to believe.   DEMOSTHENES, 348 B.C.

IT WAS A perfect night for a party. In the warm California evening the lemon trees perfumed the patio and the flickering Tiki torches cast shadows over a lavish table. The aroma of steaks sizzling on the barbecue grill was tantalizing and we were wishing someone would give the signal to eat.

To our dismay we discovered that no one else was outside. We were alone . . . with our appetites.

Crushed in a tight circle in the overheated living room were most of the guests, waiting rather impatiently for the fortune teller to read their palms. One by one they would eagerly hold out their hands, knowing they would hear flatteries, but hoping there would be some half-truth about themselves which would give them a mental uplift—an egobuilder to tell the boys at the office or the girls at the bridge table.

And so it has been from the beginning of time. People have been obsessed with the desire to know what is going to happen in the future.

From kings and rulers to servants and slaves, rich, poor, lowly and mighty people have called upon wizards, prophets, seers, magicians, the stars and the moon for powers and signs beyond the understanding of the human mind.

Astrology originated in ancient Chaldea, in the region around the Persian Gulf. All the proud kings of Chaldea, and later Babylon, had staff astrologers to advise them concerning the future.

The Greek father of historians, Herodotus, speaks of the incredible city of Babylon and mentions the enormous ziggurat from which the astrologers tracked the stars. The ruins of several of these "observatories" called ziggurats have been uncovered in the area of ancient Babylon by twentieth-century archaeologists. Obviously astrologers were VIP's in Babylon.

The Pharaohs of Egypt imported the knowledge of astrology and magic from Babylon. Some scholars have said that the Pharaohs constructed certain parts of the pyramids to line up with the stars.

The importance or position of a man has nothing to do with his superstitious concerns. Julius Caesar was the greatest of Roman leaders, and yet depended upon "augurs" for prophetic advice. An augur is a soothsayer or fortuneteller. In ancient Rome there was an official high-ranking government group, probably similar to our State Department, which was called

the "Board of Augurs." The great Roman orator, Cicero, was a member of
this board. However, it has been said that although Cicero took his duties
seriously since he was a man of great loyalty to his country, he privately
considered some of the augurs' prophecies to be absurd.

Caesar depended upon "signs in the sky" to conduct affairs of state and
rule the mighty Roman empire. As the leader of the people, he set the
example for his fellow Romans to become obsessed with horoscopes.

Many strange customs have been followed in determining the course of
people and nations. Decisions of marriage and journeys, wars and alliances,
have sometimes been made because special court seers read certain signs
of omens from the entrails of a chicken!

Starry Eyed

Many people today are discovering astrology again. Popping up on the
newsstands are so many pamphlets and books about the stars that one
would almost think it was a new phenomenon. The hippy musical, *Hair*,
has its own staff astrologer to advise the cast on personal matters and make
sure the circumstances are right for business. One of the most popular songs
of the moment is "Aquarius."

Astrology is having the greatest boom in its history. All you have to do
is look in almost any newspaper to find out from one of the syndicated stargazers what your forecast is for the day. Columns on the subject now run
in 1,220 of the 1,750 dailies in the United States.[1]

Writers have taken astrology and applied it to almost everything one can
imagine. There is *Astrology Made Practical, Astrology Made Easy, Astrology for
Everyday Living, Astrology Guide to Health and Diet*, and even *Astrology Guide
to Your Sex Life*.

A few years ago Bing Crosby starred in a movie in which one of his songs
contained the words, "Have you heard . . . it's in the stars . . .?" There was
something prophetic about that song!

Astrologers frequently guard their trade by predicting in generalities.
However, sometimes they venture beyond vagaries and are explicit in attempting to foretell exact happenings. The result may be acute embarrassment for the astrologer.

For instance, in a national publication of 1968 an article was featured that
quoted a "renowned astrologer" in her predictions about the upcoming elections in November of that year. By reading the stars this astrologer said that
Rockefeller would be the next president of the United States, and either
Ronald Reagan or John Lindsey would be vice-president. As for Hubert

Humphrey, she stated, "I've studied his chart very carefully and do not believe he will be considered as a serious contender even for the second slot on the Democratic ticket."[2]

These political gentlemen may or may not have been disappointed by the outcome of the elections of 1968, but the astrologer was probably a bit chagrined.

On Prophecy

Two hundred years ago a distinguished English statesman, Horace Walpole, said, "The wisest prophets make sure of the event first."

Many people would probably dispute that statement and draw attention to some of our famous contemporary prophets. There was Edgar Cayce, for instance, who was called America's "sleeping clairvoyant." Cayce spoke of future events while in a self-imposed hypnotic trance. He gave personal readings to guide the vocations and health and personal relationships of hundreds of persons. However, he went beyond individuals and prophesied the reversal in Japan's attitude of friendship for the U.S. before World War II, certain battles which would take place during that war, and the increase in racial tension in America.

However, Cayce's special contribution to the realm of psychic phenomena extended beyond mere prophecy. He advised others on how to develop this psychic ability, how to interpret dreams, where to find peace, and many other subjects. His telepathic statements, made during this hypnotic sleep-state, have been indexed, catalogued, and preserved by a special research society in Virginia. Although he has been dead for more than twenty years, when we called the local library to locate some of his books we were told that they were all checked out and we would have to be put on a waiting list.

What about the popularity of Jeane Dixon? Her books and articles have become national best-sellers. She has fascinated and astounded heads of nations with her uncanny skills of perception.

President Franklin Delano Roosevelt consulted Mrs. Dixon. At the height of his concern over the world crises, and plagued by his own ill health, he sought her advice. In the company of other national leaders of the past, Roosevelt sought to find out what the future would be from someone who possessed special uncanny ability to prophesy.

Jeane Dixon told President Roosevelt that eventually the U.S. would be allied with Russia against Red China. However, she warned FDR not to give Russia anything that wasn't ours to give. The president, however, evidently did not heed this advice, for it was not long afterward that the Yalta conference was held and FDR concluded a secret agreement with Russia to give the USSR certain territory which has remained under her domination ever since.

Mrs. Dixon has made some predictions which have had striking fulfillments. She sent word, it is reported, to the late President Kennedy prior to his trip to Dallas, warning him that he would be killed there. She also predicted several years ago that we would have a Republican president elected in 1968.

By her own admission, however, Mrs. Dixon says she is not infallible. For instance, she predicted that Red China would plunge the world into war over Quemoy and Matsu in October of 1958. (If you can't remember that far back, this did not happen.) She thought Walter Reuther would actively seek the presidency in 1964. (He didn't.)

High Spirits

Spiritualism and mysticism are weaving their spells among all age groups. We saw a handsomely illustrated magazine recently that featured "Prophecy, ESP news, psychic experiences, and spiritual healing." Provocative advertising included "Communications from the Sun World," and a new book which reveals "how they live in another dimension that is only an instant away from rapport with Earth."

It is a mystic time. Famous movie stars and wealthy socialites are traveling to the countries of the Far East to consult with "holy men." The influence of spiritualism in our popular songs, jewelry, and even clothing, is obvious. We received an invitation recently from an Indian spiritualist who says she "advises on all affairs of life." She also has a guarantee (money back?) to remove evil influences and bad luck from anyone who consults her.

The spirits are running in religious circles, also. A famous bishop, now deceased, stimulated interest in psychic phenomena by his communications with his dead son.

In churches and on college campuses mediums are receiving speaking invitations. The writer of a religious column in a Los Angeles paper recently reported, "Suffering from religious persecution and occasions of fakery in the ranks since its beginnings in the mid-1800s, the spiritualist movement in America is gaining new confidence today."[3]

In the field of higher education there are more than forty colleges which now conduct psychic research under the title of parapsychology. The interest in these subjects is growing in proportion to the increase in astrology and prophecy.

C'est la Vie

"The future" is big business. Frenchmen, for instance, spend more than a billion dollars a year on clairvoyants, gypsies, faith healers, seers and prophets. In Paris there is "one charlatan for every 120 Parisians, compared with one doctor for every 514 citizens and one priest for every 5,000."[4]

If you want to hear what the future has in store for you, perhaps you should see your travel agent for the fastest way to France. But try to avoid the need for a doctor or a priest—their services are rather scarce.

Escape

We were on the campus of a large university talking with some students in the comfortable lounge of one of the dormitories when we noticed a very attractive girl hesitate in the doorway. She stood for a few moments, her eyes glancing vacantly around the room, and then darted out as if she were being chased by demons. "What on earth do you think was wrong with her?" I asked my companions.

"Probably her vibrations were wrong," answered one young man. "She might have thought there was someone or something in here that was a threat. Who knows?"

Vibrations, spirits, stars, prophets—what an absorbing interest we have today in the unknown, the unseen and the future.

In our imaginations we long to step out of our humdrum existence and into worlds beyond. Take science fiction as an example. It fascinates us. We read books from the serious to the comic about men with miraculous powers of vision or perception. We sit with fascination before our television sets as we are transported out of the present and into the tomorrows.

Tell It Like It Will Be

In talking with thousands of persons, particularly college students, from every background and religious or irreligious upbringing, this writer found that most people want reassurance about the future. For many of them their hopes, ambitions, and plans are permeated with the subconscious fear that perhaps there will be no future at all for mankind.

This is a natural and prevalent attitude. Looking at the world today, it seems to be on a collision course. As the headline expressed it in a recent news magazine—"The World in a Mess."

People are searching for answers to basic questions. It is like the two young men who went into a book store and asked for "a book on the philosophy of truth." The clerk was flustered and very apologetic. She didn't want to discourage them, but she said they were asking for the impossible.

I wish I had been in that book store. It would have been so simple to walk over to a rather prominent display and pull out the Book that generations of readers have believed contains the "philosophy of truth." It not only contains truth, but also the great themes of peace, love, and hope, which are the desires of this and every other generation.

However, compared to the speculation of most that is called prophetic today, the Bible contains clear and unmistakable prophetic signs. We are able to see right now in this Best Seller predictions made centuries ago being fulfilled before our eyes.

The Bible makes fantastic claims; but these claims are no more startling than those of present day astrologers, prophets and seers. Furthermore, the claims of the Bible have a greater basis in historical evidence and fact. Bible prophecy can become a sure foundation upon which your faith can grow— and there is no need to shelve your intellect while finding this faith.

We believe there is a hope for the future, in spite of the way the world looks today. We believe that a person can be given a secure and yet exciting view of his destiny by making an honest investigation of the tested truths of Bible prophecy.

2 ○ When is a Prophet a Prophet?

Men's curiosity searches past and future.—   T. S. ELIOT

WHAT WOULD YOU think of prophets today who would be willing to stake their lives on the absolute truth of their claims? They could not allow themselves errors in judgment or mistakes in the smallest detail.

There were such prophets. They were daring men, sure of the source of their faith and strong in their belief. There is a book which boldly documents the statements of these men.

They are known as the prophets of Israel and their writings have been miraculously preserved in the Bible.

Passing the Test

Are we able to trust these old prophets? What were their credentials? In a book of the Old Testament, Deuteronomy, Moses predicted that there would be many prophets who would come to the Jewish people, culminating in the final and greatest of all prophets, the Messiah.

Moses anticipated a problem. How would people know whether a prophet who claimed to speak God's message was a true prophet? A question was asked of Moses which is still being asked today. "How may we know the word which the LORD has not spoken?" (Deuteronomy 18:21).

And Moses gave the answer—the true test of a prophet: "When a prophet speaks in the name of the LORD, if the word does not come to pass or come true, that is a word which the LORD has not spoken" (Deuteronomy 18:22).

Failure to pass the test of a true prophet was a bit severe. The only grade allowed was one of 100 percent accuracy. Anything less would doom the prophet to death by stoning, which was the method of capital punishment in those days (Deuteronomy 13:1-11).

A Greek proverb says that the best guesser is the best prophet. If the prophets of Israel had been simply "guessers," they would have had to take the cruel consequences—a slow and torturous death inflicted by flying stones.

The prophets of Israel also pointed out to their people causes of current problems. This is never very popular; true prophets would not be likely to win the "Most Beloved Citizen" award in their home town.

They not only made short-range predictions which would be fulfilled during their lifetimes, but also projected long-range predictions about events far in the future. Often they didn't understand the significance of their own prophecies (I Peter 1:10-12). However, many of these prophecies are predictions of exact historical happenings which will lead to the end of history as we know it.

The astonishing thing to those of us who have studied the prophetic Scriptures is that we are watching the fulfillment of these prophecies in our time. Some of the future events that were predicted hundreds of years ago read like today's newspaper.

Let's examine some selected Bible prophecies and apply the test of truth to them.

Accurate Short-range Prophecy

Jeremiah, a prophet of Israel, was not vague in his prophecies. He told his people that Judah, the southern kingdom of Israel, would be invaded and destroyed by Nebuchadnezzar, the King of Babylon. It was not a very cheerful prophecy, and Jeremiah probably didn't receive a standing ovation.

He said that King Nebuchadnezzar would destroy the land, that it would be desolate (Jeremiah 25:9). Jeremiah was not the type to soft pedal; he prophesied that the capital city, Jerusalem, would be destroyed and that its people would lose their capacity to laugh.

After he presented this miserable picture, Jeremiah foretold that any Jewish survivors would be carried off to Babylon as slaves. To compound the complexity of these predictions, he said that the Israelites would be Babylonian slaves for precisely seventy years (Jeremiah 25:11).

At this point Jeremiah would probably have won a contest for "The Man Least Likely to Succeed" in Israel. In fact, he made Pashur, one of the religious leaders of the time, so furious that Pashur beat him and put him in stocks (Jeremiah 20:2).

Archaeology and ancient history confirm the fulfillment of Jeremiah's prophecy. Jerusalem was destroyed, Judah was laid waste, and her people were taken captive in Babylon for seventy years.

Why did the Jewish people preserve the messages of Jeremiah? These messages which foretold of their defeat and captivity were an indictment against them. It was because Jeremiah passed the test of a prophet which was established by Moses. As despised as Jeremiah was by his contemporaries, they did not dare destroy what they believed were God's words.

Jeremiah was such a bearer of sad tidings that even today we speak of complaints as "jeremiads."

An Arrow in the Armor

One of the lesser-known men of God who achieved a straight "A" in prophetic marksmanship was Micaiah. However, this was not a time when such perfection was awarded with a gold pin and guard, or a seal on Micaiah's diploma. On the contrary, he was thrown into prison and fed bread and water. What did he do to deserve such treatment?

Micaiah lived at a time when a good king, Jehoshaphat, was reigning in the southern kingdom of Judah. In the northern kingdom of Israel ruled Ahab, a wicked king.

For some reason Jehoshaphat visited Ahab, who immediately tried to persuade him to join forces against a troublesome Syrian enemy from an area called Ramoth-Gilead.

Ahab gathered his own special prophets together—we might call them members of his Inner Security Council—and asked them whether he should go to battle against Ramoth-gilead or not. The 400 prophets were so soothing to Ahab that they should be called the "soothsayers" of his kingdom. They all agreed, without dissenting opinions, that Ahab should go into battle and that God would bring him through triumphantly.

But Jehoshaphat was not satisfied with the advice of these "prophets" in spite of their unanimous agreement. He said, "Is there not here another prophet of the LORD (Israel's God) of whom we may inquire?" (I Kings 22:7).

We can imagine how petulant Ahab must have been when he replied, "There is yet one man by whom we may inquire of the LORD, Micaiah the son of Imlah; but I hate him, for he never prophesies good concerning me, but evil" (I Kings 22:8).

Jehoshaphat insisted that Micaiah be consulted, so an officer was sent to bring him in. When the officer found him he tried to persuade the prophet to be a good fellow and go along with Ahab's "Inner Security Council" and tell the king what he wanted to hear. But Micaiah replied, "As the LORD lives, what the LORD says to me, that I will speak" (I Kings 22:14).

He realized as he said this that he was putting his life on the line.

When Micaiah was brought before the two kings, Ahab asked him if they should attack Ramoth-gilead. Micaiah answered in what must have been a tongue-in-cheek manner, "Sure, go on and win . . . the Lord will give it into your hands."

Ahab knew he was being ridiculed and commanded the prophet to say what was really on his mind. In answering, Micaiah showed the boldness that characterized a true prophet. First, he labeled all of the 400 "court prophets" as liars. Then he predicted that Ahab would be killed in the battle and that the Israeli army would be routed.

The chief of the false prophets—Ahab's "Chairman of the Security Council"—walked up and slugged Micaiah, probably with the same premonition of fear that made Pashur, the Israeli religious leader, take a whack at Jeremiah.

So Micaiah went to jail and Ahab went to battle. But first Micaiah challenged all the people to witness his grade on the test of a prophet. He said, "If you (meaning Ahab) return in peace, the LORD has not spoken by me" (I Kings 22:28).

Ahab wasn't going to take any chances with this pessimistic prophet, Micaiah, so he disguised himself during the big battle. But one of the enemy archers shot an arrow labeled "to whom it may concern" and in the most amazing and coincidental manner it struck Ahab in one small exposed place in his armor and killed him.

Micaiah passed the test of a true prophet. Ahab and all of his "yes men" flunked.

What Do You Say, Isaiah?

One of the most astounding prophets of all time was Isaiah, the son of Amoz. His brilliant, eloquent, even poetical predictions were made over a sixty-year span (740-680 B.C.) during the reign of four successive Judaean kings.

Isaiah proved himself a prophet by Moses' test many times. One striking incident was during the reign of King Hezekiah. In about 710 B.C. a mighty Assyrian army, numbering in the thousands and commanded by the vicious King Sennacherib besieged Jerusalem (Isaiah 36:1, 2).

(If you stumble over some of these unpronounceable ancient names, glance at your daily newspaper and notice the tongue twisters assigned to people today.)

Sennacherib was a crafty fellow. He sent his eloquent "mouthpiece," a fellow named Rabshakeh, to the people of Jerusalem with a powerful propaganda speech. Rabshakeh, an ancient "Minister of Misinformation," told the people of all the defeats suffered by neighboring countries. This was brainwashing in the craftiest sense. The techniques used were intended to induce the besieged citizens of Jerusalem to surrender without a fight.

When King Hezekiah heard how his people were being intimidated, he sent a delegation to Isaiah to plead with him to pray to Jehovah, the God of Israel. Isaiah then made some short-range predictions. He said that a rumor would reach King Sennacherib of internal trouble in his kingdom and that he would return without attacking Jerusalem. Furthermore, he said that Sennacherib would be assassinated in his own land.

It happened just as Isaiah predicted. Jerusalem was spared a certain defeat and King Sennacherib was killed by his own sons (Isaiah 37:36-38).

Isaiah Predicts One Hundred Years in the Future

Isaiah also predicted that Babylon would completely destroy Judah and carry away all the treasures of Israel. He foretold that the surviving sons of the royal family would be eunuchs in the palace of Babylon. This occurred just a little over one hundred years later (Isaiah 39:5-7).

One Hundred and Fifty Years in the Future

Isaiah gave an incredible prediction when he foretold that the mighty invincible Babylonians would be conquered and so completely destroyed by the Medes that Babylon would never be inhabited again (Isaiah 13:17-22).

This was an astonishing prediction at that time since the city of Babylon became one of the seven wonders of the ancient world and was considered impregnable. Yet approximately 150 years after Isaiah's prediction the Medes and Persians besieged the towering walls of Babylon. This was no small feat. Those walls were 150 feet high and so thick that five chariots · could run abreast around the top.

The Medes and Persians were cunning. They dammed the Euphrates River which ran under the Babylonian wall and through the city. While Babylon was celebrating at a drunken royal ball, the Median army marched along the dry river bed under the wall and conquered the city. This was the very night that "the handwriting on the wall" appeared to the arrogant Babylonian king. It read, "Mene, mene, tekel, upharsin." Daniel, the prophet, deciphered it to the drunken mob as follows: "Your kingdom has been weighed in the balance and found wanting. It is divided and given to the Medes and Persians." That night the Babylonian kingdom fell (Daniel 5:1-31).

Two Hundred Years in the Future

Isaiah predicted that a certain king named Cyrus would see that Jerusalem and the Temple were rebuilt by allowing those who wished to do this work to return to the land of their ancestors (Isaiah 44:28–45:4).

Almost 200 years after this prediction a certain Persian king also named Cyrus, granted royal favor to the Jewish captives left over from Babylon and sent them to Jerusalem with a requisition for materials to rebuild the city (Ezra 1:1-11).

The Prophet Preserved

Many so-called Biblical scholars today try to "late date" such predictions as Isaiah's to make his prophecies seem to be after the fact. To do this not only violates the consistent witness of the history of those times, but also makes the Jewish people religious charlatans and deceivers. The Jews would have had no reason to keep for posterity those writings of the prophets if they were a fraud.

The Israeli prophets were not popular, as we have shown. In the times of Jeremiah, Micaiah, Isaiah, and the others, the odds were against anything they wrote or said being accepted. Yet they were preserved above all the other writings of their day.

What made these prophets so special? The answer lies in the test of a true prophet which Moses gave—their prophecies must all come true. They could not be ignored. We cannot ignore them. They passed the test—summa cum laude.

3 ∘ Do We Really Live and Learn?

History teaches us that man learns nothing from history. HEGEL

IT'S IRONIC THAT man never seems to learn from past mistakes, especially when they relate to major catastrophes. World War I was called the war to end all wars, yet within a generation World War II was fought in basically the same arena. We are now running around the world desperately seeking to put out fuses which could explode into what might be the last war on earth.

Through the grim pages of history we see the record of man's constant struggle to live with his fellow man. Families fight against families, tribes against tribes, and nations against nations. Most people hate war, and yet since recorded time the world has seldom seen peace.

General Douglas MacArthur said, "Men since the beginning of time have sought peace... military alliances, balances of power, leagues of nations, all in turn failed, leaving the only path to be by way of the crucible of war. The utter destructiveness of war now blots out this alternative."[1]

Mankind has not learned the futility of war from history. However, as tragic as this is, there is another lesson, even more tragic, which has not been heeded. This involves a people whose most cherished hope had been the coming of their great Deliverer, called the Messiah.

The central theme of the Jewish prophets was that "the Messiah" would come and fulfill the promises given to their forefathers, Abraham, Isaac, and Jacob. In these promises Israel is to be the leading nation of the world under the reign of the Messiah who would bring universal peace, prosperity, and harmony among all peoples of the earth.

The paradox is that there has come a Jew who claimed to be the Messiah. He fulfilled many of the ancient predictions, but was rejected by those who should have recognized Him first. The question is this: If He was truly the long-awaited Messiah, as millions have believed, why didn't the majority of the religious leaders of His day believe His claims? These religious leaders, after all, knew the Messianic predictions. Ignorance was not their excuse. The reasons they didn't believe Him are fascinating and extremely relevant to this hour of history in which we live.

Two Portraits

Two completely different portraits of a coming Messiah were described by the Old Testament prophets. The portraits, painted by the sure hand of God, were placed on the same canvas, framed in one picture.

For those who lived prior to the birth of Jesus of Nazareth, the perspective of these two portraits of the Messiah was difficult to understand.

Imagine a man looking at a range of mountains. He is able to see the peak of one mountain, and beyond it the peak of another. However, from this vantage point, he cannot see the valley which separates these two mountains.

Men viewed the two portraits of the Messiah in the same manner. They saw two different persons, but missed the connection. They did not perceive that there could be just one Messiah, coming in two different roles, and separated by the valley of time.

One portrait of the Messiah depicts Him as a humble servant who would suffer for others and be rejected by His own countrymen. This portrait we may call "the Suffering Messiah." (Look into the prophecies of Isaiah 53 for the perfect picture of this Messiah.)

The other portrait shows the Messiah as a conquering king with unlimited power, who comes suddenly to earth at the height of a global war and saves men from self-destruction. He places the Israelites who believe in Him as the spiritual and secular leaders of the world and brings in an age free of prejudice and injustice. It's easy to see why this would be the most popular portrait.

We may call this second picture "the Reigning Messiah." We find this description in such prophecies as Zechariah 14 and Isaiah 9:6, 7.

These two portraits of the Messiah presented such a paradox that the rabbis at least a century before Jesus of Nazareth was born theorized that there would be two messiahs. They could not see how both portraits could be true of the same person. Their misunderstanding led them to believe that the suffering one would deliver the people from their sins by bearing the penalty of death for them. He would be primarily a "Spiritual Deliverer." The reigning king would conquer Israel's enemies and bring world peace. He would be primarily a "Political Deliverer."

The Big Question

Why did the majority of the Jewish people, who knew the teachings of their prophets, reject Jesus of Nazareth as their Messiah when He came? Why did they ignore the portraits of the suffering Messiah? Jesus Himself pointed out to them Old Testament predictions concerning His life and ministry which were being fulfilled in His life.

First of all, the Jews didn't take their prophets literally as far as this suffering Messiah was concerned. They took very literally the portrait of the Messiah who would come as the reigning King. However, they had degenerated in their own religious convictions to the point where they didn't believe they were sinful. They believed they were keeping the law of Moses; therefore, they saw no need for a suffering Messiah to deliver them from their sins.

The Jewish religious leaders had built up a tradition of interpretation which made keeping God's laws merely an external thing (Mark 7:1-15). Jesus, however, pointed out the true meaning of God's law in the Sermon on the Mount. He showed that murder was not just refraining from actually killing someone, but that it was being angry with your neighbor without just cause (Matthew 5:21, 22). He also pointed out that adultery in God's sight was merely looking at a woman with lust (Matthew 5:27-32).

He expounded the real meaning of "love your neighbor as yourself" as applying to your enemies as well (Matthew 5:43-48).

With each commandment Jesus emphasized the false interpretation of the religious leaders and contrasted it with the true meaning which God had always intended. He showed that God looks upon the heart and not just upon the outward performance of man.

I am sure that if you took the previous paragraph seriously you may feel a little uncomfortable right now. You may be saying to yourself what I said some years ago when the true meaning of the Ten Commandments was first pointed out to me. "Who in the world can be accepted by God if he is going to have to keep the law in his thoughts and motives?"

If this is what you are thinking, congratulations! You have just discovered the whole purpose for the law of Moses. The commandments were never intended to be used to work our way to God. The commandments were primarily given to show us how perfect we would have to be in order to earn acceptance with God by our own good deeds. This is why God says to us, "Whoever keeps the whole law and yet stumbles in one point, he has become guilty of all" (James 2:10 NASB).

It is easy to see in the light of this why the Bible says, ". . . by the works of the Law no flesh (man) will be justified in His (God's) sight" (Romans 3:20 NASB).

The law was given to show mankind why it needed a "suffering Messiah" who alone could make man acceptable to God. Any person who hasn't come to see that his most basic problem is an inner spiritual one prefers a political deliverer to a spiritual one. It is not difficult, therefore, to understand the basic attitude which rationalized away the prophetic portrait of the suffering Messiah.

Jesus presented His credentials as the suffering Messiah, but many rejected Him because they were looking for a great conqueror. They were looking for that political leader who would deliver them from the Roman oppression. In their blindness they discounted more than *300 specific predictions* in their own sacred writings about this Messiah.

The second reason why the Jewish people rejected the Messiah was one of indifference—an indifference to their spiritual need. They couldn't be bothered. They were too busy. They had a chariot race or a party to attend. Caught in the treadmill of daily existence, the deeper needs of the inner self weren't important.

In addition, they didn't bother to do any investigation for themselves. Many knew there was something unusual about this carpenter from Nazareth, but their religious leaders rejected Him and they took their opinions instead of searching for the truth themselves.

It was because people will not do their own research that Jesus made an astounding statement on the signs of the times. He showed simply and clearly how prophecies were being fulfilled by His life. And yet, to the sorrow of many, He was ignored.

Signs of the Times

The religious leaders of His day were the number one skeptics. They came to Jesus and asked Him to show them a sign from heaven. They wanted some sensational miracle which would give them proof that Jesus was their promised Messiah. They wanted Him to suddenly step out of the sky as the conquering Messiah (as He is revealed in Zechariah 14) and take over all the kingdoms of the world and defeat the Roman empire.

Jesus had already given them important signs to prove who He was. He had healed many persons and had raised at least one from the dead. But they didn't consider this sufficient evidence to prove His claim of being the Messiah.

Jesus answered these religious leaders by saying: "When it is evening, you say, 'It will be fair weather, for the sky is red.' And in the morning, 'It will be stormy today, for the sky is red and threatening.' You know how to interpret the appearance of the sky, but you cannot interpret the signs of the times" (Matthew 16:2, 3).

The signs of the times. It is important to see what Jesus was driving at. People in Palestine, even today, indulge in being amateur weather forecasters. Weather conditions are such that the particular signs given here are fair indications of what the weather will be.

Jesus said that the signs leading up to His coming were just as clear as the face of the sky. Let's examine these signs, these credentials. Let's look at specific predictions of how this man Jesus would come to fulfill the role of the Messiah, of how He would fit into the first portrait of the suffering Messiah.

The first theme of predictions relates to the circumstances of His birth. These were His credentials.

Birth Credentials: His Family

God revealed to Abraham, the father of all Jews, that he would have a direct descendant who would be a blessing to all the peoples of the earth (Genesis 12:1-3).

Furthermore, God revealed to Jacob, who was one of the descendants of Abraham, that the Messiah would come through one specific tribal state—the tribal state of Judah. The Jews established states in the land of Palestine after they took it over, and they were divided according to twelve families. These families originated from the twelve sons of Jacob (Genesis 49:10).

His family credentials were narrowed even more, from the tribe of Judah to the family of David. The prediction was given to David, the great king in the history of Israel, by the prophet, Nathan.

Nathan said, "Thus says the Lord of hosts. . . I will raise up your offspring after you, one of your own sons, and I will establish his kingdom. He shall build Me a house, and I will establish his throne for ever. I will be his father, and he shall be My Son. . ." (I Chronicles 17:11-13 Amplified).

King David was promised at least two exciting things here. First, one of his direct descendants would reign forever. Secondly, this person would not only be one of his direct descendants, but in a mysterious way He would be uniquely the Son of God.

Rabbinic tradition ascribed this to be a prediction of the Messiah. Consequently, one of the most common Messianic titles is "the Son of David."

Birth Credentials: The Place

The prophet Micah lived seven hundred years before the birth of Christ. He was a contemporary of the great prophet, Isaiah. It was revealed to Micah that the Messiah would be born in Bethlehem.

"But thou, Bethlehem Ephratah, though thou be little among the thousands of Judah, yet out of thee shall he come forth unto me that is to be ruler in Israel; whose goings forth have been from of old, from everlasting" (Micah 5:2 KJV).

This was a prophecy of the Messiah which was unmistakable because it referred to His eternal pre-existence. . . "whose goings forth have been from of old, from everlasting."

This was no ordinary man, but a supernatural person who would invade history from Bethlehem.

This prophecy is quoted in the New Testament in Matthew, in answer to Herod's question to the Hebrew theologians about where the Messiah would be born. They answered him: "In Bethlehem of Judea, for so it is written by the prophet" (Matthew 2:5).

How remarkable it is that century after century the Hebrew people handed down these detailed prophecies. They had to be revelations from God, otherwise they would not have been preserved in such a consistent manner.

Birth Credentials: The General Time

We have examined the prophecies concerning the family line of the Messiah and the place of His birth. Let's look at the time factor.

The prophet Daniel, while in captivity in Babylon, was given a precise timetable and sequence relating to the future events of the people of Israel. Daniel was told that there would be a certain number of years which would transpire between the time a proclamation was given which allowed the Jewish people to return from their Babylonian captivity back to Israel and the coming of the Messiah.

This proclamation can be established according to Scriptural history in Nehemiah 2:1-10. Also, archaeologists have uncovered evidence of this same proclamation in the ancient Persian archives.

From the time permission was given to return and rebuild the city of Jerusalem and the Temple until the Messiah would come as the Prince, the heir-apparent to the throne of David, would be 483 years (69 weeks of years—483 years). Sir Robert Anderson of Scotland Yard spent many years of his life verifying and validating the details of this prophecy. He wrote a comprehensive book of his study called, *The Coming Prince*.

Not only was Daniel given specific years, but also a sequence of major historical events which cannot be denied.

First of all, there was the proclamation given to the Jews to return from captivity and rebuild the Temple.

After that, the Messiah would come as the Prince.

Then the Messiah would be "cut off," which is an idiom for being killed.

After the Messiah was killed an army would sweep in and destroy the city and the Temple which was rebuilt previously by the returned Babylonian exiles (Daniel 9).

Daniel's prophecy shows that whoever the Messiah was He had to appear before the city and the Temple were destroyed in A.D. 70 by Titus of Rome.

There was only one person who was taken seriously as the Messiah before A.D. 70. We have the logical candidate for that role in the carpenter from Nazareth.

Credentials Relating to His Ministry

We have considered a panorama of Jesus' birth credentials to verify His claim as the Jewish Messiah. To pile proof upon proof, consider the prophecies relating to the deeds Jesus would do upon earth—prophecies about His own ministry.

The prophet Isaiah presented a vivid description of the coming Messiah when he said: "Say to those who are of a fearful heart, 'Be strong, fear not! Behold, your God will come with vengeance, with the recompense of God. He will come and save you.' Then the eyes of the blind shall be opened, and the ears of the deaf unstopped; then shall the lame man leap like a hart, and the tongue of the dumb sing for joy. For waters shall break forth in the wilderness, and streams in the desert" (Isaiah 35:4-6).

Jesus knew the Old Testament prophets. He quoted this exact prophecy from Isaiah when John the Baptist seemed to have some doubts about Him. John was the herald who announced the coming of Jesus as the Messiah, and yet even John could not reconcile the two portraits of the Messiah. When he was taken prisoner he sent some messengers to Jesus to ask, "Are You the Coming One, or shall we look for someone else?" (Matthew 11:3 NASB).

Jesus answered by quoting the predictions of the miracles He would perform. "Go and report to John the things which you hear and see: the blind receive sight and the lame walk, the lepers are cleansed and the deaf hear, and the dead are raised up, and the poor have the gospel preached to them" (Matthew 11:4, 5 NASB).

The fact that Jesus was performing these very miracles were His credentials to substantiate His claim that He was the Messiah.

Credentials Relating to His Rejection and Suffering

Probably the most phenomenal predictions relating to the suffering Messiah's portrait are the prophecies that show His rejection and suffering. One of the great passages on His rejection is Isaiah 53. This is called the "bad conscience of the synagogues" because it is no longer read in the temples on holy days, as it once was.

In Isaiah 52 there is a general look at this One who is called the servant of God. It is obvious here that the prophet is not talking about Israel, which in some passages is called the servant of God, but about one who would save Israel. "Behold, my servant, (Christ) shall prosper, he shall be exalted and lifted up, and shall be very high. As many were astonished at him— his appearance was so marred, beyond human semblance, and his form beyond that of the sons of men" (Isaiah 52:13, 14).

This was a reference to what happened at the trials of Jesus when He was repeatedly hit in the face. "So shall he startle many nations; kings shall shut their mouths because of him; for that which has not been told them they shall see, and that which they have not heard they shall understand" (Isaiah 52:15).

In this passage the prophet is saying that He would startle, or astound nations (meaning the non-Jews) and that they would see things they had never seen. The Gentiles, in other words, would begin to understand the ways of God.

However, Isaiah speaks of His rejection by the Jews, which in itself was remarkable since Isaiah was a Jewish prophet who wrote at least 700 years before Christ was born. Isaiah predicted that his people would reject the very one for whom they looked (Isaiah 53:1-3).

Notice an interesting fact. The prophet writes of this event in the past tense, which was a common literary device of the Jewish writers. . . ("many were astonished. . . his appearance was so marred"). When they wished to emphasize the certainty of a prophecy they would put it in this tense, which is called the prophetic perfect tense in Hebrew.

It was further prophesied here that the Jews would reject this Man because He didn't have the royal splendor they desired. Isaiah said He would be "despised and rejected," which is precisely what happened.

In this part of the prediction the credentials of the Messiah as a person who would be a substitute for the iniquity, or wickedness, of man are presented: "Surely he has borne our griefs and carried our sorrows; yet we esteemed him stricken, smitten by God, and afflicted. But he was wounded for our transgressions, he was bruised for our iniquities; upon him was the chastisement that made us whole, and with his stripes we are healed. All we like sheep have gone astray; we have turned every one to his own way; and the LORD has laid on him the iniquity of us all" (Isaiah 53:4-6).

Rabbis since the birth and death of Jesus of Nazareth have reinterpreted this passage to say that the third person singular pronoun does not refer to a personal Messiah, but to the nation of Israel. However, the passage speaks of this person as bearing the consequences of the transgressions of Israel. Israel could not be a substitute for itself, since the passage clearly states that the Lord hath laid on *Him* the iniquity of *us*.

Isaiah 53 continues to say that this person would not receive the true justice of the Jewish law. This, of course, was true during the trials of Jesus. They were astounded that He didn't try to defend Himself. . . "He was oppressed. . . yet he opened not his mouth" (Isaiah 53:7).

Again there is a clear prediction that the Messiah would die for the transgressions of Isaiah's people, as well, of course, as for the whole world. ". . . he was cut off (killed) out of the land of the living, stricken for the transgression of my people" (Isaiah 53:8b).

The details of prophecy relating to this portrait of the Messiah are exact. Isaiah says that He will die beside criminals. "And they made his grave with the wicked." His grave would be with the rich: "And with a rich man in his death" (Isaiah 53:9).

Did it happen? Of course. Jesus was crucified between two thieves. After His death one of the rich Pharisees, Joseph of Arimathaea, took pity on Him and buried Him in his own tomb. Joseph was the rich man predicted here.

We can picture Isaiah, standing at Calvary, looking at the panoramic view that Jesus saw and experienced on the cross. However, Isaiah saw this 700 years before Jesus was born!

To continue in this remarkable passage, Isaiah speaks of the fact that men could be declared righteous and acceptable to God because He bore their sins. In Biblical vernacular, this is the meaning of "justified."

Isaiah said that He "made intercession for the transgressors" (Isaiah 53:12). Most persons with only a slight exposure to Christian teaching will remember the words of Jesus from the cross when He said, "Father, forgive them; for they know not what they do."

Thirty Pieces of Silver

Another Old Testament prophet was Zechariah, who wrote almost 500 years before Jesus lived. In his book he gave another specific and minute prediction which could only refer to one person. He wrote: "And I said unto them, If ye think good, give me my price; and if not, forbear. So they weighed for my price thirty pieces of silver. And the LORD said unto me, Cast it unto the potter: a goodly price that I was prised at of them. And I took the thirty pieces of silver, and cast them to the potter in the house of the LORD" (Zechariah 11:12, 13 KJV).

Notice the three specific trends in this passage. First, there would be a time when the people would estimate their own God's worth at thirty pieces of silver. Then, these thirty pieces would be cast down in the house of the Lord, which is the Temple. Finally, the money would be given to the potter for the graves of the poor people.

Do you suppose any present-day "prophets" would dare make such an exact prediction?

It happened exactly as told. Matthew records this when he tells of Judas going to the chief priests who were plotting to murder Jesus and saying, "What will you give me if I deliver Jesus to you?" And the priests decided they would give thirty pieces of silver for the betrayal (Matthew 26:14, 15).

After Jesus was betrayed and Judas saw that Jesus was condemned to death, which was more severe than Judas had anticipated, he regretted what he had done. He went to the priests and tried to return the money, but the priests insulted him. Judas became infuriated. He threw the money down in the Temple (Matthew 27:3-5). (Prediction fulfilled.)

The priests took the money and piously said it wasn't proper to return to the treasury the price of the betrayal, so they decided to give it to the potter to buy a potter's field (Matthew 27:6-10). (Trying to ease their consciences, no doubt.)

Notice one very important point. Jesus had no control over this prophecy. It had to be fulfilled without any interference on His part. This fact explodes the major premise of a book which has gained some popularity, called The Passover Plot. While the writer of this book does a service by accepting the historical reality of Jesus, he claims that Jesus deliberately plotted to fulfill the predictions of the Messiah given in the Old Testament. This theory could not be valid because there is no way to explain how many predictions, such as the one about the thirty pieces of silver, could be fulfilled when the circumstances were out of Jesus' hands.

Predictions Relating to the Crucifixion

Jesus told His disciples that there were predictions of His suffering in the Psalms (Luke 24:44-46).

One of the clearest prophecies is found in Psalm 22, which was written by King David more than 1000 years before Christ. David describes events which could not have happened to himself since they were beyond the scope of his own experience.

The Psalms were accepted as the word of God and David was speaking "in the Spirit," as the ancient rabbinical schools recognized. The psalmist gives a detailed and precise prediction of a person being crucified. He speaks of the suffering of the Messiah as if he were on the cross with Him, feeling His pain, seeing the people and events around him. Speaking in the spirit of the Messiah, David says, "I am poured out like water"—he is speaking of the profuse perspiration of one hanging in the intense sun. "And all my bones are out of joint"—this is one of the most excruciating aspects of crucifixion. The ligaments stretch and the bones pop out of joint.

He tells of the intense thirst—"and my tongue cleaveth to my jaws." Jesus said on the cross, "I thirst."

"For dogs have compassed me: the assembly of the wicked have enclosed me: they pierced my hands and my feet. I may tell all my bones: they look and stare upon me. They part my garments among them, and cast lots upon my vesture" (Psalm 22:16-18 KJV).

"Dog" was a common slang expression the Jews used for the Gentiles— Jesus was surrounded by Gentiles at the crucifixion. He was crucified in the nude; this passage speaks of the shame of it. At the foot of the cross the soldiers gambled (or cast lots) for His robe.

As perfect as this passage is in its prophetic accuracy, it gains additional importance when we realize that crucifixion as a way of punishment was not known at the time David wrote this. The Jews of that time executed by stoning. It was not until about 200 B.C. when the Romans adopted this cruel practice that crucifixion was widely used—800 years after this prophecy.

Guaranteed Accuracy

If there is one thing that guarantees the historical accuracy of what the New Testament authors wrote it is the animosity of the Jewish people who crucified Jesus. The message of these prophecy fulfillments was spread by word of mouth all over the Palestinian area starting fifty days after these events happened.

If those who crucified Jesus could have disproved any of the historical realities of these events they would have done so and destroyed the whole movement from the beginning. But they didn't bring up any refutation of the facts of fulfilled prophecy; instead they put to death the persons who were proclaiming these facts.

That generation did not take seriously the credentials of the suffering Messiah. Jesus predicted the destruction of those who put Him on the cross. "For the days shall come upon you when your enemies will throw up a bank before you, and surround you, and hem you in on every side, and will level you to the ground and your children within you, and they will not leave in you one stone upon another, because you did not recognize the time of your visitation" (Luke 19:43, 44 NASB).

Was this prophecy fulfilled? As previously mentioned, Titus and the Roman legions swept down upon Jerusalem and destroyed it in A.D. 70.

Will We Learn?

Will we repeat history? Will we fail to take the prophets literally and seriously? Will we be indifferent? Will we allow those who claim to be religious leaders to explain these things away and not investigate for ourselves?

There are many more predictions about the reigning Messiah who is *yet to come* than there were about the suffering Messiah. Will we fail to weigh these prophecies for ourselves, in spite of what others may say?

The remainder of this book will present the prophecies which are related to the specific pattern of world events which are precisely predicted as coming together shortly before the coming of the Messiah the second time— coming in power to rule the earth.

Many of these predictions were in the same paragraphs as those relating to the first coming of the Messiah. Do we dare allegorize away the meaning of these?

Will these predictions be fulfilled just as certainly and graphically as those of the first coming?

This writer says positively, "Yes."

4 ○ Israel, O Israel

There are few countries which have played so central a role in world history as the Land of Israel. DAVID BEN GURION, 1965

SOME TIME IN the future there will be a seven-year period climaxed by the visible return of Jesus Christ.

Most prophecies which have not yet been fulfilled concern events which will develop shortly before the beginning of and during this seven-year countdown.

The general time of this seven-year period couldn't begin until the Jewish people re-established their nation in their ancient homeland of Palestine.

Keys to the Prophetic Puzzle

A definite international realignment of nations into four spheres of political power had to occur in the same era as this rebirth of Israel. Each sphere of power had to be led by a certain predicted nation and allied with certain other nations. The relationships of all these factors to each other is easily determined by the following clues: first, each one of the four spheres of political power is said to be present and vitally involved with the reborn state of Israel.

Secondly, each one of these spheres of power is a major factor in the final great war called "Armageddon," which is to be triggered by an invasion of the new state of Israel.

Third, each one of these spheres of power will be judged and destroyed for invading the new state of Israel, by the personal return of the Jewish Messiah, Jesus Christ.

It should be obvious that these predicted movements of history are interrelated in their general time of beginning and ending. This is why the prophecies can be pieced together to make a coherent picture, even though the pieces are scattered in small bits throughout the Old and New Testaments.

Raised Eyebrows

Many Bible students in recent years tried to fit the events of World War I and II to the prophetic signs which would herald the imminent return of Christ. Their failure discredited prophecy.

The people who have fled to the mountains to await the end of the world haven't had the faintest idea about the truths in Bible prophecy.

It is because of these unscriptural attempts at calculating dates that some eyebrows rise when we speak of Bible prophecy today.

Dream and Reality

The one event which many Bible students in the past overlooked was this paramount prophetic sign: Israel had to be a nation again in the land of its forefathers.

Israel a nation—a dream for so many years, made a reality on 14 May 1948 when David Ben-Gurion read the Declaration of Independence announcing the establishment of a Jewish nation to be known as the State of Israel.

In 1949, Prime Minister Ben-Gurion said that Israel's policy "consists of bringing all Jews to Israel . . . we are still at the beginning."[1]

What Countdown?

This seven-year period we have called the "countdown" is a period of unique events. There is more prophecy concerning this period than any other era the Bible describes.

The apostle John counted out seven years for this period when he spoke of the second half being forty-two months (i.e., 3½ years), and the first half being 1260 days (i.e., 3½ x 360 days, which is the Biblical year) (Revelation 11:2, 3).

The prophet Jeremiah spoke of the time when God would return His people of Israel and Judah from a great captivity and dispersion. He calls this period "the time of Jacob's trouble."

As Christ told of the world conditions that would immediately precede His coming, He said, "For then there will be great tribulation [affliction, distress and oppression] such as has not been from the beginning of the world until now, no, and never will be. And if those days had not been shortened, no human being would be saved" (Matthew 24:21, 22).

In other words, this period will be marked by the greatest devastation that man has ever brought upon himself. Mankind will be on the brink of self-annihilation when Christ suddenly returns to put an end to the war of wars called Armageddon.

Israel, the Fuse of Armageddon

What has happened and what is happening right now to Israel is signifi-cant in the entire prophetic picture. Men who have studied events that were to occur shortly before the great holocaust known as Armageddon are amazed as they see them happening before their eyes.

Too few Biblical scholars pay any serious attention to the proven prophetic content of Scripture. Dr. William F. Albright, eminent archaeologist and pro-fessor of Semitic Languages, noted this fact after he had verified many historic fulfillments of Bible prophecy. He said, "That the prophets were not only dedi-cated men, but also predictors of the future, is fully recognized in Biblical tra-dition but has been under-emphasized by modern Biblical scholars. . . ."[2]

The nation of Israel cannot be ignored; we see the Jews as a miracle of history. Even the casual observer is amazed how the descendants of Abraham, Isaac, and Jacob have survived as a distinct race in spite of the most formidable odds. What other people can trace their continuous unity back nearly 4,000 years?

Twice the Jews have been destroyed as a nation and dragged away as slaves under inhuman circumstances; twice the Jews returned to their ancient homeland and reestablished their nation.

What other people have preserved a distinct and separate national iden-tity in spite of a total of some 2600 years of being scattered—years of dispersion, as it is called? During all these years these men and women with-out a country have suffered the most insane and unjust persecutions ever endured by any collection of people or nationalities.

Jewish survival is a phenomenon. However, Jewish history, with all of its tragedies and triumphs, has been accurately foretold.

Setting the Stage

History may be dry bones to some, but the history of how the stage was set for the rebirth of Israel is fascinating. This history also serves as a stan-dard to test how reliable future prophecy concerning Israel will be. Let's look at the record of past prophecy fulfilled concerning Israel.

God's Woodshed

Some 3500 years ago, at a time when the Jewish people were enroute from Egypt to possess the Promised Land of Palestine, Moses predicted that they would be chastened, or disciplined, twice, as a nation, for not believing their God and rejecting His ways. The first stage of this disciplinary action came from Babylon.

Misery in Babylon

Moses predicted that a mighty nation would invade and destroy Israel. The invaders would be so fierce that they would have no respect for either the very old or the very young. Civilians would be massacred and property completely destroyed. The survivors would be taken as slaves.

As previously noted, the prophet Isaiah added details to what Moses predicted, about 150 years before it occurred. Isaiah said to a king of Judah, named Hezekiah: "Behold, the days are coming when all that is in your house, and that which your predecessors have stored up till this day, shall be carried to Babylon. Nothing shall be left, says the Lord" (Isaiah 39:6 Amplified).

The prophet Jeremiah, several years before it happened, predicted how long the Babylonian captivity would last: "And this whole land shall be a waste and an astonishment, and these nations shall serve the king of Babylon seventy years" (Jeremiah 25:11 Amplified).

Precisely as predicted, the Babylonians swept into the southern kingdom of Israel and Jerusalem and destroyed it. Those who survived the holocaust were carried off to Babylon as slaves where they remained for seventy years (II Chronicles 36:15-21).

At the end of this period of enslavement the Persian king, Cyrus, released some of the Jewish people to return and rebuild the Temple in Jerusalem (II Chronicles 36:22, 23). You will recall that this king had been predicted by name some 200 years before by Isaiah (Isaiah 44:28; 45:4).

The Winds of Rome

In the same prophecy in which he predicted the first stage of divine discipline, Moses also predicted the second stage. He said that because of continued disbelief and rejection of their God, Israel would be destroyed as a nation a second time. This time the survivors would be scattered throughout the world in every nation. They would be relentlessly persecuted—men without a country. Moses gives a graphic portrayal of the history of the Jews when he says that they will be scattered among all the people of the earth, where they "shall find no ease." The Jews will find no rest for their feet, their very lives shall "hang in doubt" (Deuteronomy 28:64-68).

Many other prophets, such as Isaiah, Jeremiah, Ezekiel, and Amos to name a few, all predicted the great world-wide exile of the Jewish people and the destruction of the Jewish nation.

Just before His arrest and crucifixion, Jesus said, ". . . for there will be a great distress upon the land, and wrath to this people, and they will fall by the edge of the sword, and will be led captive into *all the nations* . . ." (Luke 21:23, 24 NASB).

It's very important to note that this great theme of prophecy concerning the global dispersion was predicted by Jesus as occurring to the same generation that crucified Him. He said, "Truly I say to you, all these things shall come upon this generation" (Matthew 23:36 NASB).

History verifies the accuracy of these prophecies. Just as predicted by Jesus, less than forty years after His death Titus and the Roman legions destroyed Jerusalem and the nation, slaughtering hundreds of thousands. Those who survived were shipped off to the slave markets in Egypt. Soon the supply exceeded the demand and they were worthless, even as lowly slaves.

For almost 2000 years the sons of Abraham, Isaac, and Jacob have wandered around the earth with no country of their own, in constant fear of persecution and death. I am sure that they have asked the question millions of times, why all this evil for us? The true Christian has looked on with amazement and compassion, while the Jew has become a phenomenon to the world. It is no wonder that Moses wrote concerning their sufferings and punishment, "They (i.e. the judgments) shall be upon you for a sign [of warning to other nations] and for a wonder, and upon your descendants for ever" (Deuteronomy 28:46 Amplified).

Israel's history of misery which has exactly fulfilled prophetic warnings should be a sign to the whole world—a sign which among other things should teach that God means what He says, and says what He means.

Israel Reborn

The same prophets who predicted the world-wide exile and persecution of the Jews also predicted their restoration as a nation. It is surprising that many could not see the obvious: since the first part of these prophecies came true we should have anticipated that the second part would come true, also. This restoration was to come about in the general time of the climactic seven-year countdown and its finale—the personal appearance of the Messiah to deliver the new state from destruction.

Set the Record Straight

Right here a careful distinction must be made between "the physical restoration" to the land of Palestine as a nation, which clearly occurs shortly before the Messiah's coming and the "spiritual restoration" of all Jews who have believed in the Messiah just after His return to this earth.

The "physical restoration" is accomplished by unbelieving Jews through their human effort. As a matter of fact, the great catastrophic events which are to happen to this nation during "the tribulation" are primarily designed to shock the people into believing in their true Messiah (Ezekiel 38; 39).

The Scoffers

For many years prior to 1948 some Christian scholars denied the possibility of accepting the prophecies concerning the restoration of Israel as a nation in Palestine. As a matter of fact, many Bible teachers taught that all prophecy relating to Israel's future was fulfilled in Israel's past. Others taught that the promises made to Israel must be applied to the Church (since Israel rejected her Messiah.) Some theologians of the liberal school still insist that prophecy has no literal meaning for today and that it cannot be taken seriously. It is difficult to understand this view if one carefully weighs the case of Israel's rebirth as a nation.

Truth From Dusty Books

There has been down through history a group of men who diligently studied the prophetic content of the Bible and took it both seriously and literally. This writer searched through many commentaries on the subject dating back to A.D. 1611 and found that many scholars clearly understood that the Jews would return to Palestine and re-establish their nation before the Messiah would come. These men held this position in spite of mocking and ridicule on the part of the majority of Christendom.

The certainty of Israel's physical rebirth as a nation and restoration to Palestine was seen by Dr. John Cumming in 1864. Thumb through his fascinating old book, over a hundred years old, and you'll read: "How comes it to pass that as a nation they have been dispersed over every land, yet insulated, separated, and alone amid the nations? The predictions of their restoration are in words as definite only not yet fulfilled. As a nation they were cut off and dispersed, and it is *as a nation that they shall be gathered and restored.*

"But one closing act in this great dramatic history of an extraordinary people is yet wanting to complete the whole. Their restoration is predicted and demanded. Who will stretch out his hand to move the scene and call forth the actors."[3]

Was this man a prophet or a student of the prophets of God?

The fact that the Jews had to be restored as a nation before Christ could return was seen by James Grant, an English Bible scholar writing in 1866.

"The personal coming of Christ, to establish His millennial reign on earth, will not take place *until the Jews are restored to their own land*, and the enemies of Christ and the Jews have gathered together their armies from all parts of the world, and have commenced the siege of Jerusalem . . . now the return of the Jews to the Holy Land, and the mustering and marshalling of these mighty armies, with a view to capturing Jerusalem, must require a *considerable time yet.*"[4]

(This was written eighty-two years before Israel was made a nation.)

Increase Mather, a famous minister in the early colonies of America, wrote a book published in 1669 entitled, *The Mystery of Israel's Salvation*. In this book he developed many of the crucial prophecies of Israel's restoration. He, too, showed that the Jews would return to Palestine and become a nation before their spiritual conversion and the return of the Messiah, Jesus Christ.

The great contribution of these men who stood against the prevailing religious opinion of their day is obvious. They prove that these prophetic passages are clear and could be understood if taken literally. A hundred or more years ago the prospect of the nation of Israel seemed impossible. Their faith in these passages in the Bible has been verified before our eyes!

These men used what may be called the golden rule of interpretation which the Biblical record of fulfilled prophecy indicates is correct.

"When the plain sense of Scripture makes common sense, seek no other sense; therefore, take every word at its primary, ordinary, usual, literal meaning unless the facts of the immediate context, studied in the light of related passages and axiomatic and fundamental truths, indicate clearly otherwise."[5]

This is the method which this writer has diligently sought to follow.

Three Important Events

To be specific about Israel's great significance as a sign of the time, there are three things that were to happen. First, the Jewish nation would be reborn in the land of Palestine. Secondly, the Jews would repossess old

Jerusalem and the sacred sites. Thirdly, they would rebuild their ancient temple of worship upon its historic site.

The Nation Born in a Day

Some 2600 years ago Ezekiel showed that the Jewish nation would be reborn after a long world-wide dispersion, but before the coming of the Messiah to judge a great enemy who would rise up against the new nation. Here is Ezekiel—speaking prophetically to this great enemy of the revived state—"After many days you shall be visited *and* mustered for service; in the latter years you shall go against the land that is restored from the ravages of the sword, where people are gathered out of many nations upon the mountains of Israel, which had been a continual waste; but its *people* are brought forth out of the nations . . ." (Ezekiel 38:8 Amplified).

The Time of This Prophecy's Fulfillment

There are several clues in Ezekiel's words which make it possible to pinpoint the time of this restoration.

Clue one: "The latter years" is the first. Dr. Kac, a Jewish medical doctor and noted Bible scholar, sums it up this way: "The phrase 'latter days' always refers in the Old Testament to the time of Israel's final and complete national restoration and spiritual redemption."[6]

Clue two: This restoration is clearly after a long-term desolation of the land of Israel. Note the following statements in the context: "the land that is restored from the ravages of the sword . . ." And, ". . . the mountains of Israel, which had been a continual waste. . . ."

Clue three: It is also a time when the Jewish people are being returned from exile "out of many nations." Ezekiel 37 is part of this context and details the miracle of the physical restoration of the Jews to their own land, then afterward their spiritual conversion. This was predicted to occur at a time when the world would be saying, "Behold, they say, Our bones are dried up, and our hope is lost; we are completely cut off" (Ezekiel 37:11 Amplified).

Clue four: The crux of the case is that this physical restoration to the land is directly associated with triggering the hostility which brings about a great judgment upon all nations and the Messiah's return to set up God's Kingdom. In other words, it is the presence of this reborn nation of Israel, flourishing in prosperity, that excites a great enemy from the uttermost north of

Palestine to launch an attack upon them which sets off the last war of the world. This war is to be ended with such a display of divine intervention that a great many of the surviving Gentiles and Jews put their whole trust in the true Messiah, Jesus Christ.

It cannot be emphasized enough. This restoration would take place after a world-wide dispersion and long-term desolation of the land of Israel. However, it would occur shortly before the events which will culminate with the personal, visible return of the Messiah, Jesus Christ, to set up an everlasting Kingdom and bring about the spiritual conversion of Israel.

Jesus the Prophet

Jesus Christ also pinpointed the general time of His return when His disciples asked Him two important questions. "What will be the sign of your coming?" they wanted to know. And "What will be the sign of the end of the age?"

The "coming" referred to in the question above is commonly referred to as the second advent of Christ. It was only natural that they wanted to know what signs would indicate His return to set up God's promised Kingdom.

In answer Jesus gave many general signs involving world conditions which he called "birth pangs." He said that these signs, such as religious apostasy, wars, national revolutions, earthquakes, famines, etc., would increase in frequency and intensity just like birth pangs before a child is born.

One of the great signs He predicted, however, is often overlooked. He speaks of the Jewish people being in the land of Palestine as a nation at the time of His return. He speaks of "those who are in Judea" fleeing to the mountains to escape the great battles that immediately precede His return (Matthew 24:16).

Another statement of Jesus demands a national existence with even their ancient worship restored. "Pray that your flight may not be . . . on a Sabbath" (Matthew 24:20). This indicates that the ancient traditions regarding travel on the Sabbath would be in force again, thus hindering a rapid escape from the predicted invasion.

Even the Temple has to be rebuilt according to the sign given in Matthew 24:15. (More will be said about this shortly.)

Jesus' predictions regarding the nation restored to the land are extremely significant when we recall that He predicted a world-wide dispersion and complete destruction of the nation which would begin with the generation which crucified Him (Luke 21:22, 23; Matthew 23:36).

Yet when Jesus looks into the future and describes the conditions which would prevail at His coming, He puts the Jews back in the land as a nation.

It is in this context that Jesus predicts an extremely important time clue. He says: "Now learn the parable from the fig tree: when its branch has already become tender, and puts forth its leaves, you know that summer is near; even so you too, when you see all these things, recognize that He is near, right at the door" (Matthew 24:32, 33 NASB).

Perfect Parable

When the signs just given begin to multiply and increase in scope it's similar to the certainty of leaves coming on the fig tree. But the most important sign in Matthew has to be the restoration of the Jews to the land in the rebirth of Israel. Even the figure of speech "fig tree" has been a historic symbol of national Israel. When the Jewish people, after nearly 2,000 years of exile, under relentless persecution, became a nation again on 14 May 1948 the "fig tree" put forth its first leaves.

Jesus said that this would indicate that He was "at the door," ready to return. Then He said, "Truly I say to you, *this generation* will not pass away until all these things take place" (Matthew 24:34 NASB).

What generation? Obviously, in context, the generation that would see the signs—chief among them the rebirth of Israel. A generation in the Bible is something like forty years. If this is a correct deduction, then within forty years or so of 1948, all these things could take place. Many scholars who have studied Bible prophecy all their lives believe that this is so.

The Repossession of Jerusalem

Another important event that had to take place before the stage would be fully set for the "seven-year countdown" was the repossession of ancient Jerusalem. Much of what is to happen to the Jewish people at the return of the Messiah is to occur in the vicinity of the ancient city.

Zechariah some 2500 years ago predicted the great invasion against the Jewish people who would dwell near ancient Jerusalem at the time of the Messiah's second coming. Chapters 12 through 14 of Zechariah graphically describe the events in sequence.

Here is an outline of these crucial chapters:

1. The siege of Jerusalem by all nations (12:1-3).
2. A description of the battle in and around Jerusalem (12:4–9).

3. The personal revelation of Jesus Christ as Messiah to a remnant of Jews in Jerusalem (12:10).
4. The repentance and faith which occurs at this personal revelation (12:11–14).
5. The opening of the fountain of forgiveness to repentant Israel (13:1).
6. The triumphant return of the Messiah (14:1-21).

It is clear in these chapters that the Jews would have to be dwelling in and have possession of the ancient city of Jerusalem at the time of the Messiah's triumphant advent.

Jesus Christ also predicted this situation in His last great public message before His arrest. He warned the Jews who would be living in Judea to look for "the abomination of desolation," which was spoken of by Daniel, the prophet, standing in the "holy place" (Matthew 24:15).

"The abomination of desolation" has a technical Jewish meaning which is to desecrate the Temple by bringing a Gentile or an unholy thing into the holy place (a consecrated compartment where only an authorized priest is to enter). An "abomination of desolation" happened once before in Jewish history when in 165 B.C. an invading king named Antiochus Epiphanes slaughtered a pig in the holy place.

The point is this, in order for there to be a Temple, there would have to be a repossession of the Temple site in ancient Jerusalem.

In March and April of 1967 I was lecturing on this subject at many college campuses on the West coast. I said that if this was the time that I thought it was, then somehow the Jews were going to have to repossess old Jerusalem. Many chuckled about that statement.

Then came the war of June, 1967—the phenomenal Israeli six-day blitz. I was personally puzzled as to the significance of it all until the third day of fighting when Moshe Dayan, the ingenious Israeli general, marched to the wailing wall, the last remnant of the Old Temple, and said, "We have returned to our holiest of holy places, never to leave her again."

Needless to say, I received quite a few phone calls after that. Again, against incredible odds, the Jews had unwittingly further set up the stage for their final hour of trial and conversion.

The Third Temple

There remains but one more event to completely set the stage for Israel's part in the last great act of her historical drama. This is to rebuild the ancient Temple of worship upon its old site. There is only one place that this Temple can be built, according to the Law of Moses. This is upon Mount Moriah. It is there that two previous Temples were built: the first was built by Solomon 3000 years ago. The second was built by the returning Babylonian exiles 2400 years ago. This one was completely refurbished by Herod the Great later on in an effort to win the favor and acceptance of the Jews. The second Temple was totally destroyed by Titus and the Roman Legions in A.D. 70.

There is one major problem barring the construction of a third Temple. That obstacle is the second holiest place of the Moslem faith, the Dome of the Rock. This is believed to be built squarely in the middle of the old temple site.

Obstacle or no obstacle, it is certain that the Temple will be rebuilt. Prophecy demands it.

Jesus Christ predicted an event which would trigger a time of unparalleled catastrophe for the Jewish nation shortly before His second coming. This "abomination of desolation" or desecration of the inner sanctum of the Temple would occur at the midway point of God's last seven years of dealing with the Jewish people before setting up the long-awaited Kingdom of God (Daniel 9:27).

Daniel's prediction also indicates that a prince would rise up from among the people who destroyed the second Temple (who were the Romans in A.D. 70) and that he "would make a firm covenant" with the Jewish people. This treaty would guarantee the religious freedom to reinstitute the old "sacrifices and oblations" of the Law of Moses.

This "prince" must be from a revived form of the ancient Roman Empire. (More about this in a later chapter.)

The apostle Paul predicts the activities of this Roman prince in great detail and gives us insight into the act that is called "the abomination of desolation." Paul speaks of this person as one who "opposes and exalts himself above every so-called god or object of worship, so that he takes his seat in the temple of God, displaying himself as being God" (II Thessalonians 2:4 NASB). By this act, the Roman prince, who is also called "the Lawless One" and "the Antichrist," breaks his covenant with the Jewish people and causes the Jewish temple worship, according to the law of Moses, to cease (Daniel 9:27).

Tie It All Together

The main points are these: first, there will be a reinstitution of the Jewish worship according to the Law of Moses with sacrifices and oblations in the general time of Christ's return; secondly, there is to be a desecration of the Jewish Temple in the time immediately preceding Christ's return.

We must conclude that a third Temple will be rebuilt upon its ancient site in old Jerusalem.

If this is the time that this writer believes it is, there will soon begin the construction of this Temple. Are there any evidences of such intentions in Israel?

In a fascinating article written shortly after the recapture of old Jerusalem, a reporter interviewed a famous Israeli historian, Israel Eldad. In answer to the question, "Do your people intend to rebuild the Temple?" Eldad said, "From the time that King David first conquered Jerusalem until Solomon built the Temple, just one generation passed. So will it be with us."

The reporter was so startled by that answer that he asked, "What about the Dome of the Rock which now stands on the temple site?"

Eldad replied, "It is, of course, an open question. Who knows, maybe there will be an earthquake."

The hope of rebuilding the Temple that is present in the hearts of devout Jews, some of whom are in powerful positions in the Israeli government, was clearly reflected here.

With the Jewish nation reborn in the land of Palestine, ancient Jerusalem once again under total Jewish control for the first time in 2600 years, and talk of rebuilding the great Temple, the most important prophetic sign of Jesus Christ's soon coming is before us. This has now set the stage for the other predicted signs to develop in history. It is like the key piece of a jig-saw puzzle being found and then having the many adjacent pieces rapidly fall into place.

For all those who trust in Jesus Christ, it is a time of electrifying excitement.

5 ○ Russia is a Gog

The next war will not be with the Arabs, but with the Russians.

GENERAL MOSHE DAYAN, 1968

... and come from your place out of the uttermost parts of the north, you and many peoples with you, all of them riding on horses, a great host, a mighty army; you will come up against my people Israel, like a cloud covering the land. In the latter days I will bring you against my land, that the nations may know me, when through you, O Gog, I vindicate my holiness before their eyes.

EZEKIEL 38:15-16, 650 B.C.

THE NEW STATE of Israel will be plagued by a certain pattern of events which has been clearly forecasted.

Shortly after the restoration of the Jews in the land of Israel, an incredible enemy will arise to its "uttermost north." This enemy will be composed of one great nation which will gather around it a number of allies. It is this "Northern Confederacy" that is destined to plunge the world into its final great war which Christ will return to end.

When I was a teenager watching the end of World War II, facing the continued fear of another war, I wondered then how it would all end. I once heard a radio program with a minister saying that the Bible indicated that the last war of the world would be fought between nations symbolized by an eagle and a bear. That was interesting to me, but he didn't back up his remarks with any definite proof. Even though I wasn't religious or interested in the Bible, I still spent many hours in bull sessions about this subject with other men who were as irreligious as myself. Little did I realize at that time how definite the Bible is about who the nations will be that play the major roles in the last drama. There is certainly more revealed than the vague symbols of an eagle and a bear.

There are three major prophecies on this northern sphere of political power which are to be found in Ezekiel 38; 39; Daniel 11:40-45; and Joel 2:20. It is of paramount importance to identify the time to which these prophecies apply, who the leading nation of the confederacy is, and who the allies are.

Then we shall see what this Northern Confederacy will do and how it will end.

What Time Is It?

There are several clues in Ezekiel's prophecy which establish the time to which it applies.

First, several times in the prophecy it is ascribed to "the latter years" (Ezekiel 38:8) and "the latter days," which have been previously noted (Ezekiel 38:16). These are definite terms which denote the time just preceding and including the events which will be climaxed by the second advent of Jesus Christ, who will come this time as the "reigning Messiah" to set up God's promised Kingdom.

Second, this prediction is found in a context with a definite chronological sequence of events.

Ezekiel 36 and 37 speak of the final restoration of the Jews to the land of Palestine, a restoration from which they will never be scattered again. This restoration has two distinctions which show that it couldn't be speaking of the time when the Jews returned from the Babylonian exile.

The first distinction is that they are to return from a long world-wide dispersion. (The Babylonian dispersion wasn't very long nor was it world-wide.) The second distinction is that this restoration is immediately prior to and connected with the period of tribulation. This period brings about a great spiritual rebirth of the nation and the return of Jesus the Messiah to rescue them from their enemies.

Ezekiel speaks of the physical restoration of the nation when he says: "But you, O mountains of Israel, shall shoot forth your branches and yield your fruit to My people Israel; for they are soon to come home" (Ezekiel 36:8 Amplified).

And again from Ezekiel, "For I will take you from among the nations, and gather you out of all countries, and bring you into your own land" (Ezekiel 36:24 Amplified).

Ezekiel then foretells the spiritual regeneration of the people at some point *after* they are restored as a nation when he says, "Then will I sprinkle clean water upon you, and you shall be clean from all your uncleanness, and from all your idols will I cleanse you. A new heart will I give you, and a new spirit will I put within you: and I will take away the stony heart out of your flesh and give you a heart of flesh. And I will put my Spirit within you and cause you to walk in My statutes . . ." (Ezekiel 36:25-27 Amplified).

The parable of Ezekiel 37 describes these same events in this sequence: first, the physical restoration as a nation in the land and then the spiritual rebirth of the people. Ezekiel explains the prophetic vision, indicating the dry bones as "the whole house of Israel" hopelessly scattered throughout the nations of the world (Ezekiel 37:11). The bones coming together and sinews and flesh being put upon them is explained as meaning the regathering of the people into a physical restoration of a national existence in Palestine. Isn't it fascinating how graphic this physical analogy is?

Ezekiel's vision, however, goes beyond the purely physical. It says ". . . but there was no breath or spirit in them" (Ezekiel 37:8 Amplified). This indicates that the real spiritual life would come with the rebirth of the people after the restoration.

This restoration and spiritual rebirth of the nation is to be the beginning of the everlasting kingdom which the Messiah is promised to bring. Ezekiel says, "I will make a covenant of peace with them; it shall be an everlasting covenant with them . . . I will set My sanctuary in the midst of them for evermore" (Ezekiel 37:26 Amplified).

Study Ezekiel 38 and 39. The most significant part of this chain of events is established here. These chapters indicate with certainty that after the physical restoration of the nation, but before the spiritual rebirth, the great northern enemy will invade Israel (Ezekiel 38:8, 16). Then God will supernaturally judge the northern invaders, and this is the very act which will impel the Israeli people to know and believe in their true Messiah, Jesus Christ (Ezekiel 39:6-8).

Zechariah beautifully described this scene when he quotes God as saying, "And I will pour out upon the house of David and the inhabitants of Jerusalem a spirit of compassion and supplication, so that, when they look on him whom they have pierced, they shall mourn for him, as one mourns for an only child . . ." (Zechariah 12:10).

Ezekiel speaks in chapters 40 through 48 of a new worship pattern which will be established after the Messiah, Jesus Christ, comes to reign on earth over the Kingdom of God.

Since the restoration of Israel as a nation in 1948, we have lived in the most significant period of prophetic history. We are living in the times which Ezekiel predicted in chapters 38 and 39.

In 1854 a scholar named Chamberlain summed up the crux of what has just been said. In commenting on Ezekiel 38, he observed, "From all which I should infer, the coming restoration of Israel will at first be gradual and pacific; a restoration permitted, if not assisted and encouraged or protected. They will return to occupy the whole land, both cities and villages; they will be settled there, become prosperous and increasing in wealth, before this great confederacy of northern people will be formed against them."[1]

Consider that Chamberlain wrote this over one hundred years ago—long before Israel was a nation "assisted and encouraged" by other countries.

Who Is the Northern Commander?

For centuries, long before the current events could have influenced the interpreter's ideas, men have recognized that Ezekiel's prophecy about the northern commander referred to Russia.

Dr. John Cumming, writing in 1864, said, "This king of the North I conceive to be the autocrat of Russia . . . that Russia occupies a place, and a very momentous place, in the prophetic word has been admitted by almost all expositors."[2]

What's the Evidence?

Ezekiel describes this northern commander as "Gog, of the land of Magog, the chief prince (or ruler) of Rosh, of Meschech and Tubal" (Ezekiel 38:2 Amplified). This gives the ethnic background of this commander and his people.

In other words, the prophet gives the family tree of this northern commander so that we can trace the migrations of these tribes to the modern nation that we know.

Gog is the symbolic name of the nation's leader and Magog is his land. He is also the prince of the ancient people who were called Rosh, Meshech, and Tubal.

In the Biblical chapter commonly called the "Table of Nations" by scholars these names are mentioned. (See Genesis 10.) They are described as the grandsons of Noah through his son Japheth, with the exception of Rosh (Genesis 10:1, 2). Magog is the second son; Tubal is the fifth son; and Meshech is the sixth son.

You must be all excited about Magog, Meshech, and Tubal by this time! You are probably saying, "What in the world do these crusty relics of fiction have to do with Russia?" Let this writer assure you, these names are not fiction, but they have turned up in many archaeological discoveries in very early accounts of ancient history. One reason for this is that the families of these forefathers adopted their names as "tribal names." The family descended from Magog became known as the tribe of Magog, etc.

Dead Men Do Tell Tales!

It is necessary on the next few pages to establish some documentation from ancient history. Some people find this subject "a little dull," to say the least. If this is your case, you may wish to skim over the high points. For others, it will prove to be rewarding to check carefully the grounds upon which the historical case is built.

Herodotus, the fifth century B.C. Greek philosopher, is quoted as mentioning Meshech and Tubal. He identified them with a people named the Samaritans and Muschovites who lived at that time in the ancient province of Pontus in northern Asia Minor.[3]

Josephus, a Jewish historian of the first century, says that the people of his day known as the Moschevi and Thobelites were founded by Meshech and Tubal respectively. He said, ". . . Magog is called the Scythians by the Greeks." He continued by saying that these people lived in the northern regions above the Caucasus mountains.[4]

Pliny, a noted Roman writer of early Christian times, said, "Hierapolis, taken by the Scythians, was afterward called Magog."[5] In this he shows that the dreaded barbaric people called the Scythians were identified with their ancient tribal name. Any good history book of ancient times traces the Scythians to be a principle part of the people who make up modern Russia.

Wilhelm Gesenius, a great Hebrew scholar of the early nineteenth century, discusses these words in his unsurpassed Hebrew Lexicon. "Meshech," he says, "was founder of the Moschi, a barbarous people, who dwelt in the Moschian mountains."[6]

This scholar went on to say that the Greek name, "Moschi," derived from the Hebrew name Meshech is the source of the name for *the city of Moscow*. In discussing Tubal he said, "Tubal is the son of Rapheth, founder of the Tibereni, a people dwelling on the Black Sea to the west of the Moschi."

Gesenius concludes by saying that these people undoubtedly make up the modern Russian people.

There is one more name to consider in this line of evidence. It is the Hebrew word, "Rosh," translated "chief" in Ezekiel 38:2, 3 of the King James and Revised Standard Versions. The word literally means in Hebrew the "top" or "head" of something. According to most scholars, this word is used in the sense of a proper name, not as a descriptive noun qualifying the word "prince."

The German scholar, Dr. Keil, says after a careful grammatical analysis that it should be translated as a proper name, i.e., Rosh. He says, "The Byzantine and Arabic writers frequently mention a people called Rōs and Rūs, dwelling in the country of Taurus, and reckoned among the Scythian tribes."[7]

Dr. Gesenius in his Hebrew Lexicon says, ". . . Rosh was a designation for the tribes then north of the Taurus Mountains, dwelling in the neighborhood of the Volga."[8]

He concluded that in this name and tribe we have the first historical trace of the Russ or Russian nation.

In the light of the abundant evidence, it is no wonder that men long before Russia rose to its present state of power foresaw its role in history. Bishop Lowth of England was one of these men. He wrote in 1710, "Rosh, taken as a proper name, in Ezekiel signifies the inhabitants of Scythia, from whom the modern Russians derive their name."[9]

In the eighteenth and nineteenth centuries, such men as Bishop Lowth, Dr. Cumming, and Rev. Chamberlain, were ridiculed by many of their contemporaries. After all, who could have imagined then what we now see in modern communist Russia—a country founded upon atheism?

Where Is the Uttermost North?

The final evidence for identifying this northern commander lies in its geographical location from Israel.

Ezekiel puts great stress on this by saying three times that this great enemy of Israel would come from their "uttermost north." It is mentioned in 38:6 and 15, and 39:2. The King James Version doesn't translate this accurately, but the Revised Standard and Amplified Versions of the Bible do. The Hebrew word that qualifies "north" means either "uttermost" or "extreme."

You need only to take a globe to verify this exact geographical fix. There is only one nation to the "uttermost north" of Israel—the U.S.S.R.

"Thus says the Lord God: Are you he of whom I have spoken in olden times by My servants the prophets of Israel, who prophesied in those days for years that I would bring you, *Gog*, against them?" (Ezekiel 38:17 Amplified). The answer to this challenging question thrown down by God through Ezekiel centuries ago is now rather obvious, wouldn't you say?

General Dayan's statement that "The next war will not be with the Arabs but with the Russians" has a considerably deeper significance, doesn't it?

Final Exam

Just think for a moment how incredible a thing we are considering here. How could Ezekiel 2600 years ago have forecast so accurately the rise of Russia to its current military might and its direct and obvious designs upon the Middle East, not to mention the fact that it is now an implacable enemy of the new state of Israel? How could men like Chamberlain and Cumming, for that matter, one hundred years ago have so clearly seen the future rise of Russia to its present world-threatening position?

The answer is again, it seems to this writer, obvious. Ezekiel once again passes "the test of a prophet." He was guided by the Spirit of the living God. In the apostle Peter's final letter, written as he faced certain and imminent death, he stated the source of the prophets' wisdom and insight. Peter first states where prophecy did not originate; "But know this first of all, that no prophecy of Scripture is a matter of one's own interpretation" (II Peter 1:20 NASB). In other words, the prophets did not dream up their own interpretation of life and history.

Then Peter declares where prophecy did originate, ". . . for no prophecy was ever made by an act of human will, but men moved by the Holy Spirit spoke from God" (II Peter 1:21 NASB).

When a man knows that he is about to die, he usually gets around to saying the things he considers to be most important. Peter considered the certainty and relevance of the prophetic word to be the most important thing. He even warned that in "the latter times" men posing as religious leaders would rise from within the Church and deny, even ridicule, the prophetic word (II Peter 2:1-3; 3:1-18).

If you pass this book around to many ministers you'll find how true this prediction has become.

Who Are the Allies?

Ezekiel partially catalogs the ancient names of the peoples and nations who would be confederates of Russia in 38:5 and 6.

Persia

All authorities agree on who Persia is today. It is modern Iran. This is significant because it is being wooed to join the United Arab Republic in its hostility against Israel. The Russians are at this moment seeking to gain footholds in Iran by various overtures of aid. In order to mount the large-scale invasion predicted by Ezekiel, Russia would need Iran as an ally. It would be much more difficult to move a large land army across the Caucasus Mountains that border Turkey, than the Elburz Mountains that border Iran. Iran's general terrain is also much easier to cross than Turkey's. Transportation, however, will be needed through both countries.

Watch the actions of Iran in relation to Russia and the United Arab Republic. This writer believes that significant things will soon be happening there.

Ethiopia or Cush (Black African Nations)

Ethiopia is a translation of the Hebrew word, *Cush*. Cush was the first son of Ham, one of the sons of Noah.

Moses mentions "the land of Cush" as originally being adjacent to an area near the Tigris and Euphrates rivers (Genesis 2:13).

After examining many authorities on the subject, the writer discovered once again why Dr. Gesenius is recognized as one of the great scholars of history. Gesenius summarized all of the evidence as follows: (1) The Cushites were black men. (2) They migrated first to the Arabian peninsula and then across the Red Sea to the area south of Egypt. (3) All the black people of Africa are descended from Cush.

Gesenius observes, "Indeed all the nations sprung from Cush and enumerated in Genesis 10:7, are to be sought in Africa."[10]

Cush is translated "Ethiopia" twenty-one times in the King James Version, which is somewhat misleading. It is certain that the ancient Ethiopians (modern Abyssinia) are made up of Cushites, but they do not represent all of them, according to history.

The sobering conclusion is this: many of the African nations will be united and allied with the Russians in the invasion of Israel. This is in accord with Daniel's graphic description of this invasion (Daniel 11:36-45).

The Russian force is called "the King of the North" and the sphere of power which the African (Cush) force will be a part of is called "the King of the South."

One of the most active areas of evangelism for the Communist "gospel" is in Africa. As we see further developments in this area in the future, we realize that it will become converted to Communism.

Libya or Put (Arabic African Nations)

Libya is the translation of the original Hebrew word, *Put*. We have the same problem pinpointing these people as with Cush. Put was the third son of Ham (Genesis 10:6). The descendants of Put migrated to the land west of Egypt and became the source of the North African Arab nations, such as Libya, Algeria, Tunisia, and Morocco. The first settlement of Put was called Libya by the ancient historians, Josephus and Pliny.[11] The Greek translation of the Hebrew Old Testament, called the Septuagint, translates Put as Libya in about 165 B.C.

The conclusion is that Russia's ally, Put, certainly included more than what is now called Libya. Once again there are current events to show the beginning of this alliance.

The territory of Northern Africa is becoming solidly pro-Soviet.[12] Algeria appears to be already Communist and allied with Russia.

As we watch this area in the next few years we shall see indications that it is destined to join the southern sphere of power which will attack Israel along with the "King of the North."

Gomer and All Its Hordes (Iron Curtain Countries)

Gomer was the eldest son of Japheth, and the father of Ashkenaz, Riphath, and Togarmah. These people make up an extremely important part of the future Russian invasion force.

Dr. Young, citing the best of the most recent archaeological finds, says of Gomer and his hordes, "They settled on the north of the Black Sea, and then spread themselves southward and westward to the extremities of Europe."[13]

Gesenius speaks of part of Gomer's "hordes" as being Ashkenaz ... "the proper name of a region and a nation in northern Asia, sprung from the Cimmerians who are the ancient people of Gomer. The modern Jews understand it to be Germany, and call that country by this Hebrew name....[14]

Josephus called the sons of Ashkenaz, "The Rheginians" and a map of the ancient Roman Empire places them in the area of modern Poland, Czechoslovakia, and East Germany to the banks of the Danube River. The modern Jewish Talmud confirms the same geographical picture.

The conclusion is that Gomer and its hordes are a part of the vast area of modern Eastern Europe which is totally behind the Iron Curtain. This includes East Germany and the Slovak countries.

Togarmah and All Its Hordes
(Southern Russia and the Cossacks)

In Ezekiel 38:6 "the house of Togarmah, and all its hordes" are specifically pointed out as being from "the uttermost north." Gesenius says that "they are a northern nation and country sprung from Gomer abounding in horses and mules." Some of the sons of Togarmah founded Armenia, according to their own claim today, Gesenius continued.

Dr. Bauman traces evidence of some of the sons of Togarmah to the Turkoman tribes of Central Asia. This would explain the statement, ". . . of the uttermost north, and all its hordes."

The conclusion is that Togarmah is part of modern Southern Russia and is probably the origin of the Cossacks and other people of the Eastern part of Russia. It is interesting to note that the Cossacks have always loved horses and have been recognized as producing the finest army of cavalry in the world. Today they are reported to have several divisions of cavalry. It is believed by some military men that cavalry will actually be used in the invasion of the Middle East just as Ezekiel and other prophets literally predicted. During the Korean War the Red Chinese proved that in rugged mountainous terrain, horses are still the fastest means of moving a large attacking force into battle zones.

Isn't it a coincidence that such terrain stands between Russia and the Israeli?

Ezekiel indicates that he hasn't given a complete list of allies. Enough is given, however, to make this writer amazed by the number of people and nations which will be involved.

Gog, Take Command

Ezekiel, prophetically addressing the Russian ruler, commands him to, ". . . be prepared; yes prepare yourself, you and all your companies that are assembled about you, and you be a guard *and* a commander for them" (Ezekiel 38:7 Amplified).

In other words, the Russian ruler is to equip his confederates with arms and to assume command.

If you have doubts about all that has been said in this chapter, isn't it a bit unnerving to note that almost all of the countries predicted as part of this great army are already armed with weapons created and manufactured in Russia?

What's Your Game, Gog?

We have seen that Russia will arm and equip a vast confederacy. This powerful group of allies will lead an attack on restored Israel. However, Russia and her confederates will be destroyed completely by an act that

Israel will acknowledge as being from their God. This act will bring many in Israel to believe in their true Messiah (Ezekiel 38:15 ff.).

The attack upon the Russian confederacy and the resulting conflict will escalate into the last war of the world, involving all nations.

Then it will happen. Christ will return to prevent the annihilation of all mankind.

6 ○ Sheik to Sheik

Our basic aim will be to destroy Israel. NASSER OF EGYPT, MAY, 1967

They have said, Come, and let us wipe them out as a nation; let the name of Israel be in remembrance no more. PSALM 83:4 (Amplified) prophesied about 1000 B.C.

W HEN THE PHONE rings and it's the person we have just mentioned in conversation, inevitably we say, "What a coincidence, we were just talking about you." Or when we open the mail and find the check that we needed to pay an urgent bill, we enjoy the timely coincidence.

However, in writing this book too many pieces and events have fallen into place for us to believe they could all be "coincidence." This is why we believe what one vague religionist has called "the divine hand from somewhere" set the stage the week we began this chapter.

In the last chapter some of the confederates of a future Russian invasion force were documented from Biblical prophecy. The confederates who are relevant to this chapter are the Arabic nations. The Bible says that Egypt, the Arabic nations, and countries of black Africa will form an alliance, a sphere of power which will be called the King of the South. Allied with Russia, the King of the North, this formidable confederacy will rise up against the restored state of Israel.

So where is the coincidence?

As we were researching the current status of the leading Arabic nation, Egypt, we discovered that on the campus of a large university, less than ten minutes away, it was Arab Week. Obviously they must have planned it to coincide with our study.

With echos of Scheherazade humming in our subconscious, we made our way. . . .

On Campus

We found an exotic mixture of West and Middle East along the shaded walks of the beautiful university. Some students were wearing head-coverings, Arab-fashion, to indicate where their allegiance was. The vision was not quite like Lawrence of Arabia galloping across endless stretches of white sand, but the effect was striking.

Tables were everywhere around the Student Union. We were deluged with printed materials concerning the rightness of the Arab cause against Israel and their determination to liberate Palestine.

In a short while we were supplied with documents which substantiated the alliance of the Arabs and the Russians, a bond both present and actual, but also a fact which was prophesied approximately 2600 years ago!

The purpose of "Arab Week" at the university was to rally support for the Palestinian Revolution. According to the literature which was being distributed, "the Palestine Revolution draws moral support from the revolutionary movements of the world. The Arab student movement has given the revolution their total support. Arab intellectuals, joined by many world-thinkers have given their support."

This "revolutionary movement" is part of the Communist movement which has supported "wars of liberation" in countries around the world.

From the standpoint of this study of alliances which make up the King of the South we saw a valuable link in the alignment of several black African nations with the Arabs in their determined plan to "liberate" Palestine from Israel. This is another confirmation of prophecy as we have seen from Old Testament prophets.

Egypt: Leading Actor

We speak of "Arab," and yet it is obvious that the real leader in the Arabic world is Egypt. This country is in a strategic spot in the prophetic landscape, which is the reason we should follow the events in the Middle East with great interest.

Egypt is located at the southern end of "the land bridge" which connects the continents of Europe, Asia and Africa. The value of this important piece of real estate, which has been established by centuries of fighting will play an important part in events which we will show in the chapter on World War III. Conveniently for Egypt, it has an ideal location for its role of leadership in the Afro-Arab world.

"Egypt's geographical size, large population, 150,000 man military establishment, advanced industrialization, and President Gamal Abdel Nasser's military Arab nationalism make it the political, intellectual, and cultural center of the Arab world, as well as much of Africa."[1]

What about Nasser? He has become the symbol of leadership for both African and Arabic "wars of liberation from Western imperialism." Nasser's manifesto, "Philosophy of the Revolution," provides us with insight into the future direction which we can expect of the Arab and African situation.

"Nasser views the world as a stage, with Egypt as one of the principal actors. This role is three-dimensional, described in Nasser's language in terms of circles. The first of these is the Arab area with Arab unity as the main plot. Beyond this circle lies Africa, which Nasser envisages as the seat of struggle between white 'imperialists' and the indigenous Negroes for possession of its riches. Encompassing these two circles is the world of Islam, also threatened by 'imperialism.' In the past few years, Nasser appears to have expanded this conception of the third circle to include all non-Western and underdeveloped Western countries."[2]

Nasser has not swerved from his written goal to bring about a kind of "Arab Socialism." He has repeatedly said that kings, sheiks, sultans, and capitalism must all be obliterated. This has appealed to the common Arab who has been oppressed for centuries. Using the "Gospel of Materialism," plus the common bond of Arabic race identity, wedded with the Moslem religious ties, Nasser believes that he can unite the Arabs to lead the resurrection of all underprivileged nations into a mighty third world force. He envisions himself as the one to lead the nations of Africa, black and Arab, to unity.

Somehow the aims, ambitions, and worldly directions of dictators past and present never seem to change. There has never been a benevolent dictator.

How to Make Enemies and Influence People

Nasser has fallen into a trap which has ensnared all Arab leaders. It would appear that the only way to remain a popular leader in the Arab world today is to keep the flames of hatred toward the state of Israel fanned to a fever pitch. The one who can make the most elaborate and gory promises of Israel's destruction is number one on the hit parade. Whenever an Arab leader senses his popularity waning, he whips up a propaganda program about the need to liberate Palestine, according to Middle-East observers.

It is believed by most experts on the Middle East that Nasser was trapped into the June, 1967, war, playing the game of Blind Man's Bluff. He knew that he could never remain enthroned as the leader of the United Arab Republic if other aggressive Arab leaders railed against Israel in stronger terms. It is reported that he was caught unprepared when U Thant quickly complied with his order to remove the U.N. observers from the buffer zone which separated the Arabic and Israeli armies. Once this occurred, he had no alternative but to make good his threats.

Israel saw the clear danger of a large-scale Egyptian mobilization in the Sinai peninsula and also the threat of not being able to ship through the Gulf of Aqaba. The Israelites also saw the rapid unification of all Arabic nations into a formidable force surrounding them on three sides. Israeli leaders realized that unless they seized the initiative and attacked, there would be no hope of survival.

What started out to be a bold popularity stunt on Nasser's part, designed to make Israel lose face over the blockade of the Gulf of Aqaba, ended in a fiasco. Rather than be completely humiliated in the eyes of the world, Nasser carried the world to the brink of war.

It is this kind of fierce pride and smoldering hatred against Israel that will keep the Middle East a dangerous trouble spot. No Arab leader could hope to remain in power if he were willing to make concessions in negotiating with Israel.

In July, 1968, the headlines in a news magazine warned, "No Easing of Mideast War Danger." The report said that "The recent visit of Egypt's President Nasser to the Soviet Union—the country that arms him against Israel—turned attention to an area that never seems far from the explosion point."[3]

In December, 1968, the ambassador to the United States from Israel, Yitzhak Rabin, a key strategist in the six-day Arab-Israeli War of 1967, said that he couldn't be optimistic about peace in the near future in the Middle East.[4]

U Thant said of the Egypt-Israeli situation, "Never in the history of the United Nations' experience with peace-keeping has there been such complete and sustained disregard for a cease-fire agreed to by the parties." Mr. Thant went on to say that warfare along the Suez Canal had become so intense he might have to consider withdrawal of U.N. cease-fire observers.[5]

At the time this is being written Nasser is reported to be in poor health. Whether he continues to lead Egypt, or is replaced by some other leader or dead by the time this is published, the clearly predictable course of the Middle East will not be changed. There will be continual crises there and a great involvement of the world's major powers.

The King of the South

Current events in the Middle East have prepared the stage for Egypt's last act in the great drama which will climax with the finale, Christ's personal return to earth.

We are not attempting to read into today's happenings any events to prove some vague thesis. This is not necessary. All we need to do is know the Scriptures in their proper context and then watch with awe while men and countries, movements and nations, fulfill the roles that God's prophets said they would.

Long ago the prophet Daniel spoke of Egypt as "the king of the South." Egypt is identified as this power in chapter 11 where Daniel predicts a long span of history involving warfare between Egypt under the Ptolemaic dynasty and Syria under the Seleucid dynasty.

In Daniel 11:40 Daniel leaps over a long era of time to the events which lead up to the personal, visible appearance of Christ as God's righteous conqueror. The phrase "at the time of the end" speaks unmistakably of the beginning of the last great war of history.

Daniel gives great detail concerning the battles and movement of troops which will take place at the beginning of this war. (The war itself will be developed later in Chapter 12.)

Our interest here is the revelation that Egypt will attack the revived state of Israel, which will then be under the control of a false Messiah. This man will probably be a Jew who works closely with the world dictator who will come to power in Rome. (Meet the "Future Fuehrer" in Chapter 9.)

Notice what Daniel says about this attack on Israel: "And at the time of the end the king of the south shall push at and attack him" (Daniel 11:40 Amplified).

This immediately triggers another invasion of Israel by Russia who is here called "the king of the north."

The movement of Russia and its northern confederacy through "the land bridge of the Middle-East" into Egypt serves an ominous warning to Egypt. Speaking of the Russian invader, Daniel prophesies: "He shall stretch forth his hand also upon the countries: and the land of Egypt shall not escape. But he shall have power over the treasures of gold and of silver, and over all the precious things of Egypt; and the Libyans and the Ethiopians shall be at his steps" (Daniel 11:42, 43 KJV).

As we saw in the last chapter, the Hebrew words "Cush" and "Put," which are translated Ethiopia and Libya, represent the black Africans and African Arabs, respectively. Aside from the obvious evidence of a Russian double-cross of the Egyptians, this passage also indicates that the "black African" and "Arab-African" countries will be involved with Egypt and in line for Russian conquest as well. The statement, ". . . the Libyans and Ethiopians shall be at his (the Russian invader) steps," indicates one of two things: they will be next in line for conquest, or they will submit totally to the Russian will and be assimilated into the northern confederacy.

This invasion of Cush and Put, along with Egypt, and their fall together is mentioned more specifically by the prophet Ezekiel: "And a sword shall come upon Egypt, and anguish shall be in Ethiopia (Cush), when the slain fall in Egypt, and her wealth is carried away, and her foundations are torn down.

Ethiopia, and Put, and Lud, and all Arabia, and Libya, and the people of the land that is in league shall fall with them by the sword" (Ezekiel 30:4,5).

This prophecy, in the first nine verses of Ezekiel 30, refers to the judgment of Egypt and her allies during the Tribulation. The phrases, ". . . the day of the Lord" and ". . . a time of doom of nations" places it in the time just prior to the second coming of Christ. For you students of the Bible, we must add that the latter part of the chapter looks at the time when Nebuchadnezzar destroyed Egypt and her allies, but its greater fulfillment is future.

Are you discovering more pieces of this stirring prophetic puzzle? The Egyptian plan to unite the Arabs and the black Africans into a "third world force" seems to be fulfilling what the prophets have said.

Grace Goes to Egypt

After viewing such a bleak picture of the future for Egypt and its confederacy of nations it may seem as though God has written them off. The truth of the matter is, however, quite the contrary.

Isaiah, reliable prophet that he is, reveals that one of the purposes for the judgment of Egypt is to drive its people from faith in false messiahs and "religion" to faith in the one true Savior.

Isaiah warns of a terrible judgment which would fall on Egypt in the last days. He speaks of Egypt's very life source being judged: "And the waters of the Nile will be dried up, and the river will be parched and dry; and its canals will become foul, and the branches of Egypt's Nile will diminish and dry up" (Isaiah 19:5, 6).

If you think the famous Aswan Dam, which diverts the main channel of the Nile River, will help the Egyptian situation, you're mistaken. Somehow the headwaters of the Nile will be diverted and that important river will be a parched piece of real estate. Imagine the terrifying implications of this to an Egyptian!

Isaiah warns of a powerful dictator who will invade and take them over: ". . . I will give over the Egyptians into the hand of a hard master; and a fierce [merciless] king will rule over them" (Isaiah 19:4 RSV). This refers to the Antichrist of Rome who will possess Egypt after Russia is destroyed.

All of these things will happen to the Egyptians until many cry out to the true Savior, Jesus. Isaiah says, ". . . when they cry to the Lord because of oppressors he will send them a savior, and will defend and deliver them" (Isaiah 19:20).

What a great demonstration of God's loving heart! Often men won't see their need of God until He so shakes up their world that they are helpless to cope with life without Him. It's only then that they turn to trust in God's provision for their shortcomings. Then they discover that Jesus Christ has so paid the penalty for their sins that God can offer a totally free gift of forgiveness and accept them into His eternal family.

A Lesson From Egypt

As you read this book you may have reached the point where you recognize your inability to live in a way that would cause God to accept you. If this is the case, you may speak to God right now and accept the gift of Christ's forgiveness. It's so simple. Ask Christ to come into your life and make your life pleasing to God by His power.

We have found the results to be certain and exciting in our own lives.

Putting It Together

We have seen how current events are fitting together simultaneously into the precise pattern of predicted events. Israel has returned to Palestine and revived the nation. Jerusalem is under Israeli control. Russia has emerged as a great northern power and is the avowed enemy of revived Israel. The Arabs are joining in a concerted effort to liberate Palestine under Egyptian leadership. The black African nations are beginning to move from sympathy toward the Arabs to an open alliance in their "liberation" cause.

It's happening. God is putting it all together. God may have His meaning for the "now generation" which will have a greater effect on mankind than anything since Genesis 1.

Will you be ready if we are to be a part of the prophetic "now generation"?

7 ○ The Yellow Peril

. . . the great river, the Euphrates . . . was dried up, that the way might be prepared for the kings of the east . . . And they gathered them together in the place which in Hebrew is called Har-Magedon.   REVELATION 16:12, 16 (NASB)

JOHN THE APOSTLE about A.D. 90

"THE KINGS OF the East" in Biblical prophecy refers to another sphere of power which was to arise in the world at the same time as the great Northern Power (Russia) and the King of the South (Egypt and the Afro-Arabic alliance).

The original Greek words translated "east" (Revelation 16:12) are literally *anatoles heliou*, which mean, "the rising of the sun." This was the ancient designation of the Oriental races and nations. John describes this vast horde of soldiers assembled at the Euphrates River as "the kings of the sun rising" and thus definitely predicts the movement of a vast Oriental army into a war in the Middle East.

The mention of the Euphrates River brings out another important strategic clue about this Eastern confederacy. This great river has figured prominently in military history throughout the ages. It was always recognized as the ancient boundary between east and west. In the late nineteenth century a scholar said of this fact: "From time immemorial the Euphrates, with its tributaries, has been a great and formidable boundary between the peoples east of it and those west of it. It runs a distance of 1800 miles, and is scarcely fordable anywhere or at any time. It is from three to twelve hundred yards wide, and from ten to thirty feet in depth; and most of the time it is still deeper and wider."[1] This clue shows that this power is Oriental, since it comes from east of the Euphrates.

The Euphrates has presented a formidable problem for the corps of engineers of many ancient armies of the past. In this future invasion, however, God Himself will see to it that the river is dried up so that a trap is set for triggering the last great war of mankind.

Another important detail involving this Oriental army is unlocked by the clue involving the Euphrates. The apostle John speaks of the release of four vicious, depraved angelic beings which have been kept bound by God at the Euphrates River (Revelation 9:14-16). Immediately after their release an incredible army emerges from the Euphrates . . . it numbers "200 million" (Revelation 9:16). The four demonic spirit-beings somehow incite this great army to invade the Middle East and apparently they are the ones who make the river dry up so that the army can quickly cross this ancient barrier of east and west.

A terrifying prophecy is made about the destiny of this Asian horde. They will wipe out a third of the earth's population (Revelation 9:18). The phenomena by which this destruction of life will take place is given: it will be by fire, smoke (or air pollution), and brimstone (or melted earth). The thought may have occurred to you that this is strikingly similar to the phenomena associated with thermonuclear warfare. In fact, many Bible expositors believe that this is an accurate first-century description of a twentieth-century thermonuclear war.

Another Coincidence?

These predictions, made near the end of the first century, concerned an Asian confederacy which would field the greatest army ever to march to battle. This army would be raised up just prior to Christ's return to the earth.

For centuries Asia has had a tradition of backwardness. Though the peoples of Asia have always been numerous in population, they lagged behind the West in education, science and technology. For hundreds of years Asia chose to remain isolated from the world; then that isolation was broken.

Japan was the first Asian nation to push out into the stream of modern science; it was the first Asian nation in centuries to set out on a course of conquest beyond the Orient. But Japan never truly got outside of the Asian boundaries.

The Japanese navy almost brought a great invasion force into the Middle East during World War II. A convoy set sail for the Red Sea to enter the African and Palestinian campaign and break the Allied resistance there. Nothing could have stopped them. They would have defeated the British who were already extended by Field Marshall Rommel's Afrika Corps.

The British navy had only a handful of ships in the Indian Ocean and they were quickly ordered to flee to Madagascar to avert suicide. Had the Japanese continued as originally planned, World War II could have had a different ending.

It was at this point that a strange thing happened. Admiral Yamamoto, for some unexplainable reason, changed the order, and had the task force turn around in the Indian Ocean and head for the West Coast of the United States. We believe this must have been divine providence.

The intention of this task force was miraculously discovered when some sailors of the U.S. Navy intercepted their radio messages and broke the code. The battle that ensued was really the turning point of the war. With a handful of B-17 bombers and a vastly outnumbered task force, the U.S. Navy turned back the Japanese at the Battle of the Coral Sea.

Japan went on to be defeated and her dreams of world conquest have been put away.

However, the churning of upheaval was taking place in the Orient.

The Dragon Is Awake

With the Communist takeover of China, the real sleeping giant of Asia was awakened. In about 1860 an astute student of prophecy, Dr. Robinson, predicted: "Before another half century shall have rolled away in the providence of God there will be seen revolutions in the Oriental mind of which no one has even a foreboding."[2]

Dr. Cumming in 1864 also foresaw the necessity of the Orient entering the industrial age and later becoming a great scourge to the Western civilization.[3]

In the twenty odd years since the fall of China to the Communists there has been a steady relentless preparation for all-out war with the free world. Though the living conditions of the eight hundred million or more people of Red China are still basically like the nineteenth century, they have made remarkable progress in the production of weapons for war.

Concerning Red China's potential and purpose, Victor Petrov said in 1967, "China does possess all the prerequisites for being or becoming a world power. Communist China's economic growth is evident and has been on the rise. With or without Soviet help, she will be progressing toward her avowed goal of reaching the industrial level of the other major powers of the world . . . a giant, for decades half-asleep, sheepishly watching the rest of the world go by on the path of technological progress. This giant has apparently been awakened."[4]

Red China is definitely on the road to becoming a world power, but her design for the use of this stature is not peace. Within one year after the takeover of China her Communist leaders started the war in Korea. They have since fomented the war in Viet Nam and have traveled to several countries in Africa and the Middle East seeking to aggravate internal subversion and "Communist wars of liberation."

The vaunted Sino-Soviet split is over an interpretation of Communist doctrine. The Chinese insist that the world can be captured only by force of arms and violence: the Russians now believe that the free world can be captured by the relatively limited violence of internal subversion . . . while masquerading under the guise of "peaceful coexistence." It should be marked well, however, that neither have disembarked from their goal of total world conquest for Communism. This is an integral part of the Communist doctrine. Without the total destruction of the capitalist system the basic promise and goal of Communism could not be attained, that is, the changing of man's nature by the complete change of his environment. According to the Communists, as long as capitalism exists in the world it continues to infect man's environment and prevents him from being a creature that loves to work, shares equally his wealth, and loves his fellow man.

The great charge of the Red Chinese against the Russians is the most despicable word in the Communists' vocabulary—"revisionist." They believe that the Russians have "revised" the most fundamental principle of Marxist-Leninism. Lenin succinctly stated this principle. "Marxists have never forgotten that violence will be an inevitable accompaniment of the collapse of capitalism. . . ."[5]

Mao Tse-tung summarized his interpretation of this principle when he said, "Political power comes out of the barrel of a gun . . . the gun must never slip from the grasp of the Communist party."[6]

The basic difference can be described as "external invasion and takeover" versus "internal subversion and takeover."

Because of the Communist Chinese belief that the free world can only be overthrown by all-out war, they have for many years devoted approximately ten per cent of their entire military budget for developing nuclear weapons. In the February, 1969, issue of the *Bulletin of Atomic Scientists*, which was on the theme of "China's Nuclear Options," special note was made of the fantastic technological feat achieved by China's development of the H-Bomb. They went from the testing of a crude atomic bomb to the successful test firing of an H-bomb in two and one half years. This was much faster than the time taken by the other members of the world's Atomic Bomb Club.

In the same issue of the *Bulletin of Atomic Scientists*, Michael Yahuda discussed the various options which the Red Chinese have for a delivery system for H-bombs. He expressed the following opinion: "The third option— an ICBM based strategy—would be the most satisfying psychologically to the present Chinese leadership and to Mao in particular. At one fell stroke, the Chinese would have acquired the most advanced weapon . . . The American mainland would be within range as indeed would the Urals and

European Russia. Current, although incomplete, evidence suggests that the Chinese are striving for an ICBM capability."[7]

Yahuda's speculation is certainly shared by the military planners. This was undoubtedly the prime motivation behind the Nixon administration's push for an anti-ballistic missile system.

Dr. David Inglis wrote in the February, 1965, *Bulletin of Atomic Scientists* regarding this threat, "Our concern should anticipate at least two decades ahead. In such a time the large human and material potential of an upsurging China constitutes a nuclear threat so vast that no effort should be spared to anticipate this threat."[8] This was written before China's successful testing of the H-bomb.

Mao may be dead before this is read, but the course of China's path of destruction will continue. The new leaders of Communist China may be more unstable than Mao.

We believe that China is the beginning of the formation of this great power called "the kings of the east" by the apostle John. We live at a time in history when it is no longer incredible to think of the Orient with an army of 200 million soldiers. In fact, a recent television documentary on Red China, called "The Voice of the Dragon," quoted the boast of the Chinese themselves that they could field a "people's army" of 200 million militiamen. In their own boast they named the same number as the Biblical prediction. Coincidence?

Furthermore, the Chinese leaders claim that even nuclear weapons cannot stop their human wave tactics. They brag about the invincibility of the unbelievable numbers of soldiers they can expend in a given campaign. This "human wave" tactic seems to be behind the strategy of that 200 million man army predicted as invading the Middle East in the battle of Armageddon. Petrov says regarding this, "The abundant population presents an unlimited source of human material for military power, which in our age of machinery and automation has not yet been found obsolete. China's armed forces are formidable in numbers . . . that day apparently is approaching when China will definitely become a member of that small but exclusive group commonly known as the Great World Powers."[9]

The sobering fact that Red China will have ICBM's capable of delivering H-bombs by 1980 at the latest, presents another grisly potential for fulfilling prophecy regarding this Oriental power. Within a decade China alone will have the capacity to destroy one-third of the world's population just as John predicted.

Summing Up

We believe that another sphere of political power is forming its predicted role in the final stages of history. Along with the revival of Israel and the return of the dispersed Jews, the rise of Russia, the formation of the Arab confederacy, China is helping to shape the Orient into its pattern of prophecy.

History seems to be headed for its climactic hour.

8 ○ Rome on the Revival Road

Veni, vidi, vici.   CAESAR, 47 B.C.

WHEN CAESAR SENT his memorable dispatch, "I came, I saw, I conquered," the scribes of his day might have said, "We shall record these historic words immediately. Perhaps Latin students centuries from now will be required to memorize them."

Students who have struggled through Latin declensions and waded with Caesar through campaigns in Gaul know his famous words well. Certainly many other men have expressed themselves more eloquently. But there haven't been many men through the centuries who have had the power of Julius Caesar.

But Rome fell. And Caesar died as any mortal must. And the mighty Roman empire of the ancient world lost its strength.

However, the prophetic Scriptures tell us that the Roman Empire will be revived shortly before the return of Christ to this earth. A new Caesar will head this empire and "Veni, vidi, vici" will leap out of the first-year Latin books and become a reality of the times.

Twenty years ago no one would have dared to believe that Rome as an empire would be put back together. And yet we are seeing significant movements of nations today which are indications that this is what is happening.

As world events develop, prophecy becomes more and more exciting. Also, the understanding of God's prophecies becomes increasingly clear as we look at the Bible and then at the current scene.

We are told in Daniel 12 how prophecy "will not be understood until the end times, when travel and education shall be vastly increased."

We are told that "Surely the Lord God will do nothing without revealing His secret to His Servants the prophets" (Amos 3:7 Amplified).

In other words, when God is going to undertake some significant movement of history as far as His program is concerned, He will reveal it first. This writer doesn't believe that we have prophets today who are getting direct revelations from God, but we do have prophets today who are being given special insight into the prophetic word. God is opening the book of the prophets to many men. This is one reason you will find on Christian bookshelves an increasing number of books on the subject of Bible prophecy.

All Roads Lead To . . .

Where in prophecy do we find a prediction about the revival of Rome? First we shall examine the great prophet, Daniel. Chapter 7 of Daniel was written sometime in the early sixth century B.C., at a time when Babylon was still the ruling empire of the world. In the first part of this chapter the prophet Daniel was shown the successive empires which would come on the stage of history and have authority over the whole earth. A vision of these empires was also described in Daniel 2. The key to these empires is given in Daniel 2:39 where he predicts the successive empires which shall "bear rule" (literally meaning, shall have authority) over all the earth.

First of all, there was Babylon. "You (king of Babylon) are the head of gold."

Then the prophet tells us what kingdoms will rise to power after Babylon.

"And after you shall arise another kingdom [the Media-Persian], inferior to *and* earthward from you, and still a third kingdom of bronze [Greece under Alexander the Great], which shall bear rule over all the earth. And the fourth kingdom [Rome] shall be strong as iron, since iron breaks to pieces and subdues all things; and like iron which crushes, it shall break and crush all these" (Daniel 2:39, 40 Amplified).

These kingdoms would conquer everything that was worth conquering on the known earth of that time.

The Greatest Chapter in the Old Testament

The seventh chapter of Daniel, written before the coming of Jesus of Nazareth, was known by the scribes as the greatest chapter in the Old Testament. Jesus and His apostles referred to it directly or indirectly many times. Many of the predictions from Daniel's dream have been clear in their historic perspective for centuries. However, certain parts have remained obscure until recent times.

Daniel had a dream, and in this dream he saw four great beasts come up out of the sea. The first beast was like a lion, but had eagle's wings. The second beast was like a bear; the third beast was like a leopard, but had four heads. The fourth animal was "dreadful and terrible"—it had iron teeth and ten horns.

If you were an interpreter of dreams, how would you feel if you had a nightmare like Daniel's? Probably you can sympathize with the prophet when he said he was confused and disturbed. But we do not need to be confused by the outward complexity of these descriptions. Daniel had it explained to him by the angels who were the official interpreters of this vision. "These great beasts, which are four, are four kings, which shall arise out of the earth" (Daniel 7:17 KJV).

The first kingdom was Babylon, which became a world empire in 606 B.C. when it conquered Egypt. Nebuchadnezzar took over the Babylonian empire upon his father's death and made it a world kingdom.

The second kingdom, which was like a bear, was the Media-Persian empire (Daniel 8:20). The Babylonian empire was conquered by the Medes and Persians about 530 B.C. when they ingeniously built the dam in the Euphrates River.

For a time the Media-Persian empire was great. The first two kings became believers in the God of Israel. But Daniel predicted long before the Greeks grew in power, when their future leaders were obscure Macedonian hillbillies, that they would become strong and defeat the Media-Persian empire. And so they did. In 331 B.C. Alexander the Great conquered the Persian empire and took it over. The third empire, according to prophecy, became a reality in history.

As predicted in Daniel 8, the Greek empire disintegrated when the first king died prematurely. It was also predicted that four powers from within would divide the empire. And so it happened. Four generals of Alexander the Great took over the empire and divided it into four parts—they lasted until about 68 B.C. when the Romans conquered the last part of the ancient Greek empire. It was then that Rome became the greatest world power to that date.

If you are a careful Bible student you know the common sport in the classroom today, especially in courses called "The Bible as Literature," or something similar. Teachers love to tear the Book of Daniel apart—they especially like to late-date it. Some liberal professors claim that it was written in 165 B.C., in order to discredit the supernatural element of prophecy. However, the authenticity of Daniel and its early date has been carefully defended by such scholars as Dr. Merril F. Unger,[1] Dr. E. J. Young,[2] and Sir Robert Anderson.[3]

Focus on the Fourth Kingdom

The fourth kingdom, Rome, was not given the name of any animal, but it would be a beast unlike any other—more ferocious than all the rest. "Then I would know the truth of the fourth beast, which was diverse from all the others, exceeding dreadful, whose teeth were of iron, and his nails of brass; which devoured, brake in pieces, and stamped the residue with his feet" (Daniel 7:19 KJV).

This verse speaks of the first phase of this fourth kingdom. In phase 1 this kingdom gains world authority (as Rome did), and then disappears to merge again just before Christ returns to establish the Kingdom of God.

Rome: Phase 2

In phase two of the fourth kingdom, Rome, the kingdom will be in the form of a ten-nation confederacy. "And of the ten horns that were in his head, and of the other which came up, and before whom three fell; even of that horn that had eyes, and a mouth that spake very great things, whose look was more stout than his fellows" (Daniel 7:20 KJV).

The meaning of these symbols will become clearer as we continue in Daniel. To the uninitiated these Biblical pictures may seem to resemble the famous Dr. Seuss animals. However, Biblical symbolism is established in historical fact.

Daniel continues with his vision: "I beheld, and the same horn made war with the saints, and prevailed against them; Until the Ancient of days came, and judgment was given to the saints of the most High; and the time came that the saints possessed the kingdom" (Daniel 7:21, 22 KJV).

The "Ancient of Days" who is described here is identified in Daniel 7:13 as "one like the Son of Man" brought on the clouds of heaven—the One who will put down all human authority and establish His kingdom forever.

There is a cohesiveness to the Scriptures that is fascinating. Jesus knew the prophecies of His coming. When He was on trial before the Sanhedrin, which was the Jewish high court, He was put under oath by the high priest to tell who He really was. He was asked directly, "Are you the Son of God?" Jesus answered, "I am." He also said, "Ye shall see the Son of man sitting on the right hand of power, and coming in the clouds of heaven" (Mark 14:62-64 KJV).

Jesus was referring to this verse in Daniel 7:13 and everyone in that court of law knew what He was talking about. The high priests knew the prophets and their writings. They were furious with Jesus and proclaimed Him a blasphemer because He was claiming to be the "Ancient of days" who was coming to set up God's kingdom on earth.

To continue with the second phase of the Roman empire, the Scripture says that the ten horns which were just described are ten kings, or ten nations: "And the ten horns out of this kingdom are ten kings that shall arise: and another shall rise after them; and he shall be diverse from the first, and he shall subdue three kings" (Daniel 7:24 KJV).

When the Scripture says "out of" it means the ten nations (ten kings) which will come out of Rome, since Rome was the fourth kingdom. But who is "another"? This is the beast, the Antichrist.

After these ten nations arise out of the cultural inheritance of the Ancient Roman Empire, another king shall rise "diverse from the first." In other words, he will be different. He will not only be a political leader, but a religious leader. (We shall see this in the next two chapters.) When he comes to power, he will subdue three of these kings or nations. Seven of them, however, will give him authority willingly.

. . . Couldn't Put Rome Together Again

The Roman influence upon the world is so extensive that it touches Western civilization in every aspect of life. From absorbing epics like *Ben Hur* to the Roman candle we shoot on the Fourth of July, we are saturated with the glory that was Rome. However, Rome disintegrated from within; unfortunately, there is in America the same trend in moral decay that led to the downfall of Rome.

It is interesting to see in history how men have attempted to put together the old Roman Empire. Charlemagne tried to do this in A.D. 800. His "Roman Empire" included what are now the countries of France, Germany, Italy, Holland and Belgium. Charlemagne was crowned by the Pope as Emperor Charles Augustus. But his empire was not the ten-nation confederacy of the Scriptures.

Napoleon tried his strutting best to establish his own Roman Empire. Another Pope, Pius VII, made a tedious trip across the Alps to Notre Dame cathedral in Paris to place an imperial crown on Napoleon, but the new little Caesar snatched the crown from the Pope and put it on himself. His empire was not the revived Roman Empire, either.

And then there was Hitler. Does anyone doubt that he attempted to put Rome together again? He said his Third Reich would last a thousand years. God had other plans and Hitler lost.

In spite of the vain striving of man, of the bold and infamous conquerors throughout the ages who failed in their human attempts, we are beginning to see the Ancient Roman Empire draw together, just as predicted.

If you are racing for your Rand McNally, please spare yourselves the exertion. We are not speaking of a revived Roman Empire in the physical, geographical sense, although some of these countries were part of the Ancient Roman Empire, but we are speaking of those countries which are the depository of the people, the culture, and tradition of Rome.

United We . . . Must

If the formation of the European Common Market were an isolated development in the line of Biblical prophecy, then it would have no significance for our study. However, combined with the other pieces of the prophetic puzzle which we are attempting to develop for you, it takes on immense importance.

We believe that the Common Market and the trend toward unification of Europe may well be the beginning of the ten-nation confederacy predicted by Daniel and the Book of Revelation.

What particular forces are contributing to the evolvement of this federation that the conquerors of history could not command?

First, there is the threat of Communism. One of the great motivating factors in forming this economic community and NATO was the concern over a common enemy. An article about "Mister Europe at Eighty," quotes Jean Monnet, called the father of the Common Market, as saying, "As long as Europe remains divided, it is no match for the Soviet Union. Europe must unite."[4]

The second reason for the formation of the European Common Market was the economic threat of the United States. Europeans realized they could not survive the industrial might of the United States. A charismatic personality on the present-day scene is Jean-Jacques Servan-Schreiber, newspaper editor and author of The American Challenge, a book which has received great acclaim throughout Europe. Some have said that the handsome Frenchman is pushing hard for a United States of Europe because he wants to become its first president. Whether this is true or not we would not venture to guess. However, it does seem that he is "furiously trying to push a U.S. of Europe," as one writer expressed it.

Servan-Schreiber is quoted as saying that "a successful response to American technology, organization, and research demands a united European effort."[5]

The third reason this writer feels Europe will form this ten-nation confederacy is that Europeans sense the basic weakness of the United States in its will to resist Communism. They seem to realize that if Europe were really at stake the U.S. would be dragging its feet in reacting against a Russian invasion. As an American it is difficult to write these words, but Europe does not feel that it can count on us in a real showdown.

A fourth factor is that according to the prophetic outlook the United States will cease being the leader of the West and will probably become in some way a part of the new European sphere of power.

Sheath your weapons, please. We realize that the United States is not mentioned in the Bible. However, it is certain that the leadership of the West must shift to Rome, in its revived form, and if the U.S. is still around at that time, it will not be the power it now is.

In spite of many who propose alternatives to a United States of Europe, and the temporary setbacks it appears to have, it seems that the trend is ever onward. An American business magazine said, "Despite its tendency to hang dangerously over cliffs, the Common Market is here to stay."[6]

A fifth factor in the trend toward the ten-nation confederacy is the realization of the great potential of a United Europe. Many men have been preaching this, not just Servan-Schreiber. A few years ago the French foreign minister said that the Common Market will carry with its network of interests and involvements across the world such weight that it will eventually become a world system.

Former Secretary of State Dean Rusk said, "Powerful forces are moving in the European community toward political integration as well. Survival and growth force the nations of Europe to forget their historic antagonisms and unite. Through the pooling of the resources and efforts a mighty new entity is growing out of the chaos left by national rivalries and world wars."[7]

A friend who lives in Germany sent us this translated statement of Dr. Walter Hallstein, who was formerly the president of the European Economic Community. Our correspondent, knowing our interest in Bible prophecy, thought there was significance in Hallstein's words. We'll let you judge.

"Three phases of the European unification are to be noted. First, the customs union, second, the economic union, third, the political union . . . what we have created on the way to uniting Europe is a mighty economic-political union of which nothing may be sacrificed for any reason. Its value exists not only in what it is, but more in what it promises to become . . . At about 1980 we may fully expect the great fusion of all economic, military, and political communities together into the United States of Europe."

Hallstein cited 1980. The timetable may be accelerating. Developments in Europe have changed so rapidly that an American news magazine had a feature headed "Europe's Dreams of Unity Revive."

One sentence in that story leaped from the page: "Should all go according to the most optimistic schedules, the Common Market could someday expand into a ten-nation economic entity whose industrial might would far surpass that of the Soviet Union."[8]

Imagine that. A "ten-nation economic entity."

Is it any wonder that men who have studied prophecy for many years believe that the basic beginning of the unification of Europe has begun?

What Else Is New?

At the time that this Roman Empire will begin to be revived there will also be a revival of mystery Babylon. If this sounds rather spooky, bring your head out from under the skeptical covers and examine with us in a later chapter the Biblical basis and the current applications.

Heading the revived Roman Empire will be a man of such magnetism, such power, and such influence, that he will for a time be the greatest dictator the world has ever known. He will be the completely godless, diabolically evil "future fuehrer."

9 ○ The Future Fuehrer

The spirit that I have seen may be a devil; and the devil hath power to assume a pleasing shape.

HAMLET

A DICTATOR? WHO is a dictator? What makes a dictator? A dictator is a person with absolute authority, a person who has power over people. Does he appear suddenly on the scene and say, "Stop this outmoded democratic process, I am your leader now"? That isn't the way it happens.

A dictator does not thrust his rule upon people from the top down, without provocation. His tyranny is the end result of chaos in the society that results in his rise to despotic power. The dictionary describes him as a person who seizes the authority over a nation as the result of an emergency.

The chicken and egg principle does not apply here. A troubled society produces the atmosphere for the rise of a dictator, it is not the dictator who initiates the conditions which account for his rise. However, once established as the "Big Cheese," history has shown that the dictator cannot find lasting solutions to the problems.

The power-mad leader of the Third Reich, Adolf Hitler, would not have achieved his terrifying control over the lives of millions if the times had not been ripe for him. In the 1930's the German people were in despair. Economic depression was shaking the foundations of industry. Millions were out of work. Small business enterprises were collapsing. It was a desperate time, with desperate people looking for a way out. Hitler, with his evil genius, knew the mood of the German people. He saw the opportunity to pursue his Putsch in precisely the era that history demanded.

Hitler saw himself as a hero, a savior, a strong man needed by weak underlings—a "great leader" who could guide the Germans to heights of glory, according to his standards. He believed he was above the moral standards of ordinary man. Consequently, he surrounded himself with shady characters of every type. As long as they were useful to him this motley bunch of criminals and sadists were part of the ruling strength of Hitler's inner circle.

When in Rome

Hitler took the name for his empire from the all-powerful First Reich, which was the Holy Roman Empire. It was in Rome that the Caesars introduced universal Caesar worship. Their dictatorial powers, also, were absolute.

A Scottish Bible scholar has written: "The extraordinary fact is that emperor worship was not imposed on the Roman Empire from above; it grew from below."[1]

Shades of Hitler.

However, there were differences between Hitler-allegiance and emperor worship. Hitler's rise to power was rapid in comparison. Emperor worship was a gradual development which grew out of the gratitude of the provincials for what Rome had done for them. When Rome took over a country and unpredictable tyrants were booted out, Roman justice was established. The Roman peace, *Pax Romana*, was unlike anything the world had seen and people were deeply grateful.

It was not enough for the populace to appreciate Rome. This was an impersonal thing. The spirit of Rome needed to be personalized; the emperor of Rome began to be regarded as divine.

Before Christ was born, Caesar was worshiped.

"The first temple to be erected to the godhead of the emperor was built in Pergamum in 29 B.C. Caesar worship had begun."[2]

Can you imagine what happened in Rome? The empire was vast, it had many races and languages. It needed a unifying principle and "religion" can be a very unifying influence. Soon every Roman citizen was compelled to burn a pinch of incense and say, "Caesar is Lord."

Is it any wonder that Caesar worship ran head on into Christianity? When the Christians refused to call Caesar their lord, they were subjected to inhumane persecution. The gigantic movie epics showing the lions in the arena with the Christians and the public killings for the gory amusement of the Roman pagan leaders are not conjured from the imaginations of Hollywood producers.

There are many seeds which are planted in the breeding ground for dictators; anarchy, lawlessness, moral decadence, human desperation, and false hero worship fertilize the fields that produce despots. All the gold carat and two-bit demagogues of history grew out of the soil of the times.

Where Do We Fit In?

Are we living in a peaceful, placid era when people enjoy an environment free of tensions? Ridiculous question to ask, isn't it? But when we slow down our daily lives long enough to take a hard, realistic look at the generation we live in, it's a real shocker.

There are many shoulder-shruggers who say, "Always been crime and wars—always will be—why get all hot and bothered about what's going on today?"

A short time ago we saw a graph in a newsmagazine which indicated the climb in serious crimes in the United States from 1960 to 1968. If you had been an ant on that page you would have had a very steep stairway to climb each one of those eight years. While the number of crimes in America was increasing 122 per cent, the population rose only 11 per cent.[3]

Many people have stopped talking about the "crime rate." They now refer to the "crime epidemic."

Crime is waged on a grand scale by nations. Since World War II the world has been embroiled in conflict that seems to grow increasingly vicious. There has been a rebirth of guerrilla warfare; revolutions and revolutionary movements are becoming a way of life during this latter part of the twentieth century.

War and more war. Has there ever been a time when the potential for self-destruction was as great as it is today?

Another Boom

Some people feel that the concern about the population explosion is exaggerated. They point out that the marvelous technological advances of science will overcome the burgeoning boom in human beings on this earth.

They may be right. However, many experts who have studied and evaluated the population growth have arrived at statistics and conclusions which are rather awesome, to say the least. A 1969 report from the United Nations national policy panel on world population claimed that the population crisis is the world's concern and that it is as important as peace itself. This report projects the world population will reach 7.5 billion by the year 2000. Since the number of human beings on earth in 1968 was 3.4 billion, we see that if the estimate is correct, there will be more than twice as many people in the world thirty years from now.

This same report said "high fertility and high rates of population" contribute to pollution, congestion, urban sprawl, and a host of psychological ailments in developed countries and might mean widespread famine, increased illiteracy, unemployment, squalor, and unrest threatening the foundations of public order in developing countries.[4]

Chairman of the Genetics Department at Ohio State University, J. Bruce Griffing, is quoted as saying that "Unless mankind acts immediately, there will be a worldwide famine in 1985, and the extinction of man within 75 years."[5]

We may not think this will affect us personally, but in 1967 Dr. Stanley F. Yolles, director of the National Institute of Mental Health, said:

"Population movement and the increased pressures of a speeded-up society undoubtedly are causing an increasing amount of emotional disturbance. Between 1960 and 1965 the number of U.S. psychiatrists, psychologists, and other mental health workers rose forty-four per cent. Youngsters are being admitted to mental hospitals in numbers seven times their share of the total population. Many of those left on the outside proclaim loudly their 'alienation from society.'"[6]

If we complain about not being able to find "breathing space," or resent being squeezed into an impersonal computerized society, imagine what it might be like thirty years from now, if we're still around!

Men who are studying population biology, such as Paul Ehrlich, professor at Stanford University and expert in this field, are inclined to be doomsters because of the research they have done. Ehrlich, for instance, says: "Mankind may be facing its final crisis. No action that we can take at this late date can prevent a great deal of future misery from starvation and environmental deterioration."[7]

All Systems Go

It doesn't take a "religious" person to discern the fact that what is happening is setting the world in the proper frame for a dictator. We see anarchy growing in every country. We see established standards of morality thrown aside for a hedonistic brand which is attractively labeled the "New Morality." We see the super-weapons and the threats of atheistic leaders in world powers who would not hesitate to use those weapons if they would further their drive for conquest.

A view seems to be creeping into the consciousness of concerned people that the problems and the tensions of the world need to be controlled by a "strong hand from someplace."

Even Arnold Toynbee, the eminent historian, said on a radio broadcast that "By forcing on mankind more and more lethal weapons, and at the same time making the world more and more interdependent economically, technology has brought mankind to such a degree of distress that we are ripe for the deifying of any new Caesar who might succeed in giving the world unity and peace."

Who Is the "Future Fuehrer"?

The time is ripe and getting riper for the Great Dictator, the one we call the "Future Fuehrer." This is the one who is predicted in the Scriptures very clearly and called the "Antichrist."

The Bible gives a perfect biographical sketch of this future world leader.

If you will follow this Scripture from Revelation, without being bothered by the figures of speech which are used, you will see that the Bible explains the meaning.

"And he stood on the sand of the seashore. And I saw a beast coming up out of the sea, having ten horns and seven heads, and on his horns were ten diadems, and on his heads were blasphemous names.

And the beast which I saw was like a leopard, and his feet were like those of a bear, and his mouth like the mouth of a lion. And the dragon gave him his power and his throne and great authority" (Revelation 13:1, 2 NASB).

You may be saying that this doesn't sound like a human being to you, but just press on and follow carefully how the mystery unfolds.

Revelation continues with this description: "And I saw one of his heads as if it had been slain. . . ." Mark carefully the "as if" in the phrase above. ". . . and his fatal wound was healed. And the whole earth was amazed and followed after the beast; and they worshiped the dragon, because he gave his authority to the beast; and they worshiped the beast, saying, 'Who is like the beast, and who is able to wage war with him?'" (Revelation 13:3, 4 NASB).

This person, the Antichrist, is called the "beast" because from God's viewpoint that is exactly what he is. The passage is obviously talking about a person because the personal pronoun "he" is used. He is also described as a person of great authority.

In the seventeenth chapter of Revelation we are given the meaning of this description of the beast coming out of the sea. Revelation 17:15 says: "And he said to me, 'The waters which you saw where the harlot sits, are peoples and multitudes and nations and tongues'" (NASB).

The "harlot" refers to the religious system which will be tied in with this dictator. This will be described in more detail in the next chapter.

When it says that the beast will emerge out of the sea, it means that he will come out of the chaos of the nations.

In the Old Testament, Isaiah speaks of the chaos of the nations that is to come and says there is no peace for the wicked . . . they are like the "troubled sea," which is a symbolic picture of the Gentile nations (Isaiah 57:20, 21).

Like a Leopard, a Bear, and a Lion

"And the beast which I saw was like a leopard, and his feet were like those of a bear, and his mouth like the mouth of a lion" (Revelation 13:2 NASB).

To understand the meaning of this zoo which is described in Revelation, we go back to the predictive ministry of Daniel. As we studied in the previous chapter, Daniel describes his vision of four great beasts who come up out of the sea in succession. These beasts are the great Gentile empires which would rule the world. Daniel described these kingdoms using figurative expressions of wild animals.

Daniel 8 tells who the first, second, and third empires are; thus we can identify the animal figure by the order of the kingdoms. The first one of these empires which Daniel described was like a lion, which was the Babylonian empire. He said the second great kingdom was like a bear, which was the Media-Persian empire. The third kingdom would be like a leopard, and this was the Greek empire.

Then Daniel said there would arise a fourth kingdom, which would take over what was left of the Greek empire. That was Rome.

In Daniel 7:23, 24, Daniel predicts the fourth kingdom . . . and especially the person who would put it together. He says that the fourth kingdom (Rome) shall "devour the whole earth."

However, we saw in "Rome on the Revival Road" that there is a "phase 2" to the Roman Empire. Daniel says that out of the culture of the first Roman Empire ten kings shall arise, and another king after that who is different from the ten. This king is going to subdue three of the kings.

In other words, when this Roman dictator comes, he is going to take over the ten-nation confederacy. Seven of the kings or leaders will willingly give him their allegiance, but three of them will not. So he will overthrow these three leaders.

Now we are able to see how Scripture fits together. If you return to Revelation 13 and look again at verse one you will understand that the "ten horns" refer to this ten-nation confederacy and the "seven heads" are the seven leaders who form a coalition with the Antichrist.

Der Fuehrer's Personality Traits

Some people have said that they turn to the Book of Revelation to find out how it will all end . . . and then can't understand a thing that is said. Now that we know, however, who the leopard, the bear, and the lion were, we should begin to see what Revelation 13:2 means.

It is said here that the beast (the Roman dictator, the Future Fuehrer, or the Antichrist) will be like a leopard, a bear, and lion. A leopard is quick to seize his prey. The leopard was the Greek Empire. Alexander the Great, the Greek military genius, was known for the speed with which he overcame his enemies. He was fearless and strong, a human counterpart of the great leopard. Alexander was a world conqueror who led his armies to the outermost fringes of the known world of his time.

"A bear" referred to the Media-Persian Empire, which was conquered by Alexander. This kingdom, similar to the animal it exemplifies, was very strong and powerful.

The lion (Babylon) is regal. The way he walks and holds his proud head has class. Babylon was an elegant monarchy. Its palaces were splendid and the famous "hanging gardens of Babylon" were considered one of the seven wonders of the world.

Now we are beginning to see, little by little, the picture emerging of the Future Fuehrer. His conquest will be rapid, he will be very strong and powerful, and there will be an air about him which is self-assured and proud.

It is important to note as we follow in Revelation 13 that "the dragon gave him his power and his throne and great authority" (verse 2b).

Who is the dragon?

If we turn back to Revelation 12:9 we are told who he is.

It says, "And the great dragon was thrown down, the serpent of old who is called the Devil and Satan" (NASB).

We read that the dragon is going to give the Antichrist his power. In other words, Satan himself is going to give him fantastic power. He is going to be able to work all kinds of miracles. This is one reason that Christians should not get too excited when they see a miracle. It may not be a miracle of God. Satan is a miracle-worker and he has been able to work miracles from the beginning.

But there is going to be a time when Satan is allowed to work all kinds of supernatural acts through men. It is said that Satan is going to send this man, his masterpiece, with all sorts of signs and wonders and miracles (II Thessalonians 2:9).

The second thing that will be given this man is a throne. This means world government. This throne was offered to Jesus Christ. In Luke 4 it is told how Satan came to Christ during His temptation in the desert and offered Him all the authority and glory of the world. Satan said He could have all the kingdoms to rule, if He would fall down and worship him. There is only one man who could resist that kind of an offer. Satan offered Him a crown if He would by-pass the cross. But Jesus wouldn't buy it.

Now we are studying a man who will accept this throne wholeheartedly. He will be worshiped as Satan is worshiped, with forms of idolatry that we can only guess in our wildest leaps of imagination.

All around the world today the increase in the mystic, occult, and even devil-worship is so pronounced that people are beginning to question what it's all about. There are churches in some of the major cities of America which actually incorporate into their "religious ceremonies" the worship of the devil. A newspaper report said, "Moving hand-in-hand with astrology in some cities is a rising interest in witchcraft and hypnosis. Courses in the art of the history of witchcraft have popped up at a few recognized colleges and at most 'free universities' (where students design the curricula.)"[8]

A university student told this writer that he knew of several people who had signed up for a college course on witchcraft believing that it was a "how to" course, and after discovering that it was more history than mystery, dropped out of the class.

However, the Satan-worship which will be initiated at the time of the world reign of the Future Fuehrer will make today's antics of the cultists look like nursery school.

A Mortal Head Wound

We are told in Revelation 13:3 that this great world leader will have a fatal head wound which will be miraculously healed. Many people have not known just what to make of this statement. Some have thought that what this means is that one of the empires of the ancient Roman Empire would be miraculously revived and brought back to existence. That is one possible interpretation. However, I do not believe that is the right interpretation. Here is why. . . .

Look for a moment at Revelation 13:14. This is speaking of the False Prophet, who will be an associate of the Great Roman Dictator. The verse says: "And he deceives those who dwell on the earth because of the signs which it was given him to perform in the presence of the beast, telling those who dwell on the earth to make an image to the beast who had the wound of the sword and has come to life" (NASB).

Whoever this person is with this fatal wound will have a statue made of himself, and men are going to worship this idol. You do not make an idol of an empire. You make an idol of a person.

The way in which this dictator is going to step onto the stage of history will be dramatic. Overnight he will become the byword of the world. He is going to be distinguished as supernatural; this will be done by an act which will be a Satanic counterfeit of the resurrection. This writer does not believe it will be an actual resurrection, but it will be a situation in which this person has a mortal wound. Before he has actually lost life, however, he will be brought back from this critical wounded state. This is something which will cause tremendous amazement throughout the world.

We could draw a comparison to the tragic death of John F. Kennedy. Imagine what would have happened if the President of the United States, after being shot and declared dead, had come to life again! The impact of an event like that would shake the world.

It is not difficult to imagine what will happen when this coming world leader makes his miraculous recovery. This man, the Antichrist, will probably not be known as a great leader until the time of his revival from the fatal wound. After that the whole world will follow him.

He will have a magnetic personality, be personally attractive, and a powerful speaker. He will be able to mesmerize an audience with his oratory.

"Who is like the beast, and who is able to wage war with him?" These are the expressions the people who live at the time of the appearance of the Antichrist will be saying. They will accept anyone who offers peace, since this is the great cry of the world.

What does this indicate? We recall that the *Pax Romana*, the Roman peace, was the reason the provincials willingly turned to Rome and eventually initiated Caesar worship. Law and order—peace and security—freedom from war. The same needs, the same desires were expressed in ancient times that the Bible says will be prevalent before the Antichrist begins his rule. He will be swept in at a time when people are so tired of war, so anxious for peace at any price, that they willingly give their allegiance to the world dictator who will promise them peace.

There is another place in the Bible where the words of the people who are alive at the time of the coming of the Antichrist are quoted: "While they are saying, 'Peace and safety!' then destruction will come upon them suddenly like birth pangs upon a woman with child; and they shall not escape" (I Thessalonians 5:3).

This is a direct quote from the people who will live under the false security of this world dictator. It is a cry of relief—a sigh of gratitude. "Peace and safety"—at last!

The mood of the world is being developed toward the acceptance of this person. Remember what Toynbee said: "We are ripe for the deifying of any new Caesar who might succeed in giving the world unity and peace."

I Am God

The Antichrist will deify himself—just like the Caesars did. He will proclaim himself to be God. He will demand that he be worshiped and will establish himself in the Temple of God (II Thessalonians 2:4).

There is only one place where this temple of God can be and that is on Mount Moriah in Jerusalem, on the site where the Dome of the Rock and other Moslem shrines now stand. There are many places in the Bible that pinpoint this location as the one where the Jews will rebuild their Temple.

The Antichrist, who is called by many names in the Bible, but in II Thessalonians is called the "lawless one," will come in on a wave of anarchy. This is why the world will be ready to receive him.

You may be asking, "How can this possibly happen while Christians are in the world?"

It can't. As we understand II Thessalonians 2:6-12, the restraining power of the Spirit of God, within believing Christians, will hold back the rise of this World Dictator. We believe it is not until this "restrainer" is removed that his power and might will be exerted over the entire world.

We shall explain this in detail in the chapter on "The Ultimate Trip."

Authority to Act for Three and One-half Years

"And there was given to him a mouth speaking arrogant words and blasphemies; and authority to act for forty-two months was given to him" (Revelation 13:5 NASB).

Forty-two months is three and one-half years and this is the three and one-half years prior to Christ's personal, visible return to this earth. This period of time will make the regimes of Hitler, Mao, and Stalin look like

Girl Scouts weaving a daisy chain by comparison. The Antichrist is going to be given absolute authority to act with the power of Satan.

"And he opened his mouth in blasphemies against God, to blaspheme His name and His tabernacle, that is, those who dwell in heaven" (Revelation 13:6 NASB).

This is interesting. Why would he "blaspheme" or "badmouth" those who will dwell in heaven? And who are the ones who dwell in heaven; why would he even bother with them? You and I are the ones who are going to dwell in heaven, if we are true believers in Jesus Christ. If we are gone from the earth at this period, which this writer believes the Scriptures prove, how is this fellow going to explain the fact that a few million "religious kooks" are missing? He will, of course, have to discredit the Christian belief, explain it away, or "blaspheme" it and the believers.

"And it was given to him to make war with the saints and to overcome them . . ." (Revelation 13:7a NASB).

It is logical to ask at this point, how is he going to make war with the saints when they are gone from the earth? "The saints" are the people who are going to believe in Christ during this great period of conflict. After the Christians are gone God is going to reveal Himself in a special way to 144,000 physical, literal Jews who are going to believe with a vengeance that Jesus is the Messiah. They are going to be 144,000 Jewish Billy Grahams turned loose on this earth—the earth will never know a period of evangelism like this period. These Jewish people are going to make up for lost time. They are going to have the greatest number of converts in all history. Revelation 7:9-14 says they bring so many to Christ that they can't be numbered.

However, the Antichrist is going to unleash a total persecution of these people.

"And it was given to him . . . authority over every tribe and people and tongue and nation . . ." (Revelation 13:7b NASB).

He will be the absolute dictator of the whole world!

This is the Future Fuehrer.

Who Will Worship Him?

"And all who dwell on the earth will worship him, every one whose name has not been written from the foundation of the world in the book of life of the Lamb who has been slain" (Revelation 13:8 NASB).

The book of life to which this passage refers is for those who put their personal faith in Jesus Christ. Christ is the "Lamb" who was slain.

The Old Testament predicted the coming of Jesus in hundreds of prophecies. Over 300 specific predictions were fulfilled in His life and death. He is conclusively proven as the only One who could be the Messiah.

He has a book. That book contains the names of everyone who simply puts his faith in Jesus for having paid the penalty for his sins. Throughout the history of the Jewish people the Passover Lamb typified a sacrifice. What an incredible thing that so many Jews would not see Jesus as the personification of the Lamb. He was the real Lamb of God.

When John the Baptist, one of the greatest prophets of all time, first saw Jesus coming toward him, he said, "Behold, the Lamb of God that takes away the sin of the world" (John 1:29 NASB). In this statement he summarized the whole significance of the Old Testament. It all pointed to Jesus.

So we see who will worship the Antichrist. Everyone will worship him who has not put his faith in Christ.

Is it possible for a moment to project our thoughts toward that time when the entire world will look upon one human being as the supreme leader? The Antichrist will need a lot of help to carry out his diabolical schemes. His staunchest ally will be

The False Prophet

In Revelation 13:11-18 we are introduced to this infamous character. This person, who is called the second beast, is going to be a Jew. Many believe he will be from the tribe of Dan, which is one of the tribes of the original progenitors of the nation of Israel.

The False Prophet (he is called that in Revelation 19:20 and 20:10) will be a master of satanic magic. This future False Prophet is going to be a devilish John the Baptist. He will aid and glorify this Roman Dictator; he will proclaim him the savior of the world and make people worship him as God.

It is logical to ask how the False Prophet will force this worship of the Roman Dictator. He will be given control over the economics of the world system and cause everyone who will not swear allegiance to the Dictator to be put to death or to be in a situation where they cannot buy or sell or hold a job. Everyone will be given a tattoo or mark on either his forehead or forehand, only if he swears allegiance to the Dictator as being God.

Symbolically, this mark will be 666. Six is said to be the number of man in Scripture and a triad or three is the number for God. Consequently, when you triple "six" it is the symbol of man making himself God.

The cleverness of this economic vise is ghastly to contemplate. But no one could ever accuse Satan of not being clever.

O Come Now. . . .

Do you believe it will be possible for people to be controlled economically? In our computerized society, where we are all "numbered" from birth to death, it seems completely plausible that some day in the near future the numbers racket will consolidate and we will have just one number for all our business, money, and credit transactions. Leading members of the business community are now planning that all money matters will be handled electronically.

Upstage

We believe that the dramatic elements which are occurring in the world today are setting the stage for this magnetic, diabolical Future Fuehrer to make his entrance. However, we must not indulge in speculation about whether any of the current world figures is the Antichrist. He will not be known until his sudden miraculous recovery from a fatal wound.

There would be no earthly advantage in being alive when the Antichrist rules. We believe that Christians will not be around to watch the debacle brought about by the cruelest dictator of all time.

10 ○ Revival
of Mystery
Babylon

Beloved, do not believe every spirit, but test the spirits to see whether they are from God; because many false prophets have gone out into the world. 1 JOHN 4:1 (NASB)

IT IS NOT our purpose to be shocking or offensive. The prophecies of the Bible are a vital part of God's Word, but should not be used for sensationalism. Some of the symbolism in this chapter may seem very strange to modern ears, and some of the indictments of existing beliefs may trigger the defense mechanism in some readers. However, when God's Word is clear, it was never intended that man should dilute what He has to say.

All through the Scriptures we find that Christ dealt strongly with the religious leaders and false prophets who put on their many-colored coats of righteousness and led people astray. Jesus called them hypocrites, fools, and vipers, not exactly soft terms. He tipped over the tables in their places of so-called worship, which was not what men today might consider being broad-minded.

We are told in the Bible that before the seven-year period of tribulation there will be an all-powerful religious system which will aid the Antichrist in subjecting the world to his absolute authority. For a time this religious system will actually have control of the Dictator.

There are several names given to this one-world religion, all of them drawing a perfect analogy in meaning. It is called the Great Harlot, or prostitute; the "harlot" represents a religion which prostitutes the true meaning of being wedded to Christ, and sells out to all the false religions of man.

"Babylon" is another term used for the one-world religion. It is easy to see how a place could also be a system when we consider contemporary examples: Broadway means the theater today, Madison Avenue draws the mental image of the slick advertising world, Wall Street is the hub of finance.

'Tis a Puzzlement

As pieces of the prophecy puzzle appeared to fall into place there was one important part that was lost to me. The Bible outlines very specifically that there would be a one-world religion which would dominate the world in the time before the return of Christ. However, this seemed so remote, with so many different religions competing for the minds and hearts of men, how on earth could people unite in allegiance to just one religion?

Five years ago, for instance, as I surveyed the college campuses where I ministered, it seemed that most of the intellectual community was alienated by any concept of the supernatural. Many of them were not receptive to any form of "religion," which was considered a crutch for the weak, or a rigid set of rules not worth trying to follow.

We should be careful to note at this point that we are using the term "religion," not Christianity. Christianity is not a religion. Religion is the process of man trying to achieve goodness, perfection, and acceptance with God by his own efforts. Christianity, on the other hand, is God taking the initiative and reaching for man. Christianity is God saying that man cannot reach Him except through the one path He has provided—through the acceptance of His Son, Jesus Christ.

But the scene has changed rapidly in the intellectual community in the past few years. Many of those who scoffed at "religion" have become addicted to the fast-moving upsurge in astrology, spiritualism, and even drugs. What does all this mean? Does it have any significance in Biblical prophecy?

We believe that the joining of churches in the present ecumenical movement, combined with this amazing rejuvenation of star-worship, mind-expansion, and witchcraft, are preparing the world in every way for the establishment of a great religious system, one which will influence the Antichrist.

To understand the significance of these movements in relation to this one-world religious system, we should study carefully what the Bible has to say about them. As we begin to examine this in depth, there emerges a pattern which makes the Bible more up-to-date and relevant than any book today.

Origin of Astrology

Many popular American magazines have been commenting recently on astrology and its impact on the contemporary scene; most of these secular writers have done a good job of historical research into the subject. However, few touch upon the best history book of all in doing their reference work.

In Genesis we find that astrology got its beginnings in Babylon, which is verified by secular writers in their historical accounts. There is a remarkable statement in Genesis 11 about the first astrological observatory.

After the great Flood, the Bible tells us, the whole earth had one language. The people who were alive at that time settled in the land of Shinar, which is near the meeting of the Tigris and Euphrates Rivers. This was ancient Babylonia, one of the earliest centers of civilization.

"And they said, Go to, let us build us a city and a tower, whose top may reach unto heaven . . ." (Genesis 11:4 KJV).

Now the city they were speaking about was Babylon, and the tower was the famous Tower of Babel. The interesting thing is that the word "tower" is a word that can mean ziggurat, which was the ancient observatory from which the priests would gaze at the stars.

In many versions of the Bible you will find that in this verse from Genesis 11 the words "may reach" are in italics. This is because they were not in the original Hebrew writings of the Bible. When this passage is studied in Hebrew it becomes obvious that these people had enough intelligence and know-how to realize that they could not build a tower which would actually reach to heaven. It's true that the Babylonian builders were geniuses, but they were not stupid. A tower with its top in heaven meant it would be used to study the stars, chart their courses, and make predictions. Henry H. Halley, who has assembled the comprehensive *Halley's Bible Handbook*, said that the whole purpose of the ziggurats was idolatrous worship.[1]

This origin of astrology was described in what may have been among the first writing known to man, a form of hieroglyphics devised by the ancient race of the Chaldeans who began to give the stars certain meanings. They divided the heavens into the twelve sections of the zodiac and said that the stars control the destiny of men. This religion started to flourish and have its greatest glory of history in the Babylonian Empire, which was primarily made up of the priestly caste of the Chaldean people. These Chaldeans became the aristocracy of the priesthood. We know how esteemed these astrologers and magicians were because every king in Babylon built giant ziggurats for them. The astrologers were considered almost equal in power to the king.

We see God's attitude toward this star-worship when we are told that He destroyed this Babylonian observatory. Nimrod, the first world dictator, was the leader in the Tower of Babel enterprise and through this religious system established at Babylon undoubtedly wished to pursue the ambition of all dictators, and that is to have a one-world government. He did not take God into account, however. God says when you put everyone under one dictator there would be no evil which could be restrained. When the Tower of Babel was destroyed, it was a turning point in history. Where there had been but one language, now God initiated many languages and scattered the people throughout the earth.

This passage shows that God's plan for the world until the Prince of Peace returns is not an international one-world government, but nationalism. This is the one way the world can keep from falling under a dictator who could virtually destroy mankind.

The Scripture says that a Great Dictator is coming and he will be boosted to power, and strengthened in his grasp upon the world with the assistance of the ancient religion called Mystery, Babylon. This is the very religion which started in the Genesis account and made possible the first world dictator.

Some clairvoyants today, without knowledge of Bible prophecy, are saying the same things that the Scriptures tell us. In a publication which specializes in psychic phenomena there was an astounding article which said that "History and many signs of the times point to man's preparation for the coming new world leader." The writer in this magazine dealing with extra-sensory perception, prophecy (not Bible), and spiritual healing, described various events which would precede this new "Leader," among which were. . . . "Conditions shall change and, in the due course of time, people shall be led into a new Age where they have different abilities from those now existing. There shall be clairvoyance and telepathy as there was before the so-called, mis-called, Tower of Babel, in which through the abuse of special powers mankind lost its telepathic abilities *for the time being*."[2] (Emphasis is ours.)

Mystery, Babylon, Condemned

The great prophet, Isaiah, in chapter 47 of his book, gives an analysis of the Babylonian worship and religion. The description and the judgment to be brought upon this "religion" is so significant for today that we can scarcely contain our continuous excitement over prophetic pictures in the Bible.

Isaiah, speaking predictively in 47:1, says: "Come down, and sit in the dust, O virgin daughter of Babylon, sit on the ground: there is no throne, O daughter of the Chaldeans: for thou shalt no more be called tender and delicate" (KJV).

A glance down to verse 5 will indicate further condemnation of Babylon: "Sit thou silent, and get thee into darkness, O daughter of the Chaldeans: for thou shalt no more be called, The lady of kingdoms" (KJV).

(Literally, the "lady" means the "Queen of kingdoms." When we study Revelation 17 this is going to be a very important figure of speech.)

The prophet goes on to analyze the wickedness of Babylon and the reason why God is going to judge this empire. Isaiah shows how Babylon grew away from the true God and was involved in worldly pleasures. Wisdom and knowledge perverted Babylon, and the prophet says that desolation shall "come upon thee suddenly."

However, the most important thing to see is that Babylon was entangled in "sorceries" and "enchantments," two important words which we shall examine carefully . . . and that this civilization could not be saved by "the astrologers, the stargazers, and the monthly prognosticators" who were the advisers to the Babylonians.

Stay Tuned to the Facts

We are not playing a game of Biblical hopscotch when we turn from one prophet to another. If there was not a strong recurring theme in all the prophets, this book would have no validity. It is the complete agreement of all parts of Biblical prophecy which makes its study so absorbing, so filled with tingling vitality for the twentieth century that it is a wonder that every preacher in every pulpit doesn't shake the ecclesiastical rafters with this subject.

Daniel was a prophet whose themes are far-reaching and who predicted events which are yet to happen in the history of our world, events which we are studying in the context of this book. Daniel was a Hebrew nobleman who was taken captive in Babylon by the king of the empire, Nebuchadnezzar. This king had Daniel and several other Jewish noblemen who showed unusual intelligence put into a special school of the wise men. The "wise men" was a general designation given to the astrologers and magicians of the Babylonian empire and Daniel was trained in all the wisdom of the Babylonians. He became an expert in these fields, but he didn't buy it. It was a tremendous test of Daniel's faith, because he was literally brainwashed by the Babylonian religion, but he kept his belief in God, in spite of all this training.

Nebuchadnezzar had a dream which really bothered him and gave him insomnia. He called the whole gang out to help him with this—all his "magicians and astrologers and sorcerers and Chaldeans" (Daniel 2:2, 10, 27).

The first category or word which is translated "magician" means the special sacred scribes—an order of the wise men who had charge of the sacred writings which were handed down all the way from the time of the Tower of Babel. Some of the earliest-known literature on the face of this earth were these books of magic, astrology, and the black arts.

The next word, "astrologer," means literally to whisper—it came to mean "conjure." These were men who were enchanters who would cast spells through the spirit medium. They had all kinds of chants and low, muttering songs through which they thought they could cast out evil.

The "sorcerers" means the black magic art. The same word is used for the Egyptian magicians who confronted Moses (Exodus 7:11). Through their black art they duplicated several miracles which Moses performed in the court. For instance, they turned water into blood. When Moses cast down his rod and it turned into a serpent these "sorcerers" did the same thing in the court of Pharaoh. It wasn't until God enabled Moses to perform miracles that they couldn't duplicate that these magicians said that this was the finger of God. The Egyptians had all of these arts which the Babylonians exported to them.

The next word, "Chaldeans," was the priest caste of all of them. Wherever you see the word "Chaldean" it can be translated equally well as "astrology." Several great linguists unanimously agree on this point that the Chaldeans studied a person's birthday, asking the very hour a person was born, and then they would cast a horoscope of his destiny. You will find that this thinking has permeated the Aramaic world—the Arabs, the Persians, etc. This is where the idea of Kismet came from; it means it is inevitable, it is fate—what will happen will happen. The ancient astrologers believed that your fate was written in the stars before you were born and you can't alter the course of your destiny.

The Babylonian kings did not make a move without consulting their astrologers, and the Media-Persians who conquered the Babylonians did the same thing. They, too, had their court astrologers and wisemen. When the Greek, Alexander the Great, conquered the Media-Persian empire he also began to follow the astrologers and their wisdom. The practice was transported to Rome where we see the Caesars consulting the augurs, who were experts in astrology, spiritism, and the black arts.

When Nebuchadnezzar called upon his wise men for help and advice, none of them could tell him his dream or the interpretation. Daniel, however, proved he was a true prophet of God when he was able to tell the king what the dream was and then give its interpretation. Daniel really puts the bite on his fellow colleagues and shows them up for the frauds they were.

Nebuchadnezzar's dream, described by Daniel and interpreted by this prophet of God, turns out to be the whole course of world powers that would conquer the world right up to the second coming of Jesus Christ.

Daniel shows that astrologers cannot accurately predict the future. As a matter of fact, God condemns astrology. In Deuteronomy 18 astrologers were commanded in that day under the law of Moses to be put to death.

Astrology is the backbone of the ancient religion of Babylon, but there is no such thing as a man's fate being controlled by the stars.

Man's fate is controlled by God alone.

Whenever a person gets sold out by things like astrology, it will be like the Israelis. Israel was judged and virtually destroyed and taken to Babylon in 606 B.C. because the people became devoted to idolatry, especially astrology. II Kings 23 makes this clear when it says that God wiped out the high places and all of the places where they burned incense to the stars of heaven, or to the constellation (the twelve signs of the Zodiac).

Emergence of the One-world Religion

Now we are coming to some of the most important pieces of the prophetic puzzle which are shown in the Scriptures. In Revelation 17 the apostle John has a vision which shows the future and precisely what is going to happen on earth the last seven years before Christ returns. In Revelation 17 John is given one of the most important prophecies for us to understand because he is exposing a one-world religious system which will bring all false religions together in one unit. Through this system Satan's Antichrist will take over the world—and he is going to do it first with Rome as home base and then from Jerusalem.

Scarlet O'Harlot

Look what John says in Revelation 17:3-5: "And he carried me away in the Spirit into a wilderness; and I saw a woman sitting on a scarlet beast, full of blasphemous names, having seven heads and ten horns. And the woman was clothed in purple and scarlet, and adorned with gold and precious stones and pearls, having in her hand a gold cup full of abominations and of the unclean things of her immorality, and upon her forehead a name was written, a mystery, 'BABYLON THE GREAT, THE MOTHER OF HARLOTS AND OF THE ABOMINATIONS OF THE EARTH'" (NASB).

It is sometimes difficult for the Bible reader to grasp this symbolism. Understanding "the mother of harlots," or the great harlot, is important to the basic understanding of the Christian belief, versus all religions. This church which the prophet describes claims to be united to Jesus Christ in mystical marriage, but is really an adulteress in the spiritual sense. This church professes an allegiance to God, but worships a false religious system.

The main thrust of this passage in Revelation 17 is about Mystery, Babylon, who is typified by this woman. "And I saw the woman drunk with the blood

of the saints, and with the blood of the witnesses of Jesus. And when I saw
her, I wondered greatly. And the angel said to me, 'Why do you wonder?
I shall tell you the mystery of the woman and of the beast that carries her,
which has the seven heads and the ten horns'" (Revelation 17:6, 7 NASB).

We know the meaning of the "beast," for we studied this in the chapter
on "The Future Fuehrer." The ten horns, as we have seen, refers to the revived Roman Empire, or a ten-nation confederacy.

The fact that this woman, who is the Mystery, Babylon, is riding upon
this beast shows that she controls him. Historically this "religion" has
controlled many empires. Notice what John the Apostle, writing in about
A.D. 95, says about these empires which the "woman" has controlled: "Here
is the mind which has wisdom. The seven heads are seven mountains on
which the woman sits, and they are seven kings; five have fallen, one is,
the other has not yet come; and when he comes, he must remain a little
while" (Revelation 17:9, 10 NASB).

We must look at this from the apostle John's perspective. He speaks of
seven kingdoms, five of which have fallen. We must examine what five kingdoms over which this mystery religion of Babylon exerted authority have
fallen. The first great kingdom where the Babylonian religion had great sway
was the Chaldean. The second world power which was virtually controlled
by this religion was Egypt. The great Egyptian pyramids had astrological
significance, as well as being a burial place for the kings, and the sphinx is
the key to where the earth starts in the twelve sections of the Zodiac. The
head of the sphinx is a woman, with the body of a lion. The word "sphinx"
means to "join together" in Greek—it shows that the first part of the circle
of the zodiac is the woman, Virgo, and the last part is the lion, Leo. What
the sphinx does is to put the two together and show the beginning and the
end of the Zodiac.

The next great world kingdom to be controlled by the mystery religion
was, of course, Babylon itself under the great Babylonian rulers. The fourth
kingdom was the Media-Persian empire, and the fifth was the Greek empire.

John says that "five have fallen, one is." The kingdom which was present
at the time John wrote this was Rome. The mystery religion of Babylon was
in Rome, exerting its great influence over the decisions of the empire. The
other kingdom which "has not yet come" is referring to the revived Roman
Empire.

The Antichrist will come up out of the culture of the ancient Roman
Empire. He will come to the ten-nation confederacy, take it over, and make
it an eighth form of power.

We believe that we are seeing, with all of the other signs, the revival of Mystery, Babylon—not just in astrology, but also in spiritism, a return to the supernatural, and in drugs.

More insight into this last one-world religion is given in Revelation 9:20: "And the rest of mankind, who were not killed by these plagues, did not repent of the works of their hands, so as not to worship demons, and the idols of gold and of silver and of brass and of stone and of wood, which can neither see nor hear nor walk" (NASB).

Some may scoff at the idea that idol worship will become prevalent. Even in America, however, there are growing cults which actually do worship stone and metal idols. At one of California's colleges some young men were seen at dawn, indulging in a primitive sort of sun-god worship on the lawn of a fraternity house. When they were questioned about their rather strange activities they said, "There's a bunch of us up at Big Sur who worship idols and stuff."

And what else will be seen during these times preceding Christ's return? "And they did not repent of their murders nor of their sorceries nor of their immorality nor of their thefts" (Revelation 9:21 NASB).

One of the words here is extremely important—the word "sorceries." It comes from the Greek word *pharmakeia*, which is the word from which we get our English word, pharmacy. It means a kind of occult worship or black magic, associated with the use of drugs. This word is mentioned several times in the Book of Revelation. It is said of the great religious system that "all the nations were deceived by your sorcery" (Revelation 18:23).

If there is anyone today who is not conscious of the spread of drug addiction, particularly among college and high school students, and now reaching down into the junior high and even the grade school level, then they are blind to what is happening. The increase in the use of narcotics and all forms of dangerous drugs has spiralled to such an extent that statistics written today would be out of date by the time this book is published.

A newspaper we saw recently quoted narcotics officials in the juvenile division of a police department saying that they were so alarmed that they thought the situation should be labeled a "Drug Epidemic" and treated by drastic and swift measures before it was more out of hand than it is now. One officer said that whatever they say about the arrests of young people on drug charges is like an iceberg. All they are able to see is what protrudes above the surface. Lurking beneath the known dangers are thousands and thousands of users and pushers that haven't been caught.

I used to wonder how on earth people could see the supernatural things which would occur during the Great Tribulation, the seven-year period before the return of Christ, and still not turn to God. I have seen a graphic example of how minds can be clouded from a person I met in a fraternity house at one of our major universities. He was an outstanding young man and expressed the desire to know more about Christ. I met with him for several weeks and he said, "I believe it, but I just don't want to commit my life to Christ."

When I met him a few months later he looked completely different. He said, "I'm really religious now—I feel sorry for you—I've been taking trips and I've really seen God. Only this God is the King of Darkness—this is the one we worship."

This man had completely blown his mind. He is at this point, apart from a miracle, completely beyond reach. Satan uses these hallucinatory drugs to take man to a deeper level of approach with him. You talk to some people who have been on drugs for a long time and they will tell you, "I know the devil is real—I've seen him."

We believe these drugs reduce a man's thinking and mentality to a point where he is easily demon-possessed. Demons are under the control of Satan and the Bible speaks about them in abundant terms, so we're not talking about spooky things.

There are all sorts of new spirit groups which are worshiping Satan. A newspaper feature article told of "Modern Witches: Old Black Magic but a New Spirit." The story concerned the upsurge in witchcraft in England and told how people take it very seriously. "So ostensibly do the hundreds, perhaps even a few thousand, of witches in Britain who are riding again since the centuries-old Witchcraft Act was repealed in 1951. Covens, assemblies of witches are even said to be thriving in Los Angeles and New York."

As one modern witch describes, "For us it's our religion—we worship a horned god, the prince of darkness, and this makes some people say we're devil-worshipers."[3]

A major television station had a potpourri of news and showed the great interest high school students have in witches. The commentator said, "Nearly every respectable high school these days has its own witch." The program pictured a pretty 16-year-old, eyes staring and voice chanting incantations, conjuring up all sorts of spells. A psychiatrist intoned that he thought the trend toward witchcraft was "healthy" for some because it helps relieve aggressive feelings.

The upsurge of interest in astrology was documented in the first chapter of this book. Man seems to be on this great quest for knowledge and assurance of the future with such intensity that all types of mystic ideas are being accepted today.

Where Is the Church?

We have developed the various forms of religious expressions which we believe constitute a revival of Mystery, Babylon, but have not included the organization which the Bible says will be a definite part of this one-world religion. This is the visible church which is characterized by increasing unbelief and apostasy.

This description of the visible or physical church is given with sadness. We find it difficult not to be disheartened when we see what is happening in the churches which call themselves "Christian." However, if we follow Bible prophecy carefully we see that it is made absolutely clear that in the time preceding the return of Christ there would be a "falling away" from the basic doctrines of Christ by the churches. Some churches are not just falling away, they are plunging recklessly toward destruction with their disbelief and blasphemous programs.

It's not uncommon to hear someone say, usually in a state of anger over some real or imagined injustice, "Why doesn't the church do something about it?"

It is imperative for us to have a clear understanding of who and what "the church" is before we can understand its apostasy. ("Apostasy" means an abandonment or desertion of principles or faith.)

The apostate church is, always has been, and will be, the visible, physical gathering of people who may call themselves Christians. These churches may be of any denomination. They may be magnificent cathedrals or storefront missions, a congregation of thousands or a gathering of a few. However, no matter what sacred or holy name is applied to the visible church, this is no guarantee that it teaches and preaches the truth of God.

The true church, on the other hand, includes all believers in Christ. Many places in the New Testament speak of those who are joined to Christ, the Head of the body. In other words, Christ is the Head of the true church.

"He is also head of the body, the church" (Colossians 1:18 NASB).

"For even as the body is one and yet has many members, and all the members of the body, though they are many, are one body, so also is Christ. For by one Spirit we were all baptized into one body, whether Jews or Greeks, whether slaves or free, and we were all made to drink of one Spirit" (I Corinthians 12:12, 13 NASB).

An organized church may have among its members those who are true believers and those who merely claim to be believers in Christ. We must not make the mistake of saying that everyone who belongs to a church which has strayed far away from the teachings of the Bible is a non-believer. A true believer can be surrounded by apostasy in the church or denomination or the council of churches to which he belongs. Usually, if the believer is aware of what is happening at the policy-making level of his church, he is pretty miserable—or angry—or disgusted.

Some of you may be thinking that every generation has seen this apostasy in the church. This is true, but the Bible says that as the countdown before Christ's return comes closer, the teachings of the false leaders of the church will depart farther and farther from God's Word.

"But false prophets also arose among the people, just as there will also be false teachers among you, who will secretly introduce destructive heresies, even denying the Master who bought them, bringing swift destruction upon themselves" (II Peter 2:1 NASB).

The Harlot

This one-world religious system is not described in delicate terms. A harlot, or a prostitute, is one who is unfaithful. She has prostituted her God-given womanhood. In the same manner, the church which says it belongs to God, but joins in worshiping through a false religious system, is prostituting its purpose.

How can we recognize the apostasy in the church today? What are the characteristics of this harlot?

Peter writes that in the "last days" there would be "mockers" who would say: "Where is the promise of His coming?" (II Peter 3:4 NASB).

John, the apostle of love, spoke strongly about false teachers who deny the fact that Christ will return bodily to earth the second time. He wrote: "For many deceivers have gone out into the world, those who do not acknowledge Jesus Christ as coming in the flesh. This is the deceiver and the antichrist" (II John 7 NASB).

We need to be alert. When we hear church leaders, teachers, or preachers questioning the visible return of Christ, this is a doctrine of apostasy.

The Bible teaches from beginning to end that man is basically sinful. Since this is contrary to so much of the humanistic teachings that surround us today, it is hard for some to swallow. But it does not make it any less true. "If we say that we have no sin, we are deceiving ourselves, and the truth is not in us" (I John 1:8 NASB).

There are many who admire Jesus of Nazareth as a great man, an outstanding teacher, but scoff at His deity. This is another form of apostasy. This is a denial of God, since the doctrine of the trinity is a basic tenet of

Christianity. John says: "Whoever denies the Son does not have the Father . . ." (I John 2:23 NASB).

We have often had people say to us, "Sure, I believe in God, but you certainly don't think Jesus was God, do you?" Of course we do. The Bible also says Jesus was born of a virgin; to deny this is a denial of the miracles of God, what traditional Christianity has said throughout the centuries.

What is happening today in many of our standard brand denominations? One of the first exposés of the beliefs of our future ministers was made by *Redbook* magazine in August of 1961. The publishers hired one of the top pollsters in the nation to survey a full representation of our seminaries which are supposedly preparing men for Christian service in the Protestant churches. Here are some of the results—compare them carefully with what the Bible says about apostasy.

Of the ministers in training, 56 percent rejected the virgin birth of Jesus Christ, 71 percent rejected that there was life after death. 54 percent rejected the bodily resurrection of Jesus Christ. 98 percent rejected that there would be a personal return of Jesus Christ to this earth.

"But false prophets also arose among the people, just as there will also be false teachers among you, who will secretly introduce destructive heresies . . ."(II Peter 2:1 NASB).

We are seeing "destructive heresies" bought in wholesale lots. In the 1968 annual of the *Encyclopedia Brittanica* in a special section on religion the writer wrote that this marks a turn in the history of American theology, for not only are they saying that God is dead, but men who still claim to be Christian theologians are saying that there is no such thing as a personal God at all.

In the February, 1968, issue of *McCall's* a survey of major denominations showed that a considerable number rejected altogether the idea of a personal God. How, may we ask, can a man be a minister today if he does not believe in a personal God?

Although this trend has been accelerated in recent years, this has been going on for a long time. When people move away from Christianity the church will lose its power and influence to a great religious movement, a satanic ecumenical campaign.

The Ecumenical Mania

Years ago when we first heard about the ecumenical movement, we couldn't pronounce it, but we thought it sounded like a great idea. It seemed plausible that all the "good guys" in the churches should join together to fight all the evil on the outside. There are many fallacies in that way of thinking. When all of the various churches begin to amalgamate in one unwieldy body, soon the doctrinal truths of the true church are watered down, altered, or discarded. In their place we see political pronouncements and ecclesiastical shenanigans that astound the believer and repel the non-believer. The mass movement of the National Council of Churches and the World Council of Churches toward an umbrella-like structure which would cover all sorts of beliefs and camouflage its motives with "broad-mindedness," seems to say: "Come unto me all ye that are weary and heavy-laden and I will give you—controversy!"

In May of 1969 the World Council of Churches, for instance, recommended that the churches should support violence if it is the last way to overthrow political and economic tyranny. This group also recommended that churches confess that they are "filled with blatant and insidious institutional racism."[4]

The news media carry stories every day about churches being invaded by pressure groups who "demand" money or recognition. Churches are joining forces with those who oppose everything that is known as traditional Christianity. "Marxist-Christian dialogue" is very popular; not for the purpose of extending the love of God to the atheistic Marxists or Communists, but with the idea of exchanging "truths" and reaching a common ground of understanding.

When Gus Hall, one of the best-known spokesmen for the Communist Party in the United States, says that the current red goals for America are "almost identical" to those espoused by the liberal church, then perhaps it is time (really far past time) that people begin to wake up to what is going on in the apostate church.

"A big and growing trend toward unity is developing in many of America's churches at this time. That trend, some clergymen are saying, could lead to a 'superchurch' of immense religious and political power."[5]

Satan's real intention is not to have a godless political situation, he wants a religious situation. Satan loves religion, which is the reason he invades certain churches on Sunday. Religion is a great blinder of the minds of men.

Where Does Apostasy Lead?

Christ calls His followers, the true Christians, the salt of the earth. If the salt is removed this important preservative will no longer be able to stop the decaying process. When false teachings and doctrines become predominant there will be a decline in the moral climate, for the preservative has been taken away.

Hear what the Bible has to say about the time before Christ's return: ". . . in the last days difficult times will come. For men will be lovers of self, lovers of money, boastful, arrogant, revilers, disobedient to parents, ungrateful, unholy, unloving, irreconcilable, malicious gossips, without self-control, brutal, haters of good, treacherous, reckless, conceited, lovers of pleasure rather than lovers of God . . ." (II Timothy 3:1-4 NASB).

That is a strong indictment of the era in which we live, isn't it? Continuing in that passage, Paul says that learning or intellectualism will increase, but men will not come to the "knowledge of truth."

We have increased in technology so rapidly in the past few years that our grandfather's heads would be spinning at what we take for granted. However, all the educational advances have not brought mankind one step further toward solving the basic needs of love, security, and true happiness; on the contrary, civilization seems more removed from these concepts than ever.

In this letter to Timothy, Paul also cites that there will be a pretense of worship, at the same time denying godliness. When we read of some of the magazines that fall under the category of "religious publications," we can understand what is meant by this pretense. God is not a living, vital reality, personified by Christ, He is hardly more than a "Thing," a "Reality," a "Ground of Being," a "Voice from Somewhere." When there is little to separate the church from a nightclub, a school, a social gathering, a political meeting, even a philanthropic group, then the salt has been taken away, its flavor is no different from any secular organization.

The Power Without the Salt

Although this great religious system of the time of the Tribulation, or the final seven-year period before the return of Christ, will be godless, it will also be powerful.

John says in Revelation 17 that this system would dominate the beast, or the Great Dictator who will be the head of the ten-nation confederacy. As we have said, it would seem that fear of Communism and the need for a common defense against the "King of the North" would drive the one-world political system into the arms of the "harlot" or the one-world religious system. The "harlot" will be "clothed in purple and scarlet, and adorned with gold and precious stones and pearls . . ." (Revelation 17:4 NASB). In other words, this religious system will be splendid on the outside, but corrupt to the core.

This harlot, as described in Revelation, is not only a system, but also a city. There is no question about where the city would be—it was Rome. It says that the woman sits (or rules) on seven mountains. Most elementary students of history or geography know that Rome is the city of seven hills. It is there that the religious system will reign for a time in coalition with the political system.

However, the Bible tells us about the end of this system. The political system and its dictator will hate this religious system after a time, because it controls the Antichrist and he wants to proclaim himself to be God, without any interference. The Great Dictator is not going to be a puppet; if strings are to be pulled, he wants to do the manipulating.

Revelation 18:2 shows that the destruction of the religious system will take place in two phases. "Fallen, fallen is Babylon the great." The first "fallen" refers to the destruction of the religious system by the dictator. This will take place in the middle of the Tribulation, at the end of three and one-half years. The second "fallen" refers to the sudden destruction of the city of Rome.

God-given Compassion

There is a tightrope which is walked by everyone who condemns the actions of churches, their leaders, or any belief which is no more than unbelief. One is accused of being "anti-church," "narrow-minded," or "dogmatic." However, in proclaiming the truths of God, revealed by the Bible and its prophets, we cannot dilute what is said. On the other hand, while loathing the actions and motives of any system which is religious, without knowing Christ, we do at the same time want to introduce persons within these systems to the only way to God, to Jesus Christ Himself. This is a distinction which is difficult for a non-Christian to understand, and sometimes equally difficult for the Christian to follow. It is against human nature to separate the man from the beliefs he appears to follow. We cannot do it alone. Only Christ, working in and through our whole being, can possibly give us compassion and love for what we ourselves have labeled unloving and despicable.

11 ○ The Ultimate Trip

One small step for a man—one giant leap for mankind.

APOLLO 11 COMMANDER NEIL ARMSTRONG
20 JULY 1969

AND THE WORLD caught its breath. Science fiction had prepared man for the incredible feats of the astronauts, but when the reality of the moon landing really hit, it was awesome.

On that historic Sunday in July we watched TV, laughing as Armstrong and Buzz Aldrin loped on the moon's surface. We walked out the front door and looked up at the Old Man and said, "It's really happening—there are a couple of guys walking around up there right now. Amazing."

Astounding as man's trip to the moon is, there is another trip which many men, women, and children will take some day which will leave the rest of the world gasping. Those who remain on earth at that time will use every invention of the human mind to explain the sudden disappearance of millions of people.

Reporters who wrote the historic story of Apollo 11 told how the astronauts collected rocks which may reveal the oldest secrets of the solar system. Those who are alive to tell the story of "Project Disappearance" will try in vain to describe the happening which will verify the oldest secrets of God's words.

What Will They Say?

"There I was, driving down the freeway and all of a sudden the place went crazy. . . . cars going in all directions . . . and not one of them had a driver. I mean it was wild! I think we've got an invasion from outer space!"

"It was the last quarter of the championship game and the other side was ahead. Our boys had the ball. We made a touchdown and tied it up. The crowd went crazy. Only one minute to go and they fumbled—our quarterback recovered—he was about a yard from the goal when—zap—no more quarterback—completely gone, just like that!"

"It was puzzling—very puzzling. I was teaching my course in the Philosophy of Religion when all of a sudden three of my students vanished.

They simply vanished! They were quite argumentative—always trying to prove their point from the Bible. No great loss to the class. However, I do find this disappearance very difficult to explain."

"As an official spokesman for the United Nations I wish to inform all peace-loving people of the world that we are making every human effort to assist those nations whose leaders have disappeared. We have issued a general declaration of condemnation in the General Assembly concerning these heads of state. Their irresponsibility is shocking."

"My dear friends in the congregation. Bless you for coming to church today. I know that many of you have lost loved ones in this unusual disappearance of so many people. However, I believe that God's judgment has come upon them for their continued dissension and quarreling with the great advances of the church in our century. Now that the reactionaries are removed, we can progress toward our great and glorious goal of uniting all mankind into a brotherhood of reconciliation and understanding."

"You really want to know what I think? I think all that talk about the Rapture and going to meet Jesus Christ in the air wasn't crazy after all. I don't know about you, brother, but I'm going to find myself a Bible and read all those verses my wife underlined. I wouldn't listen to her while she was here, and now she's— I don't know where she is."

Rapture—What Rapture?

Christians have a tendency sometimes to toss out words which have no meaning to the non-Christian. Sometimes misunderstood terms provide the red flag an unbeliever needs to turn him from the simple truth of God's Word. "Rapture" may be one of those words. It is not found in the Bible, so there is no need to race for your concordance, if you have one. There are some Christians who do not use the word, but prefer "translation" instead.

The word "rapture" means to snatch away or take out. But whether we call this event "the Rapture" or the "translation" makes no difference—the important thing is that it will happen.

It will happen!

Someday, a day that only God knows, Jesus Christ is coming to take away all those who believe in Him. He is coming to meet all true believers in the air. Without benefit of science, space suits, or interplanetary rockets, there will be those who will be transported into a glorious place more beautiful, more awesome, than we can possibly comprehend. Earth and all its thrills, excitement, and pleasures will be nothing in contrast to this great event.

It will be the living end. The ultimate trip.

If you are shaking your heads over this right now, please remember how many "impossibles" you have said in your lifetime—or how many "impossibles" men throughout the ages have said to many things God has revealed through His spokesmen. And yet they were possible, because nothing is impossible for God.

We have been examining the push of world events which the prophets foretold would lead the way to the seven-year countdown before the return of Jesus Christ to earth. The big question is, will you be here during this seven-year countdown? Will you be here during the time of the Tribulation when the Antichrist and the False Prophet are in charge for a time? Will you be here when the world is plagued by mankind's darkest days?

It may come as a surprise to you, but the decision concerning your presence during this last seven-year period in history is entirely up to you.

God's Word tells us that there will be one generation of believers who will never know death. These believers will be removed from the earth before the Great Tribulation—before that period of the most ghastly pestilence, bloodshed, and starvation the world has ever known.

Examine the prophecies of this mysterious happening—of the "Rapture." Here is the real hope for the Christian, the "blessed hope" for true believers (Titus 2:13-15).

As we see the circumstances which are coming on the world, this hope gets more blessed all the time. This is the reason we are optimistic about the future. This is the reason that in spite of the headlines, in spite of crisis after crisis in America and throughout the world, in spite of the dark days which will strike terror into the hearts of many, every Christian has the right to be optimistic!

You may be thinking now, "Count me out. I like it right here and I have a lot of plans for my future."

Exactly. This is what we are talking about—your plans for the future. In fact, this is what Christ was talking about when He said: "Let not your heart be troubled; believe in God, believe also in Me. In My Father's house are many dwelling places; if it were not so, I would have told you; for I go to prepare a place for you. And if I go and prepare a place for you, I will come again, and receive you to Myself; that where I am, there you may be also" (John 14:1-3 NASB).

According to all the Scriptures we are told that the place He is preparing for us will be utterly fantastic. Eternal life will surpass the greatest pleasures we have known on earth.

I Tell You a Mystery

To avoid confusion, we will refer to the event when the church (those who believe in Jesus Christ as Savior) will meet Christ in the air as the Rapture. If you have grown in a school of Christian thought that uses the "translation," simply substitute this word when you are reading.

In I Corinthians 15:50 important things are revealed about the Rapture. We are told that Christians cannot inherit the Kingdom of God in the type of bodies we now have—that is, in bodies of flesh and blood.

However, according to the gospels and the Old Testament, there will be certain people who will inherit for a time the Kingdom of God in their mortal bodies. This is the Kingdom that Christ will establish after He returns to earth. This does not contradict the previous statement. The Bible is speaking of two separate events.

The distinction between God's dealing with the church and His dealing with another group of believers who are largely gathered around Israel is very important. Revelation 20 and Matthew 25 speak of the time when Jesus will return to the earth and separate the believers from the nonbelievers. For us, as believers, our hope is different from Israel's. This will be clear when we distinguish between the second advent, or the second coming of Christ, and the Rapture.

We are told that we cannot enter the Kingdom of God until we are changed from the type of body we now have into a new model. Then we have this fascinating verse: "Behold, I tell you a mystery; we shall not all sleep, but we shall all be changed" (I Corinthians 15:51 NASB).

The word "mystery" in the original Greek means something which has not been revealed before, but is now being revealed to those who are initiated. It was from this word that the concept of Greek fraternities came— everyone who has been in a fraternity or sorority knows there are certain secrets which are not disclosed until after initiation.

To draw the analogy, every believer in Jesus Christ is initiated into Christ's fraternity. Then, and only then, can he understand some of the secrets of God. These secrets the rest of the world will not accept as those who believe in Christ will accept them and understand them.

What is the secret that had not been revealed anywhere in the Scriptures before Paul wrote this letter to the Corinthians? Here is where the mystery gets exciting.

It says, "We shall not all sleep." Sleep is the word for Christian death. "Sleep" does not mean that your soul, your consciousness sleeps. There are some who believe that when you die your soul, your personality, the real you goes into some strange limbo. However, we are told that the moment a believer breathes his last breath and dies his soul goes immediately to be with Christ—to be face to face with the Lord (II Corinthians 5:1-10; Philippians 1:21-23).

So what does sleep? Your body. The body that disintegrates, Christ will raise into a body which can never see corruption again. "For our citizenship is in heaven, from which also we eagerly wait for a Savior, the Lord Jesus Christ; who will transform the body of our humble state into conformity with the body of His glory, by the exertion of the power that He has even to subject all things to Himself" (Philippians 3:20, 21 NASB).

What about the mystery? The mystery has to do with the believers who will be *alive* when Christ comes for them. "In a moment, in the twinkling of an eye, at the last trumpet; for the trumpet will sound, and the dead will be raised imperishable, and we shall be changed" (I Corinthians 15:52 NASB).

Words are fascinating—and the basis for understanding. The word translated "moment" is the Greek word *atomos*, which is the word from which we get "atom." In the Greek it means that which is indivisible, in other words, it will happen so quickly, in a flash of time which is so short it can't be divided. At that point those who are alive will be brought into the presence of the Lord.

This will take place "at the last trumpet," which refers to something which was the practice of God in the Old Testament. When the Israelites were on their march from Egypt over to the land of Palestine, every morning before they started on their journey they would have seven trumpets blow—to prepare to break camp, fold up their tents, etc. When the seventh trumpet, which was the last trumpet, sounded, this meant—move out!

The idea in this passage is that when God has the last trumpet blow it means He will move out all the Christians—and at that point we shall be changed.

What's in a word? "Changed" means to be changed in essence, but not to be completely changed in appearance. This strengthens the truth which is spoken of in other places that in eternity we are going to recognize people we knew here on earth. If you're not too satisfied with the face or body you now have, you will have a glorious new body. However, you will be recognizable, just as you will recognize others.

We won't have to eat to be sustained, but the Scripture says we can eat if we want to—and enjoy it. For those who have a weight problem, that sounds rather heavenly in itself. Our eternal bodies will not be subject to aging, or pain, or decay.

Just think how excited a woman can get about a new wardrobe. How much more excited we should be about acquiring a new body!

When the Scripture says, "the dead will be raised imperishable" and "for this perishable must put on the imperishable," it refers to the Christians who have died physically. They will be resurrected to meet Christ in the air.

However, when it says, "this mortal must put on immortality," it is referring to those who are alive at the coming of Christ. That's the mystery, the Rapture or translation. That is the hope that Paul offered for the generation which will be alive when Christ returns.

Who Goes First?

The Thessalonians were evidently worried about something that might be concerning you also. They wondered if those who had died and would be resurrected when Christ returned might be in some separate part of God's Kingdom. No Christian would want to miss seeing their loved ones throughout eternity.

However, the apostle Paul assured them that God's plan was perfect: those who had "fallen asleep in Jesus," or the Christians who had died, will join the Lord first. Then the Christians who are alive at that time will be caught up "together with them in the clouds" to meet the Lord in the air (I Thessalonians 4:13-18).

What a great reunion that will be!

The world will not know what has happened, because it occurs in an atom of time.

Debating Another Mystery .

Christians sometimes have a theological debate about whether the Rapture occurs at the same time as the second coming of Christ or whether it takes place before the second coming, even before the Tribulation.

It is only fair to sincere Christians who differ about this time element for us to develop the reasons why we believe the Bible distinguishes between the Rapture and the second coming of Christ and why they do not occur simultaneously.

First, there is a great distinction between God's purpose for the nation of Israel and His purpose for the church, which is His main program today. The church is composed of both Gentiles and Jews. We are now living during the church age and the responsibility for evangelizing the world rests upon the church. We should reemphasize here that we are speaking of the true meaning of the church, which is the body of believers in Jesus Christ.

In the Old Testament evangelizing was the task of the Jew. Of course he seldom fulfilled that obligation, which is one of his great failures. But the Scriptures give a vast distinction between God's dealing with the church and that time of Tribulation which seems to be a resumption of God's dealing with Israel. During the Tribulation the spotlight is on the Jew—in the Book of Revelation the Jew is responsible for evangelizing the world again (Revelation 7:1-4).

Another reason why we support the idea that the Rapture and the second coming are separate events is that the second coming is said to be visible to the whole earth (Revelation 1:7). However, in the Rapture, only the Christians see Him—it's a mystery, a secret. When the living believers are taken out, the world is going to be mystified.

Furthermore, we are told when Christ comes at the second coming it is at the height of a global war. Everyone will know that this is the great war predicted by the prophets. There will be no doubt about it. But when Christ comes for the believers, it will not necessarily be at the time of a war.

More proof—when Christ comes to earth for the second time we are told in Matthew 25 that He will divide the believers from the unbelievers. Now if the Rapture were to take place at the same time as the second coming how could the believers and unbelievers be separated on earth? At the Rapture all the living believers will be caught up to join Him in the clouds.

Here is the chief reason why we believe the Rapture occurs before the Tribulation: the prophets have said that God will set up a Kingdom on earth over which the Messiah will rule. There will be mortal people in that kingdom. If the Rapture took place at the same time as the second coming, there would be no mortals left who would be believers; therefore, there would be no one to go into the Kingdom and repopulate the earth.

We need to understand that during the seven-year Tribulation there will be people who will become believers at that time. In spite of persecution as described in the previous chapter, they will survive this terrible period of history and will be taken by Christ to reign with Him for 1000 years. This is the Kingdom which is God's prelude to eternity.

The Church Disappeared

The largest descriptive volume of the Tribulation is found in Revelation 6 through 19. Here is a fascinating revelation about Revelation. In the first five chapters of this book, the church is mentioned thirty times. In fact, in chapters 2 and 3, at the end of each letter to the churches, John says "let him hear what the Spirit saith unto the churches." This is repeated seven times. Then we have the beginning of the description of the Tribulation, and there is not one mention of the churches. The church is conspicuous by its absence. Why? Because the church will be in heaven at that time.

If you are a believer, chapters 4 and 5 of Revelation describe what you will be experiencing in heaven. Talk about mind expansion drugs! We are told we shall expand in understanding and comprehension beyond that of any earthbound genius.

Be Alert

When will the Rapture occur? We don't know. No one knows. But God knows. However, we believe that according to all the signs, we are in the general time of His coming. "But you, brethren, are not in darkness, that the day should overtake you like a thief" (I Thessalonians 5:4 NASB).

In other words, you shouldn't be surprised when Christ returns to take you with Him. Unfortunately, this does not refer to all believers. We may have to go over to some of them and say, "I told you so, friend." It will be a surprise because they don't study the prophetic word. What an exciting time they may have missed on earth! The study and understanding of prophecy is an experience we pray all Christians will have.

"We are not of the night, nor of darkness . . ." (I Thessalonians 5:5 NASB). Darkness refers to the persons who do not have Christ, who cannot understand these things at all.

If you have not accepted Christ in your life this chapter will probably sound like the biggest farce you've ever read.

". . . so then let us not sleep as others do, but let us be alert and sober" (I Thessalonians 5:6 NASB). The idea of sleep is that a person just doesn't know what is going on. He may rationalize along his merry way, not paying any attention to the indications that the world can't go on much longer in the way it is going. He will say, "Something will happen—science will pull something out of the hat." So he puts his faith in science.

If you know what the prophets have said, and if the spirit of God has spoken to you, then you should be alert.

There's nothing that remains to be fulfilled before Christ could catch you up to be with Him.

What's Important?

Have you ever found an electric train, or a bedraggled doll that belonged to you as a child and remembered how terribly important it was to you years ago? When we meet Christ face to face we're going to look back on this life and see that the things we thought were important here were like the discarded toys of our childhood.

What a way to live! With optimism, with anticipation, with excitement. We should be living like persons who don't expect to be around much longer.

12 ○ World War III

There is no defense in science against the weapons which can now destroy civilization.   ALBERT EINSTEIN

In the next war, none of us can count on having enough living to bury our dead.
                                                                J. ROBERT OPPENHEIMER

Mankind must put an end to war—or war will put an end to mankind.
                                                                JOHN F. KENNEDY, 1961

A war would be an irreversible and fatal occurrence. It would not be the end of difficulties but the end of civilization.   POPE PAUL VI

. . . you will be hearing of wars and rumors of wars—then there will be a great tribulation, such as has not occurred since the beginning of the world until now, nor ever shall. And unless those days had been cut short, no life would have been saved.   JESUS CHRIST, A.D. 33

FROM THE BEGINNING of man's history he has sought peace, but war has been his chief legacy. Among certain people today the peace sign has become an outward expression of their revulsion against war. This desire is like the people of Jeremiah's day who said, ". . . peace, peace, when there is no peace" (Jeremiah 6:14).

The great men of our day warn us about the insanity of another major war. Many experts, however, feel that it is inescapable. Whether we agree with the conclusions or theories of some of these experts or not, it is important to know what they are saying.

Several years ago a number of Nobel prize-winning scientists from various countries prepared a document and sent it to the leaders of all the world powers. They warned: "Here, then, is the problem which we present to you, stark and dreadful and inescapable: shall we put an end to the human race or shall mankind renounce war? We appeal, as human beings to human beings; remember your humanity, and forget the rest. If you can do so, the way lies open to a new paradise; if you cannot, there lies before you the risk of universal death."[1]

Many of the scientists who were most responsible for the development of the H-bomb signed the document quoted above.

War has greatly increased in frequency and intensity in this century. It has kept pace with the acceleration of technological advances. Some people have undoubtedly become callous to the continuous fighting on our globe, but it is shocking to review the statistics since World War II:

"Since World War II there have been 12 limited wars in the world, 39 political assassinations, 48 personal revolts, 74 rebellions for independence, 162 social revolutions, either political, economic, racial or religious."[2]

Since these statistics were written there have been more major assassinations and several more revolts.

In spite of all the oratory and books that have been aimed at steering man away from another world conflict, all-out war continues to be an ever-impending possibility. Any one of the limited wars such as Viet Nam or the Middle East crisis could at any time strike the spark that ignites World War III.

Why is it that in spite of the terrible lessons learned from history about war and the terrifying predictions of a future war, man keeps playing on the precipice of complete destruction? Jesus predicted that man would not learn from the past nor heed the warnings of the future; man would ultimately plunge the whole world into a war so vast, so utterly destructive, that only the personal return of Jesus Christ Himself to stop it would prevent the total annihilation of all life.

Here is the further solemn prediction of Jesus Christ as He described the world situation that would be present at the moment of His return:

"And unless those days had been cut short [abruptly ended], no life would have been saved . . ." (Matthew 24: 22 NASB).

Why Can't Man Live Without War?

We believe the answer to that question is important to consider before presenting the predicted path that man will take to the last great war which the Bible calls Armageddon.

Man cannot stop war because he will not accept the basic reason and cause for war—nor will he accept the cure for this basic cause. God says: "From whence come wars and fightings among you? come they not hence, even of your lusts that war in your members? Ye lust, and have not: ye kill, and desire to have, and cannot obtain: ye fight and war, yet ye have not . . ." (James 4:1, 2 KJV).

Inside of man there is a selfish, self-centered nature. This is the source of what God calls sin. Sin is basically self-centered seeking and striving—going our own way, with our backs turned on God. It is because of this selfish nature with which we were born that we cannot have consistent peace with ourselves, our family, our neighbor, or, on a broader scale, with other nations.

As one man has said, "What's wrong with the world?" And answered himself truthfully, "I'm wrong with the world."

God didn't intend for man to have this condition. Man was created originally to have fellowship with God. This fellowship is so vital that without it man is like a jet aircraft flying in a dense fog and suddenly losing all its instruments.

God warned man of the consequences when He gave man one simple prohibition. Man understood that to disobey God on this one command was to reject fellowship with God. In spite of all the evidences of God's love and veracity, man went his own independent way and lost fellowship with the only One who can give him the true fulfillment for which he was created.

Man has been turned in upon himself; he has become self-centered and discontented. No matter how much he gets of fame or wealth or power, he is not satisfied. Why? Because he cannot fill the vacuum once filled by God with any other thing. So he fights with himself, with his mate, with his family, and with other nations.

Solution

The only cure for war is to change the hearts of men. Jesus came into the world to bring men back to fellowship with God and consequently make that change in their hearts. The Bible promises, "For Christ also died for sins once for all, the just for the unjust, in order that He might bring us to God . . ." (I Peter 3:18 NASB).

Jesus took the just rap due our sins and died under its penalty so that God might forgive us and receive us back into fellowship. When this occurs God gives us a new heart that desires to follow Him and a love for our neighbor. He gives us a new dimension of life with which we can perceive and know Him. He puts His Spirit within us to live so that He motivates and empowers us to follow God's purpose for our lives.

We begin to experience peace of mind, a new stability, a new sense of purpose, an awareness of Christ's presence, and a healing of our personality that makes us a whole person. We find ourselves concerned about the interests of others. A new kind of love impels us to place others before ourselves. This cannot be done by any system of government, education, psychology, or outer environmental changes. It can be done only by a personal invitation of Christ into the heart and an acceptance of the gift of forgiveness which He gave His life to provide.

Right where you are, as you read this chapter, you can make this decision in the quiet of your heart.

General Douglas MacArthur was eternally right when he said on the deck of the battleship Missouri at the close of World War II: "We have had our last chance. If we will not devise some greater and more equitable system, ARMAGEDDON will be at the door. The problem basically is theological and involves a spiritual recrudescence and improvement of human character that will synchronize with our almost matchless advances in science, art, literature, and all material and cultural developments of the past 2000 years. It must be the spirit if we are to save the flesh."[3]

The sad prediction of the Bible is that mankind will not accept God's diagnosis or His cure. Therefore, they will seek to solve the problem themselves. Fear of war will grow until it prepares man to accept the Antichrist's solution for preventing war. Paul predicts the false hope the world will have in the Antichrist: "While they are saying, 'Peace and safety!' then destruction will come upon them suddenly like birth pangs upon a woman with child; and they shall not escape" (I Thessalonians 5:3 NASB).

Where Are We Going?

In the previous chapters we have shown the predicted powers that would arise shortly before the return of Jesus Christ and how these powers are simultaneously developing in current history. We have outlined how world conditions in this generation are launched into a countdown that will end in the final collapse of man's efforts to run the world without God.

In this chapter we will trace consecutively the predicted events that lead to the Armageddon campaign: the various sequence of battles, the particular powers who fight each other, and how in turn each is destroyed. The crucial prediction of the revived state of Israel's part in triggering Armageddon will also be shown.

The Fuse Was Primed

When the Jews re-established their nation in Palestine they created an unsolvable problem; they displaced Arabs who had dwelt in Palestine for several centuries. All the legal debates and logical dissertations that can be advanced will never change the basic state of hostility that exists between the Israelis and the Arabs.

The Jews will never be convinced that they should leave the land that God gave to their forefathers. They believe that they were robbed of their inalienable right to the land by the Romans. Centuries of persecution have taught them that there is no country in the world where they can be assured of continuing acceptance, much less safety. Remaining as a nation in Palestine is a matter of survival of the race for the Israeli. He feels that it is his only hope in a hostile world.

The Arabs are equally implacable in their unwillingness to accept the Israeli occupation of what they consider to be their land. It has become a matter of racial honor and sacred religious duty to drive out the Israelis.

Israel's Treaty With Hell

According to the Bible, the Middle East crisis will continue to escalate until it threatens the peace of the whole world. The focus of all nations will be upon this unsolvable and complex problem which keeps bringing the world to the precipice of a thermonuclear holocaust. This is apparently the first major problem that the incredible Roman leader will solve after taking over the ten-nation confederacy of European nations.

Some 2500 years ago the prophet Daniel said that a prince would come to power from the people who would destroy the city of Jerusalem and the second Temple (Daniel 9:27). The Romans under Titus did the destroying, so the coming prince would have to be someone out of the Roman culture. This Roman prince, as we described in "The Future Fuehrer," will come to power just before the return of Christ. He will make "a strong covenant" with the Israelis, guaranteeing their safety and protection. The word translated "strong covenant" has the idea of a treaty or mutual protection pact. The Israelis will then be permitted to reinstitute the sacrifice and offering aspect of the law of Moses. This demands that the Temple be rebuilt, because according to the law of Moses, sacrifices can be offered only in the Temple at Jerusalem. Apparently all this will be done under the protection of the Antichrist of Rome.

(P.S. The Arabs are not going to like this idea of rebuilding the Temple one bit.)

According to Daniel's prophetic chronology, the minute the Israeli leader and the Roman leader sign this pact, God starts His great timepiece which has seven allotted years left on it. This event marks the beginning of the period of Biblical history previously noted as the Tribulation.

Isaiah prophetically expressed warning to the Jews concerning this covenant when he declared: "Because you have said, 'We have made a covenant with death, and with Sheol we have an agreement; when the overwhelming scourge passes through it will not come to us; for we have made lies our refuge, and in falsehood we have taken shelter'; Then your covenant with death will be annulled, and your agreement with Sheol will not stand; when the overwhelming scourge passes through you will be beaten down by it" (Isaiah 28:15, 18).

It is through an ingenuous settlement of the Middle East problem that the Antichrist will make good his promise to bring peace to a world terrified of war. After this he will rapidly bring all nations under his control. The world will experience great hope and put its full trust in the genius of Rome. He will begin to bring in fantastic plans of economic prosperity, even to the underdeveloped countries. War will seem to be a curious game that men used to play. The world will be universally acclaiming the Dictator.

"Who is like the Dictator, and who is able to make war with him?"

After three and a half years of remarkable progress, the Antichrist will become worshiped for his brilliant statesmanship and the wonderful progress in the world. The believers in Christ will oppose his rule and be ruthlessly exposed. Publicly, they will not be able to buy, sell, or hold a job. They will be executed en masse as examples to those who would hinder the "brotherhood of man," because they will insist that Christ is the only lasting hope for man.

Riding upon the crest of public worship the Roman Dictator will go to Jerusalem and in the Temple proclaim himself to be God incarnate (II Thessalonians 2:4; Matthew 24:15). As mentioned, this will be the great warning sign to the believers of that day that Armageddon is about to begin. The residents of Israel who believe in Jesus will flee to the mountains and canyons of Petra for divine protection, as promised (Matthew 24:16; Revelation 12:6, 14).

The Red Horse Unleashed

"And another, a red horse, went out; and to him who sat on it, it was granted to take peace from the earth, and that men should slay one another; and a great sword was given to him" (Revelation 6:4 NASB).

Almost immediately after the Antichrist declares himself to be God, God releases the dreaded second of the four horsemen of the Apocalypse. This is a figure of the unleashing of war upon the earth.

That beautiful balance of power established by the Antichrist is suddenly ruptured. God begins to show man that the Antichrist's promises cannot stand. The thing which man feared most, an all-out war, now rushes upon him.

The Beginning of the End

"At the time of the end the king of the south shall attack him (Israeli leader)" (Daniel 11:40a).

We have identified the characters of this passage. The Arab-African confederacy headed by Egypt (King of the South) launches an invasion of Israel. This fatal mistake spells their doom and begins the Armageddon campaign. ". . . but the king of the north shall rush upon him (the Israeli leader) like a whirlwind, with chariots (mechanized army) and horsemen (cavalry), and with many ships" (Daniel 11:40b).

Chart one shows the movement of troops.

Russia and her allies use this occasion to launch an invasion of the Middle East, which Russia has longed to do since the Napoleonic wars. Ezekiel 38 describes the development of this great Russian force, and its plan to attack Israel.

Twenty-six centuries ago Ezekiel described the plot of the Russian leaders against revived Israel: "Thus says the Lord GOD; On that day thoughts will come into your mind, and you will devise an evil scheme and say, 'I will go up against the land of unwalled villages; I will fall upon the quiet people who dwell securely, all of them dwelling without walls (i.e. fortifications), and having no bars or gates'; to seize spoil and carry off plunder; to assail the waste places which are now inhabited, and the people who were gathered from the nations, who have gotten cattle and goods, who dwell at the center of the earth" (Ezekiel 38:10-12).

The Russians will make a great tactical blunder by invading Israel. They will construe the defenseless posture of Israel, who will be trusting in the Antichrist's protection, as an opportunity to finally conquer the great land bridge of the Middle East. They will be motivated by the great material wealth of the restored nation of Israel. Their purpose is thus revealed by Ezekiel ". . . to seize spoil and carry off plunder. . . ."

The wealth of Israel is also predicted: ". . . the people who were gathered from the nations, who have gotten cattle and goods."

True Bible scholars have recognized that some day there would be a vast concentration of wealth in Israel. Harry Rimmer wrote in 1940, when the land was scrub brush in comparison to what it is today: ". . . The development of the resources of that land has only commenced. Ten years of uninterrupted industry there will make Palestine the richest concentration of treasure this world has so far witnessed. Even five years of unbroken application to the cultivation of her natural resources would make Palestine the envy of the world, and a land very well worth robbing, indeed."[4]

The prophetic indication is that Israel will become one of the most prosperous nations on earth during the reign of the Antichrist. It is also said to be, ". . . at the center of the earth." Geographically, this is approximately true, but more seems to be meant here than physical location. Israel will become a cultural, religious, and economic world center, especially at Jerusalem. The value of the mineral deposits in the Dead Sea alone has been estimated at one trillion, two hundred and seventy billion dollars. This is more than the combined wealth of France, England, and the United States!

I was talking to a prominent Los Angeles engineer after a message on this subject and we discussed the need for a cheap source of energy by which these Dead Sea minerals could be refined. He said that he is certain that there is enough steam trapped under the numerous faults in the earth around Israel to provide power to run turbines to produce electricity very economically. He called this new process geo-thermal energy. In the near future Israel will discover a way to produce cheap energy to develop this gold mine of riches.

One of the chief minerals in the Dead Sea is potash, which is a potent fertilizer. When the population explosion begins to bring famine, potash will become extremely valuable for food production.

It is strategic wealth of this sort that will cause the Russian bloc to look for an opportunity to invade and conquer Israel, according to Ezekiel.

The strategic military importance of "the land bridge of the Middle East" which begins in the north with the Bosphorus (the narrow channel which divides Turkey connecting the Black Sea with the Mediterranean), and extends southward to Egypt, has been established by centuries of military conflicts. The one who would control Europe, Asia, and Africa must control this area, which literally connects the three continents. This must figure into the Russian motivation for future conquest. Since Israel lies in the center of this land bridge, it has been made a battleground innumerable times.

This writer is indebted to Col. R. B. Thieme, Jr., a man who is uniquely qualified to explain this passage, since he is both a scholar in military history and in the original languages of the Bible, for pointing out the military aspects of this war.

The Classic Double-cross

When the Russians invade the Middle East with amphibious and mechanized land forces, they will make a "blitzkrieg" type of offensive through the area. As Daniel saw it centuries ago: ". . . and he [Russians] shall come into countries [of the Middle-East] and shall overflow and pass through. He will come into the glorious land [Israel]. And tens of thousands shall fall" (Daniel 11:40b, 41a).

Ezekiel describes the same invasion as follows: "Therefore, son of man, prophesy, and say to Gog [the Russian leader], Thus says the Lord GOD: On that day when my people Israel are dwelling securely, you will bestir yourself and come from your place out of the uttermost parts of the north [Daniel's king of the North], you and many peoples with you [i.e., the European iron curtain countries], all of them riding on horses, a great host, a mighty army; you will come up against my people Israel, like a cloud covering the land. In the latter days, I will bring you against my land . . ." (Ezekiel 38:14-16).

As previously quoted the Russians will make both an amphibious and land invasion of Israel. The current build-up of Russian ships in the Mediterranean serves as another significant sign of the possible nearness of Armageddon. They now have more ships in the Mediterranean than the United States, according to several recent news releases. The amphibious landings will facilitate a rapid encirclement of the middle section of "the land bridge."

The might of the Red Army is predicted. It will sweep over the Arab countries as well as Israel in a rapid assault over to Egypt to secure the entire land bridge. It is at this point that Russia double-crosses the United Arab Republic leader, Egypt. After sweeping over tens of thousands of people Daniel says of the Red army: "He shall stretch out his hand against the countries [i.e. Arab countries of the Middle East], and the land of Egypt shall not escape. He [Russian leader] shall become ruler of the treasures of gold and of silver, and all the precious things of Egypt; and the Libyans [African Arabs] and the Ethiopians [African blacks] shall follow in his train" (Daniel 11:42, 43).

As we saw in Chapters 5 and 6, this prediction indicates that the Russian bloc will double-cross the Arabs, Egyptians, and Africans, and for a short while conquer the Middle East. At this time, with the main Russian force in Egypt, the commander will hear alarming news: "But rumors from the east [the Orient mobilizing] and from the north [the Western Europeans mobilizing] shall alarm and hasten him. And he shall go forth with great fury to destroy and utterly to sweep away many" (Daniel 11:44 Amplified).

As shown in Chart two, the Russian force will retrace its steps from Egypt to consolidate for a counter-attack in Israel. The Russians will be alarmed at the news of the Roman Dictator mobilizing forces around the world to put down this breach of peace. Apparently it will surprise the Russian leader who underestimated the revived Roman Empire's will to fight.

CHART TWO

Daniel 11:43-45

Phase IV

Russian commander hears tidings out of the "East" (Orient mobilizing) and out of the "North" (Roman confederacy mobilizing) and regroups his troops.

Phase V

Russian army returns to Israel from Egypt and is destroyed there.

ROME

Roman Confederacy Attacks

Russian army commander

Phase III

Russian Confederacy initiates conquest of Africa, attacking to the West and South.

African Arabs (LIBYA)

EGYPT

African Blacks (ETHIOPIA)

It is conjecture on this writer's part, but it appears that the Oriental powers, headed by Red China, will be permitted to mobilize its vast army by the Roman Dictator, thinking that they would be loyal to him against Russia. However, the Orientals will eventually double-cross him, and move a 200 million man army against the Antichrist, as we have seen in Chapter 7.

This Russian double-cross of the Arabs is predictable by any astute observer of the Middle East situation today. It is obvious that the Russians are playing games with the Arabs in order to accomplish the old Russian dream of year-round seaports and oil supplies. The Arab leaders think that they can accept Russian loans and supplies without strings, but there are steel cables of conditions behind every Russian ruble given in aid and they are used eventually to pull a country behind the iron curtain.

The Russian force will establish command headquarters on Mount Moriah or the Temple area in Jerusalem. Daniel pointed this out when he said: "And he shall pitch his palatial tents between the seas [Dead Sea and Mediterranean Sea] and the glorious holy mount Zion; yet he shall come to his end with none to help him" (Daniel 11:45 Amplified).

As the Russian commander confidently prepares to meet the forces of the revived Roman Empire in Palestine, he seeks to utterly destroy the Jewish people. This is the apparent meaning of verses 44 and 45. Perhaps no other great army of history has ever been so totally destroyed as this one will be.

The Russian Waterloo

Ezekiel sounded the fatal collapse of the Red Army centuries ago when inspired by the Spirit of the living God he said: "But on that day, when Gog shall come against the land of Israel, says the Lord GOD, my wrath will be roused. For in my jealousy and in my blazing wrath I declare, On that day there shall be a great shaking in the land of Israel; the fish of the sea, and the birds of the air, and the beasts of the field, and all creeping things that creep on the ground, and all the men that are upon the face of the earth, shall quake at my presence, and the mountains shall be thrown down, and the cliffs shall fall, and every wall shall tumble to the ground. I will summon every kind of terror against Gog, says the Lord GOD; every man's sword will be against his brother. With pestilence and bloodshed I will enter into judgment with him; and I will rain upon him and his hordes and the many peoples that are with him, torrential rains and hailstones, fire and brimstone" (Ezekiel 38:18-22).

"... then I will strike your bow from your left hand, and will make your arrows drop out of your right hand. You shall fall upon the mountains of Israel, you and all your hordes and the people that are with you; I will give you to birds of prey of every sort and to the wild beasts to be devoured. You shall fall in the open field; for I have spoken, says the Lord GOD" (Ezekiel 39:3-5).

The description of torrents of fire and brimstone raining down upon the Red Army, coupled with an unprecedented shaking of the land of Israel could well be describing the use of tactical nuclear weapons against them by the Romans. It explicitly says that this force would fall "in the open field," so apparently this position enables the use of nuclear weapons.

God consigns this whole barbarous army, which will seek to annihilate the Jewish race, to an utter and complete decimation. Ezekiel speaks of the Russians and "... all your hosts and the peoples who are with you ..." being destroyed in Israel.

Nuclear Exchange Begins

A fearful thing is predicted as occurring at the time of the Red Army's destruction. God says, "I will send fire on Magog [Russia] and upon those who dwell securely [false hope] in the coastlands [various continents] ..." (Ezekiel 39:6 Amplified). According to this, Russia, as well as many countries who thought they were secure under the Antichrist's protection, will have fire fall upon them. Once again, this could be a direct judgment from God, or God could allow the various countries to launch a nuclear exchange of ballistic missiles upon each other.

What About the United States?

The United States may be aligned with the Western forces headed by the ten-nation Revived Roman Empire of Europe. It is clear that the U.S. cannot be the leader of the West in the future. It is quite possible that Ezekiel was referring to the U.S. in part when he said: "I will send fire—upon those who dwell securely in the coastlands...."

The word translated "coastlands" or "isle" in the Hebrew is *ai*. It was used by the ancients in the sense of "continents" today. It designated the great Gentile civilizations across the seas which were usually settled most densely along the coastlands. The idea here is that the Gentile nations on distant continents would all experience the impact of sudden torrents of fire raining down upon them. This can include prophetically the populated continents and islands of the Western hemisphere as well as the Far East. It pictures cataclysmic events which affect the whole inhabited earth.

The Greatest Battle of All Time

With the United Arab and African armies neutralized by the Russian invasion, and the consequent complete annihilation of the Russian forces and their homeland, we have only two great spheres of power left to fight the final climactic battle of Armageddon; the combined forces of the Western civilization united under the leadership of the Roman Dictator and the vast hordes of the Orient probably united under the Red Chinese war machine.

The Mobilization

There may be a short lapse of hostility in the world after the destruction of Russia and allies while the armies mobilize. The apostle John predicts the mobilization of the oriental power as mentioned in Chapter 7. "And the sixth angel poured out his bowl upon the great river, the Euphrates; and its water was dried up, that the way might be prepared for the kings from the east" (Revelation 16:12 NASB).

The Chinese, as previously discussed, will be the most logical leader of this great army. They will use the chaos caused by this conflict in the Middle East to march against the Roman Dictator in a challenge for world control.

As this incredible Oriental army of 200 million soldiers marches to the eastern banks of the Euphrates, the Roman Dictator will begin to prepare his armies to meet them for the showdown in the Middle East. The apostle John predicts the supernatural power that the Antichrist and the False Prophet will use to gather all remaining nations together to confront the Oriental armies: "And I saw coming out of the mouth of the dragon [Satan] and out of the mouth of the beast [Roman Dictator] and out of the mouth of the false prophet, three unclean spirits like frogs; for they are spirits of demons, performing signs, which go out to the kings of the whole world, to gather them together for war of the great day of God, the Almighty. And they gathered them together to the place which in Hebrew is called Armageddon" (Revelation 16:13, 14, 16 NASB).

Several things must be noted from this passage. First, this whole sequence of events constitutes the final judgments of God against the Christ-rejecting world. They are called in the Book of Revelation the seven bowl or vial judgments and they occur just before and during the visible return of Jesus Christ to the earth. Secondly, the passage shows that the Roman Dictator and his sensational religious cohort, the False Prophet, will speak a satanically originated message to the non-oriental world—a message energized with great demonic power. They will persuade the nations of the whole world (i.e. not aligned with China) that they should send armies to the land of Palestine to destroy the last great warlike force on earth. They will probably promise an age of everlasting peace after the troublesome communist forces of the Orient are destroyed. Thirdly, the passage indicates that "leaders of the whole world" will send armies to the Middle East to fight under the Antichrist's command against "the kings of the east." Such countries as Western Europe, the United States, Canada, South America, and Australia undoubtedly will be represented.

Fourthly, these armies will be assembled and deployed for battle in the place called "Armageddon" or "Harmageddon."

What and Where Is Armageddon?

Armageddon is a byword used through the centuries to depict the horrors of war. Dr. Seiss sums up its true significance as follows: "Harmageddon (Armageddon) means the Mount of Megiddo, which has also given its name to the great plain of Jezreel which belts across the middle of the Holy Land, from the Mediterranean to the Jordan. The name is from a Hebrew root which means to cut off, to slay; and a place of slaughter has Megiddo ever been."[5]

In Biblical history countless bloody battles were fought in this area. Napoleon is reported to have stood upon the hill of Megiddo and recalled this prophecy as he looked over the valley and said, ". . . all the armies of the world could maneuver for battle here." In the Old Testament book of Joel this valley was called the "valley of Jehoshaphat."

Today this valley's entrance has the port of Haifa at its Western end. This is one of the most accessible areas in Palestine for amphibious landing of troops. It also affords a great area for troop assembly, equipment, and organization. Some troops will doubtlessly be airlifted in as well, and this large valley is suited for that, too.

The Valley of Decision

Some twenty-seven centuries ago the prophet Joel focused upon this same scene and said: "Proclaim this among the nations: Prepare war, stir up the mighty men. Let all the men of war draw near, let them come up. Beat your plowshares into swords, and your pruning hooks into spears; let the weak say, 'I am a warrior.' Hasten and come, all you nations round about, gather yourselves there. Bring down thy warriors, O LORD. Let the nations bestir themselves, and come up to the valley of Jehoshaphat; for there I will sit to judge all the nations round about. Put in the sickle, for the harvest is ripe. Go in, tread, for the wine press is full. The vats overflow, for their wickedness is great. Multitudes, multitudes, in the valley of decision! For the day of the LORD is near in the valley of decision" (Joel 3:9-14).

Joel reveals that it is in this very place that the Messiah will destroy the armies of the world and establish his kingdom of true peace and everlasting happiness. He also confirms the world-wide assemblage of armies there.

It is extremely important to note the accuracy of Bible prophecy in relation to this last conflict. In this day of H-bombs and super weapons, it seems incredible that there could ever be another great land war fought by basically conventional means, yet the Chinese believe that with a vastly superior numerical force, they can absorb devastating losses and still win a war. They also believe that all war is still determined on the ground by land forces.

Another interesting fact is that a force of 200 million soldiers could not be transported by China and its foreseeable allies by air or sea. They do not possess the industry to produce a transportation system for such an army. This necessitates the movement of troops across the land as is indicated in Revelation 16:12.

India has revealed recently an important development. It is reported that 12,000 Chinese soldiers are at work inside Pakistan-held Kashmir on the road which would give Chinese troops in Tibet a shortcut to the subcontinent. India calls the Chinese road-building activities a "threat to peace in Asia." It was said that "a flurry of road-building throughout the Himalayas is taking on increasing strategic importance."[6]

When this road is completed, it will make possible the rapid movement of millions of Chinese troops into the Middle East. It will literally pave the way for John's prophecy to be fulfilled: ". . . unless those days had been cut short, no life would have been saved . . ." (Matthew 24:22 NASB).

So here it is—the last great conflict. After the Antichrist assembles the forces of the rest of the whole world together, they meet the onrushing charge of the kings of the East in a battle line which will extend throughout Israel with the vortex centered at the Valley of Megiddo.

According to Zechariah, terrible fighting will center around the city of Jerusalem (Zechariah 12:2, 3; 14:1, 2).

Isaiah speaks of a frightful carnage taking place south of the Dead Sea in ancient Edom (Isaiah 63:1-4).

The apostle John predicts that so many people will be slaughtered in the conflict that blood will stand to the horses' bridles for a total distance of 200 miles northward and southward of Jerusalem (Revelation 14:20).

It seems incredible! The human mind cannot conceive of such inhumanity of man to man, yet God will allow man's nature to fully display itself in that day. No wonder Jesus said: ". . for then there will be a great tribulation, such as has not occurred since the beginning of the world until now, nor ever shall" (Matthew 24:21 NASB).

World-wide Destruction

The conflict will not be limited to the Middle East. The apostle John warns that when these two great forces meet in battle the greatest shock wave ever to hit the earth will occur. Whether by natural force of an earthquake or by some super weapon isn't clear. John says that all the cities of the nations will be destroyed (Revelation 16:19).

Imagine, cities like London, Paris, Tokyo, New York, Los Angeles, Chicago—obliterated! John says that the Eastern force alone will wipe out a third of the earth's population (Revelation 9:15-18).

He also predicts that entire islands and mountains would be blown off the map. It seems to indicate an all-out attack of ballistic missiles upon the great metropolitan areas of the world.

Prophecy indicates that U.S. Representative John Rhodes was right when he said concerning the danger of Red China and nuclear weapons, ". . . anyone who expects restraint from Red China ignores history and imperils future generations of Americans."[7]

Isaiah predicts in Chapter 24 concerning this time: "Behold, the Lord will lay waste the earth and make it desolate, and he will twist its surface and scatter its inhabitants."

"The earth lies polluted under its inhabitants." (Perhaps this refers in part to water and air pollution.)

"Therefore, a curse devours the earth, and its inhabitants suffer for their guilt; therefore the inhabitants of the earth are scorched [burned], and few men are left" (verses 1, 5, 6).

In the same chapter Isaiah says: "The earth is utterly broken, the earth is rent asunder, the earth is violently shaken. The earth staggers like a drunken man, it sways like a hut . . ." (verses 19, 20).

All of these verses seem to indicate the unleashing of incredible weapons the world over.

A Bright Spot in the Gloom

As Armageddon begins with the invasion of Israel by the Arabs and the Russian confederacy, and their consequent swift destruction, the greatest period of Jewish conversion to their true Messiah will begin. Ezekiel predicts that the destruction of the great Russian invading force will have a supernatural clement to it which will cause great numbers of Jews to see the hand of the Lord in it. Through the miraculous sign of the destruction of this enemy who sought to destroy all Jews they come to see the name of their true God and Messiah, Jesus Christ.

Ezekiel quotes God as saying: "I will send fire on Magog [Russia] and on those who dwell securely in the coastlands; and they shall know that I am the LORD. And my holy name I will make known in the midst of my people Israel; and I will not let my holy name be profaned any more; and the nations shall know that I am the LORD, the Holy One in Israel. Behold, it is coming and it will be brought about, says the Lord GOD. That is the day of which I have spoken" [i.e., in the prophecies] (Ezekiel 39:6-8).

Zechariah predicts that one-third of the Jews alive during this period will be converted to Christ and miraculously preserved.

"In the whole land, says the LORD, two thirds shall be cut off and perish, and one third shall be left alive. And I will put this third into the fire, and refine them as one refines silver, and test them as gold is tested. They will call on my name, and I will answer them. I will say, 'They are my people'; and they will say, 'The LORD is my God'" (Zechariah 13:8, 9).

The Greatest Moment

As the battle of Armageddon reaches its awful climax and it appears that all life will be destroyed on earth—in this very moment Jesus Christ will return and save man from self-extinction.

As history races toward this moment, are you afraid or looking with hope for deliverance? The answer should reveal to you your spiritual condition.

One way or another history continues in a certain acceleration toward the return of Christ. Are you ready?

13 ○ The Main Event

The purposes of the United Nations are: to maintain international peace and security, and to that end: to take effective collective measures for the prevention and removal of threats to the peace. U. N. CHARTER, 1945

These things I have spoken to you, that in Me you may have peace. In the world you have tribulation, but take courage; I have overcome the world. JESUS CHRIST

WRITTEN UPON THE cornerstone of the United Nations building is a quotation of part of a prophecy. It reads: ". . . they shall beat their swords into plowshares, and their spears into pruning hooks; nation shall not lift up sword against nation, neither shall they learn war any more" (Isaiah 2:4).

This is a noble thought and has been quoted often by men who seek peace for this troubled world. There is a problem in the phrase, however, and we believe this is why the United Nations will never bring a lasting peace to the world. This quotation has been taken out of context. The meaning of the passage speaks of the time when the Messiah would reign over the earth out of Jerusalem and judge between the nations in a visible, actual, and historic Kingdom of God on earth. The people of the earth will come to the Lord in that day and ask Him to teach them His ways. Knowledge of God will be universal (Isaiah 2:3). This is the era for which Jesus taught us to pray in the Lord's Prayer, ". . . Thy kingdom come, thy will be done on earth as it is in heaven" (Matthew 6:10).

Men today vainly seek after peace while they reject and shut out of their lives the Prince of Peace, Jesus Christ. The name of Christ is not mentioned at the close of prayer in the United Nations. In fact, Jesus has been excluded from the premises. Man has shut out the only hope of peace, according to the Bible. The spirit of "antichrist" reigns in the governments of the world, for Christ is said not to be relevant to the problems we face.

Peace is available to the individual today as he invites Christ into his heart and allows Him to reign upon the throne of his life. But the Bible teaches that lasting peace will come to the world only after Christ returns and sits upon the throne of David in Jerusalem and establishes His historic kingdom on earth for a thousand years (Revelation 20:4-6).

The rulers of the world are told by many prophecies that God would send His king to rule over the earth and establish a reign of peace, righteousness, and justice in place of their godless, selfish, and violent rule. Jesus will return at a time of world-wide catastrophe, when man is on the brink of self-destruction. Men, for the most part, will have utterly rejected the true God and His Son, Jesus the Messiah, as predicted long ago by the psalmist: "The kings of the earth set themselves, and rulers take counsel together, against the LORD and his anointed [Christ], saying, 'Let us burst their bonds asunder, and cast their cords from us'" (Psalm 2:2, 3).

In spite of all that man will try to do to establish his rule and push God out of the world, God will establish His king, the Messiah Jesus, as the psalmist goes on to predict: "Yet have I set my king upon my holy hill of Zion" (Psalm 2:6 KJV).

Many so-called Christian leaders today do not believe that Jesus Christ will literally and physically make a personal return to the earth. Some teach that Christ returns spiritually when people accept Him and say that this is all that is meant by the various predictions of His return. Others teach that Jesus may return some day, but that it is irrelevant to study or to talk about it. The latter are worse than the former, for one out of every twenty-five verses in the New Testament is related to the second coming of Christ, and the survival of mankind as well as the fulfillment of hundreds of unconditional promises especially made to the believing remnant of the Jewish race are dependent on the second coming of Christ to this earth. As a matter of fact, in the Old Testament there were more than 300 prophecies regarding Christ's first coming (all of which were literally fulfilled), but more than 500 relating to His second coming. Many of these two different themes of prophecy were disclosed in the same sentence.

We have read that the apostle Peter clearly warned that in the days just prior to Christ's return false teachers would arise in the church and say: "Where is the promise of His (Jesus') coming? For ever since the fathers [apostles] fell asleep, all continues just as it was from the beginning of creation" (II Peter 3:4 NASB).

Characteristics of Christ's Return

Immediately after Jesus physically departed from the Mount of Olives and while His disciples were staring after Him with awe and amazement, the following promise was given: "And as they were gazing intently into the sky while He [Jesus] was departing, behold, two men in white clothing stood beside them; and they also said, 'Men of Galilee, why do you stand looking into the sky? This Jesus, who has been taken from you into heaven, will come in just the same way you have watched Him go into heaven'" (Acts 1-10, 11 NASB).

The word in the original translated "in just the same way" means "in exactly the same manner." Just as Jesus departed physically, visibly and personally from the earth, so He will return. Just as Jesus departed with clouds, so He will return.

His Return Will Be Visible, Personal, and Physical

The apostle John said: "Behold, He [Jesus] is coming with the clouds, and every eye will see Him, even those who pierced Him; and all the tribes of the earth will mourn over Him" (Revelation 1:7 NASB).

Zechariah predicted the same picture 500 years before Christ was born: ". . . and they [believing Israelites] shall look upon me [Jesus] whom they have pierced, and they shall mourn for him, as one mourneth for his only son . . ." (Zechariah 12:10 KJV).

To mourn over the one who was pierced necessitates that man recognizes Jesus who was crucified and rejected. This demands a dramatic personal and physical appearance.

Jesus promised under oath before the high priest at His trial: ". . . nevertheless I tell you, hereafter you shall see the Son of Man sitting at the right hand of Power [God], and coming on the clouds of heaven" (Matthew 26:64 NASB).

This statement was the official ground of His condemnation for blasphemy and the death sentence. Jesus dared to be the One who would fulfill two of the best-known prophecies concerning the Messiah's coming in glory to rule the earth. The first is from the Psalms, predicted before 1000 B.C.: "The LORD [God, the father] said unto my Lord [God, the Son], Sit thou at my right hand, until I make thine enemies thy footstool" (Psalm 110:1).

The second is from Daniel, predicted about 550 B.C.: "I saw in the night visions, and behold, one like the Son of man came with the clouds of heaven, and came to the Ancient of days, and they brought him near before him. And there was given him dominion, and glory, and a kingdom, that all people, nations, and languages should serve him: his dominion is an everlasting dominion, which shall not pass away, and his kingdom that which shall not be destroyed" (Daniel 7:13, 14 KJV).

No wonder the Jewish supreme court (the Sanhedrin) went into orbit. When Jesus made such a fantastic claim as that in one terse sentence, they either had to fall down and worship Him or kill Him. They chose the latter.

His Coming Will Be Sudden and Startling

Jesus predicted the suddenness of His return as follows: "For just as lightning comes from the east, and flashes even to the west, so shall the coming of the Son of Man be" (Matthew 24:27 NASB).

And again He said: ". . . and then the sign of the Son of Man will appear in the sky, and then all the tribes of the earth shall mourn, and they will see the Son of Man coming on the clouds of heaven with power and great glory" (Matthew 24:30 NASB).

Perhaps the "sign of the Son of Man" will be a gigantic celestial image of Jesus flashed upon the heavens for all to see. This would explain how all men suddenly recognize who He is and see the scars from His piercing at the cross.

His Coming Will Be With the Saints

It is significant to note that many references to Christ's return speak of His return accompanied with "the clouds of heaven." We believe that the clouds refer to the myriads of believers who return in white robes with Jesus. Believers are referred to as "a cloud of witnesses" in Hebrews 12:1. The clouds then would be all of the church age believers, you and I, returning in immortal glorified bodies, having been previously caught up to meet Christ in the air in "the ultimate trip," prior to the seven years of Tribulation on earth, and the resurrected saints of the Old Testament (Revelation 19:14).

The word "saint" means someone who is set apart as God's possession. It is used to designate all who have believed in Christ as Savior. This word is used many times to refer to those who will accompany Christ at His return.

As Zechariah referred to the Messiah's second coming he said: ". . . and the LORD my God, shall come, and all the saints with thee" (14:5 KJV).

The apostle John speaks of the apparel of the saints as they return with Christ: "And the armies which are in heaven, clothed in fine linen, white and clean, were following Him on white horses" (Revelation 19:14 NASB).

John explains the white linen robes: "And it was given to her [the church made up of all believers who have been caught up in the Rapture] to clothe herself in fine linen, bright and clean; for the fine linen is the righteous acts of the saints" (Revelation 19:8 NASB).

His Coming Will Be With Violent Judgment

When Jesus came the first time it was not to judge the world, but to save it. He came as the Lamb of God who gave His life to take away the sin of the world. The one thing that God has established for man to do is to believe in His Son as Savior. When Jesus returns the second time it will be as a lion to judge those who rejected the free gift of salvation from sin. Man will have completely demonstrated his worthiness of judgment.

According to Zechariah, "all nations will be gathered against Jerusalem to battle." The Jews who live in the area will be on the verge of annihilation when God gives them supernatural strength to fight. Then the Lord will go forth to fight for them and save them.

Jesus' feet will first touch the earth where they left the earth, on the Mount of Olives. The mountain will split in two with a great earthquake the instant that Jesus' foot touches it. The giant crevice which results will run east and west through the center of the mountain. It will go east to the north tip of the Dead Sea and west to the Mediterranean Sea (Zechariah 14).

It was reported to me that an oil company doing seismic studies of this area in quest of oil discovered a gigantic fault running east and west precisely through the center of the Mount of Olives. The fault is so severe that it could split at any time. It is awaiting "the foot."

Zechariah predicts a strange thing with regard to the ensuing split in the earth. The believing Jewish remnant in Jerusalem will rush into the crack instead of doing the natural thing of running from it. They will know this prophecy and realize that this great cavern has opened up for the Lord to protect them from the terrible devastation that He is about to pour out upon the godless armies all around. It will be used as a type of bomb shelter.

The nature of the forces which the Lord will unleash on that day against the armies gathered in the Middle East is described in Zechariah 14:12: "And this shall be the plague wherewith the LORD will smite all the people that have fought against Jerusalem; Their flesh shall consume away while they stand upon their feet, and their eyes shall consume away in their holes, and their tongue shall consume away in their mouth" (KJV).

A frightening picture, isn't it? Has it occurred to you that this is exactly what happens to those who are in a thermonuclear blast? It appears that this will be the case at the return of Christ.

His Return Will Be to Set Up God's Kingdom on Earth

After Christ destroys all ungodly kingdoms, Zechariah says, "The Lord shall be king over all the earth; in that day shall there be one Lord, and His name one."

Most ministers and religious leaders today reject even the possibility that Christ will establish an actual physical kingdom of God upon the earth.

Many who believe in a personal return of Christ reject that He will establish a thousand year kingdom of God and rule mortals from the throne of David out of Jerusalem after His return.

The Latin word for "1000" is "millennium" and down through history the teaching concerning this earthly kingdom came to be known as the "millennial kingdom." Those who reject that Christ will establish a 1000 year kingdom after His return are known theologically as "amillennialists," meaning "no millennium." Those who believe that Christ will return and set up a 1000 year kingdom are called "premillennialists," meaning Christ returns first, then establishes the kingdom on earth.

There used to be a group called "postmillennialists." They believed that the Christians would root out the evil in the world, abolish godless rulers, and convert the world through ever increasing evangelism until they brought about the Kingdom of God on earth through their own efforts. Then after 1000 years of the institutional church reigning on earth with peace, equality, and righteousness, Christ would return and time would end. These people rejected much of the Scripture as being literal and believed in the inherent goodness of man. World War I greatly disheartened this group and World War II virtually wiped out this viewpoint. No self-respecting scholar who looks at the world conditions and the accelerating decline of Christian influence today is a "postmillennialist."

We are "premillennialists" in viewpoint. The real issue between the amillennial and the premillennial viewpoints is whether prophecy should be interpreted literally or allegorically. As it has been demonstrated many times in this book, all prophecy about past events has been fulfilled literally, particularly the predictions regarding the first coming of Christ. The words of prophecy were demonstrated as being literal, that is, having the normal meaning understood by the people of the time in which it was written. The words were not intended to be explained away by men who cannot believe what is clearly predicted.

The opponents of the premillennial view all agree grudgingly that if you interpret prophecy literally it does teach that Christ will set up a literal kingdom in time which will last in history a thousand years and then go into an eternal form which will never be destroyed.

To us the biggest issue is over the question, "Does God keep His promises?" For God unconditionally promised Abraham's descendants a literal world-wide kingdom over which they would rule through their Messiah who would reign upon King David's throne. The Jews who believe in the

Messiah will also possess the land which is bordered on the east by the Euphrates River, and on the west by the Nile (Genesis 15:18-21).

It is promised that Jerusalem will be the spiritual center of the entire world and that all people of the earth will come annually to worship Jesus who will rule there (Zechariah 14:16-21; Isaiah 2:3; Micah 4:1-3). The Jewish believing remnant will be the spiritual leaders of the world and teach all nations the ways of the Lord (Zechariah 8:20-23; Isaiah 66:23).

Paradise Restored

God's kingdom will be characterized by peace and equity, and by universal spirituality and knowledge of the Lord. Even the animals and reptiles will lose their ferocity and no longer be carnivorous. All men will have plenty and be secure. There will be a chicken in every pot and no one will steal it! The Great Society which human rulers throughout the centuries have promised, but never produced, will at last be realized under Christ's rule. The meek and not the arrogant will inherit the earth (Isaiah 11).

Prelude to Eternity

As it was mentioned in Chapters eight and nine, Daniel predicted the four great world ruling kingdoms that man would set up during the time from the sixth century B.C. until the coming of the Messiah. We noted these four human empires as Babylon, Media-Persia, Greece, and Rome, with its revived form in the last days. The fifth world kingdom, which according to Daniel will conquer the revived form of the Roman Empire, is the Messianic kingdom (Daniel 7:13-27).

This kingdom will begin in time with mortal subjects (Revelation 20:4-6), last 1000 years, and at the end of that time some of the children of the believers who started in the kingdom will apparently prove to be unbelievers and start a rebellion against Christ and His rule. Christ will bring swift judgment upon them before the rebellion reaches the actual fighting stage (Revelation 20:7-10).

After this event there will be no more human history with mortal men. All unbelievers, it seems, will be judged in the crushing of the last rebellion which is led by God's old adversary, Satan. Satan will have been bound for a thousand years, but is released momentarily so that he could reveal the rebellion in the unbelieving hearts of those who rejected Christ as Savior

(Revelation 20:7, 8). All who remain as mortals will be changed into immortality at this point, and the Kingdom of God will not cease, but simply change form and be reestablished in a new heaven and a new earth (Revelation 21).

The sequence is clear in the last chapters of Revelation. First there is the return of Christ at the climax of the greatest war of all time. Second, Christ separates the surviving believers from the surviving unbelievers; the unbelievers will be judged and cast off the earth (Revelation 20:1-6; cf. Matthew 25:41-46). Third, Christ establishes the millennial kingdom and the surviving believers go into it as mortals and repopulate the earth (Revelation 20:11-15; cf. Matthew 25:31-40). Fourth, at the end of a thousand years the unbelieving children rebel, Christ judges them, then He completely changes the old heaven and earth and creates a new one (Revelation 21; Isaiah 65:17; II Peter 3:8-13). This is the ultimate destiny of all persons who are redeemed by Christ.

How many times have we wondered what heaven will be like? According to such passages as Revelation 21 and 22, heaven is a real and breathtaking place. We will not wander about as disembodied spirits, playing harps throughout an ethereal expanse. We shall live forever in the presence of God, fellow heirs with Christ, as kings and priests forever, with no more sorrows or tears. We shall know an ecstatic, endless joy surrounded by an earth and heaven of indescribable beauty. If you can think of the most beautiful place you have ever been, then amplify its beauty beyond your comprehension and imagine what it would be like without death, disease, or any curse upon it, you may have an inkling of heaven.

The word translated "new" in Revelation 21:1 means "new in kind or order" as distinguished from merely new in point of time. Peter describes the process the Lord will use in renovating the heaven and earth that now exist: "But the day of the Lord will come like a thief, in which the heavens will pass away with a roar and the elements will be destroyed with intense heat, and the earth and its works will be burned up. Since all these things are to be destroyed in this way, what sort of people ought you to be in holy conduct and godliness, looking for and hastening the coming of the day of God, on account of which the heavens will be destroyed by burning, and the elements will melt with intense heat. But according to His promise we are looking for new heavens and a new earth, in which righteousness [only] dwells" (II Peter 3:10-13 NASB).

The word translated "elements" is *stoicheiov*, which means the most basic element of nature. Today we know the atom is the smallest building block of nature. Now Peter says that these elements will be "destroyed." The literal meaning of the word "destroyed" is "to loose something." It was frequently used for untying a rope, or a bandage as in John 11:44. In other words, Christ is going "to loose" the atoms of the galaxy in which we live. No wonder there will be a great roar and intense heat and fire. Then Christ will put the atoms back together to form a new heaven and earth, in which only glorified persons without their sinful natures will live. There will be no more rebellion of man's will against God; only righteousness, peace, security, harmony, and joy.

That's where we want to be!

14 ○ Polishing the Crystal Ball

> *Go your way, Daniel, for the meaning of the words of prophecy is shut up and sealed until the time of the end. Many shall travel about and knowledge shall increase. None of the wicked shall understand these words, but those who are wise shall in the last days understand.*   GOD TO DANIEL ABOUT 520 B.C. (LITERAL TRANSLATION)

NO OTHER PROPHET has ever had more numerous, far-reaching prophecies revealed to him than Daniel; and yet a great deal of what he received in God-given visions and revelations he didn't understand. Many of his predictions had to do with "the end times" or the events immediately preceding the coming of the Messiah-Jesus to set up God's kingdom.

At the close of Daniel's written account of his prophecies, he reveals his bewilderment about when and how all the things he had predicted would occur: "How long shall it be to the end of these wonders?" (Daniel 12:6 Amplified).

A special angelic messenger replied to Daniel and said, ". . . when the shattering of the power of the holy people [Israel] comes to an end all these things would be accomplished" (Daniel 12:7).

Daniel replied, "I heard, but I did not understand." Then he said, "O my lord, what shall be the issue and final end of these things?" (Daniel 12:8 Amplified).

The messenger replied, "Go your way, Daniel; for the words [of prophecy] are shut up and sealed till the time of the end" (Daniel 12:9 Amplified).

In other words, God revealed to Daniel that his prophecies would not be clearly understood *until* the end times, i.e., the times when the events predicted would begin to take shape. The key that would unlock the prophetic book would be the current events that would begin to fit into the predicted pattern.

Christians after the early second century spent little time really defining prophetic truth until the middle of the nineteenth century. Then there seems to have been a great revival of interest in the prophetic themes of the Bible. Today, Christians who have diligently studied prophecy, trusting the Spirit of God for illumination, have a greater insight into its meaning than ever before. The prophetic word definitely has been "unsealed" in our generation as God predicted it would be.

Now I am about to walk into the lion's den. Perhaps it would be wise to follow Churchill's tactic when he said, "You know I always avoid prophesying beforehand, it is much better policy to prophesy after the event has already taken place." However, in this chapter I will make a number of forecasts about the future which are based on a careful study of the prophetic truth and the writings of many scholars on the subject. I believe that these forecasts are based upon sound deductions; however, please don't get the idea that I think that I am infallibly right in the same way that a Biblical prophet speaking under the direct inspiration of God's Spirit was. I believe that God today gives us illumination to what has been written, but that He doesn't give us infallible revelation as He gave the authors of the Bible. Here, then, are the things that I believe will happen and develop in the near future.

The Religious Scene

In the institutional church, composed of professing Christians who are in many cases not Christian, look for many things to happen:

With increasing frequency the leadership of the denominations will be captured by those who completely reject the historic truths of the Bible and deny doctrines which according to Christ Himself are crucial to believe in order to be a Christian. In some of the largest Protestant denominations this has already taken place. The few remaining institutions which are not yet dominated by the disbelievers will go downhill in the same manner.

There will be unprecedented mergers of denominations into "religious conglomerates." This will occur for two reasons: first, most denominations were formed because of deep convictions about certain spiritual truths. As more of these truths are discarded as irrelevant because of unbelief in Biblical authority, there will be no reason to be divided. Unity is certainly important to have, but never, according to the teachings of Christ, at the expense of the crucial truths of Christianity.

Secondly, as ministers depart from the truths of the Bible they lose the authority and power that it has to meet real human needs, and as many ministers are not truly born spiritually themselves and are consequently without the illumination of God's Spirit, they no longer will be able to hold their present congregations, much less attract others. So they resort to "social action gimmicks," super-organization, and elaborate programs as a substitute.

As Paul predicted concerning these ministers in the last days: "holding to a form of godliness [literally religion], although they have denied its power. . . ." And again he says, ". . . they are always learning and never able to come to the knowledge of the truth" (II Timothy 3:5, 7 NASB).

Young people will continue to accelerate their exodus from the institutional churches. Several surveys taken by church leaders indicate this. Youth today reject impersonal, highly structured organizations with their emphasis upon buildings and material affluence. In talking with many young people from various backgrounds I have found that the institutional churches are viewed by them as a reflection of all they despise in what they consider materialistic, hypocritical, and prejudiced elements within our American culture.

Above all, young people want a simple, personal, and relevant answer to life that isn't based upon self-centered materialism, but upon real life, selfless love. When they are shown that this idealistic view of life cannot be achieved by various shades of welfarism, socialism, or drugs, but only through a personal relationship with Christ that is not tied to joining an institutional church (or religious country club as they call it), then many respond and receive Jesus Christ.

Some traditional churches have learned to provide the personal ministry of God's truth to the youth and you will find their youth departments are flourishing. But they are the exception, unfortunately. Most churches seem to be on the wrong wave length altogether. Some have the truth, but can't communicate it to today's youth; others simply don't teach the truth, and though they try "underground church" approaches, they can't compete with the radical political organizations.

Many youth are going to be on the front edge of a movement toward first century-type Christianity, with an emphasis upon people and their needs rather than buildings and unwieldy programs.

There will be an ever-widening gap between the true believers in Christ and those who masquerade as "ministers of righteousness." I believe that open persecution will soon break out upon the "real Christians," and it will come from the powerful hierarchy of unbelieving leaders within the denominations. Christians who believe in the final authority of the Bible, salvation through the substitutionary atonement of Christ alone, the deity of Jesus Christ, etc., will be branded as prime hindrances to "the brotherhood" of all men and the "universal Fatherhood of God" teaching, which is so basic to the "ecumaniacs" who don't believe in the very heart of Jesus' teachings. Jesus taught that God is the Creator of all, but the Father of only those who believe in Him (John 8:44; Galatians 3:26).

Because of the persecution of believers, there will grow a true underground church of a believing remnant of people.

Look for vast and far-reaching movements toward a oneworld religious organization, spearheaded mostly by the unbelieving leaders of the institutional churches; also look for this movement to become more politically oriented than it is now.

Look for movements within Israel to make Jerusalem the religious center of the world and to rebuild their ancient Temple on its old site.

The Political Scene

Keep your eyes on the Middle East. If this is the time that we believe it is, this area will become a constant source of tension for all the world. The fear of another World War will be almost completely centered in the troubles of this area. It will become so severe that only Christ or the Antichrist can solve it. Of course the world will choose the Antichrist.

Israel will become fantastically wealthy and influential in the future. Keep your eyes upon the development of riches in the Dead Sea.

The United States will not hold its present position of leadership in the western world; financially, the future leader will be Western Europe. Internal political chaos caused by student rebellions and Communist subversion will begin to erode the economy of our nation. Lack of moral principle by citizens and leaders will so weaken law and order that a state of anarchy will finally result. The military capability of the United States, though it is at present the most powerful in the world, has already been neutralized because no one has the courage to use it decisively. When the economy collapses so will the military.

The only chance of slowing up this decline in America is a widespread spiritual awakening.

As the United States loses power, Western Europe will be forced to unite and become the standard-bearer of the western world. Look for the emergence of a "United States of Europe" composed of ten inner member nations. The Common Market is laying the groundwork for this political confederacy which will become the mightiest coalition on earth. It will stop the Communist take-over of the world and will for a short while control both Russia and Red China through the personal genius of the Antichrist who will become ruler of the European confederacy.

Look for the papacy to become even more involved in world politics, especially in proposals for bringing world peace and world-wide economic prosperity.

Look for a growing desire around the world for a man who can govern the entire world.

Look for some limited use of modern nuclear weapons somewhere in the world that will so terrify people of the horrors of war that when the Antichrist comes they will immediately respond to his ingenious proposal for bringing world peace and security from war. This limited use could occur between Russia and China, or upon the continental United States.

On the Sociological Scene

Look for the present sociological problems such as crime, riots, lack of employment, poverty, illiteracy, mental illness, illegitimacy, etc., to increase as the population explosion begins to multiply geometrically in the late '70's.

Look for the beginning of the widest spread famines in the history of the world.

Look for drug addiction to further permeate the U.S. and other free-world countries. Drug addicts will run for high political offices and win through support of the young adults.

Look for drugs and forms of religion to be merged together. There will be a great general increase of belief in extrasensory phenomena, which will not be related to the true God, but to Satan.

Astrology, witchcraft, and oriental religions will become predominant in the western world.

Where Do We Go From Here?

We believe that in spite of all these things God is going to raise up a believing remnant of true Christians and give one last great offer of the free gift of forgiveness and acceptance in Jesus Christ before snatching them out of the world as it plunges toward judgment.

After considering the incredible things in this book, what should our attitude and purpose be?

First, if you are not sure that you have personally accepted the gift of God's forgiveness which Jesus Christ purchased by bearing the judgment of a holy God that was due your sins, then you should do so right now wherever you are. It may be that you are bothered because you can't understand it all, or you feel that you don't have enough faith. Don't let either of these things stop you. The only thing you need to understand is that God offers you in Jesus Christ a full pardon and new spiritual life. If you truly desire to receive Jesus Christ into your life, then you have enough faith to enter God's family and change your eternal destiny.

Jesus put the whole thing in a very picturesque way when He said: "Behold, I stand at the door [of your heart] and knock; if any one hears My voice and opens the door, I will come in to him, and will dine [have fellowship] with him, and he with Me" (Revelation 3:20 NASB).

Right at this moment, in your own way, thank Jesus for dying for your sins and invite Him to come into your heart. The door of the above illustration is your desire and will. You open the door by inviting Jesus Christ into your life.

Did you do it? If you did, then where is Jesus Christ right now? According to His promise (and He can't lie), He is in your heart.

Jesus further promised, "I will never desert you, nor will I ever forsake you" (Hebrews 13:5 NASB).

He has come into your heart to stay and to bring new purpose, peace of mind, stability, in spite of circumstances, and true fulfillment to your personality as well as eternal life.

Secondly, if you have received Jesus Christ as Savior, then He wants to change your desires about life to God's desires, and empower you to live for God. God doesn't want us to try to clean up our own lives, but rather to be available to His Spirit who now lives personally within us.

As we trust Christ to deal with our temptations and to work in us His will, then He produces a real life righteousness in us which is characterized by an unselfish love for God and for others. The more we learn of God's love and unconditional acceptance of us, the more we want to please Him and the more we are able to trust Him to work in us. We also will desire to learn His Word which renews our minds to His viewpoint.

Ask Christ to teach you God's Word as you study it and He will.

Third, far from being pessimistic and dropping out of life, we should be rejoicing in the knowledge that Christ may return any moment for us. This should spur us on to share the good news of salvation in Christ with as many as possible. The Holy Spirit is working upon men in a dramatic way and He will lead you to people who are ready or who will be shortly if you trust Him.

Fourth, we should make it our aim to trust Christ to work in us a life of true righteousness. We all grow in this, so don't get discouraged or forget that God accepts us as we are. He wants our hearts to be constantly set toward pleasing Him and have faith to trust Him to help us. John said it this way: "See how great a love the Father has bestowed upon us, that we should be called children of God; and such we are. For this reason the world does not know us because it did not know Him. Beloved, now we are children of God, and it has not appeared as yet what we shall be. We know that, if He should appear, we shall be like Him, because we shall see Him just as He is. And every one who has this hope fixed on Him purifies himself, just as He is pure" (I John 3:1-3 NASB).

Fifth, we should plan our lives as though we will be here our full life expectancy, but live as though Christ may come today. We shouldn't drop out of school or worthwhile community activities, or stop working, or rush marriage, or any such thing unless Christ clearly leads us to do so. However, we should make the most of our time that is not taken up with the essentials.

Right after one of the major passages of the apostle Paul concerning the Rapture, he gave this promise: "Therefore, my beloved brethren, be steadfast, immovable, always abounding in the work of the Lord, knowing that your toil is not in vain in the Lord" (I Corinthians 15:58 NASB).

As we see the world becoming more chaotic, we can be "steadfast" and "immovable," because we know where it's going and where we are going. We know that Christ will protect us until His purpose is finished and then He will take us to be with Himself. We can "abound in His work" as we trust Him to work in us and know that it is not in vain because He will give us rewards to enjoy forever for every work of faith.

So let us seek to reach our family, our friends, and our acquaintances with the Gospel with all the strength that He gives us. The time is short.

In the early centuries, the Christians had a word for greeting and departing; it was the word, "maranatha," which means "the Lord is coming soon." We can think of no better way with which to say good-by—

MARANATHA!

NOTES

CHAPTER 1

1. *Time*, March 21, 1969.
2. *Family Weekly*, July 14, 1968.
3. *Los Angeles Times*, November 19, 1968.
4. *Time*, January 15, 1965.

CHAPTER 3

1. Douglas MacArthur, *Reminiscences* (McGraw-Hill: New York, 1964).

CHAPTER 4

1. *U.S. News and World Report*, Oct. 30, 1967.
2. William F. Albright, *From the Stone Age to Christianity* (Doubleday & Co.: Garden City, New York, 1946).
3. John Cumming D.D., *The Destiny of Nations* (Hurst & Blackette: London, 1864).
4. James Grant, *The End of Things* (Darton & Co.: London, 1866).
5. David L. Cooper, *When Gog's Armies Meet the Almighty in the Land of Israel* (Biblical Research Society: Los Angeles, 1940).
6. Arthur W. Kac, M.D., *The Rebirth of the State of Israel* (Marshall, Morgan and Scott: London, 1958).

CHAPTER 5

1. Walter Chamberlain, *The National Resources and Conversion of Israel*, (London, 1854).
2. John Cumming, M.D., *The Destiny of Nations* (Hurst & Blackette: London, 1864).
3. Chamberlain, op. cit.
4. Louis Bauman, *Russian Events in the Light of Bible Prophecy*, (The Balkiston Co.: Philadelphia, 1952).
5. Cumming, op. cit.
6. Wilhelm Gesenius, D.D., *Hebrew and English Lexicon*.

7. C. F. Keil, D.D. and F. Delitzsch, D.D., *Biblical Commentary on the Old Testament* (Eerdmans Publishing Co.: Grand Rapids, Michigan).

8. Gesenius, op. cit.

9. Cumming, op. cit.

10. Gesenius, op. cit.

11. Gesenius, op. cit.

12. W. S. McBirnie, *The Coming Decline and Fall of the Soviet Union* (Center for American Research and Education: Glendale, California).

13. Robert Young, LL.D., *Young's Analytical Concordance* (Eerdmans Publishing House: Grand Rapids, Michigan).

14. Gesenius, op. cit.

CHAPTER 6

1. *Current History*, "Nasser's Egypt," Gordon H. Torrey, May, 1965.

2. Ibid.

3. *U.S. News and World Report*, July 22, 1968.

4. *Santa Monica Evening Outlook*, December 3, 1968.

5. *Los Angeles Times*, July 9, 1969.

CHAPTER 7

1. J. A. Seiss, *The Apocalypse* (Zondervan Publishing House: Grand Rapids, Mich., 1962).

2. Cumming, op. cit.

3. Ibid.

4. Victor Petrov, *China: Emerging World Power*, (D. Van Nostrand Co., Inc.: Princeton, N.J., 1967).

5. W. Cleon Skousen, *The Naked Communist*, (The Ensign Publishing Co.: Salt Lake City, 1961).

6. *Quotations from Chairman Mao Tse-Tung*, "Problems of War and Strategy" (November 6, 1938), Selected Works, Vol. 11, P. 224. Quoted from a research pamphlet of the Center for American Research and Education, Glendale, Calif.

7. *Bulletin of Atomic Scientists*, "China's Nuclear Options," Michael Yahuda, February, 1969.

8. David Inglis, February, 1965.

9. Petrov, op. cit.

CHAPTER 8

1. Merrill F. Unger, *Introductory Guide to the Old Testament* (Zondervan Publishing House: Grand Rapids, Michigan, 1965).

2. Dr. E. J. Young, *The Prophecy of Daniel* (Eerdmans Publishing Co.: Grand Rapids, 1949).

3. Sir Robert Anderson, *Daniel in the Critic's Den* (New York, n.d.) .

4. *Look*, November 26, 1968.

5. *New York Times Magazine*, May 19, 1968.

6. *Nation's Business*, November, 1966.

7. "Trade and Atlantic Partnership," Dept. of State Publication 7386, Secretary of State Dean Rusk at the Conference on Trade Policy, Washington, D.C., 1962.

8. *Time*, July 4, 1969.

CHAPTER 9

1. William Barclay, *The Revelation of John* (Westminster Press: Philadelphia, 1960).

2. Ibid.

3. *U.S. News and World Report*, August 25, 1969 (source: F.B.I.).

4. *Los Angeles Times*, May 25, 1969.

5. *Columbus Dispatch*, August 21, 1969.

6. *U.S. News and World Report*, November 6, 1967.

7. *Natural History*, May, 1968.

8. *Los Angeles Times*, May 28, 1969.

CHAPTER 10

1. Henry H. Halley, *Halley's Bible Handbook* (Zondervan Publishing House: Grand Rapids, Michigan).

2. *Chimes*, October, 1968.

3. *Los Angeles Times*, May 18, 1969.

4. *Los Angeles Times*, May 25, 1969.

5. *U.S. News and World Report*, July 25, 1966.

CHAPTER 12

1. Bertrand Russell, *Has Man a Future?* (Simon & Schuster: New York, 1962).

2. *U.S. News and World Report*, December 25, 1967.

3. Douglas MacArthur, *Reminiscences* (McGraw-Hill: New York, 1964).

4. Harry Rimmer, *The Coming War and the Rise of Russia* (Eerdmans Publishing Co.: Grand Rapids, Michigan, 1940).

5. J. A. Seiss, *The Apocalypse* (Zondervan Publishing House: Grand Rapids, Michigan, 1962).

6. *Los Angeles Times*, August 20, 1969.

7. *Human Events*, August 26, 1967.

SATAN IS

ALIVE & WELL

ON

PLANET EARTH

O O O o o o O O O

In memory of Kent Carlson, the son of my dear friends, Carole and Ward Carlson. Kent, eighteen, was killed in a plane crash on the day this book was being completed. His life was a tribute to a godly home where he was taught the love of Christ, his fellow-man, and his country. Earth is poorer, but heaven is richer because of the entrance of this wonderful young man.

CONTENTS

Introduction   *165*

1   What's Happening?   167
2   Perilous Tide From the Other Side   179
3   Birth of the Black Prince   187
4   "D" Day Earth   195
5   Three Dimensional Warfare   207
6   Thought Bombs   221
7   Mind Manipulators   233
8   Angels of Light   245
9   Signs and Wonders   257
10   Diagnosing Demon Possession   273
11   Doctrines of Demons   287
12   The Guilt Trip   301
13   Weapons of Warfare   319
14   On a Note of Triumph   337
   Appendix   *349*
   Notes   *353*

INTRODUCTION

A FEW YEARS ago I came face to face with a complete reversal in the academic community. An unusual change came over many who had denied any belief in the power of a supernatural God. The indifferent, the scoffers, the proud agnostics in the Age of Rationalism, began to turn to another form of the supernatural. They became involved with psychic research, parapsychology, ESP, mystic philosophies, and Eastern religions. Recently there has been an upsurge in all forms of the occult!

Witchcraft and Satan worship spread throughout campuses and cities. In America, a so-called civilized country, people are involved in weird rites and rituals.

This book is an attempt to define a personal enemy who rules our world system. Whether we know it or not, he also influences every life to some degree. Until recent years his very existence has been doubted. Our churches have denied or underestimated him. But he is here—alive and well!

My wife Jan and I were having dinner with Carole and Ward Carlson, my co-author and her husband, when we first discussed *Satan Is Alive and Well.* A restaurant overlooking the Pacific didn't seem to be the right scene for the subject; the world and its problems were too remote. However, I felt compelled to warn them that anyone involved in this project would be a target for the central character.

We all discovered the reality of our adversary.

At times I thought I'd shelve the whole idea, but every time the progress on the manuscript was slowed down, I was shown another reason for the urgency of this message. I have never before come under such personal attack. It was not my imagination.

We are all part of an unseen conflict in the world and within ourselves. Yet we don't have to lead defeated lives, no matter what is thrown at us.

Consider what is said about this clever character, Satan. Anyone who has dominated history as he has cannot be ignored, especially in these days. To do so may be at the peril of your very life.

1 ○ What's Happening?

"Millions of spiritual creatures walk the earth unseen, both when we wake, and when we sleep."
JOHN MILTON, *Paradise Lost*, A.D.1667

WHAT A CHANGE! I had shelved my usual life style of teaching among the youth culture of California for a few quiet days with my wife, Jan, and a group of professional people at a conference in Indiana. No pressures, an easy pace, a chance to recharge the batteries.

If I had known what was going to happen in that reserved atmosphere, I probably would have belted back to the refuge of the mad West.

We had two days of lectures which were calm enough. No past midnight rap sessions, no crisis calls at 2:00 A.M., no emergencies that couldn't wait while we ate dinner. We had unwound and were feeling great.

The last day we decided to have breakfast with some women who had come to the conference together. One of them had attracted our attention because every day she wore an unusual plaid skirt. All of the women were high fashion, but this one was a striking individualist.

The comments at the breakfast table drifted to prophecy, and the Scottish kilt gal dropped a bomb in the conversation when she said, "I've always been able to look into the future and foresee what is going to happen."

I gulped my coffee and snapped to attention. I began to question her.

"This isn't something new. . . . I've had a gift of psychic power all my life—inherited it from my mother and grandmother, I guess."

To this day I have a difficult time describing the change in the atmosphere. I looked at her more closely and realized that she was a woman with deep problems.

After we had discussed some of the results of this psychic ability, one of her friends said, "I know she has something unusual. She's told me things about my life she couldn't possibly have known by natural means."

The psychic woman added, without any attempt to boast, "I've always believed this power is from God."

Before I had really thought about it, I blurted out, "This is not of God. And if you don't reject this power, it will destroy you."

Everyone at the table was startled. I almost choked, but as soon as I had said it, I knew it was right. There had been a growing sense of uneasiness (that's an understatement—it was a sensation of the presence of evil) from the time the woman had mentioned her psychic ability.

Then I noticed she was wearing an unusual ring. I recognized the head of the ram with a woman's breasts, the symbol usually worn by Satan worshipers.

The group broke up quickly—whether out of embarrassment at my rudeness or as an excuse to go to the morning seminars, I don't know.

Our friend in the plaid skirt remained, however, obviously willing to hear me out. As a conversation opener, I asked her about the ring, and she said that she had been attracted to artifacts like this since childhood and possessed hundreds of dollars' worth of these things. She didn't seem to be aware of their Satanic significance.

It was a bright morning, yet I could feel an uncanny oppression around us. We talked about her life, and she began to confide that she was having some real personal heartaches. She told me her husband had left her recently; when I asked her if she knew why, she began to reveal some eerie things.

In recent years, she said, she had times of depression when she would like to sit alone in her darkened house. She said that "a spirit" began to come to her at night, trying to totally possess her being. A couple of times she went into convulsions. She began to drink heavily. Her life became restless and disoriented, and in the midst of all this her husband walked out.

As I talked with her, a sense of unexplainable fear kept gnawing at me. I wanted to run and forget this whole thing. It wasn't that the woman herself was evil; it was extrasensory, some sort of unnerving spiritual presence.

I knew, as I had from the beginning but didn't want to admit to myself, I was dealing with something that until this time had been only a doctrine from my seminary training. I knew what the Bible had to say about such manifestations, but I had never been called upon to deal with someone who was under the influence of an evil spirit.

What happened during the following hours was an amazing experience, and I'll tell you more about it later in the book. At this point, it is sufficient to say I witnessed a miracle! This woman was freed from an evil spirit. Not in Africa, not in the remote regions of the Amazon, but in the sunshine of an American college campus.

This incident awakened me to the widespread phenomenon of the occult. It alarmed me that the increase in astrology, extrasensory perception, witchcraft, black magic, fortunetelling and Satan worship, which you might expect among the youth of the West Coast, was evident in other places. The occult influence went deeper into American life than I had imagined.

American Jungles

The drug epidemic was the alarm sounded in the middle and late 1960s by law enforcement officials. Statistics mounted to fever level and realistic, compassionate men like Commander Bob Vernon of the Los Angeles police force watched the sickening results on young lives. The disease started largely in the West and quickly spread from coast to coast.

An interview with Commander Vernon in the early 1970s revealed a shifting scene, a new upsurge. This time the infection was bizarre. Some of the events he related were happening right at our doorstep.

As we sat in Commander Vernon's office, listening to the incredible stories he told us, we found our shockproof constitutions were beginning to shatter.

By the time this book is published these stories may have become so commonplace that most of us will have developed attitudes which are beyond the realm of being surprised by anything.

I would like to repeat parts of the interview verbatim, without comment. Add your own exclamation points.

"Do you see indications of witchcraft or Satanic cults in the Los Angeles area?"

"Yes, and they're increasing all the time. We've found evidence of animals, mostly dogs, who have been skinned and all the blood drained from them. We discovered through talking with some of the cult members that the blood is put into caldrons, mixed with LSD, and then used as a drink during their rites or ceremonies."

"What are some of the actual cases of Satan worship and these blood sacrifices?"

"Not too long ago a woman called us and said that she had seen a van pull up to the beach and some of the occupants take out a box and bury it in the sand. She thought they were trying to dispose of a baby. We arrived on the scene and found that the box contained the remains of an animal that had obviously been skinned.

"We have also encountered a case where a part of the ceremony required skinning a dog without killing it. It was a careful job and one of the most pitiful sights I've ever seen."

"Where are some of these cults located?"

"Many live in communes. Our Metro squad made a raid into a canyon near here where they had to let down ropes to get into the area and haul up the occupants. They were living in the most primitive way you can imagine—just a short distance from one of the most affluent neighborhoods in the country—indulging in acts of sexual deviation, pagan ceremonies, and rites which defy imagination."

"Is Satan worship tied into the drug scene?"

"It's a part of it. However, some of these procedures have little or no relationship to drug usage. Not too long ago there was a 'Kiss-In' on a Santa Monica beach. I walked into the area and was struck by the similarity between what I saw and what I knew of the rites of African savages. There were about four hundred people, so tightly packed together that they were just one big mass swaying to the throb of drums and weird music. Although it was early in the afternoon and we found little drug evidence, they soon became glassyeyed—transported, so to speak, into another world. Some of them began to peel off their clothes. Some began to indulge in open sex, oblivious to any around them. We noticed that most of them wore charms around their necks. They believe in the spirit world and will readily tell you that the Devil is very real to them."

"Are there leaders in these groups of Satanists or Devil-worshipers?"

"Usually. We had a strange one in the station not too long ago. He said his name was 'Om' and that he was God. He had a following who believed that the only way to worship was through sexual deviations, and they practiced all of them. 'Om' has a group of followers who are so perverted it's impossible to describe. We asked him how old he was and he replied, 'Before the world was, I am.' We pressed him for his age and he replied, 'Through the illusion of time the way you mortals view it, I am thirty-two.'"

"You've talked about animal blood sacrifices. Have you ever found evidences of human sacrifices?"

"A highway patrolman apprehended a man who was said to have killed another man and eaten his heart. When the officer searched him, he found knuckles of a human in the suspect's pocket. He was part of a Satanic cult,"

"Do you have an explanation for the trend toward witchcraft, Satanism, and some of these other bizarre cults?"

"For one thing, I know there is a spiritual hunger among people today. Many of them have gone to a church and haven't found the answer to that hunger. Someone comes along and offers them a feeling of belonging, a sense of being loved by a group, and they fall for it. There are other reasons, of course, but longing for acceptance and a place in the world is what I see as being a very important part of the insane direction many are taking into the supernatural."

Commander Vernon is a no-nonsense man. He reports it as he sees it.

The Satanic Age

Are we in a new age of Satan? Many people would be revolted by the so-called churches which openly worship Satan. The most widely publicized establishment of this kind is the First Church of Satan in San Francisco, headed by Anton LaVey, the High Priest.

The bald, narrow-eyed LaVey was quoted as saying, "The Satanic Age started in 1966. That's when God was proclaimed dead, the Sexual Freedom League came into prominence, and the hippies developed as a free sex culture."[1]

Satanic cults are expanding in every major city in the United States. "We have received reports from other California cities which show the existence of three Satanist groups in Berkeley, two of them communes, one in Big Sur, one in Venice, five in San Francisco, and one in San Diego. The number of Satanist circles gathering in Los Angeles County is indeterminate."[2]

Some of the churches of Satan are brazenly open, such as LaVey's establishment, an impressive three-story Victorian home, while others are camouflaged by storefronts or meeting halls.

In Europe Satanic masses are held in ruined churches and monasteries, but we should not be deceived by creaking castles or shadowy figures in musty rooms. Satanism is not just an old-world phenomenon.

Arthur Lyons says, "Satanism is not only present in Europe, but in the United States as well. In fact, the United States probably harbors the fastest-growing and most highly organized body of Satanists in the world."[3]

In the "churches" entangled in Satan worship the rites are opposite from those of a Christian church. Every desecration of Christianity is emphasized, from the upside-down cross to the flagrant use of sex and sexual stimuli. In Hollywood the altar was a glass tank filled with formaldehyde, containing the body of a dead baby. Lyons reported that the "high priest" had a hypnotic effect upon a teen-age girl. The ritual in which she became involved was so debasing he couldn't describe it.

We are reminded of the sordid spectacle of the girls who were mesmerized by Charles Manson. In a personal interview with a former Manson family member, I found they indulged in all types of Satanism and witchcraft. Manson was said to have had visions and magic powers. There were stories of his being physically transported from one end of the Spahn ranch to the other. Group sexual experience, an indulgence of some witch covens, was commonly practiced by the Manson cult. The twisted reversal of Christianity was evident. Manson was called "God," "Jesus," and "Satan" by his followers.

After Manson's conviction for the seven Tate-LaBianca murders, five members of his "family," girls with their heads shaved to prove their loyalty to their leader, led a trek through Hollywood on their knees "in witness to the second coming of Manson."[4]

Bubble, Boil, and Trouble

The steps which separate witchcraft and Satanism are almost invisible. Their histories, rites, and followers are intermingled. Statistics of witch covens given today would be out of date in a month. *Life* magazine reported in 1964, "It is difficult to estimate numbers as not all covens are known to one another, but the interest appears to be growing."[5]

Seven years later a Ph.D. from Harvard wrote, "It is undeniable that the rising addiction to mysticism has swelled to a veritable epidemic."[6]

In Switzerland an ex-priest and his mistress were charged with the murder of one of their followers. They said she had been sexually and physically possessed by the devil.[7]

In France 60,000 sorcerers are taking in $200,000,000 a year.

In Frankfurt, Germany, there are reportedly tens of thousands who believe in witches.[8]

The bishop of Exeter said that more Britons are turning toward black magic as their interest in traditional religion declines.[9]

The chairman of the psychology department at the University of the Pacific in Stockton, California, advertised for a woman who felt she was a witch or had unusual psychic powers to assist in a course on extrasensory perception.[10]

"The Golden State is the new holy land of Satanism, and its occult flood has divided itself into two main streams, two types of witches—the drugged and the drugless."[11]

One estimate says there are five hundred witches in Manhattan.[12]

Why Witch?

Louise Huebner, who claims to be Los Angeles County's official witch, describes the recent revival of the "Old Religion," as witchcraft is often called, and its attraction to young people in this way:

"You see, witchcraft is a participatory religion. This isn't a religion where you go somewhere and sit to listen to a sermon. We all get involved.

"This attracts the young person, because he or she is sick of the organized and recognized religions. They want to be active—to take part. Witchcraft offers them just such an opportunity.

"Witchcraft is actually a return to nature, a worship of the natural gods as opposed to the chrome and glass gods you find in society. We're more interested in finding powers within ourselves, in broadening our own minds."[13]

In Orange County, California, an area known for its family living, Knott's Berry Farm and Disneyland, an attractive witch housewife, Cassandra Salem (an assumed name), made another observation on witchcraft.

"Our whole religion is based on the lunar cycle, moon worship, and we really were the first ones interested in ecology, which you are hearing so much about right now.

"We're the ones who are pushing for a return to nature, and we may be on the right track. At least witchcraft seems to be growing faster right now than any other religion."[14]

Unhook My Nose

Many witches are seriously concerned about their image. They make it clear that there are, according to their views, good witches. Dr. Robert Ellwood, assistant professor of religion at the University of Southern California, recently offered a course on "New Religious and Philosophical Movements in Southern California." He said that a meeting he attended of eight or nine witches, magicians, and Satanists "took on aspects of a Protestant church meeting." In describing the witches he commented:

"They rejoice in being witches and being pointed out, but at the same time they expressed concern to one another about their bad 'image' because of publicity about the Manson family, a recent article in *Esquire* magazine, and the motion picture *Rosemary's Baby*."[15]

Merry England

The image concern among the witches extends to England, where spooky castles and eerie happenings have long been a rather romantic part of legend and life. Tourists are delighted if they can stay in a haunted house.

Modern English witches are different. For one thing, they insist that they have a vital and growing religion. According to one report, there are as many as 6,000 witches meeting regularly in small groups throughout England.[16]

The witches of England work at their religion seriously. They meet regularly and perform their rituals in a manner of worship, not of magic-making as many in America are doing. The witches' deities are a sun god and a moon goddess, and according to one "high priestess," who is a housewife and a manager of a home for the aged, "We witches are simple people with simple beliefs." She describes candidly the type of people in their covens.

"We are just ordinary people going about our own particular jobs. We are reasonably intelligent. We have doctors, teachers, businessmen, farmers, nurses, theatrical people, office workers, and housewives among us. Most of us have studied comparative religion. We do not try to convert others, but we do encourage people who have a leaning towards our craft. We do not take everybody who wants to come in."[17]

This would imply that witchcraft is a rather exclusive club of believers.

Brooms Are Out

When witchcraft is mentioned today in many circles, some people become defensive and say, "You really don't believe in witches, do you? That went out with the Salem trials."

It is true that any study of witchcraft revives scenes of a medieval inquisition where many innocent victims were self-righteously judged in the name of "Christianity" or "The Church." However, this is not the impression the witchcraft devotees want to give us. It must appear to be exciting, sophisticated, inviting, or perhaps just a little amusing.

No one is attracted by fangs and raspy cackles.

Trust Hollywood

I was introduced to a clever place in Hollywood by a calling card announcing the "Sorcerer's Shop." The shop was appealing in every way with an atmosphere of quality. A raven with the predictable name of "Lucifer" greeted me, while a large owl with the equally appropriate name of "Solomon" ogled me from his perch near the door.

The shopkeeper was about twenty-two years old; he told me he was a college graduate with a degree in political science. He was dignified, gracious, and serious.

Some of the usual accouterments of witchcraft were visible: the cauldron, the jars containing special herbs for spells, the various types of incense and candles. There were dozens of instruction books on witchcraft, potions, spells, astrology, tarot, and the occult. The host told me that some spirits had been there a few nights previously and that a sword had flown off the wall. He said that this was probably the work of a poltergeist (a spirit that causes solid objects to move from one place to another).

Covens on the Campus

Witchcraft has become so widespread that most high schools and colleges have their own special witches. They live in dorms, go to class, and on the side meet in their covens. A coven is a circle of witches and warlocks (male wizards or witches) numbering thirteen. The rites, rituals, and literature of witchcraft are ancient and established.

In the Bible Belt of the Midwest at a girls' college, conservative in outlook and rated high academically, the school newspaper which was issued at the beginning of the fall semester contained an editorial that told of a strange occurrence. Thievery was evidently a severe problem at the school library, because almost 2,000 books were missing after the inventory was taken at the end of the summer. The part of the editorial which caught my attention was the information that all of the books on witchcraft had been taken—completely removed from the shelves.

On the same campus I watched a televised talk show on the college station featuring a coed who said she was a witch. It was an impish interview, leaving the audience with the impression that this was not something we should take seriously.

The pretty coed said, "To be a witch I had to say the Lord's Prayer backwards three times while staring at a candle."

When asked about Christian beliefs, she became quite animated, but also defensive.

"I have nothing against Christianity," she said. "You're wrong if you think witchcraft is against Christianity. It isn't."

She continued to say that there was a "pyramid" that must be ascended in graduating steps before you could become a witch. That witch's pyramid involved faith, will, and imagination. However, she could not divulge how to become a witch.

The *New York Times*, in commenting on the campus scene, described a certain Catholic university where a coven of warlocks was discovered. The dean of the institution said, "We've really become progressive around here. A couple of hundred years ago we would have burned them at the stake. Twenty-five years ago I would have expelled them. Now we simply send them all to psychiatrists."[18]

Witchcraft and Sorcery Convention

I could have registered at the Witchcraft and Sorcery Convention and no one would have thought it was strange. It was held in the plush suites of one of the major Los Angeles hotels. The registrants were a cross section of respectable America with the intent smiles and programmed schedules of any convention. Most of them were promoting supernatural comic books or occult artifacts. The majority of speakers were members of the publishing industry specializing in weird tales. However, beneath the businesslike surface was an undercurrent which emerged after a few meetings. Then the big announcement was made: Nick Nocerino (not his real name) was going to speak; as a parapsychologist teaching in the occult, he was considered an expert in the field. He announced that he was a wizard ("Not a warlock, please. That is a perversion of my craft.") and proceeded to describe in a series of lectures some fascinating trade talk.

Nocerino differentiated between what he called "witchcraft" (of which he is a part) and "wickedcraft," which is what he termed a perversion of his art. He called witchcraft a religion and said that ten years ago he could not find five good books on the subject, but that today he knows of at least five hundred books on the market. He said witches are everywhere. There are ten million in the United States, and about two thousand in Los Angeles. However, he added secretively, "What is known publicly about the number of witches is just what has to be known."

He said that in the past few years he had seen an outpouring of "wickedcraft" in the national magazines, such as *Esquire* and *McCall's*, and "it scared me . . . and I've been around for a long time." He thought it was a crime that his craft was being perverted by bad publicity. He indicated there are witches in every part of the world, but they are more open in France, Germany, and England. In Italy, he said, witchcraft is practiced in conjunction with the church, but the church will not admit it.

"There is a move today," explained the famous wizard, "to bring witchcraft into the open as a religion."

"Many witches are very active in their churches," said Nocerino, "but no witch says, 'I'm a witch.' The stigma is too great."

Nocerino does not associate true witchcraft, as he called it, with Satanic cults. He explained that people are selected very carefully for a coven of witches and not just anyone who would like to be a witch or a wizard is accepted.

You Can't Be Serious

Many regard witchcraft with the same degree of amused tolerance they granted to goldfish swallowing, telephone booth cramming, and other fads. The news media is giving it an aura of gentle fun. If a self-proclaimed witch is blonde and shapely, this is good copy. A recent wire story in one of the West Coast's leading newspapers told about a beautiful witch who was raising funds to combat the effects of movies that portray witches in a bad light.

"We get such bad publicity from crummy movies. Black witches are the bad witches who practice voodoo, for one thing. White witches are your goodie two-shoes who read your palm for $2."

This lovely lady is a gray witch, she says, which is neither good nor bad.[19]

To get the message to the public there are record albums of "how to's" concerning witchcraft. One of them has a seductive advertisement featuring "The Gray Witch," who will tell you what you can gain today from practicing witchcraft.

"She introduces you to witches and warlocks who'll describe everything from the appearance of a demon to the everyday problems of witchcraft in a modern society. Barbara will tell you how to develop and practice your witchcraft ability even if you're only a mortal."

The Teen-Age Witch

Cheryl may have answered an ad on how to be a witch. Who knows? She didn't tell me that, but as we sat on the floor of the coffee house rapping about her experiences, she told me she was sixteen—well, almost sixteen. She was pretty, spoke softly, and had a sharp mind.

Cheryl had traveled the drug route since she was twelve or thirteen. She had uppers and downers, bad trips and good ones. Most of her associates were older, and as she watched them in the moments when her mind was clear, she decided that unless she split she'd fall apart. So Cheryl took another route. She became a witch.

At first she pretended it was just a prank. Someone bought her a crystal ball, and she spent hours staring into it and interpreting the visions she saw.

One day she told one of her friends in school that her friend's father was going to die. When he met with an accidental death two days later, Cheryl felt little sadness; she was high with power!

"It shook me at first," she said, "but I was fascinated by it. I had something no one else had! I had been doing a lot of reading about potions and chants, and I knew that I had this power over people. I could burn a hole right through someone by just looking at them."

A few years ago I might have listened to Cheryl and thought that she was a cute teen-ager with a lively imagination.

Not any more.

"Recent history has shown terrifyingly enough that the demonic lies barely beneath the surface, ready to catch men unawares with new and more horrible manifestations."[20]

Witches and Satanists, spirits and demons have surfaced in our generation. But underneath is the cauldron of cults, claiming for its victims the gullible and the young.

Who will be the victims? And the victorious?

2 ○ Perilous Tide From the Other Side

"There is a way which seems right to a man, but its end is the way of death."

Proverbs 14:12

A WASHINGTON NEWSPAPER reporter and a dead man have written a best seller about the "first inside, eyewitness account of the Hereafter."

Ruth Montgomery, one-time friend and confidant of Jeane Dixon, and Arthur Ford, deceased spiritualist and the medium the late Bishop Pike used to contact "the other side," are the co-authors of a book which is supposed to answer every major metaphysical and theological question that has plagued mankind since the beginning of time.

Ruth Montgomery sat at her typewriter in a trance and Ford transmitted through her fingertips the information about what is going on in the beyond. Evidently the world-famous personalities who have passed on are involved in the same interests they had on earth. Robert Kennedy is occupied with civil rights. J.F.K. is peacemaking in the Middle East. Churchill is arguing world politics with Franklin Roosevelt.

Arthur Ford says (through Montgomery's automatic writing) that in the spiritual realm everything is basically the same as on earth, except thought patterns replace physical form.

Ruth Montgomery explains why she believes she was chosen to write about the hereafter: "I guess Arthur and the others decided that because of my journalistic background, I'd be good to write it . . . and it's the Age of Aquarius, so the time was right for revelations about the unknown."[1]

Travels Back With A. Ford and J. Pike

In 1967 Arthur Ford, probably the best known medium of modern times, went into a public, televised trance on a program with Bishop James Pike. The Bishop's direct involvement with spiritualism was revealed to people across the country. Interest in the occult was given a new boost by Pike's testimony that he had communicated with his deceased son, Jim. Ford gave credence to Pike's revelations.

The publication of Pike's book, *The Other Side*, popularized spiritualism. Through seances, mediums, and other spiritualistic phenomena Pike claimed to have had many dealings with the spirit world. He believed that communication with the dead was possible and during his lifetime wrote and lectured extensively on this subject.

Now Pike is dead, too. His body was found in September of 1969 in the desert area surrounding the Dead Sea. I have no way of knowing what drew him into that bleak area where he met his death. A friend of mine who was in that vicinity a month after the mishap questioned some of the inhabitants, and they said no one in his right mind would have gone into that remote region without skilled and knowledgeable guides.

Ford is supposed to have seen Pike struggling for his life in the wilderness. He probably did, because Ford was not a fraud! If that statement surprises you, hold your fire until we have investigated the amazing evidence together.

Dr. Merrill Unger, a renowned archaeologist and theologian, writes, "This human spirit does possess mysterious powers, but the *greater* power of demonic spirits to delude humanity is the unrecognized peril surrounding parapsychologists and spiritualists."[2]

On the other hand, Hans Holzer, assistant professor of parapsychology at the New York Institute of Technology and the author of twenty-six books on psychic phenomena, says, "Psychic phenomena don't hurt anyone. In fact, they're good for you. They expand the mind, expand your sense of man's purpose."[3]

Chris Pike, the son of the late Bishop Pike, would not agree with Holzer. Pike, who speaks cautiously of his famous father, told me in a personal interview that while practicing yoga and meditation he became possessed by spirit beings who nearly destroyed his life. He has denounced that way of life and today is a witness to the transforming power of Jesus Christ. His own life has been completely changed, and I believe the world will soon hear from this brilliant young man.

Look Inward, Angel

Meditation is very big. The president of the National Center for the Exploration of Human Potential said, "Many young people today are engaged in an extensive search for the meanings and values of life. They are endeavoring to make peace, love, and tranquillity part of their daily lives.

They are rediscovering the spiritual dimensions of their being. There is a widespread interest in meditation, and the Transcendental Meditation Movement currently has 30,000 members on U.S. campuses."[4]

A study made over a period of three years of twenty-two communes in the United States shows that "widespread reports of psychic phenomena can be attributed to the altered states of consciousness induced by drugs in some cases and by yoga-type meditation in others."

These mental states, according to Dr. Stanley Krippner, tend to make a person become skeptical of God, doubt any concept of life after death, and discard many beliefs he may have had before he delved into meditation and psychic phenomena.[5]

It's in the Tarot Cards

The ancient art of reading tarot cards has been revived in our time. One expert on the subject says that tarot is derived from the pages of the oldest book in the world, originating in Egypt at a period when magic, astrology, and other mystic sciences flourished.

The object is to be able to read the cards as they fall in relation to one another, to solve a person's problems or read his future. An expert who has made a great study of this subject and has written several popular books on the art of reading tarot cards advises her readers to "Go deep within in meditation; find your own divine center, and you will understand by direct intuition that which the Tarot only hints at. . . . Prepare to pass through the beautiful gate of symbolism into the starry world beyond."[6]

The Tarot is supposed to have its own "divinatory powers and its own spiritual content." The reader, who interprets the cards, is particularly interested in your character analysis, your future, and solutions to immediate problems, much as the palmist or the fortuneteller. It is emphasized that "there are also those who will value the Tarot's help in meditation."[7]

Nichiren Shoshu

This Buddhist sect began a few years ago with most of the membership being in their teens and twenties. In the past few years older persons have been drawn into membership. A typical meeting is a cross section of Americans, all seated lotus-fashion, chanting the same words over and over again. One report said that in the United States there were 25,000 followers in 1965 and 200,000 in 1971.[8]

Willie Davis, an outfielder for the Los Angeles Dodgers, is involved in Nichiren Shoshu. He chants all the time. Davis said he does most of his chanting to a scroll at home with his family, but that he "might be chanting at all times during the day."

"It scares people when you say Buddhism," he said, "because right away they think it's some kind of witchcraft. It's a philosophy, a true philosophy."[9]

An owner of a grocery store in Manhattan chants at a Nichiren meeting because "Going makes me feel good, it's soothing, it calms me down. . . . Nichiren Shoshu is nice because you participate. Let's face it, the church has lost it. They lost most of my generation and I would say all of the next generation."[10]

Eastern religions, their chants and meditations, are flourishing in Western soil.

How Does a Guru Grow?

On a speaking tour in Texas I was invited to appear on a television show with Peter Max, the well-known pop artist. Max, whose psychedelia in the art media has influenced many of the art forms of the youth culture, told me how he was one of the first persons to bring gurus from the East to teach meditation, reincarnation, and transcendentalism.

Entertainers have been leaders in this movement, seeking the advice of "holy men" and even making pilgrimages to India to consult with their own special guru of the moment.

Along the sun-drenched shopping malls of our California cities is another sect from the Eastern religions called Hare Krishna. Mingled with the long-hairs of their own generation, the shaved heads and long yellow robes of this group present sharp contrasts. The Krishna devotees approach anyone who hesitates in his walk and try to sell their magazine. They sing, dance, and chant, seemingly immune to any criticism or ridicule.

Los Angeles is fair game for touring gurus. A thirteen-year-old guru visiting from India sent out publicity releases stamped "Top Sacred," which described the youth as "empowered to impart the imperishable word of God to all sincere aspirants who seek for perfect tranquillity of mind through spiritual insight."[11]

It was reported that millions believe the "world's youngest guru" is the new son of God. He travels by jet as the "Lord from Heaven," bringing what he says are messages of hope and wisdom to troubled souls. Some of his devotees who come to worship him say they are saved in his presence.

McCandlish Phillips, of the *New York Times*, writes, "Demons of the East are coming into the United States now, bringing with them the religious teachings and the occult arts with which they have long deceived the people there."[12]

Religions of the East may seem alien to the life style of many Americans, but other cults are acceptable in the urge for self-improvement and fulfillment.

Scientology

Most cults have a strong founder-image. L. Ron Hubbard, the man who dreamed up Scientology, is practically worshiped as being an indestructible force. He is an authoritarian leader with a missionary zeal to spread the word of his discoveries. The literature of the cult declares that "In 1950 one man, one book touched off the spark that has become a star for all of Mankind."[13]

Not to be outdone in modesty, another Scientology publication states that Hubbard is author of the book *Dianetics, The Modern Science of Mental Health* which has done more than any other book to change the fate of Mankind.[14]

Scientology claims to be both a religion and a science. It has coined its own vocabulary, which is weird to the uninitiated. They have "dianetics" courses, "power processing," and steps to follow to achieve their goal to "Go Clear."

Scientology claims, "We are evolving Man to a higher state."[15]

Its membership and new centers are growing at an astonishing rate. The eager young man I spoke with at one of the centers said that Scientology has doubled every six months since 1966. When asked how he accounted for this amazing growth, he said simply, "It works."

A *Life* magazine writer traveled some of the steps recommended by the cult and arrived at some personal conclusions. He wrote, "Scientology is scary—because of its size and growth, and because of the potentially disastrous techniques it so casually makes use of."[16]

The young writer said, "I have Hubbard to thank for a true-life nightmare that gnawed at my family relationships and saddled me with a burden of guilt I've not yet been able to shed."[17]

Christian ? Spiritualism

Spiritualism has found a home in many churches. One spiritualism denomination called the Universal Church of the Master began in 1966 and now has 125 active churches. In the Los Angeles phone book there are eight congregations listed.[18]

Raphael Gasson, a former member of a spiritualism church and a medium, writes, "Many people are unaware of the challenge which spiritualism presents to the true Church of God, and they should be warned not to treat too lightly what is one of the diabolical delusions that Satan is using. Many have suffered greatly because they started investigating into this thing and have eventually been brought to distraction when they have attempted to free themselves from it."[19]

A friend of mine, a successful young banker, became involved in a spiritualist church which is well advertised—Rosicrucians. He recognized evil in the movement, but thought there was enough good in it to offset some of its more unsavory aspects.

This particular thought-line is called "Christian Metaphysics." As we sat in a brightly lit restaurant having an informal lunch, the young executive told me of some of the strange happenings in this movement. He spoke of auras surrounding the bodies of participants, of spirit-controlled men and women. For anyone who has once been deep into the occult, it's difficult, if not dangerous, for him to tell of his experiences. To relive the past involves unnecessary discomfort, and for this reason I stopped him from relating some of his experiences when he became definitely uneasy.

Passport for a Psychic Tour

On a recent trip to the Middle East I noticed an interesting sign of our times in a Pan American Airlines magazine. Pan Am is pushing a tour to explore the occult revival in Great Britain. The psychic scene is a fourteen-day package including a banquet given by the Spiritualist Association of Great Britain.

I'm sure it is not a coincidence that one of the highlights of the tour will be lectures by Ena Twigg, who was the go-between when Bishop Pike wished to talk with his departed son. Twigg is also said to have established contact between Mrs. Pike and the Bishop after he died in the desert.

The tour company promises personal astrological/numerological charts prepared for the participants.

Psyched Out in Russia

Some remarkable research has been done on the extensive use of psychic phenomena in Russia. These studies do not involve the ghoulishness or foolishness of witchcraft, but are careful works done by men of science. Some of these findings bear ominous warnings to the free world of the type of mind and thought manipulations which are being employed today in an anti-God society. It's interesting that the occult realm has been made scientifically respectable under the academic guise of "parapsychology."

In forces which are more scientific or refined than Satan worship or witch covens we find effects which could be more insidious. In a recent book, *Psychic Discoveries Behind the Iron Curtain*, the writer-researchers say: "In the early sixties, the Stalinist taboo against all things psychic vanished with a bang. Top-level physiologists, geologists, engineers, physicists, and biologists abruptly plunged into work on ESP. A freewheeling, little known psychic renaissance hit Russia. Bankrolled by their governments, not just Russians, but Bulgarians, Czechs, and Poles are pursuing clues to telepathy, prophecy, and psychokinesis, the ability to move matter with mind alone."[20]

This is the same Russia of sputnik—the Russia of the scientific man, where leaders since the Communist revolution have been wary of anything that could not be seen in the materialistic manner.

Russia's extensive interest in researching "inner space," just as the scientific community has sought to conquer outer space, has ominous undertones. For instance, the authors say: "Highly placed Soviet scientists take parapsychology seriously, not snickeringly. . . . It was hoped that suggestion at a distance could induce individuals, without their being aware of it, to adopt the officially desired political and social attitudes."[21]

Does that sound like brainwashing through telepathy? It was further described in this book that confidential reports have been seen that indicate the Soviets are attempting to train clairvoyants for spy purposes.

Is It All a Bad Joke?

Witchcraft, Satan worship, cults, occult, spiritualism, psychic phenomena—should we take any of these movements seriously? Is it just a passing trend? Will they ever touch our lives or influence our future?

I believe that man's search for truth and reality may take him into realms of mind expansion where serious harm may be done to his mental health and his ability to cope with real life situations. The *Journal of the American Medical Association* said, "The new occult craze—and that is just what it is— has given rise to all manner of flimflam and hocus-pocus with people's health. In this Age of Aquarius, quackery is thriving as a surprising number of people, young and old, are fleeing into superstition and unreality."[22]

All of these cults, ventures into spiritualism, fortunetelling, and psychic avenues, have a common danger: they open the mind to associate with the spiritual realm and to seek contact with the world beyond. The will is made available to any experience which is beyond the senses. Whether it is realized or not, the person exposed in this manner can be brought under the direct influence of powerful spiritual personalities who are dedicated to enslaving his life.

There are phenomena beyond the realm of the senses. They are beginning to be accepted in scientific circles, and we may scoff or laugh at our own peril. They are not related to the true God, but to the one whom Jesus Christ called "the god of this world."

I believe that people are being given superhuman powers from Satan in order that they may promote his work on earth. *We are only at the beginning of this explosion.* There will be inventions which will come from the spirit world and fantastic displays of miracles and wonders that the ancient Scriptures predicted would occur in the days just before this present civilization would end.

We should not be fooled by miracles worked through the extrasensory powers of Satan. This is a time when people need to know what is behind the eruptions that are disfiguring our world. More important, we need to know *who* is behind it all.

In the following pages I will take you back into the dawn of history to an account which is stranger than fiction; but without a knowledge of it you could never understand the mess in which the world finds itself.

Some of the propositions in the next few chapters may seem fairly heavy to you. On the other hand, the food for thought may taste unusual. Whatever your background, if you approach this subject boldly and openly, I believe you will find that the conclusions are justified.

3 ○ Birth of the Black Prince

"How you have fallen from heaven, O star of the morning, son of the dawn!"
ISAIAH 14:12

*"You were blameless in your ways from the day you were created, until unright-
eousness was found in you."*
EZEKIEL 28:15

IN 1966 A friend of mine submitted a manuscript to a well-known pub-
lisher. It was rejected with the explanation that the subject was a dead issue
and no one believed in that sort of thing any more. The book was entitled
The Dark Prince, and it presented a very real spiritual being who is sometimes called Satan.

Would anyone dare to say this is a dead issue today?

Recently a brilliant young Englishman named Os Guinness began searching through the vast libraries of London for literature on witchcraft, magic,
and the occult. He found that most major works on history listed these
subjects as phenomena which were almost extinct and had been dealt a
deathblow by the Renaissance and modern science. However, beginning
about 1967 he discovered a veritable explosion of literature and documentation on the subject.

I am convinced that the vast majority of people today, even those directly
involved in ESP, astrology, the occult, and various forms of Eastern religions, do not realize with whom they are dealing.

How many believe they are making contact with a powerful, incredibly
intelligent spiritual being who heads a vast, highly organized army of spiritual beings like himself? This host is dedicated to blinding men's minds to
the gift of forgiveness and love which God offered through Jesus Christ and
to destroying or neutralizing those who have already believed in Him.

Just how clever this spiritual being is (he is often called Satan) may be
comprehended by the strategy he has used in modern history. Beginning
in the Renaissance period and extending to the first two-thirds of the twentieth century, men progressively rejected phenomena which were beyond
their senses. Many medieval superstitions related to demons and devils were
exposed as foolish by scientific discoveries and education, as they should
have been. However, from the seminaries of Germany in the 1800s came a

group which called itself the "Higher Critical School." These liberal biblical scholars began to question the historicity of the Bible. Using subjective literary methods of analysis (not based on hard facts of history or archaeology), they dissected the books of Moses and attributed them to a host of different writers. Many of these critiques were made on the basis of different names for God being used in various sections of Moses' writings. On this tenuous basis, these men rejected all of the witness of history which attributed the first five books of the Bible to Moses and ignored the fact that all through the books themselves it is repeatedly stated that they are the writings of Moses.[1]

From Moses to Myth

From the books of Moses, the "Higher Critical School" went on to attack other crucial books of the Old and New Testaments. The effect was to render the entire Bible a mass of unhistorical myths and folklore of the Jewish people. Each of these biblical mythologists more or less denied the possibility of the supernatural. Some were less subtle and blatantly denied all supernatural manifestations.

This type of teaching began to spread, and young theologians from the rest of Europe and the United States who studied under the influence of these intellectuals returned to their seminaries and churches and began to introduce these new doctrines. By 1925, many of the major seminaries of America had taken this point of view. In the colleges and universities of the United States it became the vogue to cast out the Bible as unhistorical and unfit for honest academic consideration.

In universities today, Bible courses are often taught by men who are biased against a normal, historical approach and who usually show hostility toward acceptance of the miraculous. In some of the "Bible as Literature" courses that I have observed, the teachers were agnostics.

Over the past fourteen years hundreds of students have reported to me that they felt their faith was deliberately and relentlessly attacked or discredited in university religion and philosophy courses. Some actually received poor grades on papers which were well done simply because they expressed a Christian point of view which centered on believing the Bible as literally true.

What began in the "Higher Critical Schools" of Germany has brought about an almost universal rejection of the Bible as a historically reliable document in the colleges and universities of the world today.

The irony is this: the Bible was discredited and discarded because of a general rejection of the supernatural. However, beginning with the late 1960s a new trend began to grow with the acceptance of ESP and other forms of the supernatural. Unfortunately, the Bible has been left out of this acceptance.

Now we have some members of the academic community as well as our youth experimenting with ESP and the occult without any reliable criteria to understand the origin of the phenomena they may experience.

A professor at the prestigious Massachusetts Institute of Technology describes an experience he had in a seminar with some of the best students of that institution. He said the progression of topics ran from Asian philosophy to meditation, yoga, Zen, then to *I Ching* (a book presenting an ancient Chinese divination device which supposedly enables one to make decisions), the yang-yin macrobiotic diet, Maher Baba, astrology, astral bodies, auras, U.F.O.'s, tarot cards, parapsychology, witchcraft, and magic. He added that the students were not dallying with these subjects, but were involved in them.

"And they weren't plebeians," the professor said. "Intellectually they were aristocrats with the highest average math scores in the land, Ivy League verbal scores, and two to three years of saturation in M.I.T. science."[2]

I do not believe this trend of history has happened by chance. Satan does not want a world that rejects the supernatural; he wants a world that is "religious" and accepts supernaturalism because it sets the stage for him to be worshiped in the person of a coming world leader known as the Antichrist.[3] The first step was to discredit the Bible so that Satan's true nature and plan would not be discovered. Satan wants a religious world, but one which rejects God's offer of a personal relationship with Him through Jesus Christ.

If you are having trouble accepting some of these assertions, if you are saying, "How can any educated person really believe in a personal Devil?" I dare you to read on with an open mind and ask God to reveal what is true. There is historical evidence of the reality of this being, and the evidence is increasing.

I realize that in man's long attempt to explain the continual existence of evil in the world, many myths and superstitions have sprung up. But the account that we are investigating here is found in the record of the ancient Hebrew Scriptures. I believe that this account has proved to be the most consistent explanation of the rebellious nature of man and society.

To understand what is happening today and in the near future, we must reach back into these ancient documents and look into events that occurred before man came into existence. The account of how an exalted supernatural being of incredible beauty, power, and intelligence named Lucifer came to be Satan is stranger than fiction. The Bible chronicles the origin of Satan with the same factual precision as any other historical event it covers. The key to understanding man's purpose and destiny is related to the pre-history conflict that began with Lucifer's revolt against God.

Curtain up on Pre-history

Ancient history can be pretty dull. I'm sure some of you may have dozed through classroom lectures on the subject. However, God's ancient history is something else. It's exciting because it has meaning to every one of us; it hits us where we are today.

Let's examine the Book of Job, for instance, which was written about four thousand years ago. Job was a fellow who had a few problems. As things started to pile up, he began to do what a lot of us do—he began to question God's judgment.

God asked Job some pointed questions designed to show him that he didn't have enough wisdom to sit in judgment upon God. Consequently, God revealed some fantastic information about the creation of this planet and all its surrounding galaxy.

"Where were you when I laid the foundation of the earth!
Tell Me, if you have understanding,
Who set its measurements, since you know?
Or who stretched the line on it?
On what were its bases sunk,
Or who laid its cornerstone,
When the morning stars sang together,
And all the sons of God shouted for joy?" (Job 38:4-7)

Here we are introduced to some interesting descriptions: "morning stars" and "sons of God." A careful study of these titles reveals that in the Old Testament they are used only in regard to angels. Angels are higher than man; they have greater intelligence and more power than man. They have a personal audience with God.

Now when God created the universe, these spirit beings, these spirit personalities "shouted for joy" at the demonstration of God's tremendous power. What a great picture!

They weren't fighting or arguing about their positions in God's kingdom. This passage says clearly that they *all* shouted for joy, indicating complete harmony among the angels. Obviously no rebellion had taken place at this time.

Lucifer the Perfect

The highest and most exalted position of this spirit realm was held by Lucifer, a creature who was perfect in all of his ways from the day he was created. The way we are introduced to him is important in itself.

In Ezekiel 28:1-2 a ruler is introduced as the *prince* of Tyre. He is described as a man who became so vain about all of his riches and intelligence that he claimed to be God. In Ezekiel 28:12 we are introduced to someone who, according to the description, is a different person. He is called the *king* of Tyre. The king of Tyre is the real power behind the prince of Tyre.

Again the word of the Lord came to me saying, "Son of man, take up a lamentation over the king of Tyre, and say to him, 'Thus says the Lord God, "You had the seal of perfection, full of wisdom and perfect in beauty. You were in Eden, the garden of God; every precious stone was your covering: The ruby, the topaz, and the diamond; the beryl, the onyx, and the jasper; the lapis lazuli, the turquoise, and the emerald; and the gold, the workmanship of your settings and sockets, was in you. On the day that you were created they were prepared. You were the anointed cherub who covers; and I placed you there. You were on the holy mountain of God; you walked in the midst of the stones of fire. You were blameless in your ways from the day you were created, until unrighteousness was found in you"'" (Ezekiel 28:11-15).

God truly mourned over this person; he is described as "having had the seal of perfection," which in the original Hebrew means a pattern of perfection. He is even described as having been "full of wisdom and perfect in beauty," the most beautiful and wise of all God's creation!

We will be able to understand how perfect is perfect (which is in no way a relative term when God is describing Lucifer) by some of the descriptions applied to him. He is called "the anointed cherub who covers." A cherub is an angelic being of high rank, associated with God's holy presence and His glory. Cherubs are celestial beings who proclaim the righteousness of God.

He is called "the anointed" one, which indicates supreme favor from God. "Anointed" is the same word that is used of the Messiah, God's anointed king. This person was the ruler and leader of the angelic beings and apparently led them in their praise of God and shouts of joy. The Hebrew word translated "who covers" in Ezekiel 28:14 and 16 literally means "who leads."

All the fabulous jewels were given to him, further indicating his exalted rank. He had been in "Eden, the garden of God" and "on the holy mountain of God." He had walked "in the midst of the stones of fire," which is a symbol often used of God's holy presence. Such a description could not be applied to a mere human.

This passage is speaking of the greatest being God ever created, one who had unequaled strength, wisdom, beauty, privilege, and authority. This is the one who according to Isaiah was named "Lucifer" and "the Son of the Morning." His name literally means "the shining one" and is a word for great beauty.

The crisis point of the universe is described in Ezekiel 28:15 where it says, "You were *blameless* (literally perfect) in your ways from the day you were created...."

Could this have been an ordinary man? No. First of all, man is not created; (since Adam) he is born. Second, no man is born perfect. The blameless, perfect Lucifer was created without any form of evil, which is something which could not have applied to any *man* after Adam.

What happened to Lucifer?

The Big "Until"

Lucifer was perfect in his ways *until* "unrighteousness was found in him." This marked the fall of Lucifer and the birth of Satan. What this unrighteousness or evil was is described more fully in Isaiah 14:12-14.

It is important to note that God addresses Satan through the person of the prince of Tyre. Satan is the unseen source of this prince's arrogance and self-deification. Scofield describes other instances of indirectly addressing Satan through a man or another creature: when God addressed the serpent in the garden in Genesis 3:14; when Jesus spoke to Satan through Peter in Matthew 16:23. "The vision is not of Satan in his own person, but of Satan fulfilling himself in and through an earthly king who arrogates to himself divine honors" (*Scofield Reference Bible*, page 871).

Five "I Wills"

In Ezekiel we have the key to the origin of evil. In Isaiah 14:12-14 there is a description of the same supernatural being who introduced all the suffering into the universe. When this passage was written in the original Hebrew, it was a song of sorrow. God was mourning over this creature whom He had created and loved.

How art thou fallen from heaven, O Lucifer, son of the morning! how art thou cut down to the ground, which didst weaken the nations! For thou hast said in thine heart, I will ascend into heaven, I will exalt my throne above the stars of God: I will sit also upon the mount of the congregation, in the sides of the north: I will ascend above the heights of the clouds; I will be like the Most High (Isaiah 14:12-14, KJV).

He was described first as Lucifer, the "shining one." He was so beautiful he literally shone, and he was no stranger to holiness because apparently he was created with the very glory of God. However, when the verse in Isaiah begins "For thou hast said in thine heart," this is the real description of evil. This is where sin originates—in the heart. Five times he said in his heart, "I will!"

Lucifer filled his heart with the violence of rebellion; he wanted to act independently of God. He was saying to God, "After all, since *I* am so magnificent, so beautiful, so filled with power, why shouldn't *I* have some of the worship of the universe for myself?"

He said, "I will ascend to heaven." In other words, "Move over, God, I'm going to be in charge here." He said, "I will make myself like the Most High." He wanted to be God!

God Doesn't Manufacture Robots

When God created the angelic realm (and apparently Lucifer was the leader of all the angels), He took a calculated risk. He created Lucifer with the greatest intelligence of any created being, endowing him and the other angelic beings with self-determination. God did not want robots. He wanted creatures who could respond to His love and have spontaneous fellowship with Him.

God believed it was worth the risk to create these beings with the ability to act independently of His will and have the choice of rejecting or obeying Him. Lucifer, realizing how beautiful he was, inflated with power and pride, rebelled against God. He broke his relationship with God when he said, "I will be like the Most High."

Apparently a great rebellion erupted throughout the universe at that time. Lucifer led a revolution among the angels. We are told in Revelation 12 that one-third of the angelic realm followed Lucifer in this revolt. After Lucifer rebelled and became the first sinful creature, he lost none of his great intellect, beauty, or power. He used this to entice many angels to join his ranks. However, he lost the one trait which would make him function correctly, and that was a personal relationship with God.

When the perfect Lucifer, the one who had authority over all of God's creation and walked in unity with God, became inflated with pride and fell from his high position, God's perfect universe became impure. Pollution entered in such a rush that God brought the greatest polluter of all time to trial and pronounced judgment upon him and all those angels who had revolted with him.

Satan Was Born!

Evidently when God judged the crimes of Lucifer, He changed his name to Satan, the Devil, the Evil One. "Satan" means "the resister or adversary"; the name "Devil" means "the accuser and slanderer."

Satan was sentenced to eternal banishment. In Matthew 25:41 Jesus says that hell was created for the Devil and his angels.

After God pronounced Satan's judgment, His first act was to clear off one of the planets of the universe, beautify it, and call it "earth." This little planet was to become the arena of the mightiest contest of all time: a contest where God Himself would be wounded in a life-and-death struggle with the powers of darkness. God had a plan, a method to resolve this pre-history rebellion led by Satan, which involved the creation of another creature with whom all of you are familiar.

I realize that this account may appear to some as wild conjecture based on only a few verses, but I have projected the light shed by the rest of the Bible into an area where little is actually disclosed. However, as you read on you will see that it is consistent with all that is revealed of God's working in human history.

4 ∘ "D" Day Earth

"In the beginning God created the heavens and the earth. And the earth was formless and void, and darkness was over the surface of the deep; and the Spirit of God was moving over the surface of the waters. . . . And God created man in His own image, in the image of God He created him; male and female He created them."

GENESIS 1:1-2, 27

WHEN GOD MADE Planet Earth, He established a giant, complex research and development center where a strange creature called "man" was going to be tested. However, before man was created, God restored the earth from the chaotic mess caused by Satan's rebellion and brought forth life in the form of animals, fish, and fowl to inhabit that earth.

God could have left the earth as a gigantic perpetual zoo, but instead He did something about which many have mixed emotions—He gave us our first parents.

Why would God do a thing like that? Why did God create man? These are the most basic questions of all time: Why is man? Why does he exist? Why are we here?

Footnote in the Sands of Time

I don't want to inject heavy theology here, but instead will attempt to answer some speculations concerning the universe of eternity past.

Some believe that God created the world in six stages, at six intervals separated by long expanses of time. This is called the age-day theory. Others believe that God spaced different stages of evolution which developed into the world of today.

Another belief centers upon the concept that Genesis 1 and 2 describe an original and recent (in relationship to eternity) creation of the world.

I believe that chapters 1 and 2 do not explain the original creation of Planet Earth and the universe, but assume their prior existence. If we consider this view, then these two chapters describe a *reconstruction* of the earth and its galaxy by God in six literal solar days.

The chronology of Job 38:4-7 indicates that God created the material universe before the angelic revolt and consequently before man's appearance on the planet. In Job 38:4 the context begins, "Where were you when I laid the foundation of the earth?" and continues to speak of the great acts of creation. Then in verse 7 God says, "When the morning stars sang together, and all the sons of God shouted for joy?" As mentioned in chapter 3, this refers to angels. The passage also indicates that *all* the angelic beings were in harmony as they shouted for joy at this demonstration of God's great power. Two vital things are involved here: the earth was created *after* the angels were and yet *before* the angelic rebellion. I believe, after carefully piecing together the few rays of light from the Scripture about things prior to Genesis 1, that the earth was somehow devastated when God rounded up Satan and his cohorts and brought them to judgment.

The only original acts of creation in Genesis 1 and 2 are described by the Hebrew word "bara," which is used in the sense of bringing something into existence out of nothing. It is used in Genesis 1:1, where it refers to the original act of creation in the undisclosed past; again in Genesis 1:21, where the creation of all subhuman creatures is described; and in Genesis 1:27, where the creation of the life and personality of man is described.

Other words which are used in connection with creation do not necessarily imply any original acts, but rather *restoration* of a galaxy which is described in Genesis 1:2 as being in a state of chaos. This chaotic condition is the literal meaning of the Hebrew words "tohu-wa-bohu," translated "without form and void." This expression doesn't just mean "undeveloped," but rather something that is the result of a catastrophe.

This is sometimes called the "gap" theory, so named because of the expanse of time which elapsed between Genesis 1:1 and Genesis 1:2.

Barnhouse describes the time between the original creation of the earth and its restoration from chaos as "The Great Interval." One of the most cogent statements he makes to substantiate this view is, "If a perfect God should create a very imperfect world, chaotic, waste and desolate, a wreck and a ruin, it would be a violation of one of the great spiritual principles stated by the Holy Spirit Himself: 'A fountain cannot send forth sweet water and bitter (James 3:11)'"[1]

After the subsequent formation or reconstruction of the same earth which had been turned into chaos, God *created* man, and he has the center stage now.

Footprints in the Sands

In eternity past there was only one will, the will of God. There was no evil whatsoever, only harmony, holiness, and righteousness. When the second will entered the universe, generated by the heart of Lucifer, rebellion broke out. Time, as we know it, began with two wills in existence.

One great Bible scholar says that the shortest definition of sin is simply, "I will."[2]

When Satan was born and stated his proud "I will's," God didn't hesitate; God ousted Satan from his position of authority in His government.

The declaration of war had been made, but God was not taken by surprise. He had His plan ready to be launched with Operation Man.

Doubtless God had many reasons for creating man which we cannot fathom, but I believe the following are primary. God wanted to prove His perfect love and to show the angelic beings who chose to stay with Him that He had been neither unjust nor unloving to Satan and his followers by sentencing them to eternal banishment. God demonstrated this love to the fullest at Golgotha.

Perhaps another reason was to show the complete folly of choosing to reject God's will. And finally, God wanted to elevate man above the angelic realm and to fellowship with Him.

In the Book of Hebrews God shows that man will rule the world to come; angels will actually be under man's rule: "For He did not subject to angels the world to come, concerning which we are speaking. But one has testified somewhere, saying, 'What is man that Thou rememberest him? Or the son of man, that Thou art concerned about him? Thou hast made him for a little while lower than the angels; Thou hast crowned him with glory and honor, and hast appointed him over the works of Thy hands; Thou hast put all things in subjection under his feet'" (Hebrews 2:5-8).

The Apostle Paul says the same thing in 1 Corinthians 6:3: "Do you not know that we shall judge angels? How much more, matters of this life?"

But man is not just a pawn for a divine demonstration. He has destiny himself. God has great love and concern for each person and total forgiveness for the man who places his faith in the reconciliation God offers.

God's Crown of Creation

Out of the millions of galaxies of the universe God chose one galaxy for His great creative efforts. He set apart one of the planets to be the stage of testing, a complex experimentation center, more comprehensive than any progressive corporation board of directors could imagine.

God chose to construct the world in six days. (Although I believe He could have created it in a split second if He had chosen.) On the sixth day we read of God's greatest creation—man.

"Then God said, 'Let us make man in our image, according to our likeness; and let them rule over the fish of the sea and over the birds of the sky, and over the cattle and over all the earth, and over every creeping thing that creeps on the earth.' So God created man in His own image, in the image of God He created him; male and female He created them" (Genesis 1:26-27).

The important part is that man's immaterial being was created in the very image of God. God doesn't have arms or legs or a body in His essential being; the image of God in man is the possession of will, intellect, emotion, moral reason, and everlasting existence. All of this is part of what the Bible calls the soul of man.

Angels also possess these qualities, with a few superior additives which set them apart from humans: angels have greater mobility and intelligence than man. However, men and angels have a vitally important quality in common—they both possess freedom of choice and the intellect to make choices.

No Place to Hide

Once man had been created, he was watched by both the angels of God and the fallen angels. Fantastic thought, isn't it? We believe that we can take ourselves to a remote Pacific Island or an isolated mountain retreat and get away from everybody and everything. However, we still are being watched by angels. We know this from many passages in the Bible.

In Luke 2:8-14 the angels visited the shepherds and told them of the birth of the Savior. In Ephesians 3 it says that God is teaching "rulers and the authorities in the heavenly places" (terms used only about angels, describing their rank and order) many things about Himself through man.

If man is the object of a great deal of study on the part of angels, we must ask "why?" What are they observing? What are they learning? I believe that God is demonstrating to angels that He was perfectly just in His eternal judgment of them and that His love is so great it cannot be fathomed by any created being.

Paradise Found

Man's immaterial being will always exist; it will always live. In that sense, man is also in the image of God. At the time of his creation man was given legal authority to rule himself and all of the earth. The responsibility is spelled out clearly in Genesis 1:28: "And God blessed them; and God said to them, 'Be fruitful and multiply, and fill the earth, and subdue it; and rule over the fish of the sea and over the birds of the sky, and over every living thing that moves on the earth.'"

That is an important fact to remember: when God gave man that legal right, he was put into a garden where he was provided with every conceivable need that he might have. We may allow our human imaginations to take over here, visualizing what a perfect environment would have been. There would have been no need for Earth Day advocates, Federal Water Quality boards, or Air Pollution Control departments in the Garden of Eden.

When God created man, He saw that he was going to need a companion with whom to share Paradise, so He created the loveliest creature in the form of a woman. Eve must have been the most gorgeous female ever to exist. Too often today we think of ancient man looking quite inferior to modern man. However, the very reverse was true. Adam and Eve were the most beautiful specimens of Homo sapiens ever to walk this planet, according to the Bible. They were the direct creation of God. The idea is often embraced by man that if he had the most beautiful woman as a mate, all problems would fade away; the woman thinks if she had the perfect, handsome man her problems would be solved. Others think, *If only we had a secure society with a perfect ecological balance of nature and all material needs provided, we would have no problems.* Adam and Eve had all this plus personal fellowship with God, but they threw it away.

Rebel With a Cause

What a drama in Genesis 3! No clever playwright with all the skills of manipulating characters and providing psychological tricks of suspense could dream up a better plot than the one that happened in the Garden of Eden.

On stage we see Adam and Eve, living in fellowship with God, seeing the evidence of God's love on every side. However, there was one prohibition: man was not to eat the fruit of a certain tree in that garden. The tree was called "the tree of the knowledge of good and evil." (The Hebrew word for knowledge means "experiential knowledge.") We do not know the kind of fruit the tree had on it, but it was to provide the test which would determine whether man wanted to stay in perfect fellowship with God or not. The test would set the stage for God to demonstrate His justice and His love to the angelic realm.

Man was told that if he ate from this tree, he would die. The evil was not in the tree—it was not sprayed with some lethal insecticide which would poison the fruit. The evil was in rejecting God's revealed will and consequently rejecting fellowship with God.

The stage was set, and Satan was allowed to enter the scene. He was off-stage in the wings all the time, waiting for his entrance cue, plotting how he could make man rebel against God just as he had done. He apparently thought that the whole onstage contest revolved around this act, the act of making man fall.

Satan may be extremely wise, but he is battling against a far wiser being. For when Satan made man fall, he played right into the hand of God. Far from defeating God, he set a trap for himself. He set up a situation through which God could demonstrate His justice and His love to the infinite degree.

God did not want man to fall, but He wasn't surprised when he did. And He had a plan—a plan to save man from his own rebellious state.

How Did Satan Make Man Fall?

Genesis 3 is probably one of the most important chapters in the Bible. We must understand it to grasp anything of history. In Genesis 3:1 it says: "Now the serpent was more subtle than any beast of the field which the LORD God had made." (KJV)

This does not mean "subtle" in the sense of being clever, although we know he is that. In this case subtle means graceful and lovely. We tend to think of a serpent as a slimy thing which wiggles around on its belly, but that wasn't what the serpent looked like then. The word "serpent" in the original Hebrew means something shining and beautiful. It is similar in meaning to "Lucifer."

Apparently at that time the serpent walked around on legs, as indicated by the description "beast of the field." It was shrewd, an extremely wise and cunning member of the animal kingdom. As Satan began to work his wiles, it was obvious he had done his homework thoroughly. He studied man and woman to see how he could make them rebel against God; he analyzed the situation and saw that the more susceptible of the two might be the woman. Satan also saw that if he could get Eve to rebel, Adam would probably follow after her rather than follow God.

Satan was a master of timing in this first encounter in the garden. He waited until the perfect moment to fire his temptation at Eve. He knew that if the temptation didn't work, it would be twice as hard to fool her the second time. Also, he didn't come directly to tempt Eve, but he used a beautiful creature.

Where was Eve when all of this took place? It is obvious from the context of the chapter that she was by the tree of the knowledge of good and evil. She was already curious about it, a trait which has meant trouble for many!

Poor Eve didn't sense that powerful and evil dignitaries were breathlessly watching as she eyed the forbidden tree. She was just standing there, probably thinking, *I wonder why God doesn't want us to eat from this tree.*

Satan had already put into her mind the suggestion to look at the tree. This is how he works upon man—planting an idea here, an innuendo there.

Satan, the super-intelligent being, invented one of the cleverest attacks of all time. He invented the power of suggestion, the ability to put thoughts into our minds about things we already desire. He knows our natural weaknesses; he knows the areas where desire is strongest in us. He knew Eve and her basic curiosity, and he hit her at just the right time. We see how adroit and fiendishly clever this foe is when we understand that the original Hebrew in which Genesis 3:1 was written gives just the right inflection to the serpent's words. Try asking this question out loud and see how it sounds:

"Indeed, has God *really* said, 'You shall not eat from *every* tree of the garden?'" (Literal translation.) Wow! Satan can really get it together when he wants to tempt! He doesn't come to a person with a dogmatic statement, "God's word isn't true." Rather, he will ask a question carefully designed to start the doubt gnawing at our minds. Notice how he said to Eve, "You shall not eat from *every* tree of the garden." How many trees could she use to satisfy her hunger, her desire, and her needs? Every tree but one, we are told. So what was Satan focusing upon? The one limitation, of course. This question was planned to take Eve's eyes off all that God had given her and make her center upon the one thing He had forbidden. Satan is a master at this.

The Poison Planter

Satan is a master at planting seeds of doubt. He fogs us in and we become confused. This is exactly what he did with Eve.

When Eve answered the serpent's question about eating from the tree, we see that Satan's poison had begun to work. She said, "From the fruit of the trees of the garden we may eat; but from the fruit of the tree which is in the middle of the garden, God has said, 'You shall not eat from it or touch it, lest you die'" (Genesis 3:2-3).

Wait a minute! There's only one problem. Eve added her own embellishment to the original command in Genesis 2:17. She said, "or touch it." She showed that she didn't know what the real issue was; she thought there was something in the material of the tree that was evil. God didn't say, "Don't touch." She was making sin something material or tangible, rather than a choice of the mind. She was psyched out! Already she had the wrong issue.

Satan saw that he had her where he wanted her and zeroed in with an outright denial of the word of God. It is his special technique: first he makes suggestions in an area where we are uncertain or doubtful; then he will come along with a direct repudiation of what God said. In Genesis 3:4 he said, "You surely shall not die!"

Eve was probably gazing at the tree, listening to Satan's smooth talk, and the next thing she thought was, "What is God's *motive* for not wanting me to eat from this tree?" Satan was right on the spot with the reason. He said: "For God knows that in the day you eat from it your eyes will be opened, and you will be like God, knowing good and evil" (Genesis 3:5).

What Satan was saying to Eve was that God's motive was jealousy. Satan implied, "Look, Eve, He's holding out on you because if you eat from this tree you'll have the experiential knowledge of good and evil and you'll be like God."

This is another of Satan's methods: he takes clear truth and drops just enough poison in it to kill us. It was true that if Adam and Eve ate from the tree they would get the experiential knowledge of good and evil, but it was not true that they would be like God. See how clever Satan is? He got this woman, who was already confused and missing the point, to reject God's Word outright and to accept the idea that God had impure motives and was holding out because He didn't love mankind. Once that insidious thought was planted, Satan had his ally—the lust of the eye.

Arsenic in the Race

Eve ate from that tree and immediately things began to happen. For one thing, I believe there was a visible change in Eve. Before this she was covered with light, a beautiful glow from God, but after she ate she lost this ethereal shine. What is more amazing, she "also gave some to her husband, and he ate."

We can say that the woman was confused, that she was deceived and therefore wasn't legally responsible for sin. However, there was no excuse for the man at all. "And it was not Adam who was deceived, but the woman being quite deceived, fell into transgression" (1 Timothy 2:14).

Adam gave in without a fight! There was not one word given directly to the man, not one temptation. He walked into transgression with his eyes wide open. It seems that he simply chose to stay with Eve rather than continue with God. He made a cool and calculated decision to reject God. Adam had the legal power of attorney over himself and the world, but he betrayed the trust God had given him and forfeited his authority to Satan.

Satan, this fantastically superhuman being, achieved what he thought was a great victory—leading man to go against the will of God. Things really happened when Adam and Eve rejected God and obeyed Satan; in a flash of time mankind had some drastic results.

Man: Down for the Count

One, man died instantly, just as God had said, "... *in* the day that you eat from it you shall surely die" (Genesis 2:17). He lost spiritual life, the most important sphere of life we have. Man is made up of body, his material being; soul, his immaterial life; spirit, his spiritual life with which he is able to communicate with God. The instant man disobeyed God, he lost this spiritual life and severed that direct line of communication with his Maker. As it is written, "... you were dead in your trespasses and sins" (Ephesians 2:1), "being darkened in their understanding, excluded from the life of God" (Ephesians 4:18).

Two, man received a nature of self-centeredness and rebellion against God. We see this result throughout the history of mankind. God describes it this way: "The heart is more deceitful than all else and is desperately sick; who can understand it?" (Jeremiah 17:9). This rebellious nature is the root of what the Bible calls sin.

Three, Satan became man's absolute master; man became the slave. It's really a heavy scene, but according to the Bible Satan is ruling all those who have rejected God. Jesus Christ brought this out clearly when He commissioned Paul: "... I am sending you, to open their eyes so that they may turn from darkness to light and from the dominion of Satan to God ..." (Acts 26:17-18).

Four, when man rebelled, the world was legally handed over to Satan. Adam actually became the Benedict Arnold of the universe. When he obeyed Satan, he turned the title deed of himself, all his dominion, and all his descendants over to Satan. This is why Jesus called Satan the "ruler of this world" (John 12:31).

God: Into the Arena

Satan won the first round in the garden. He thought the fight was all over, but it was just beginning. We are a part of this massive conflict which is settling an ancient battle between these extraterrestrial beings and God, because after man fell God gave the promise that the seed of woman would ultimately triumph over Satan (Genesis 3:15). Those today who plant doubt about the virgin birth of Jesus Christ should mark well that it was the seed of woman, not the seed of man, that God promised would eventually conquer Satan. Jesus Christ, the Promised One, would be greatly wounded in this battle with His adversary, but would later give Satan a mortal wound.

When man fell into Satan's hands, God immediately launched His plan to redeem man from this helpless situation. What Satan didn't count on was that God would be so just that He wouldn't forgive man unless divine justice was satisfied. And something much more incredible—that God would be so loving that He would be willing to step down from heaven and temporarily lay aside all of His divine rights and become a man. Satan didn't anticipate that God, as a man, would later go to a cross and bear His own righteous judgment against the sin of the whole universe.

Just Thinking . . .

Perhaps Satan figured if he could get God's new creation to sin, rather than condemn man, God would bend His justice and let Satan go free as well.

Satan may have reasoned: *If I can get enough of mankind to reject God, then God will not be able to bring Himself to judge them all, and ultimately He will let them go free. Once God compromises His justice with man, He will have to do the same with me and my angels.*

Have you ever heard someone say, "I *can't* believe that God would condemn *all those people*"? Now where do you think they get that line of reasoning?

God, taking the form of man, poured out upon Himself all of the just wrath that was due the whole human race, so that anyone who gets beneath the cross with Jesus will be shielded from that wrath. To be brought into God's family, all we need to do is accept the fact that Jesus Christ died in our place with our sins and simply receive this gift of forgiveness which our Substitute provided for us. The Spirit of God describes it beautifully: "When we were utterly helpless with no way of escape, Christ came at just the right time and died for us sinners who had no use for him. Even if we were good, we really wouldn't expect anyone to die for us, though, of course, that might be barely possible. But God showed his great love for us by sending Christ to die for us while we were still sinners. And since by his blood he did all this for us as sinners, how much more will he do for us now that he has declared us not guilty? Now he will save us from all of God's wrath to come. And since, when we were his enemies, we were brought back to God by the death of his Son, what blessings he must have for us now that we are his friends, and he is living within us!" (Romans 5:6-10, *Living Bible*).

When God accomplished this on the cross, it showed conclusively that He is perfectly just because He didn't bend His justice to salvage man out of this whole conflict; He showed how great His love is because He was willing to become a man and bear His own judgment to set man free.

"God showed how much he loved us by sending his only Son into this wicked world to bring to us eternal life through his death. In this act we see what real love is: it is not our love for God, but his love for us when he sent his Son to satisfy God's anger against our sins" (John 4:9-10, *Living Bible*).

This is the ultimate demonstration of both the justice and the love of God! All this was done that God might be both "just and the justifier of the one who has faith in Jesus" (Romans 3:26).

Satan thought if he could destroy the Man who was the Son of God, if he could destroy the humanity of Jesus Christ, he would win. He thought that Man would never be able to be raised from the tomb. Once dead, He would stay buried!

The resurrection of Jesus sealed Satan's defeat. It was God's proof that Jesus had completely paid for every sin that would ever be committed. Even one sin not paid for would have held Christ in the grave. The fact that Jesus is alive proves that all who believe in Him are declared righteous before a Holy God (Romans 4:25).

Now Satan has no legal authority over the believer.

Satan's Blindfolds

Satan may have won a battle in the garden, but he has not won the war. He has already been defeated, and he knows it! However, he is going to use every tactic in his bag of deceptions to keep as many individuals as possible from knowing it, especially those who are believers in Jesus. He already has the unbelievers in his grasp by blinding them to the good news of the pardon that God freely offers through Jesus Christ.

"If the Good News we preach is hidden to anyone, it is hidden from the one who is on the road to eternal death. Satan, who is the god of this evil world, has made him blind, unable to see the glorious light of the Gospel that is shining upon him, or to understand the amazing message we preach about the glory of Christ, who is God" (2 Corinthians 4:3-4, *Living Bible*).

Right . . . Right Now

Where do you stand in this conflict? Perhaps you're having trouble accepting these things. If you are, guess who is helping you think that way?

The most important thing to realize is that you don't have to believe everything to become a member of God's forever family. All you need is faith enough to call out to God in your heart and thank Him that Jesus Christ died for *your* inability to measure up to His perfect standards. Receive the forgiveness of your sins and thank Him for it. Tell Jesus Christ that you want Him to come into your life right now and begin to make it pleasing to God.

If you did this, on the authority of God's Word, I assure you that you have eternal life right now.

5 ○ Three Dimensional Warfare

"For thou didst gird me with strength for the battle...." KING DAVID, PSALM 18:39

DR. FRANCIS SCHAEFFER, the Christian scholar of L'Abri Fellowship, Switzerland, recently told me, "This is not an age to be a soft Christian."

He shared with me his concern for something which has stirred me also. He feels there is a tremendous need to reach out to the tens of thousands of young men and women who are turning to Christ in the Jesus Revolution and give them in-depth training in their new faith.

I believe that Dr. Schaeffer is right on! It has greatly thrilled me to observe firsthand the amazing work the Spirit of God is doing among the youth of America and other parts of the world, especially in what was once known as the hippie and drug culture. I have seen youth delivered from hopeless addiction to acid and heroin through faith in Jesus Christ. Radicals for Mao Tse-tung's principles have become radicals for spreading the love of Jesus. Weathermen and Hell's Angels are now true disciples of Jesus Christ. No man or group can take credit for what is happening. It's a work of God.

But great as this is, I fear that unless mature and trained teachers who can communicate with the "Jesus People" begin to influence and instruct them, they will be swept into terrible error and excesses. Few Christians today realize that we are engaged in a three-dimensional warfare. At stake is whether we will enjoy the tremendous sense of inner peace, purpose for life, and new source of strength that is the heritage of every believer.

Either your life will count for God or it will be sidetracked and neutralized through the opposition of little-understood enemies.

Battlefield Strategy

If we have come to a point in our lives where we believe in Jesus Christ and accept Him as the One who is our Savior, one of the first desires that comes to us is that we want to live a life which is pleasing to Him. This comes from a new nature He puts within us. At this point we all find there are many handicaps which hinder us from being the type of person we want to be.

We are, whether we know how to express it or not, fighting a warfare on three fronts. These have been called the world, the flesh, and the Devil.

Throughout history leaders have never approached an enemy in warfare like a child brandishing a stick, flailing in all directions. They have used careful strategy and have studied the way in which the enemy maneuvers. General Albert Wedemeyer, a top military strategist of World War II, told of attending the German War College in the late 1930s and learning from the very men who would later become his opponents in war. He said, "The Germans stressed the campaigns of Frederick the Great, Napoleon, Caesar, Alexander and Philip of Macedon.

"When we studied a campaign of Frederick the Great or Napoleon, we generally went to the area where the battle had been fought," General Wedemeyer wrote. "The military history instructor reviewed the situation, analyzed dispositions and tactical decisions, and injected interesting anecdotes."[1]

If we are to understand and study the warfare we are in, we must know the area where the battles are being fought. The "flesh" is one battlefield where our enemy Satan constantly hinders us from doing what God wants.

The Flesh Trap

The term "flesh" ("sarx" in the original Greek) is used in many ways in the New Testament. Sometimes it is used to mean simply the stuff that covers our bones, as in Luke 24:39. "See My hands and My feet, that it is I Myself; touch Me and see; for a spirit does not have flesh and bones as you see that I have."

Sometimes flesh is used to represent the whole body, as in Acts 2:26. "Therefore my heart was glad and my tongue exulted; moreover my flesh also will abide in hope."

And sometimes flesh is used in the sense of our physical, earthly limitations, as in Second Corinthians 10:3-4. "For though we walk in the flesh, we do not war according to the flesh, for the weapons of our warfare are not of the flesh, but divinely powerful for the destruction of fortresses."

But the sense in which it is used as an area of warfare is most fully developed by the Apostle Paul. Drs. Arndt and Gingrich comment as follows: "In Paul's thought especially, the flesh is the willing instrument of sin and is subject to sin to such a degree that whatever flesh is, all forms of sin are likewise present, and no good thing can live in the flesh itself."[2]

A careful study of the many passages on the "flesh" when it is used in this sense reveals the following facts:

1. It is a basic nature or principle which operates within us from the time we are born physically. This nature is in rebellion against God; it is self-centered and wants its own way (Romans 7:14-24; 8:5-9).

2. It is an inseparable part of our material body and cannot be eradicated until we receive our transformed resurrection bodies (Romans 7:25; 1 John 1:8, 10).

3. Though it cannot be eradicated, its power to *operate* in the life of the Christian has been neutralized by our being united with Christ in His death to sin. The flesh has no right to reign in the Christian's life any longer, and its power is broken in our lives when we count this as being true (Romans 6:1-14).

The attitude of believing that God has already broken sin's and/or the flesh's power over us sets the Spirit of God free to make victory a reality in our experience (Romans 8:1-4).

Here is just a partial list of what the flesh does in our lives when we don't consider its power broken and depend upon God's Spirit: "Now the deeds of the flesh are evident, which are: immorality, impurity, sensuality, idolatry, sorcery, enmities, strife, jealousy, outbursts of anger, disputes, dissensions, factions, envyings, drunkenness, carousings, and things like these, of which I forewarn you just as I have forewarned you that those who practice such things shall not inherit the kingdom of God" (Galatians 5:19-21).

Most of these words which are used for the deeds of the flesh need amplification. Briefly, here are some of the specifics:

Immorality: from the word "porneia," it means all sexual intercourse outside of marriage.

Impurity: impure thoughts and actions, especially in the area of sex.

Sensuality: living primarily to please the senses (out-of-control appetite for foods, music, sex, creature comforts, etc.).

Idolatry: anything that we place ahead of Christ as an object of our attention and devotion; this could be a girl friend or a boyfriend, our children, a job, an education, a beautiful home, clothes, a sleek body, or a fast car.

Sorcery: from the word "pharmakia"; the practice of witchcraft and occultism in association with drugs.

Enmities: to be at odds with people; carrying grudges.

Disputes: modern man calls these "personality conflicts," but "selfishness" is more accurate.

Dissensions: literally division; causing conflicts and taking of sides between people.

Factions: literally heresies; leading astray with false doctrine and forming sects.

Envyings: attitudes of dissatisfaction which cause you to desire what others have.

Drunkenness: any loss of normal judgment and awareness through the use of alcohol or drugs. The idea of better living through chemicals instead of the Spirit of God.

Carousings: seeking to escape reality through excessive pursuit of entertainment.

These are only some of the deeds of the flesh, not all of them! When the apostle says that those who practice such things "shall not inherit the kingdom of God," he means that those who *habitually* indulge in them are evidencing the fact that they have never received the new nature which hates sin.

It is impossible for a Christian to regularly practice the deeds of the flesh without a change of heart before God. Because of the fact that the Holy Spirit dwells inside of us, we can't be continually happy in sin. Sooner or later the Christian will acknowledge his sin and turn back to trusting Christ to deliver him from its power; and from the standpoint of his happiness, the sooner the better.

Continuous, unbroken toleration of the deeds of the flesh should cause a person to question whether he has really been born spiritually. A true Christian can and does experience these deeds of the flesh, but he will have a desire to be delivered from them for Christ's sake. A non-Christian just wants to be delivered from the consequences.

Deeds of the Flesh and Demons

Some well-meaning Christians today have a tendency to go overboard about demons. I want to be sure no one falls into the trap of attributing to demons what is actually the work of the flesh.

You may have heard people speak about the "lying demon," the "lust demon," the "envy demon," and others. I do not believe that there are specific demons such as these who can only do one thing.

Consider a fellow who is constantly thinking about sex. He is consumed by lascivious thoughts every day. If he has heard of such things, he may begin to think, "Maybe I have a lust demon."

He shares his thoughts with some of his Christian friends, and they have a little prayer meeting and "cast the demon out." Sanctimoniously they may say, "We've cast out the lust demon. Praise the Lord."

Our Christian friend, thus assured by his own feelings and the pronouncements of his friends, takes his wife to a restaurant, smug in his victory over himself. A curvaceous waitress in a mini-skirt comes to the table, and in a flash the old demon is back.

The danger in this concept is that a deed which is actually a part of the flesh or the old sin nature is attributed to a demon. It is vital that we assign things to their proper cause. There is no "lust demon" per se. Lust is a sin which comes from the flesh. But there are demons who will use the lust of the flesh to guide us into moral disaster. Satan can take a natural drive and use it, but he is not the originator of it. He capitalizes on something which is already going on in our hearts

Along with many other doctrines which become distorted in popular usage, the theme of Satan probably has more false clichés attached to it than any other.

"The Devil made me do it" is a cop-out.

When Satan takes the desire which you have and uses it for his purposes, he doesn't force you. If you really express the truth when overtaken by a sin of the flesh, you would say, "I did it because I chose to follow the desires of my old nature." Now that is not as easy to say as "The Devil made me do it," but it is more honest.

Puzzled Apostles

Mark 7 gives a good description of the flesh. Jesus had told the disciples a parable, and they questioned Him about it. We can almost see Him shaking His head when He said, "Are you so uncomprehending?" Then He explained: "That which proceeds out of the man, that is what defiles the man. For from within, out of the heart of men, proceed the evil thoughts and fornications, thefts, murders, adulteries, deeds of coveting and wickedness, as well as deceit, sensuality, envy, slander, pride and foolishness. All these evil things proceed from within and defile the man" (Mark 7:20-23).

Jesus is talking about the flesh, the source of this sinful nature. He shows that our major problem is not our environment but our inner nature of the flesh.

It's not a sin to have an evil thought flash into the mind; it is only a sin when we fail to say "no" to it and do not rely upon Christ to put it down. Temptation and sin are different. The old saying applies, "You can't stop a bird from landing on your head, but you can stop it from building a nest in your hair."

When the Bible speaks of the temptations of the flesh, it is always in terms of a continued need to overcome them. It is a matter of moment-by-moment reliance upon the Holy Spirit by deliberate choice to overcome the lusts of the flesh. Victory is never achieved by freedom *from* temptation, but by overcoming temptation through the power of the indwelling Holy Spirit.

Galatians 5:16 says: "But I say, walk by the Spirit, and you will not carry out the desire of the flesh."

To walk in the Spirit means to have a continuing attitude of reliance upon the Holy Spirit and not on your own human resources. Note: it does not say that if you walk in the Spirit you will not *have* temptations; it does say that you will not fulfill them. The Spirit-controlled believer will be tempted, but it is not sin until you stop trusting the Spirit to fight it.

The Bible talks about overcoming the flesh, or going to battle with it in dependence upon the Holy Spirit who lives in every believer. However, as the Bible speaks of "the world," it talks of claiming victory which has already been won.

Christ has won a victory over the world and Christians are to claim that victory. This will be amplified later in the chapter "Weapons of Warfare."

The World

In most cases the term "world" as used in the Bible comes from the word "kosmos." Basically it has three ideas in its verbal form: to put things into order, to systematize, and to adorn or decorate. In the latter form the word became used as "cosmetics," which is the concept of adorning the outer appearance.

First idea: in the New Testament, "world" is used in the sense of the planet Earth, the material planet. This is the way it is used in Acts 17:24 and John 1:10.

Second idea: "world" is used to mean the inhabitants of the Earth. First, referring to people in general, not viewing them as good or evil, as in John 3:16—"God so loved the world"; and second, referring to all unbelievers, alien toward God, as in John 14:17 and John 15-18.

Third idea: vital to our study, it is used to describe the world *system*, beautifully organized and arranged to function without God, opposed to all that is true in Jesus Christ. The world system is adorned with the beautiful concepts of culture, music, art, philosophy, knowledge, social concerns, programs of welfare, science, politics, religion, and pleasure. It embraces all these things in an orderly system. These are not evil in themselves, but Satan weaves them into a world order so that he can take man's heart away from a true relationship with God and center him on those things which are both temporal and material.

Beginning of the World System

In the Garden man gave the title deed of the world to Satan, and since then the world has been under his control. Before man's rejection of God, there was no "cosmos" in the sense of an ordered world system alien to God. There was only the planet Earth and God's appointed regent, man. When man chose to reject fellowship with God and follow the lie of Satan, he not only handed over to Satan the title deed to man's life, but to that of the Earth itself. It was then that the world system began to develop.

Adam had been given authority over Planet Earth, including its creatures and elements. "And God blessed them; and God said to them, 'Be fruitful and multiply, and fill the earth and subdue it; and rule over the fish of the sea and over the birds of the sky, and over every living thing that moves on the earth'" (Genesis 1:28). Adam had complete power of attorney; when he chose to reject God and follow Satan, legal ownership of mankind, animals, and the Earth was transferred to Satan.

God, being just, had to honor this legal right, even to Satan. Man and the world could not be taken back until sin, which caused the forfeiture of ownership to Satan, was paid for.

Jesus certainly knew Satan had won legal right to the world. When Satan personally tempted Jesus, displaying at that time his ability to deceive, the Scriptures say, "And the devil said to Him, 'I will give You all this domain and its glory; for *it has been handed over to me*, and I give it to whomever I wish'" (Luke 4:6).

Our earthbound minds can't comprehend the mysterious power it took to show Jesus all the kingdoms of the world in a moment. Satan probably made it look like the most dazzling movie production, combining a panorama of nature's beauty and the pomp and glory of kingdoms. Satan can make the things of the world appear so good that men would give their lives for them—and some do. (See 2 Timothy 4:10 for the tragedy of a promising young minister, Demos.)

Jesus didn't dispute Satan's claim to the world; He knew that Adam had handed over the legal ownership to the whole planet and all on it.

The Arch Architect

Satan lost no time in beginning to set up a whole scene that would carry man's mind away from God. Genesis 4 records the beginning of the system.

One of the most basic parts of the world system is religion. Religion is based on man's pride. It assumes that man can do something to earn God's acceptance. True faith says you can only be accepted with God through receiving forgiveness as a gift on the basis of a God-provided substitute bearing the penalty for sin. Abel approached God the true way. He brought the appointed animal sacrifice as a substitute to die for his sins. Cain, on the other hand, came the way of the world system. He brought the fruit of his own works. Abel was accepted—Cain wasn't.

God even reasoned with Cain and sought to get him to come the true way. "Then the Lord said to Cain, 'Why are you angry? And why has your countenance fallen? If you do well, will not your countenance be lifted up? And if you do not do well, sin is crouching at the door; and its desire is for you, but you must master it'" (Genesis 4:6-7).

Cain's pride was inflamed. Rather than come by faith in God's provision, he did what religion has been doing for centuries; he murdered the one who represented God's truth. Religion can't stand the truth because it is a rebuke to man's self-centeredness and pride. This is why some of the greatest crimes in history have been done in the name of false Christianity and religion. The false cannot stand the true.

The world system began with the underlying principles of pride, rejection of God's truth, and force.

What Cain Raised

We see the world system further developed as Cain "... went out from the presence of the Lord" (Genesis 4:16). Cain established a highly developed society and culture which left God out; he built the first city mentioned in the Bible, called Enoch.

In the generations that immediately followed, many advancements were made. "Jabal ... was the father of those who dwell in tents and have livestock" (Genesis 4:20). Agriculture began to develop and flourish.

"Jubal ... was the father of all those who play the lyre and pipe" (Genesis 4:21). Music, art, and culture were introduced to take their places in the world system.

"Tubal-cain (was) the forger of all implements of bronze and iron ..." (Genesis 4:22). And now we see the development of industry becoming involved in the early world system.

These things were not evil in themselves, but there was one glaring problem—they left out God. Man's achievements became a snare to take his heart further away from God. Here was an entire civilization organized and developed around the material and temporal. Man's proud self-sufficiency, rejection of God's truth, and violence permeated the whole system.

It wasn't until Adam's son Seth had a son named Enosh that it says, "*Then* men began to call upon the name of the Lord" (Genesis 4:26).

The first world system became so permeated with every kind of evil that God had to destroy it (Genesis 6-7).

Alienation of Affections

The real battle with the world has to do with something as basic as our affections. When Satan can't reach a person through temptations to do the more obvious gross sins of the flesh, he will switch to such innocent and worthwhile avenues as education, careers, nature, money, fame, or a myriad of other pursuits. If he can shift anything from the world system into being first in our affections, taking Christ's place of priority, he has effectively sidetracked us into the web of worldliness. This is why John warns, "Do not love the world (cosmos), nor the things in the world. If any one loves the world, the love of the Father is not in him. For all that is in the world (system), the lust of the flesh and the lust of the eyes and the boastful pride of life, is not from the Father, but is from the world (system)" (1 John 2:15-16).

Friendship with the world is hostility toward God because the philosophy of the world, its whole life view, is in contradiction to God's viewpoint of life. Embracing the world and its ways will inevitably drive our affections away from God. There is no neutral ground. This is why John warned, ". . . if any one loves the world, the love of the Father is not in him."

Behind all that is tangible in the world system there is the intangible genius of Satan, the master deceiver. Behind "the things of the world system" is the mastermind who uses them to shift our focus from devotion to Christ to devotion to things. Once this is done, the inevitable ever-increasing force of greed sets in. Because things can never take the place of fellowship with God, we are never satisfied. The more we get, the more we want. James zeroed in on this when he said, "You lust and do not have; so you commit murder. And you are envious and cannot obtain; so you fight and quarrel. You do not have because you do not ask. You ask and do not receive, because you ask with wrong motives, so that you may spend it on your pleasures. You adulteresses, do you not know that friendship with the world is hostility toward God? Therefore whoever wishes to be a friend of the world makes himself an enemy of God" (James 4:2-4).

Satan: Ruler of This World

The diabolical mastermind backing up the world system deceives and ensnares the minds of people. He does a good job with those who do not believe in Christ and a fair job with those who do.

Three titles describe Satan's work: first, he is "the ruler of this world," which means he is constantly at work in human government and its political systems.

Before you accuse me of being an anarchist, I don't mean that every government is totally evil or immoral, but that Satan is capable of manipulating all forms of government for his purposes.

Jesus gave us many details about this person who pulls the political strings of the world system. Even those who see Jesus as only a historical figure or a great teacher must admit He wouldn't have taught anything which He couldn't prove by experience. Here are a few passages where Jesus speaks of "the ruler of this world":

"Now judgment is upon this world; now the ruler of this world shall be cast out" (John 12:31).

"I will not speak much more with you, for the ruler of the world is coming, and he has nothing in Me" (John 14:30).

"And concerning judgment, because the ruler of this world has been judged" (John 16:11).

The Greek word for ruler in the previous passages is "archon." The Greeks were specific in their meanings, and when "archon" is used it stresses the vise that Satan has upon the world. It literally means a political ruler. It emphasizes Satan's control over the political systems of this earth.

Let's look at an example of this from the Book of Daniel. Daniel was one of God's great prophets. At one time he was given a prophetic vision which he couldn't interpret. He prayed that God would reveal its meaning to him.

Daniel spent twenty-one days in prayer. Then an angel appeared to Daniel and told him that he had come to reveal the meaning of the vision. The angel explained to Daniel that he had been detoured in an unusual manner. "The prince of the kingdom of Persia was withstanding me for twenty-one days" (Daniel 10:13).

At that time Persia was ruling the world. It was no mere human who held up one of God's angels, but a demon (or fallen angel), one of Satan's generals, who was controlling the prince of Persia. This mighty spiritual power behind the Persian prince actually withstood the angel for three weeks, until God sent Michael, one of His chief angels, to overcome the demon and send the messenger on his way to Daniel.

This is not just ancient history, something we delegate to Daniel's time. According to the Bible, an unseen warfare is being waged behind world events all the time. The Bible describes this "invisible warfare" from Genesis to Revelation. The vast, highly organized army of demons behind the world system is clearly revealed in Ephesians 6:12: "For our struggle is not against flesh and blood, but against the rulers, against the powers, against the world-forces of this darkness, against the spiritual forces of wickedness in the heavenly places."

Prince of the Power of the Air

Satan's second title is "prince of the power of the air." Before a person becomes a Christian, he is spiritually dead and ruled by this prince. "And you were dead in your trespasses and sins, in which you formerly walked according to the course of this world, according to the prince of the power of the air, of the spirit that is now working in the sons of disobedience" (Ephesians 2:1-2).

The word translated "air" literally means the air we breathe. However, in this context it is obviously not used in a literal sense. The clause prior to it, ". . . the course of this world," looks at the world in the sense of the thought forms and environment of the world view of this godless world system.

The clause following it, "the spirit that is now working in the sons of disobedience," looks at the energizing spirit of evil within the unbelieving world. Both clauses speak of the dynamics that motivate and shape the way men think and act. Therefore, in context the word "air" must be speaking of the "mood" or "atmosphere of thought." We often use the term "atmosphere" in this sense. For instance, "Paris has a romantic atmosphere" or "The atmosphere in the room was oppressive."

Satan is said to be the prince and power behind the atmosphere of the thoughts of this world system that are hostile to God. Before we believe in Jesus Christ and are born spiritually, we are unwittingly dominated by this atmosphere of thought.

As "prince of the air," Satan rules over the thoughts of the world system. He originated the concept of brainwashing long before human rulers used it to manipulate prisoners of war.

In this role Satan injects his treachery into the educational system, the philosophy, the mass media, the arts, the style, and the culture. He will use a lake of truth to disguise a pint of poison. His deceptions about life and its purpose are lethal. Any flirting with the ways of the world can lead to spiritual adultery (James 4:4).

When we think that he is the ruler over all of these thought forms and realize the ways in which we are bombarded every day by these sources, we begin to see how deadly the world system can be. At the same time, we begin to understand the importance of the promise of 1 John 5:4: "For whatever is born of God overcomes the world; and this is the victory that has overcome the world—our faith. And who is the one who overcomes the world, but he who believes that Jesus is the Son of God?"

With our hearts focused on Jesus, we are constantly having our minds renewed with God's view of life, which is alien to the human viewpoint of the world system.

The human viewpoint of life looks at the daily problems as well as all the complications of living in this world from the standpoint of the human ability to cope with them. The divine viewpoint looks at life from God's ability to handle it through a yielded you. It is His job to deal with your temptations and needs. There is peace of mind, stability, and power for the one who has the divine viewpoint.

This is why Romans 12:2 says: "Don't let the world around you squeeze you into its own mold, but let God remold your minds from within" (Phillips' translation).

God of This Age

Satan's third title is "the god of this *age*," which is from the Greek word "aion." This often means the prevailing thought of a particular era. Satan is constantly changing the "in thing" so that when you get "where it's at" you find you're where it was. The pace is accelerating; the world system is changing so fast that even the world can't keep up with it.

In the future, old institutions are going to change so rapidly that people will reach a tremendous state of instability and emotional disturbance resulting in psychological problems. Nothing will be dependable, stable, or certain.

"The god of this age" also refers to Satan's activity in relation to religion. He loves religion. It's his ace trump for blinding our minds to the truth. He is *the god* of all those who do not follow Jesus Christ. Those who worship in any religious form apart from Christ are ultimately being deceived by Satan.

It is comforting to know, however, that Satan can't permanently blind the minds of those who are truly seeking to know God. Wherever a person may be, whether in Lapland or Africa, Dubuque or Denver, the Scripture says that he can come to a God-consciousness. "But God shows his anger from heaven against all sinful, evil men who push away the truth from them. For the truth about God is known to them instinctively; God has put this knowledge in their hearts. Since earliest times men have seen the earth and sky and all God made, and have known of his existence and great eternal power. So they will have no excuse" (Romans 1:18-20, *Living Bible*).

If a man sincerely wants to know God, then God will move heaven and earth to get enough light to him so that he will have the knowledge to throw himself upon the mercy of God. "And you will seek Me and find Me, when you search for Me with all your heart" (Jeremiah 29:13).

Although Satan can't blind the mind of the person who is sincerely seeking God, he does blind those who reject the light that they have. This is a hard fact which each person, no matter how good he is in his own opinion, no matter what good principles he obeys, no matter how many good works he performs, should confront. If he is not following Christ, he is unwittingly following Satan, "the god of this age."

"If the Good News we preach is hidden to anyone, it is hidden from the one who is on the road to eternal death. Satan, who is the god of this evil world, has made him blind, unable to see the glorious light of the Gospel that is shining upon him, or to understand the amazing message we preach about the glory of Christ, who is God" (2 Corinthians 4:3-4, *Living Bible*).

Traveling Incognito

"The Devil's cleverest ruse is to make believe that he does not exist."[3]

This is the reason we see the ridiculous pictures of Satan with his horns and red suit, sporting a tail and an evil grin. If he is a comic figure or a mythical villain, there is little harm he can do except give us an occasional nightmare.

Satan's incognitos are cleverer than movie star disguises. He hides behind religion, intellectualism, poetry, art, music, psychology, human understanding, and even our human "self." The Bible says, "The whole world lies in the power of the evil one" (1 John 5:19).

All men are under Satan's rule until they are brought to Jesus Christ.

That's heavy! When we are faced with an "either-or" situation or a black and white choice, most of us would like to wiggle in the center with a "maybe" or charge through the middle wearing a gray hat. Modern thought rejects the antiquated idea that Satan is the origin of evil and has the world in his control. Man has so many explanations for evil: poverty, pollution, politicians, police, parents, employers, unions, racial minorities, racial majorities . . . choose your cause! Put the rap on someone, man says, but don't tell me about Satan. That's negative—unpleasant.

Christians are not exempt from this inability to understand where and how Satan is working. In fact, because his doctrine has been neglected for so long, they are sometimes the least discerning of all in understanding the world system. Young Christians are particularly vulnerable. As Francis Schaeffer has said, "We have left the next generation naked in the face of 20th century thought by which they are surrounded."[4]

Satan is not the man below, heaping coals into an eternal furnace. He's the original "jet-setter"; he's "right on" with the latest cause. When God asked Satan a direct question, his answer showed outrageous arrogance: "And the Lord said to Satan, From where do you come? And Satan—the adversary and the accuser—answered the Lord, From going to and fro on the earth, and from walking up and down on it" (Job 2:2, *Amplified Bible.*)

What a picture! Satan trucking all over the earth, constantly doing his thing in every spot he can! He's working in our world system through governments, education, business, and culture. You name it—he'll tame it.

This modern "promoter" has had some help from his advance men who began planning his twentieth century campaign a few hundred years ago. Stand by for the shock waves from the nineteenth century thought-bombs that are threatening to bring the whole civilization into Armageddon.

6 ○ Thought Bombs

"For the wisdom of this world is foolishness before God."

APOSTLE PAUL TO THE CORINTHIANS

"Our dialectical philosophy abolishes all the notions of absolute and definitive truth."

FREDERICK ENGELS IN A EULOGY TO KARL MARX

DATELINE WASHINGTON, NOVEMBER, 1971.

"The 5-megaton atomic explosion set off by the United States beneath Amchitka Island Saturday caused the largest earth tremor produced by man but resulted in no apparent damage outside the immediate vicinity of Amchitka."[1]

Who remembers Amchitka? The explosion on that remote island made Hiroshima look like a firecracker. And yet the blast from Amchitka was minor compared to the thought bombs set off by a few eighteenth and nineteenth century men who dreamed up ideas which have sent shock waves to rock our thinking today.

The contamination of these explosive ideas has been so devastating that it has completely permeated twentieth century thinking. The men who devised these thought bombs are the subject of this chapter. Satan took their concepts and wired the underlying frame of reference for our present historical, educational, philosophical, sociological, psychological, religious, economic, and political outlook. You and I and our children have been ingeniously conditioned to think in terms that are contrary to biblical principles and truths in all of these areas—and without our even realizing it.

There is only one person who had anything to gain by so radically conditioning the thinking of mankind, and that person is Satan. He was the real genius and impetus behind each of these men and their ideas which we are going to discuss.

I realize it is a serious charge to imply that these brilliant men, who in many ways made significant contributions to our world, were instruments of Satan to lead men's thinking away from eternal truths, but as the case against them unfolds I believe the conclusions will be justified.

You may find some of this pretty heavy reading, but it is absolutely essential that we understand how we have come to this present hostility toward God's viewpoint of life. The analysis of each man and his philosophy will be brief and confined to the specific areas where his thinking came into conflict with the Bible.

Bomb One: Kant

Immanuel Kant was a German philosopher. He never traveled more than sixty-nine miles from his home in Prussia, where he lived from 1724 to 1804, and yet his original thinking formulated principles which still sway the civilized world.

Until Kantian philosophy began to influence the intellectuals of the age, classical philosophy was based upon the process of antithesis, which means that man thought in terms of cause and effect. This means if A is true then non-A cannot also be true. According to classical philosophy, values were absolute.

The world at large accepted these possibilities of absolutes in both knowledge and morals. Before Kant you could reason with a person on the basis of cause and effect. However, this one man and his critiques began to question whether people could actually accept things which were beyond their five senses.

A modern French philosopher describes the Kantian thinking this way: "Kant was able to go definitively beyond scepticism and realism by recognizing the descriptive and irreducible characteristics of external and internal experience as the sufficient foundation of the world."[2]

In Kant's analysis of the process of thought he proposed that no one can know anything except by experience. He believed that individual freedom lies in obedience to the "moral law that speaks within us."[3]

Kant, therefore, finding no personal basis for accepting absolutes, triggered the ideas which would result in the philosophy introduced by another German.

Bomb Two: Hegel

Hegel took the ideas of Kant and began to press them forward. He lived from 1770 to 1831 and left a heritage of brutal and violent fallout which has invaded our century.

He was called the philosophical dictator of Germany. He believed that one fact or idea (thesis) working against another fact (antithesis) would produce a new fact (synthesis). This philosophy was the basis of the communistic political and economic ideas of Karl Marx and the National Socialism of Adolf Hitler.

Hegel glorified the state. He taught that the state did not have to obey moral laws, nor did governments have to keep agreements. Hitler followed this philosophy to perfection.

According to the Hegelian thought, everything was relative. This gave man an approach to truth, an approach to life, in which there were no absolutes, only terms of relativity.

When Hegel introduced the philosophical basis for relative thinking and rejected absolutes, he literally altered the future course of the world. Absolutes are unchangeable truths from which you can reason from cause to effect. In relative thinking you are dealing with subjective thought in which cause and effect have no part. Relativity is based upon changeableness. When you think in this manner, you say, "Well, how do you feel about it now?"

As Hegel did away with cause-and-effect logic, there was no need for ultimate truth. With the elimination of an ultimate cause or truth, man could plunge headlong away from any necessity of believing in a Creator-God.

This philosophy of relative thinking soon permeated the higher educational systems of Europe and America. The sad progress (?) afterward was simple: the more educated people became, the more they rejected absolutes of God, truth, and morals. Even those who had a true faith in Jesus Christ found their faith weakened in college, but it was hard to discover why.

Dr. Francis Schaeffer in his great book, *The God Who Is There*, shows that it wasn't so much that truth was being attacked as it was the very presuppositional basis for truth. This was much more subtle.

Today the average college student who hasn't been born spiritually through personal faith in Jesus Christ doesn't believe in the possibility of absolute truth. Relative thinking has now been brought down to the earliest levels of elementary education. It is a Trojan Horse which few Christian parents understand, much less actively fight.

Bomb Three: Kierkegaard

Out of Denmark in the nineteenth century came a philosophical theologian, Soren Kierkegaard. Although he came from a Christian environment, he rejected the generally accepted beliefs of the Lutheran Church, the established church of Denmark.

Kierkegaard was a great influence in the theology of his time and is considered the father of contemporary existentialism. His writings are a denial of the basic tenets of the Christian faith and show a disdain for those who do not agree with his intellectual pursuits. He was the first man to launch a system of thought in which despair was the underlying current. In two books which Kierkegaard himself called "the most perfect books I have written," *Fear and Trembling* and *The Sickness Unto Death*, the very titles reflect that mood of despondency.

Kierkegaard believed that a man comes to a point in his life when he concludes that he cannot find any definite reasons for truth or for life. To find purpose he has to take a leap of faith which has no rationality behind it at all.

In the writings of Kierkegaard there is contempt for those who do not think on his intellectual plane. It is understandable that his philosophy would not accept biblical truths. For instance, in his volume *Fear and Trembling* he wrote scornfully, "One not infrequently hears it said by men who for lack of losing themselves in studies are absorbed in phrases that a light shines upon the Christian world whereas a darkness broods over paganism. This utterance has always seemed strange to me, inasmuch as every profound thinker and every serious artist is even in our day rejuvenated by the eternal youth of the Greek race."[4]

Kierkegaard was one of the foremost proponents of the philosophy which has swept the intellectual world right down to our time. He introduced the tenets of Kant and Hegel into the theology of the Christian faith. The idea that there is no rational basis for things beyond the five senses, but that we must take an irrational leap of blind faith to find purpose in life came out of Kant's teaching. The idea that there is no absolute truth and we must therefore find relative reasons upon which to base our life resulted from Hegel's teaching. This was the beginning of "existential thought."

I believe this gave a philosophical framework for "the doctrines of demons" which Paul said would sweep the world in the latter times before the return of Christ. When Karl Barth came along in the early twentieth century and developed a "new" system of theology called "Neo-Orthodoxy" (which was neither new nor orthodox), this existential, relative thinking became thoroughly spread throughout the Christian church.

Bomb Four: Marx

Karl Marx, one of the most influential men to explode his ideas onto the world scene, was a German who was born in 1818 and came from a long line of outstanding scholars and rabbis. His father broke his religious family tradition and became a Protestant when Karl was a child.

Karl was a brilliant student and, from what we learn from his biographers, a man who did not make or keep friends. Hot-tempered, brooding, and intense, he allowed his wife and half-starved children to live in cruel poverty while he devoted himself to his intellectual studies.

Marx and the only close friend he ever had, Friedrich Engels, were co-workers for many years in the movement which has changed the course of modern history.

As we see the vast chain of influence established by the philosophers and writers in the nineteenth century, it shouldn't be surprising that Marx became involved at the University of Berlin with a left-wing group which followed the philosophy of Hegel. Their main thrust at that time was to throw out Christianity. Marx was inspired in his intellectual quest to start a movement to remake the world. (At least that desire was partially fulfilled generations after his death.)

When Marx and Engels got together to formulate the great blueprint which would make this warring planet a utopia, they had already decided that the main way it could be achieved was through a classless society. They saw the proletariat (the class of wage labor) in a state of war, or conflict, with the bourgeoisie (the class of property ownership). According to Marxist thinking, the property owners were the exploiters, and the workers were the exploited.

Marxism applies the principle of dialectics, or the art of reasoning, to this inevitable class struggle in a manner in which we may readily see the influence of Hegel. Three elements are at work: the thesis (a positive force) and the antithesis (the opposing force) resulting in a clash which would produce a new idea of force (a synthesis). This clash would provide the dynamics which would catapult society into some new development.

Marx and Engels believed that this great and glorious class struggle would eliminate the cause of all past conflicts in society. They thought that the cause of all the human struggles and war could be traced to that terrible evil—private property. If the great class uprising overthrew private property, then there would be nothing to fight over and everyone could live happily ever after.

To remake the world along the lines of this classless society, Marxism employs every weapon: not just bombs, guns, and tanks, but also the weapons of education, religion, trade, economics, and culture. The material improvement of society will be brought about by whatever methods are useful to the cause. The end justifies the means.

Goals established by Marx were: abolish private property; centralize all power in the hands of the state; control the world. Collectivize, centralize, control.

Marx believed the property class used religion as a device to suppress the "exploited class." This extended into the philosophy of modern Communism which has a few basics: everything can be explained by matter (the

Russian cosmonaut who saw no signs of God in the stratosphere); materialism is the beginning and end of reality.

"The communist intellectual believes that everything in existence came about as a result of ceaseless motion among the forces of nature. Everything is a product of accumulated accident. There is no design. There is no law. There is no God. There is only matter and force in nature."[5]

Marx justified violence to achieve the new classless society, although he expounded the social and economic ideals of utopian Communism. His ideas and his aims have permeated every aspect of twentieth century thought and life.

The late J. Edgar Hoover said, "Communism is many things: an economic system, a philosophy, a political creed, a psychological conditioning, an educational indoctrination, a directed way of life."[6]

It is time for the world to realize that Communism is not just another political philosophy, but a religion--a religion which promises utopia to its devotees. The state is worshiped in place of God. Communism deals with such basic issues as: What is man? What is man's most basic problem? How can man be delivered from his problem? What is man's destiny? In all these points Communism gives answers which are diametrically opposed to God's truth.

Bomb Five: Darwin

When Charles Darwin, an Englishman of the nineteenth century, came on the scene, he caused a real sensation in the scientific and nonscientific world. Darwin amassed a vast amount of scientific facts and presented a theory dealing with the development of plants and animals. This theory, in simple form, said that living things increase more rapidly than people realize. Earth cannot provide room and food for all the offspring of these living things; members of each species then compete for a chance to live. This competition brings about a process called natural selection, or the preservation of those life forms best adapted to survive in the struggle for existence. In essence, this is the belief that lower forms advance to higher forms in this struggle for existence.

When Darwin took his theories out of the plant and animal kingdoms and transferred them to man, the sparks flew that ignited educational fires right into our time. On one hand was Darwin's widely held theory that all life, including man, evolved from lower forms, and on the other was the

Bible which in the Genesis account states that God created man, animals, and plants "after their kind"; they did not evolve from lower forms.

Conflict! Hegel and Marx would be happy—a scientist using their theories of thesis, antithesis, and synthesis.

Today, although we hear a great deal about the *theory* of evolution, even some reference books place it in the category of fact. A new reference series says, "The popular conception that Darwinism is simply the theory of evolution applied to the origin of man is far from correct. Its novelty lies not in the conception of evolution, but in an explosion of a probable cause of evolution so clear and cogent as to remove the theory from the sphere of philosophical speculation to that of practical life."[7]

In *The Naked Ape*, a book which has been widely recommended by high school and college teachers to their psychology students, the author states, "If we accept the history of our evolution, then one fact stands out clearly: namely that we have arisen essentially as primate predators."[8] This nurtures the idea that since man is no more than an animal, he should act like one.

Hegel introduced the philosophical basis for man to see no necessity for a Creator-God. Darwin introduced what seemed to be a scientific basis for not believing in a Creator-God to whom man was responsible. The impact of this thought bomb is that since man had no special beginning, he has no special purpose or destiny. This thinking leads many to sink into amoral behavior, disorientation, and despair.

Bomb Six: Freud

Sigmund Freud, born in the middle of the nineteenth century in Austria, was "very attracted to Darwin's theories because they offered the prospect of an extraordinary advance of human knowledge."[9]

Freud, the founder of psychoanalysis, was an atheist. His ideas, his teachings, his concept of the unconscious have become so fundamental to the mental attitude of the twentieth century that "without them much of modern life is unintelligible."[10]

Freud defines psychoanalysis as a "method of treatment for those suffering from nervous disorders."[11] The doctrine which promoted this type of treatment is based upon Freud's fundamental views of human nature—views which have formed the basis for the permissive society in which we live today.

Whether a person today knows anything about Freud or not, whether he only thinks Freud is someone who invented those "slips" we hear mentioned so frequently, or whether he is a student who has studied his works for years, all are products of the Freudian ethic.

What did Freud believe? The human race is motivated chiefly by pleasure; everything starts and ends with sex. Man is repressed by society in the fulfillment of his unconscious drive for gratification of his erotic desires; this repression makes him unhappy. The consequence of the conflict between our pleasure-seeking instincts and the repression exerted by our society is neurosis.

"Freud's doctrines, and particularly his ethics, are the product of his concept of the human race. There is no purpose in man's existence. There is no goal in mankind's presence on earth. There is no God . . . and if this is so, all is permitted."[12]

Freud firmly laid the groundwork for extreme permissiveness. He simply set forth the logical conclusions of behavior for man as the highest form of the evolutionary chain.

A prominent doctor has written, ". . . the intellectuals and the wealthy promote and defend an extreme permissiveness without even realizing that they are contaminated by the Freudian ethic, the ethic which declares that all is permitted, that the permissiveness syndrome is the natural drive of a human being to be free from society and that it should not be repressed or even controlled."[13]

The interest in sex, which was just getting a fleshhold in the beginning of American Freudianism, has exploded in our time. It is ironic, however, that the influence of the Freudian ethic is growing fast while his brainchild, psychoanalysis, seems to be dying.

Freud's Fruits

We are reaping the fruits of permissiveness. There is a criminal homicide every thirty-three minutes in the United States. America is "maintaining its long held, unhappy distinction of leading advanced Western nations in the rate at which its citizens destroy one another. . . . It has led many behavioral scientists to begin talking about a national 'crisis of violence'."[14]

The pattern we see is from permissiveness to disintegration. The state of disarray in the American family, fostered in our permissive society, has contributed to the runaway phenomenon. Each week more than 10,000 American children run away from homes, schools, and institutions. Why? The shock waves from these thought bombs are beginning to rip our society apart.

One young runaway said, "I was really spoiled by my mother. She should have said 'No' to me when I was small. Now she's trying to correct the mistake and says 'No' to everything, but it's too late."[15]

A police officer in an upper-class Chicago suburb said, "It becomes a form of blackmail that the kids use on the parent. Maybe the parent won't let the kid stay out as late as he wants, so he runs away. Some of these parents have taken threats from their kids from the time they were small. They ought to call the kids' bluff and not give in."[16]

Many of our modern mind manipulators, the educational theorists of twentieth century America, don't know the difference between a free society and a permissive society. One syndicated columnist wrote: "Under their mushy tutelage, we have raised two generations of children to suppose that discipline is cruel, that obedience is a sometime thing."[17]

The advocates of the permissive school are watching with horror the grades which are being handed out in the form of violence, alienation of their children, and tragic disintegration of families.

Evolution to Revolution: Lenin

The thought bombs are coming closer to our age. Lenin died some fifty years ago, leaving a heritage of brutality and violence to following generations. Probably more than any other man, Lenin is the builder of modern Communism. He took a philosophy and added the activism.

Lenin was not a simpleton. He had an outstanding record as a law student and became a staunch Marxist. He had one very basic belief: atheism. He referred to religion as the "opiate of the people."

Lenin used terror, murder, and secret police to crush all opposition to his counter-revolutionary ideas and emerged the dictator of Soviet Russia. He believed that to be successful revolution must be masterminded by a small, utterly loyal group of trained revolutionaries, and with this intensity of belief he succeeded in creating a force which would cross national boundaries and unite socialists in a universal class. This group would settle for nothing less than a world-wide Communist victory.

In 1917 Lenin declared, "We will destroy everything and on the ruins we will build our temple! It will be a temple for the happiness of all. But we will destroy the entire bourgeoisie, grind it to a powder. . . . I will be merciless with all counter-revolutionaries."

Since 1917 history has witnessed the impact of what Lenin meant: Hungary, Czechoslovakia, East Germany, The Balkans, Cuba, China.

In the Communist philosophy, man is treated with the cold logic of "survival of the fittest." Since there is no God, and since man has no special destiny or purpose, but is simply matter in motion, he can be disposed of without conscience. Individual life is unimportant. The State is all.

Demons on the Front Line

At times Satan works openly in the world system through the governments and leaders of countries. It has frequently been said, even by those people who have little knowledge or belief in supernatural beings, that Adolf Hitler was demon-possessed. However, the extent of influence upon the course of Germany's history by another strange and little-known man, who by his own admission was demon-possessed, is an astonishing fact shared by William L. Shirer. "It is probably no exaggeration to say, as I have heard more than one follower of Hitler say, that Chamberlain (Houston Steward Chamberlain, one of the strangest Englishmen who ever lived) was the spiritual founder of the Third Reich."[18]

Here is Shirer's description of Chamberlain, the man who inspired Hitler and his insane reign of terror and power: "Hypersensitive and neurotic and subject to frequent nervous breakdowns, Chamberlain was given to seeing demons who, by his own account, drove him on relentlessly to seek new fields of study and to get on with his prodigious writings. One vision after another forced him to change from biology to botany, to the fine arts, to music, to philosophy, to biography, to history. Once, in 1898, when he was returning from Italy, the presence of a demon became so forceful that he got off the train at Gardone, shut himself up in a hotel room for eight days and, abandoning some work on music that he had contemplated, wrote feverishly on a biological thesis until he had the germ of the theme that would dominate all of his later works: race and history.

"Since he felt himself goaded on by demons, his books (on Wagner, Goethe, Kant, Christianity, and race) were written in the grip of a terrible fever, a veritable trance, a state of self-induced intoxication, so that, as he says in his autobiography, *Lebenswege*, he was often unable to recognize them as his own work.

"But it was on the Third Reich, which did not arrive until six years after his death but whose coming he foresaw, that this Englishman's influence was the greatest. His racial theories and his burning sense of the destiny of the Germans and Germany were taken over by the Nazis, who acclaimed him as one of their prophets. During the Hitler regime books, pamphlets and articles poured from the presses extolling the 'spiritual founder' of National Socialist Germany."

The Deep Things of Satan

As I examined the philosophies of the men and movements which have influenced the past two centuries, I began to understand what Revelation 2 means when it speaks of the deep things of Satan (Revelation 2:24). There are very deep things behind the thought patterns of our time, introduced by many of the philosophical munitions-makers from the past. These are the men who led the way for man's approach to truth today.

Most secular education (apart from that which is related to the Christian form of truth which is in the Bible) is based upon these concepts. When we think about morality in the world, there is no way of establishing what is right and what is wrong because there is no way of relating it to God. Morality becomes a system based on the Gallup Poll. That's where we're at. That is the kind of thinking that has spread throughout the educated world.

The world system has established this atmosphere of thought that subtly seeks to gain footholds in the believer's thinking. Once this is done, a steady pressure is exerted to pull him away from the divine viewpoint of life.

Thank God that ". . . the weapons of our warfare are not of the flesh (i.e. human resources), but divinely powerful for the destruction of fortresses. We are destroying speculations and every lofty thing raised up against the *knowledge of God*, and we are taking every *thought* captive to the obedience of Christ" (2 Corinthians 10:4-5).

As we simply keep our eye of faith focused upon Jesus' ability to work within us and keep trusting Him to teach us God's Word, we find that "greater is He who is in you than he who is in the world (system)" (1 John 4:4).

7 ○ Mind Manipulators

THOUGHT CONTROL REVOLTS me. Free men should be able to think for themselves.

I remember a science fiction movie which impressed me with its far-reaching implications. It was probably grade B, rated G—scarcely a contestant for an Academy Award—but I'll never forget it.

Creatures from outer space invaded this planet, captured human beings, and took them to their space ship. When they had the earth people bound and anesthetized, they planted little electrical receivers in the back of their heads. The invaders held the controlling transmitters and returned the earthlings to their jobs and society. Some of the people on remote control killed their own husbands and wives, committed despicable crimes, and changed their life styles into parodies of their former selves because their thoughts and actions were being controlled by these extraterrestrial invaders.

That describes Satan exactly. He is an extraterrestrial invader who has planted his receiver deep in every human heart. This receiver is called "the flesh" or the sin nature. He also flashes his messages into our minds through the vast, highly organized world system he controls. This is why God tells us, "For the weapons of our warfare are not of the flesh, but divinely powerful for destruction of fortresses. For our struggle is not against flesh and blood, but against the rulers, against the powers, against the world-forces of this darkness . . ." (2 Corinthians 10:4; Ephesians 6:12).

Extremes of criminal behavior are not the only ways in which Satan works. His control of the atmosphere of thought in the world system is more deadly than the cold steel of a gun in your back. His *modus operandi* has been so successful that even Christians are constantly being lured from the divine viewpoint of life into Satan's web of deceit. Bombarded from every direction, undermined by the philosophy, education, art forms, music, mass media, styles, and fashions of the day, the world system will whirl us into its cesspool if we do not understand how we are being pushed and where we can slip.

Satan has always created confusion in the world. Nineteen centuries ago the Apostle Paul emphatically warned Christians: "See to it that no one takes you captive through philosophy and empty deception, according to the tradition of men, according to the elementary principles of the world, rather than according to Christ" (Colossians 2:8-9).

This is the warning: we are not to be taken captive by Satan through philosophy, which he has always used as a subtle, logical means of leading the minds of men away from the Truth. Today these philosophical deviations are more powerfully used than at any other time.

Twentieth century mind manipulation takes many forms. In the fields of psychology and sociology one of the modern social planners to hit the scene in a big way is B. F. Skinner.

Skinner Dipping

In 1971 *Time* magazine had a cover story about the man who says "we can no longer afford freedom, and so it must be replaced with control over man, his conduct and his culture."[1] This thesis, proposed not by a fiction writer, but by a man of science, raises the specter of a 1984 Orwellian society that may become reality.

B. F. Skinner, called by *Time* the "most influential of living American psychologists," reasons that free will is an illusion; he claims that since man is already controlled by external influences, he should plan his environment so that desired behavior will be guaranteed. In the Skinnerian world, utopia would be achieved by conditioning man to serve group interests.

How could this be done? Skinner believes that "human behavior can be predicted and shaped exactly as if it were a chemical reaction." The way to do it, he thinks, is through "behavioral technology," a developing science of control that aims to change the environment rather than people, that seeks to alter actions rather than feelings, and that shifts the customary psychological emphasis from the world inside men to the world outside them.

Skinner is said to believe that an "inner man is a superstition that originated, like belief in God, in man's inability to understand his world."[2] This leading exponent of behaviorism would deny the very existence of a soul-life, much less the possibility of needing a spiritual birth.

This is an extreme view of manipulating man, and many reputable psychologists reject Skinner's methods. However, the frightening thing about Skinner's book, *Beyond Freedom and Dignity*, is that some young intellectuals are beginning to take it seriously. Who would have dreamed that the writings of Karl Marx would find such dedicated adherents—or that Chamberlain's mad thesis of a master race would inspire fanatic zeal for its principles within one generation?

All that radical new panaceas for world problems need in order to flourish are crisis times and satanically inspired leaders like Lenin and Hitler. Could it be that the long-dreaded figure of Bible prophecy, the Antichrist, will rise up to implement Dr. Skinner's basic tenets into reality? According to the latest projections of scientists, scholars, and statesmen, the times just ahead will be right for such a phenomenon. The greatest crises in the history of man are a mathematical certainty according to the computerized projects of "Project Predicament of Man," sponsored by the prestigious international group called the Club of Rome.[3]

But before the young intellectuals of high school and college age are confronted with some of the more advanced techniques of a Skinner, they have been made pliable by the mind-bending in their pre-school and public school years.

Never Bend Over

Perhaps nowhere does the modern world viewpoint become more obviously opposed to God's viewpoint than in the area of the parent-child relationship. Basic concepts of discipline, respect for authority, absolutes, and morality have been radically changed in the concepts of child-rearing and the public educational system.

The permissive syndrome is not something new, but recent generations have been nurtured on it from the seeds planted by such men as Freud, Dewey, and Spock. These men led the way in applying relative thinking and life patterns without rules at the child level.

Freud's philosophy is complex, but is best described by his theory of "repression." Again and again in his writings, Freud returns to the question of man's repression by the society in which he lives. "Repression is the basic factor in man's unhappiness, in his inner conflicts, for society represses the individual, and thus the individual is forced to repress himself."[4]

Freudian thinking is that problems from childhood to adulthood are the result of being repressed, but the Bible says: "Correct your son, and he will give you comfort; He will also delight your soul" (Proverbs 29:17).

John Dewey, a man who threw out the traditional concepts of a few generations ago (that there are fixed moral laws and eternal truths), was a man who rejected God and the idea that man has a soul. His educational theories scorned individualism and promoted the idea that man should lose his individuality by finding acceptance and absorption in the great mass. Dewey's educational philosophy was built upon permissive principles, although the ideas were termed "progressive education," not permissive education. The Progressive Education Association, inspired by Dewey's views, put some of his doctrines into their code by expressions such as these: "The conduct of the pupils shall be governed by themselves, according to the social needs of the community," and "Interest shall be the motive for all work."[5]

What does all this mean? Erich Fromm, well-known psychologist, wrote: "The basic principle of such self-determination was the replacement of authority by freedom, to teach the child without the use of force by appealing to his curiosity . . . this attitude marked the beginning of progressive education and was an important step in human development."[6] Certainly a teacher should strive to be interesting and to capture the child's natural curiosity. But what these men proposed was education without specific requirements or structure.

Diametrically opposed to this way of thinking stands God's instructions, "Foolishness is bound up in the heart of a child; the rod of discipline will remove it far from him" (Proverbs 22:15).

Dr. Benjamin Spock, the pediatrician turned politician, in his famous handbook for parents, *Baby and Child Care*, advised the parents of the present generation not to restrict the permissiveness complex of children. Spock's advice was followed by thousands of inexperienced parents who raised their children with his book under one arm and the baby in the other. Parents were told not to spank, but to reason. According to the Dewey-Spock school of thought, the old-fashioned strap and woodshed principles were not a demonstration of love.

God wants us to discipline our children, but He certainly doesn't condone brutality. Some of the cruel beatings and punishments which are practiced by those who vent their own frustrations and hatreds upon children are despicable.

Children will test their parents to the limit. They will irritate, misbehave, and disobey until parental authority is backed up with action, not occasionally, but consistently.

God is not cruel; He is just—which is why He disciplines His children with love. And this is how He commands us to discipline our children—in love, not anger.

The Bible says, "He who spares his rod hates his son, but he who loves him disciplines him diligently" (Proverbs 13:24).

To discipline diligently means steadily, constantly, tirelessly, and patiently. It is not a sometime thing.

Radical Result in Education

Although the permissive philosophy of the Dewey followers has seeped through our educational system in various ways, there are few who would admit that the extreme theories of a comparative unknown by the name of A. S. Neill are acceptable in our public school systems. However, if you ask most college students in teacher-education courses if they have heard of "Summerhill," they would say "yes."

A. S. Neill started his radical approach to child rearing at his school, "Summerhill," in England. The Summerhill method has spread to the United States and is being used in many private schools and experimental public schools. If Neill's ideas were not required reading in so many college courses and were not so widely accepted in intellectual circles, they might not be important in this section about education. But what B. F. Skinner is to the extreme in psychological thought, Neill is to the extreme in educational circles.

At Summerhill, and the other schools patterned after it, there are no rules, no established courses of study. Freedom is the ultimate; happiness is the aim. "There is no need whatsoever to teach children how to behave. A child will learn what is right and what is wrong in good time . . . provided he is not pressured."[7]

Neill believes that all children are born good; therefore, there is no need for redemption. He believes that moral instruction makes a child bad, that "there is no case whatever for the moral instruction of children."[8]

The man who has spawned this radical approach to education writes: ". . . I repeat that parents are spoiling their children's lives by forcing on them outdated beliefs, outdated manners, outdated morals."[9]

The Bible says, "Train up a child in the way he should go, even when he is old he will not depart from it" (Proverbs 22:6).

Train . . . in the Way He Should Go

A cartoon in the Los Angeles Times showed a bound and gagged Statue of Liberty with a professor leaning over her saying, "Look, all I want is the truth, the whole truth, and nothing but the truth . . . as I see it."

Much of the formal education we have today is a product of "the truth . . . as I see it." As the permissive school of education has been built, the social engineers have been the builders—striving for a new world, a better society through guiding man and his behavior.

Bertrand Russell said: "Man now needs for his salvation only one thing: to open his heart to joy. He must lift up his eyes and say: 'No, I am not a miserable sinner.'"[10]

The Bible says, "It is a trustworthy statement, deserving full acceptance, that Christ Jesus came into the world to save sinners . . . for all have sinned and fall short of the glory of God" (1 Timothy 1:15; Romans 3:23).

H. G. Wells said: "It is the triangle of Socialism, Law and Knowledge which frames the Revolution that may yet save the world."[11]

The Bible says of Jesus, "And there is salvation in no one else; for there is no other name under heaven that has been given among men, by which we must be saved" (Acts 4:12).

These men will never come up with an adequate cure for man's basic problems because they have started with a wrong diagnosis.

And so the social planners and educational engineers continue, believing man is basically good and that he can somehow elevate society and create a better world by his own efforts. Meanwhile, the school system abolishes absolutes and rips moral values as it is caught in the grip of the world system.

Students and parents must wake up! We need to carefully evaluate what the educational system is advancing in the methods of the mind manipulators. As further effort is made to centralize and control education, there is more urgency than ever to learn and understand what God's truth is.

Mind Manipulators . . . in Art

It's "in" to be arty. There is no doubt that art has a real impact on the times. Or perhaps we should say that the times have an impact upon art.

A professor of fine art at the University of Edinburgh said, "Art is a mirror of its age . . . each age gets the art it deserves."[12]

A man's world view will permeate everything he creates. If the artist accepts a philosophy of life where there are no absolutes, no way of knowing definite purpose, his art will reflect this. This is one reason why a psychoanalyst will ask a patient to draw a picture. The way the patient sketches his surroundings and life can be very self-revealing.

Much art today ranges from the lewd to the absurd. You don't have to be a connoisseur to be hit in your subconscious by the obscenities which are expressed by some modern artists. Art is one of the most powerful mediums which affect the way a person thinks about life.

In analyzing some of the leading exponents of the new art, an art critic wrote: "There is some evidence that the climate of New York may now have become almost too favorable for heresies and radical experiments of all kinds. The appearance of a large and militantly avant-garde audience, a shockproof public that greedily accepts whatever is offered in the name of art so long as it is certifiably new and it has impressed Duchamp, among others, is proof that the long decline of Western art has now reached its nadir."[13]

H. R. Rookmaaker, an art history professor in Amsterdam, in documenting the main art trends from the Renaissance to the twentieth century, says, "Modern art in its more consistent forms puts a question mark against all values and principles."

Modern art, according to Rookmaaker, has won the battle and become the official art of today. "If in the wake of this avalanche of modern work of all kinds there is a strong anarchistic trend among the younger generation we must not be surprised." He believes that the modern movement of revolution in art has won because Christians were not alert. He says that his fellow Christians have not understood that art and literature, philosophy and even popular music are the agents of the "new spirit of the age" and have "left these alone or optimistically assumed they were too remote to be of influence."

Music . . . for the Masses

Satan works subliminally in the area of music. We are being bombarded, and we don't know what is hitting us. I was astounded as I began to study this subject. Basically I'm ignorant about music, and yet I realize that it is a powerful means of provoking emotions. Henry Thoreau, the new-old hero of many youth, prophesied in *Walden*: "Even music may be intoxicating. Such apparently slight causes destroyed Greece and Rome, and will destroy England and America."

I heard a professor of sociology speak on trends in music, and about rock in particular. This man was not an ivory-tower member of the academy speaking without experience. He was a member of the musician's union and had been a professional trumpet player for fifteen years. He explained that harmonic and rhythmic fabrics of rock music are critically important. And it's not necessary to comprehend the intricacies of music to understand what's being done with it.

This former jazz man described how changes in rhythm and other musical techniques can be used to sell attitudes and concepts. Many of Pavlov's experiments were conducted with a metronome to research the effects of rhythms as a conditioning agent.

By changing the rhythm within a musical piece, you may have a strong impact on the listener. The subconscious effect is to push the message more strongly.

The ability of music to excite and incite is nothing new. In primitive societies music's chief function is arousing emotion and action. However, in civilized countries music is more a means of communicating pleasurable emotions, not creating havoc.

Today, in some of our popular music at least, we seem to be reverting to savagery. The most dramatic indication of this is the number of times that rock concerts have erupted into riots.

I'm not trying to blast all modern music, but I think we should be aware of the fact that Satan can use it as his tool to pull us away from God and into chaotic thinking.

Poison in the Popcorn

When movie critics open their reviews with a social analysis of cinema artlessness, it is a sign that the concern for the evil impact of the media is widespread. A reviewer on one of America's largest dailies wrote: "As has often been observed, the loss of faith in technology in these perilous times is reflected in the resurgence of interest in astrology, psychic phenomena and even Satanism.

"The new preoccupation with the occult is also reflected in movies. The overwhelming success of *Rosemary's Baby* showed that film makers no longer needed to come up with rational last-reel explanations for seemingly supernatural goings-on. . . . In short, what several years ago most people would have dismissed as superstition in its ugliest form is in some quarters being taken seriously, regarded as 'purifying' or 'enlightening'."[15]

It's not difficult to see how Satan is using the world of entertainment to advance his kingdom. When movies are not presenting sex, violence, or Satanic themes, we see blatant mocking of the Christian faith. One movie rated GP (which means parents send their children in blind confidence) was *The Reincarnate*. The advertisement blared "No Heaven . . . No Hell . . . No Guilt! Eternal life is the only reality!" The subtitle to the film announced it was "A fascinating tale of the occult."

We've come a long way since the old Clark Gable era when the most daring escapade in the movies was a scene in "It Happened One Night" where Gable and Claudette Colbert made a curtain out of a blanket and put it between their beds when they were forced to spend the night in a cabin. They called the blanket the "Walls of Jericho," but today the movie makers have torn down the walls and turned them into crumpled bed sheets.

Reel life is supposed to depict real life, but the themes of some of the films are unreal. Counterfeit Christianity is one favorite. One issue of *Time* magazine carried two reviews, one of a film called *Black Jesus*, the other *Sweet Savior*. The first described a scene in which an African leader, a world-famous apostle of nonviolence, was brought before the local Pontius Pilate, cast into jail with a thief, and tortured with nails driven into his hands. The *Sweet Savior* description said: "The movie gloats over its scenes of degenerate sex and reaches a climax in human butchery . . . a symptom of a social disease."[16]

To their credit, many movie makers are trying to cure this social disease, but the virus has a head start.

The Eye in Our Living Room

Nowhere is the theme of permissiveness more subtly presented than through television. One popular comedy program shows "love" as the inevitable chase in and out of the bedroom, enjoyed in unmarried bliss. Many programs glamorize the social drink and burlesque the social drunk. The media is sanctimonious about eliminating cigarette advertising but liberal with suggestive jokes.

Talk shows have a way of reflecting the bias of the interviewer and the opinions of the audience. On one interview show a much-married celebrity was telling about a wedding ceremony he had recently attended where the vows exchanged between the bride and groom ended ". . . as long as we both shall love." The comments from Mr. Celeb were: "Isn't that a groovy idea. None of this Victorian idea of repeating 'as long as we both shall live.' " The audience reacted with applause, and the master of ceremonies agreed.

From cartoons to comedy, the mind benders use the television controls to channel us in the mold of the world system.

One World Economic System

Satan . . . the unifier. System and control are essential ingredients in his world system. In the vast area of economics and business, a trend toward a world economy with a centralized money exchange would be one tool which could be used to manage the purse strings of the world.

Is a world economic system possible?

A UPI report in 1968 said: "Rune Hoglund, president of Sweden's largest bank, said the long-term solution of international gold and monetary problems is establishment of an international paper currency issued by the International Monetary Fund."[17]

Most of us have little knowledge of the machinations of international banking or what effects it has upon our personal lives. However, one trend toward a moneyless society should be obvious to all of us with our bulging billfolds. Credit card living is a future probability. "Bankers in one city after another refer to it as 'the credit card revolution'."[18]

According to a 1967 report, in a two-year span of time the number of banks offering credit card services jumped from one hundred to fifteen hundred. Two years later *U.S. News* reported "an upheaval now going on in banks across the country."[19] This involved setting up holding companies which own a bank in addition to other businesses. The chairman of the Federal Reserve Board feared that holding companies might lead to undue concentration of economic power in the hands of the banks.

Many other economic manipulations can be used to centralize control in the hands of a few: industry taken from the free market economy and placed under state control; destruction of individual initiative through excessive taxation; regulatory laws which strangle private enterprise; government intervention into every aspect of private affairs.

A future world ruler will have his stage set if a one-world economic system is within his grasp.

Short Change

This whole system of thought has one fatal presupposition. "You can cure all of man's ills by changing or manipulating his environment."

The center of Jesus Christ's teaching was that man's problem is in his very heart and nature, and that you can only heal man by giving him an inner transformation, a new nature. Such a thing is possible only by a miraculous working of God's power called "the new birth." Jesus explained that man must be born spiritually because he is born into this world with a vacuum at the center of his being. He has physical life by which he can relate to the phenomena of this world, but he is without a spiritual dimension through which he can know God personally.

Jesus said, "Men can only reproduce human life, but the Holy Spirit gives new life from heaven; so don't be surprised at my statement that you must be born again!" (John 3:6-7, *Living Bible*).

Stop the World, I Want to Get Off

Any normal, sane person must be saying by now, "Stop the world, I want to get off!" But we can't stop the world or the world system. What can we do then? Mainly, we must be aware of how Satan is using art, music, philosophy, education, economics, and the mass media to entice us away from God's view of life. I think it's about time that we realize what is meant in James 4:4: "You adulteresses, do you not know that friendship with the world is hostility toward God? Therefore whoever wishes to be a friend of the world makes himself an enemy of God."

Why does James use the word "adulteresses"? If you have personally believed in Jesus Christ and accepted forgiveness from Him, you are married to Christ in a spiritual sense. When you go back to the world's way, figuratively you are committing adultery.

"Do you not know that friendship with the world is hostility toward God?" means that anyone who makes a friend of the world system is an enemy of God.

The world is a real battlefield in the area of our minds and our affections. We need the Spirit of God to give us careful discernment about what we allow to bombard our minds. This is why the Scripture says: "Do not love the world, nor the things in the world. If any one loves the world, the love of the Father is not in him" (1 John 2:15).

What Wavelength Are You On?

If we think we can get into these deceptive things of the world and still remain on intimate terms with God, we are deluding ourselves. We won't lose our relationship with God, but we will get so disoriented spiritually that we cannot think God's thoughts. We can't be intimate with God when our affections are dominated by the world. We are on a different wavelength.

When Jesus told us we are to be *"in* the world but not *of* it," He meant that we are not to cop out or drop out but to reject the world's hold on our affections and mental attitudes. Then we can be part of the solution for the world instead of part of the problem.

We need more Christian writers, artists, business people, and educators who will produce works that express God's viewpoint. This is not a time for withdrawal; this is a time for involvement!

Needed: A New World

H. G. Wells said, "Either Mankind collapses or our species struggles up by the hard, fairly obvious routes I have collated in this book to reach a new level of social organization."[20]

The philosophers of the day try to find unity and reason in this mixed-up world. However, they shut themselves off from the only hope—Jesus Christ.

More and more I see what Jesus meant when He said, "You shall know the truth, and the truth shall make you free" (John 8:32).

Jesus Christ is not a concept of truth; He is Truth. That is why He is the only one who can set us free from the established world order. He is the only one who can give us the freedom to find the full potential that God intended us to have. He is the only one who can give meaning and definition and purpose to life.

I am not speaking theoretically. I am speaking out of experience.

By the time I was twenty-six years old, I had tried everything and was saying, "Okay, now what do I do for an encore?" I'd run out. I began thinking about committing suicide. It was only then that I reached out, with no faith at all, to read the third chapter of John. To my amazement, Someone took my hand; He turned on the lights, and I found that Someone was Jesus Christ.

In this world where men have cut their moorings from God and values, there is only one real hope: to be born spiritually by faith in Jesus Christ. For those who are, it is the most exciting time to be alive. Things are happening so quickly today that I can hardly keep them catalogued—no one can.

Revolutionaries, social planners, humanistic philosophers . . . attention, please! A New World order will be established someday. When Jesus Christ returns, He is going to throw out the garbage of the world system and then —and only then—we will see perfect equality and peace.

That time is coming when believers in Jesus Christ are going to walk upon this earth and see it in perfect condition. Pollution will be passé.

Jesus Christ is going to recycle the late great Planet Earth.

8 ∘ Angels of Light

"...for even Satan disguises himself as an angel of light. Therefore it is not surprising if his servants also disguise themselves as servants of righteousness...."

2 CORINTHIANS 11:14-15

As THE MASS media bombards us with instant news, it also programs us with future forecasts. Modern-day prophets manipulate minds by anticipating things to come.

Newspaper columns, best seller lists, and television talk shows are spouting prophecies, and the current prophets are prolific in their outpourings. The late Edgar Cayce, known as "the sleeping prophet" because his "readings" came to him during periods of trancelike slumber, left so many prophecies in stenographic records that there is a special library devoted to them.

How should the public evaluate these people and their pronouncements? Each individual has the freedom to discredit or believe them, but the Christian must judge these prophecies on the basis of God's standards.

What About Jeane Dixon?

If that question has been asked me once—well, you know the rest. Mrs. Dixon is perhaps the best known psychic of modern times with an impressive list of amazing predictions, some of which have come true and were fairly detailed.

In her book, *The Call to Glory*, which deals with her views of Jesus Christ, among other things, Mrs. Dixon claims that: "It is my belief God has given me a gift of prophecy for His own reasons, and I do not question them."[1]

How does she receive these prophetic powers?

"I empty my mind in order that I may be filled with the Spirit of God. Finally, during my meditations, when my spirit is calm and He is ready, God talks to me. I know then, beyond all doubt, that the channel is coming directly to me from the Divine, the Lord our God, because *I feel it* and sense it. I know it is not the channel of Satan, because his channel I have felt and sensed too; and I definitely know the difference. So according to my wisdom I follow the Lord's channel...."[2]

She claims, "The future has been shown to me to 2037 A.D."[3]

She predicts such things as the rise of the Antichrist, major world conditions leading up to and following this, the Second Coming of Christ and a time of unprecedented blessing to follow.

Many of her new predictions are very close to biblical prophecies of these events, but the whole timetable for their occurrence does not fit with the biblical pattern. According to my understanding of the biblical prophets, all of the events which are associated with the Second Coming of Christ will occur within a time period of seven years immediately preceding His visible and personal return to the earth (Daniel 9-11).

She also speaks authoritatively about how to know Jesus Christ and enter God's kingdom.

When a person makes the sort of claims for herself that Jeane Dixon has made, either she is a remarkable modern-day prophet of God and we should analyze her prophetic utterances as new revelations from God on the level with Scripture, or she is a counterfeit prophet who, though appearing as an angel of light, is setting up the unwary for great deception.

Appointment Arranged

To be as fair and discerning as possible with Mrs. Dixon, I prayed that God would somehow get me an interview with her. This was next to impossible, but through an incredible set of circumstances, not long after my prayer I found myself in a face to face encounter with her, an interview which lasted for some time.

Mrs. Dixon is a charming and sincere person who is genuinely interested in people and speaks of God in a natural and easy manner. I liked her immediately and enjoyed several hours of fascinating conversation with her.

As I had anticipated our meeting I had searched the Scriptures to find what is most important in discerning whether a modern-day prophet is really a true prophet of God or not. I found that the most important issues are what one believes about Jesus Christ and what one thinks the requirement is to become a true Christian. Therefore, I was concerned about Mrs. Dixon's view of what a person must believe to be forgiven of sin and accepted into God's kingdom. This is a most crucial issue, and I could not find a clear statement on this subject in any of her books. In her many illustrations of prominent people whom she had helped get right with God, she told of emphasizing to them that they could find God by finding their talent in life and using it in the service of humanity.

Mrs. D. and Salvation

In *The Call to Glory* Mrs. Dixon makes the nearest thing to a definitive statement about her view of how to become a Christian. In the chapter on "Getting to Know Him," she says, "The present Jesus Christ becomes known by bringing the knowledge of His historical life and teaching into our lives; this is the way we bring Jesus Christ into our lives, for was it not He who said, 'I am the way, the truth and the life.'"[4]

In another section of the same chapter she says, "His (Jesus') major message was if we follow His teachings and strive for the kingdom of God while on earth, then we will have a much better life on earth, and the assurance of eternal life in heaven."[5]

Mrs. Dixon confirmed this thinking in our conversation. But the above statements are not the Gospel that Jesus Christ has given us to share with man so that he may enter God's kingdom. They set forth a salvation by works plus faith and exactly what we are to believe is not made clear.

The Bible declares, "For by grace you have been saved through faith; and not of yourselves, it is the gift of God; not as a result of works, that no one should boast" (Ephesians 2:8-9).

This verse shows that if we *strive* to gain God's acceptance by our own works, we won't make it.

When some sincere religious seekers asked Jesus what works they could do to inherit eternal life, Jesus said, "This is the work of God, that you *believe* in Him whom He has sent" (John 6:29).

The only way to come to God is to accept the work which Jesus did for us at the cross and believe in Him as our personal Savior from sin and its consequence, which is eternal separation from God.

We are saved by grace, not by works or human merit. "But if it is by grace, it is no longer on the basis of works, otherwise grace is no longer grace" (Romans 11:6).

The only possible way of receiving grace is through the agency of faith. Faith is the one thing that man can do and still not accomplish anything meritorious. Biblical faith is receiving the work of another on my behalf based on the realization that I can't help myself.

Even my works for God as a Christian must be done in my life through faith. For the Bible says, "And without faith it is impossible to please Him . . ." (Hebrews 11:6).

As I depend upon Christ for strength and direction, the following becomes true: "For it is God who is at work in you, both to will and to work for His good pleasure" (Philippians 2:13).

Mrs. D. and Faith

Not once does Mrs. Dixon make clear the object of saving faith, which is the significance of Christ's substitutionary death, bearing our judgment for not being able to measure up to God's perfect law.

The Bible says, "He made Him who knew no sin to be sin on our behalf, that we might become the righteousness of God in Him" (2 Corinthians 5:21). "Even the righteousness of God through faith in Jesus Christ for all those who believe; for there is no distinction; for all have sinned and fall short of the glory of God, being justified as a gift by His grace through the redemption which is in Christ Jesus" (Romans 3:22-24).

To be justified means to be declared righteous and blameless in God's sight.

In talking with Mrs. Dixon, I asked her why she hadn't made salvation and faith clear in her books, and she said, "Because the world is not ready for that yet."

Is the world not ready to hear a message which God commanded to be preached to every creature?

In all fairness, I must state that when I went through the facts of the true Gospel of Christ with Mrs. Dixon she said that she had always known and believed those things. Assuming that she actually does believe them, it is difficult for me to understand why she doesn't make them clear, but rather stresses a message of works.

A prophet's chief goal should be to lead people to a saving faith in Jesus Christ. "For the testimony of Jesus is the spirit of prophecy" (Revelation 19:10).

Is She a Prophet of God?

Rene Noorbergen, the writer of Mrs. Dixon's book, *My Life and Prophecies*, raises twenty issues in the prologue which are designed to lead the reader to the conclusion that Jeane Dixon has a God given gift of prophecy which is in accord with the Scriptures.

At the close of this list, Noorbergen writes, "Jeane Dixon's record of accuracy is unequaled."[6]

I would like to raise the question, "Unequaled in comparison to whom?"

If Noorbergen is comparing Jeane Dixon's record to the records of modern-day prophets such as Edgar Cayce, Maurice Woodruff, and others, Mrs. Dixon *is* the most accurate. If Noorbergen means to compare her with the biblical prophets, there is no contest. A biblical prophet was a person called of God and given a unique gift and commission which always fit into God's ultimate goal of bringing men to a change of heart and faith in His provision for salvation from sin.

One of the chief credentials of a true prophet of God was that he had to be 100 percent accurate on all predictions. Noorbergen and Jeane Dixon left this credential out of the list of twenty given in *My Life and Prophecies*.

While talking with Mrs. Dixon, I brought up the passage in Deuteronomy 18:9-22 which gives the description of a true prophet of God. She said that she knew the passage well; however, I observe that it was strangely absent in all of her books.

In this portion of Scripture Moses warned the Israelites about seeking to obtain secret information and guidance through the occultic practices common to the people whom they were expelling from the land of Canaan. Instead of looking to these forbidden pursuits, they were to obtain all their guidance and understanding through prophets who would be sent from God, as Moses was.

Moses put it this way: "When you enter the land which the Lord your God gives you, you shall not learn to imitate the detestable things of those nations. There shall not be found among you anyone who makes his son or his daughter pass through fire, one who uses divination, one who practices witchcraft, or one who interprets omens, or a sorcerer, or one who casts a spell, or a medium, or a spiritist, or one who calls up the dead. For whoever does these things is detestable to the Lord; and because of these detestable things the Lord your God will drive them out before you" (Deuteronomy 18:9-12).

Divination

This is a term from the previous passage which needs careful definition. There are many means of divination, but all forms seek to obtain secret knowledge of past, present, and especially future events by supernatural means. The most amazing display of divination is called "inspirational divination" in which the medium is given direct communication from demons of events that could not have been known by normal means. In this form of divination, the medium is conscious of contact with real spirit beings, though erroneously thinking that it is the Spirit of God.

The pagan world was filled with diviners, which were a counterpart of God's prophets. Every king of the ancient world had his cabinet of diviners, soothsayers, magicians, and astrologers. Daniel mentions this practice throughout his book. (See also Leviticus 19:26, 31; 20:6; Joshua 13:22; Jeremiah 27:9.)

If a person receives accurate secret knowledge which cannot be attributed to fakery, then there are only two possible sources. The person is either a prophet of God and receiving revelation from the Holy Spirit, or he is a divining medium receiving revelation from a demon, called in Acts 16:16 "a spirit of divination." The Bible leaves us no other option.

Whispering Wizards

Isaiah lashed out against the nation of Israel because they had departed so much from their true faith that they were turning from the true prophets to the occult diviners. Listen to his inspired warning: "And when they say to you, 'Consult the mediums and the wizards who whisper and mutter,' should not a people consult their God? Should they consult the dead on behalf of the living? To the law and to the testimony! If they do not speak according to this word, it is because they have no dawn" (Isaiah 8:19-20).

The challenge of Isaiah is appropriate for our day. As the nation Israel had been drawn away from the true faith, so America is rushing headlong into apostasy today. For discernment as to what is true and false we must evaluate all things by "the law" and "the testimony," which means the Bible. If any phenomenon, no matter how seemingly moral, religious, and supernatural, doesn't jibe with God's Word, it is because these false prophets have "no dawn," or literally "have no light" (i.e., they don't have light from God's Spirit).

As Moses condemned all forms of occult practice and predicted that other prophets like himself would be sent to give God's Word to Israel, he perceived a question that was already in everyone's mind: "How shall we know the word which the Lord has not spoken?" (Deuteronomy 18:21). In other words, how are we to tell who is a "diviner" and who is a "prophet sent by God"?

Test of a True Prophet

Moses gave the acid test: "When a prophet speaks in the name of the Lord, if the thing does not come about or come true, that is the thing which the Lord has not spoken . . ." (Deuteronomy 18:22).

Two important things are to be observed here. First, nowhere is there any authorization for obtaining secret knowledge of past, present, or future things except by the sovereign will and inspiration of the Spirit of God. "For no prophecy was ever made by an act of human will, but men moved by the Holy Spirit spoke from God" (2 Peter 1:21).

God says again on this matter, "The secret things belong to the Lord our God, but the things revealed belong to us and to our sons forever, that we may observe all the words of this law" (Deuteronomy 29:29).

Only God's prophets are authorized to reveal secret things and only with a purpose of bringing men into obedience to His Word.

Whatever God's Spirit reveals to a prophet is always spoken in the Lord's name. This is why the statement, "Thus says the Lord," appears hundreds of times throughout the Bible.

A New Testament prophet named Agabus said, "This is what the Holy Spirit says. . ." (Acts 21:11).

Everything spoken in the name of the Lord, or the Spirit of God, must come true exactly as predicted. In Israel, before her apostasy, a prophet was either 100 percent accurate or he was stoned (with rocks, that is)!

No prophet called of God was given authorization to hedge his predictions! Nowhere does a Bible prophet claim that some predictions are the thoughts of men and thus, because men can change their minds, may be excused for inaccuracy. God, who has perfect foreknowledge of all things, is never fooled by men changing their minds. He even knows when this will occur, and His prophecies take it into account.

Mrs. D. and the Bible

Let's examine Jeane Dixon's claims in the light of the biblical standards of accuracy and purpose.

Her prophecies do not all come true. Though the accurate predictions are greatly publicized, the inaccurate ones are usually ignored. Just a few of her failures are listed here:

World War III would begin in 1958.

Red China would be admitted to the United Nations in 1958.

The Vietnam War would end in ninety days (i.e., from 7 May 1966) on terms not satisfactory to the U.S.

On 19 October 1968 she said that Jacqueline Kennedy was not thinking of marriage. The next day she married Onassis.

How does she explain her failures? Mrs. Dixon gives a curious answer. She has several categories of prophecies which she makes. First, she claims that divine revelations are always accurate. The other categories are based on "tuning in" on the thoughts of men via mental telepathy through a number of methods, such as touching their fingertips, getting them to look into a crystal ball while she reads their thoughts, putting her hand on a deck of cards she received from a gypsy fortuneteller, or dreams and visions.

Mrs. Dixon claims that at the time she reads the person's thoughts, she accurately predicts what he intends to do. But since these are only the plans of men, intentions can change and then the prediction does not come true.

As fascinating as this explanation may be, it does not square with the Word of God. She may receive secret information, but if she does it is not from the Spirit of God. If it were from God, it would be accurate in spite of any change of mind on the part of men.

The Bible does not authorize hedging a prophetic bet with qualifications. Any prediction of the future must come true or it is not from God.

Her prophecies are not given in the name of the Lord. God-given revelations of the future must be given in the name of the Lord; no other kinds of predictions are authorized. All other prophets are branded false prophets and divining mediums. Even pagan prophets used to predict some things accurately, but not in the Lord's name (see Deuteronomy 13:1-5).

She obtains secret information supernaturally, but not through the Spirit of God. This is an intrusion into an area expressly forbidden by God. "The secret things belong to the Lord."

Mrs. Dixon's prophetic insight into the lives of people both for present and future events is clearly occultic.

Her prophecies do not line up with the biblical purpose for prophecy. True prophecy has two purposes: first, it should bring people to obedience to God's Word (Deuteronomy 29:29); second, it should bring people the testimony about Jesus Christ (Revelation 19:10).

Mrs. Dixon makes predictions about such things as fashion changes, horse races, and prominent celebrities. When she tells the future of well-known personalities, no attempt is made to bring them to a personal faith in Jesus Christ or to challenge some of their moral and spiritual problems.

She gives a lot of political advice but doesn't consistently exhort people for failing to believe in Jesus Christ as personal Lord and Savior. Some leaders from the East come to her, and no issue is made concerning personal faith in Jesus Christ instead of their false religions. Yet the Bible declares, "And there is salvation in no one else; for there is no other name under heaven that has been given among men, by which we must be saved" (Acts 4:12).

Jesus Christ is the theme of all true prophecy (Revelation 19:10). All prophecy must either bear direct witness or authenticate a witness as to how men can be forgiven of their sins and be born again spiritually.

Mrs. Dixon's predictions are about everything from the mundane to international political affairs, with no true witness to the Gospel of the grace of God attached to them.

She uses artifacts of the occult to receive her prophecies. I questioned Mrs. Dixon at length about why she uses a crystal ball, a deck of cards from a gypsy fortuneteller, palmistry, astrology, numerology, etc, and she had an explanation for each of these things.

About the crystal ball: she said that she doesn't ever receive visions in the ball itself, but rather uses it as a means of helping the person whom she is "reading" to clear his mind and concentrate. Then she reads his mind by "vibrations" or "telepathy." Both are contrary to the teaching of Scripture.

Both cases are an example of intruding by human will into the area of "secret things" which the Lord has forbidden. God says, "But know this first of all, no prophecy of Scripture is a matter of one's own interpretation" (2 Peter 1:20). This means that God's prophets didn't initiate or give their own interpretation of life and history. It continues, "For no prophecy was ever made by an act of human will, but men moved by the Holy Spirit spoke from God" (2 Peter 1:21).

Furthermore, no prophet of God made a practice of using artifacts to receive a vision or a prophecy, especially things that have been historically associated with the occult such as Mrs. Dixon uses.

Contradictions in the Crystal Ball

Mrs. Dixon seems to contradict her own claim of "not seeing things in the crystal ball."

As she described her meeting with the gypsy at age eight when she first received the crystal ball, she said, "I looked into it and what I saw was so beautiful it almost made me cry. I saw a wild, rocky coast in a far-off land and a turbulent sea crashing into the jagged edges of the crumbling rocks."[7]

The fortuneteller was deeply moved and said that Jeane had just described her homeland. On this basis she gave Jeane the crystal ball. If words mean anything, Jeane Dixon said she "looked into the crystal ball and saw" that vision.

Mrs. Dixon describes another incident which happened in 1948: ". . . suddenly the crystal ball was filled with tumult. I saw helmeted police and heavily armed soldiers leading and dragging sullen and belligerent men through angry crowds, etc."[8]

Note that she said, "the crystal ball was filled with tumult . . . etc."

My question is this: if Mrs. Dixon doesn't see her visions in the crystal ball, why does she need it at all? Aren't there other means of helping a person to relax and concentrate? Why use something that is contrary to any biblical pattern of prophecy and which has always been associated with the occult?

The partial deck of "blessed cards" was given to Jeane when she was a young girl by the gypsy fortuneteller, who was clearly a medium, possibly demon-possessed. "Cartomancy," described by Kurt Koch, is the technique of fortunetelling by means of cards. Koch cites many examples (he has examined over 20,000 case histories) of a pattern of occult involvement being established by experiences with mediums.[9]

The fortuneteller's cards are examples of the types of artifacts clearly condemned in the Scriptures. In witchcraft, for instance, certain artifacts carry a strong presence of demon influence. This is why it is reported in Acts 19:18-19: "Many also of those who had believed kept coming, confessing and disclosing their practices. And many of those who practiced magic brought their books together and began burning them in the sight of all; and they counted up the price of them and found it fifty thousand pieces of silver."

To be delivered from demonism these people confessed their practice of black magic and burned their artifacts. Whenever I lead a person to Christ who has been involved in the occult, I immediately urge him to confess his complicity with demons to God and get rid of all artifacts associated with the occult such as crystal balls, tarot cards, books on the occult, jewelry of the occult, ouija boards, astrology paraphernalia or fortunetelling bric-a-brac.

The use of astrology plays a role in Mrs. Dixon's analysis of a person. One of the first things she asked me was, "What is the date of your birth?"

She has a regular syndicated astrological column in over three hundred newspapers in the United States.[10] Mrs. Dixon said that she began the horoscope column because this was a way of giving helpful advice about life to many people who were requesting her help.

God condemns the practice of astrology, which began in ancient Babylon along with all kinds of witchcraft and black magic. It grew out of the pagan belief that each star was a god who exercised control over men's lives. It was a pseudo-science as well, which has been proven absurd in the light of modern science.

The prophet Daniel clearly declared that the things of God could not be understood or predicted by the occult representatives of his day: "Daniel answered before the king and said, 'As for the mystery about which the king has inquired, neither wise men, conjurers, magicians, nor diviners are able to declare it to the king. However, there is a God in heaven who reveals mysteries, and He has made known to King Nebuchadnezzar what will take place in the latter days" (Daniel 2:27-28).

Astrology was the chief means of divining in the kingdom of Babylon. The king financed the building of elaborate towers for the astrologers to use in their study of the stars. The ruins of these "observatories" are still visible today in Iraq.

Isaiah condemned the astrologers and sorcerers in Babylon and predicted their destruction. "Stand fast now in your spells and in your many sorceries with which you have labored from your youth; perhaps you will be able to profit, perhaps you may cause trembling. You are wearied with your many counsels, let now the astrologers, those who prophesy by the stars, those who predict by the new moons, stand up and save you from what will come upon you. Behold, they have become like stubble, fire burns them; they cannot deliver themselves from the power of the flame; there will be no coal to warm by, nor a fire to sit before!" (Isaiah 47:12-14).

No child of God has any business toying with astrology, much less practicing it as Mrs. Dixon does.

So As to Mislead

In conclusion, I believe many lessons should be learned from the case of Jeane Dixon. This is why I have gone into so much detail about her. I believe many prophets like her will appear in the near future. Jesus said, ". . . false prophets will arise and will show great signs and wonders, so as to mislead, if possible, even the elect. *Behold, I have told you in advance*" (Matthew 24:24-25).

With real regret I told Mrs. Dixon that I believed her prophetic ability was *not* from God. I told her I sincerely believed that if she didn't reject this psychic power, it would lead to her destruction.

She said she was certain her gift was from God and that she knew beyond doubt the "feeling" of God's presence.

When I left her, I quoted Proverbs 14:12; "There is a way which seems right to a man, but its end is the way of death."

When our "feelings," no matter how right they may seem, contradict Scripture, we must conclude that our feelings are wrong.

May God graciously touch Jeane Dixon and bring her fully to the truth.

In the meantime, reader, be discerning.

9 ○ Signs
and Wonders

"Bread obtained by falsehood is sweet to a man, but afterward his mouth will be filled with gravel."   PROVERBS 20:17

W E ARE LIVING in a time when history is racing toward a climax. The pattern of events which the prophets said would occur before the Second Coming of Christ are coming together rapidly.

After hundreds of years of being scattered throughout the world, the Jews have returned to their homeland to establish a nation again. They have recaptured Old Jerusalem and have sustained sovereign possession of it for the first time in 2600 years.

The Arabs have united with the mutual desire of attacking Israel to regain their land.

To the north of Israel a great military power has formed in Russia.

In the Orient there is a great power that can field an army of 200,000,000 men—Red China.

There are rumblings of the revival of the ancient Roman culture in Europe uniting to form a ten-nation confederacy in the Common Market.

Scientists, confronted with the reality of the world situation, are predicting famines on a scale never seen by man—in the next ten to fifteen years.

Earthquakes are increasing mysteriously; pollution promises to be a greater and greater problem.

All of these things are predicted in the Bible, and they are fitting together simultaneously. We are in an unparalleled time in human history in which the most wonderful event of all, Jesus Christ coming secretly to snatch out all of those who truly believe in Him, could happen at any moment.*

Prophecy of Deceptions

Along with these events, there is another great prophetic sign of the imminent return of Christ: the emergence of Satanic deceptions through the activity of counterfeit miracles and false prophets.

* For a more detailed account read *The Late Great Planet Earth.*

The Bible gives a series of sober warnings both to those who know Jesus Christ personally and to those who don't know Him or may be putting off this decision.

The first warning was given by Christ Himself in one of His last great public messages. As Jesus was about to be arrested and taken to the cross, He said that we should watch because there would be great deceptions during the last times; there would be false messiahs, people who would come in with a plan for saving the world, for bringing about a utopian society (Matthew 24:4-5). He warned that there would be false prophets who would mislead many (Matthew 24:11).

These warnings are not just to the world, but to the believers—to those who know Jesus Christ. He said, "For false Christs and false prophets will arise and will show great signs and wonders, so as to mislead, if possible, even the elect" (Matthew 24:24).

The Apostle Paul prophesied that these counterfeits would be a part of the activities which would prepare the way for the great world dictator known as the Antichrist. "That is, the one whose coming is in accord with the activity of Satan, with all power and signs and false wonders, and with all the deception of wickedness for those who perish, because they did not receive the love of the truth so as to be saved" (2 Thessalonians 2:9-10).

The prelude to this dictator will be a build-up of supernatural phenomena through Satanic power. The same words used to describe the miracles of Christ in the gospels are used here, which clearly indicates that in the last days Satan will be permitted a greater freedom to counterfeit the miracles and gifts of the Holy Spirit.

What/Who Is a False Prophet?

A false prophet claims to have a revelation from God, but doesn't; he appears to be someone sent from God, but isn't. He doesn't simply step out on the center stage of humanity and say, "Behold, I am a false prophet, so don't listen to what I have to say." He comes in sheep's clothing, but inside he's a ravening wolf. He makes proclamations and predictions mixed with just enough truth to make them plausible.

The Scriptures clearly tell us that false teachers and prophets have the ability to mix truth with deception.

As the days draw near for the return of Christ, the Bible says that God will allow these false prophets to work miracles in the power of His archenemy—Satan himself. They will work great signs, so that even those who know Jesus Christ will be deceived—but not utterly deceived, for that's not possible.

In the Power of Satan

What kinds of miracles can we expect to see in the last days? In Acts 8 we find one example of the power of Satan. "Now there was a certain man named Simon, who formerly was practicing magic in the city, and astonishing the people of Samaria, claiming to be someone great; and they all, from smallest to greatest, were giving attention to him, saying, 'This man is what is called the Great Power of God'" (Acts 8:9-10).

Here was a man who through black magic had performed such things before people that they thought it was the power of God, but he did it by the power of Satan!

We have examples from the days of Moses when God sent him into the court of Pharaoh and he worked some real wonders before the Egyptian people. We are told that the magicians who practiced black magic duplicated the first several signs that Moses worked; they were able to counterfeit the miracles of God.

Many people do not realize that Satan has this power. He has the power to come as an angel of light; he has his own ministers. He may work through someone who appears to be righteous. He may perform feats of the supernatural which appear to be direct acts of God.

I do believe that God is working miracles today and that we haven't seen anything yet! We are in the day of a special outpouring of the Spirit of God that will parallel the early days of the Church. God is beginning to show the miraculous in reauthentication of His Word and His message. However, Satan is also going to be allowed to counterfeit these miracles.

And, this is why we must . . .

Be Discerning

Christian, be warned! You may see and be involved in acts which appear to be supernatural. You may be inclined to think, "Wow, this must be of God; it's miraculous!"

Watch out.

One of the ways in which great deceptions are going to capture individuals is through the popularity of the occult.

At the check-out counter in a supermarket you can buy a 25¢ booklet on *Everyday Witchcraft.* The cover shows a white cat, a black candle, and the enticing words, "Love magic, charms and spells, fortunetelling; everything you need to know to enjoy occult power!"[1]

What a come-on. So innocent. So appealing.

Women, especially, are going in for palmistry and fortunetelling in a big way. Political, charitable, and philanthropic organizations, searching for the newest in modern motifs for their luncheons or fund-raising events, are turning to the occult theme.

If you have read this far and still do not believe in the danger of these things, the following is a true story about a man who was equally hard to convince.

A Little Dabble Do Ya

A young minister wanted to expose the folly of astrology to his congregation. Rather than showing them the demonic spirit behind astrology, he figured the best way was through involving himself, so he had his horoscope cast. *Why not,* he thought. *This is all ridiculous, and I'm going to show my people how absurd it is.*

He told his church what he had done and even told them what had been predicted about his life. To his amazement, those things started coming true. He began to have periods of terrible fear; he lost his discernment. He read the Bible but didn't have the understanding he had had previously. As the conflict in the spiritual realm became almost unbearable, he finally went to God on his knees and confessed that he had sinned by dabbling in this art, realizing that it wasn't just a bunch of fakery.

When he went to God and confessed, he was delivered from his spiritual oppression and immediately the remainder of that horoscope began to be wrong.

There are many case histories of this type in Dr. Kurt Koch's book *Between Christ and Satan.*[2]

Any time you submit yourself unreservedly to the spiritual realm, turn off your mind and cease to be discerning, you are opening yourself up to possible demon deception. As you study the Scriptures on this, you will find that even though you may be sincere, earnestly seeking God, not immoral or involved in some gross sin, this will not keep you from being deceived.

Jesse Penn Lewis tells how a great revival in Wales was completely neutralized by an invasion of demonic power.[3] The demons began to get into this movement through people who sincerely wanted to know God in a deeper way and began to open themselves up for all kinds of spiritual contact and leading. You may say, "Well, if that's true, should I ever open myself up to God?" Of course you should. We are commanded to submit ourselves to Him. However, since there's more than one spirit which will try to contact us in the spiritual realm, we are warned to "try the spirits" to see whether they are of God or not. As we depend on the Holy Spirit and have the Word of God in our hearts, the Holy Spirit will never lead us contrary to His written word.

Sometimes this discernment will take time; we may not understand what the Holy Spirit is seeking to reveal to us. Our hearts may cry out, "I want to have something dramatic happen—something which will show me God's power in a fantastic way. I want to know it all—right now!"

Instant Maturity

A deceiving spirit can get into a person's life when he begins to believe there is some experience which is going to give him instant maturity.

The Scripture tells us that when we become believers in Jesus Christ we have the Holy Spirit indwelling us. As believers we must come to understand that we can walk in dependence upon the power of the Spirit of God Himself. We can have His power to live for Christ, to understand God's Word, to minister for Christ according to our spiritual gifts, and to overcome temptation. Any believer can have this. A babe in Christ who submits himself to God and walks by faith and dependence upon Christ can be empowered by the Spirit.

However, there is no such thing as instant perfection or instant maturity!

When, as a young believer in Christ, I first learned I could have the power of the Holy Spirit in my life, I claimed this by faith and God began to overcome hangups in my life. He began to do things through me that I had never seen before in my whole life. As I look back with the mature perspective I have now, I know God was blessing my faith and my understanding as far as it went, but there were big areas that I didn't understand, and God just didn't hold me accountable for those areas.

The Christian life is a maturing process. We are to keep growing in grace and knowledge of Christ. There are many Christians, especially young Christians today, who want everything now. Some seek an experience by which they instantly have total victory over the flesh—no more temptations. They want to have great power and wisdom so that they suddenly know more than the Bible teachers, more than their pastors.

God may graciously grant us an experience that will give our faith such a jolt that we start believing in Him. We may suddenly come to realize for the first time that the Holy Spirit is dwelling in us and that we can count on Him for power. For many people this may come as such a welcome revelation that they would describe it as a "second blessing." Some even conclude that they must have received the Holy Spirit for the first time because His indwelling Presence has become so real to them. This, of course, is unscriptural. Every believer has the Holy Spirit indwelling him, but not necessarily filling or empowering him.

When we initially become aware of His personal power and Presence within us and yield to His control, we may experience anything from a quiet sense of assurance to an emotional sense of release. The point is, however, that we still have to grow in knowledge; we have to know how to apply the truth of the Scripture to our life day by day; we have to grow in our ability to depend upon God in our daily circumstances and to live by faith, claiming His promises. If we try to jump over this process of growth, we can get into a situation where we can be badly deceived.

One of the most controversial subjects in the Christian world today, and one which I write about only after years of study and much prayer, is this matter of the supernatural gifts of the Spirit, particularly tongues. Now and then I run into people who have never heard about this phenomenon. Many others are confused by the profusion of books on the subject—both pro and con—and are genuinely seeking a calm, reasonable, and biblical approach to this issue. For this reason I feel that it is necessary to deal with the subject in a book such as this. Mine is by no means an exhaustive study; a whole book would be necessary for that. But I do want to set forth some of the prevalent thinking about this matter and my own conclusions.

There are different views among those who speak in tongues regarding the purpose of tongues, kinds of tongues, what tongues indicate, and who must speak in tongues. The old-line Pentecostals and a new breed of articulate writers and speakers who have sought to be the spokesmen for the new tongues phenomenon, usually referred to as the charismatic movement, do not agree on all points.

Similarly, many evangelicals have spoken out strongly against this modern-day manifestation, and their denunciation ranges from accusations that "all tongues are of the Devil" to "God may be giving the gift today, but you're better off staying away from it."

As the present charismatic phenomenon began to grow to epidemic proportions in many areas of the world, I felt I needed to take a second look to see if any of it was of God and for the church today. I had previously believed that all of the sign gifts such as healing, miracles, tongues, and prophecies ceased as bona fide gifts of the Spirit about the end of the first century, just after the New Testament was completed.

The Scripture usually cited to prove this thesis is First Corinthians 13:8-12: "Love never fails; but if there are gifts of prophecy, they will be done away; if there are tongues, they will cease; if there is knowledge, it will be done away. For we know in part, and we prophesy in part; but when the *perfect* comes, the partial will be done away. When I was a child, I used to speak as a child, think as a child, reason as a child; when I became a man, I did away with childish things. For now we see in a mirror dimly, but then face to face; now I know in part, but then I shall know fully, just as I also have been fully known."

There are many biblical scholars who believe that the "perfect" in this passage refers to the completed New Testament canon of Scriptures. This school of thought contends that after the New Testament was written there was no longer any reason for God's message to be authenticated by special supernatural signs, so the gifts were taken away. For this reason, they look sceptically upon any present-day manifestation of these sign gifts.

This is admittedly a difficult passage of Scripture, but I have come to believe that the "perfect" refers to a condition which will be true of us when Christ returns for the Church and gives us glorified bodies like His own. Then we will see Him face to face and know as we have been known. Therefore it is my opinion that this passage alone is not enough to warrant the forbiddance of tongues today.

What Is "Tongues" Anyway?

From passages in both Acts and First Corinthians, "tongues" appears to have been an actual language which had never been learned by the speaker. In First Corinthians 14 the believers were both speaking and praying in an unknown tongue. I don't believe it was gibberish. I believe it was the same phenomenon as on the day of Pentecost—an actual language. If used in public worship, it needed an interpreter; but not if used in private prayer.

There are some who believe that there are two different kinds of tongues: the first a heavenly language (sometimes called a prayer language), which is unintelligible to anyone on earth, and the second the gift of tongues, which is a language unknown to the speaker but intelligible to someone, somewhere in the world.

However, the same words are used in the original language throughout the New Testament to describe the manifestation of tongues, thus showing its unity of meaning. I am not convinced that there is solid biblical ground for asserting that there is a genuine phenomenon of tongues that is other than the gift of tongues which is an actual language.

Speaking in tongues is first recorded in the New Testament in the Book of Acts. Following Christ's resurrection, He told His followers (about 120 of them) to wait in Jerusalem until they were given the Holy Spirit. When the Holy Spirit came, He would give them power to become bold witnesses to the whole world.

In Acts 2 we read of the fulfillment of this promise. The Holy Spirit filled all of the believers in the upper room, and they all began to speak in different languages, languages which they had never learned. They went out into the streets and began telling the wonderful works of God and praising Him, and everyone heard the message in his own language. In this instance the major purpose of tongues was to enable the disciples to preach the message of Christ to the mass of foreigners in the city during that religious festival. There were dozens of dialects represented in the crowds, and many hardened heathen were astonished at hearing the message of a Jewish Savior in their own language.

The Real Miracle

But the real miracle on the day of Pentecost was that after weeks of discouragement and cowardice, these believers were now filled with an overwhelming boldness to witness, and it was this boldness which confirmed to them that they had received the Holy Spirit—NOT just the fact that they had spoken in tongues or that tongues of fire and rushing winds had also been present.

I remember a story Dr. J. Edwin Orr used to tell student groups. He told of speaking with a college boy about his drinking habits. The boy would get drunk on Monday night on gin and soda. On Tuesday night he got high on whiskey and soda. Wednesday night his inebriation was brought on by vodka and soda. On Thursday it was vermouth and soda. Then Dr. Orr would ask the question, "What do you suppose it was that got the boy drunk? Obviously it was the soda."

In the same way, people often draw the conclusion that since tongues were associated in *some* cases with the filling of the Spirit in the Book of Acts, that obviously tongues are the evidence of having received the fullness of the Spirit. But if we are going to believe the witness of the Book of Acts, *power* and *praise* are the chief evidence of having been filled with the Spirit since they are the *common* factors mentioned each time a believer was filled. The same thing can be said of the epistles' witness on this matter.

Original Purpose of Gifts

I believe that the primary reason God originally gave the gifts of the Spirit to believers is what Paul painstakingly tries to point out in First Corinthians 12-14. Paul paints a beautiful word picture of what the Church is really like. He says that we're like a body: Christ is the head, and each of us has been placed, ever so lovingly and conscientiously, into our proper place in the body by the Holy Spirit. He picks out the role that each of us is to play in the body. Everyone can't be an eye and everyone can't be an ear. I'm sure that there are certain parts of any body which are more glamorous than others, and no one is really excited about being a big toe. But Paul says that the Spirit has placed us in the body, *as He wills,* on the basis of the gift. He has given us. In other words, your place in the body is determined by your gift, and we won't all have the same place because we don't all have the same gift.

The very thing Paul was dealing with in this letter to these carnal Corinthian believers was that they were "big-timing" one another with their gifts and especially the gift of tongues. In effect he was saying, "Look, the Spirit doesn't make any mistakes. He knows what gift you need to function properly in the body. It isn't necessary to beg Him for this gift or that, or to flaunt it in people's faces once you've discovered it. Just stay a healthy member of the body and God will use your gift to edify you and the rest of the body and to bring more members into it."

The Sign Gifts—What and Why?

In the list of spiritual gifts which Paul enumerates in Romans 12 and First Corinthians 12 there are about ten that would be considered fairly normal abilities, although any spiritual gift is attended with divine power when exercised in the Spirit. However, there are several gifts mentioned that are definitely supernatural in their manifestation: the gifts of healing, miracles, tongues, prophecies, and interpretations.

In Hebrews 2 the writer spells out clearly why the supernatural gifts were given. "For this reason we must pay much closer attention to what we have heard, lest we drift away from it. For if the word spoken through angels proved unalterable, and every transgression and disobedience received a just recompense, how shall we escape if we neglect so great a salvation? After it was at the first spoken through the Lord, it was confirmed to us by those who heard, God also bearing witness with them, *both by signs and wonders and by various miracles and by gifts of the Holy Spirit* according to His own will" (Hebrews 2:1-4).

The Gospel of redemption in Christ had to have strong authentication for the Jew to accept it as a message which superseded what he had always been taught. The pagan world also had to be convinced that the disciples were not just bringing a story about another god among many, but that their message was from the one true God.

It is an undeniable fact that these gifts ceased to be widely known from around the middle of the second century until modern times. This can't be explained away by saying that all the believers down through those centuries just wouldn't believe God for those gifts. More likely, the truth is that there was simply not the same need for authenticating the gospel message as there had been prior to the completion of the New Testament. This is why there is little if any record of public use of the gift of tongues during those centuries. Perhaps there was private use of the gift as a secondary purpose, since the primary need no longer existed.

Resurgence of Tongues

Our present day seems to be another era when strong authentication for God's Word is needed. The "sign" gifts have made a remarkable inroad into the Jesus Movement. There are many reasons for this, and not all are good. Many young people who have been turned on to drugs have had supernatural experiences with demons and Satan, and they might not have much use for a God who couldn't pull off some miracles bigger than those they've already experienced.

Another place where a renewed validation for the Scriptures is needed is in many church denominations which have swallowed the liberal theologian's destructive views of the validity and historicity of the Bible. Neo-orthodoxy seeks to find spiritual values in the Bible while siding with the liberals against its historical accuracy. The results have been a bewildered group of sincere seekers after God who can't find Him in the institutional churches.

In some of the major old-line denominations where these conditions have existed to the greatest degree, a strange phenomenon sprang up. People began to receive the gift of speaking in tongues. Even ministers who had been in the ministry for years began experiencing this gift of the Spirit as they came alive in Christ, many for the first time. A true revival has resulted in many areas. Thousands have come to experience new life in Jesus Christ and are excited about living and witnessing for Him. This has also split churches and divided friendships of long standing, but there is no denying that many impotent, defeated Christians have come gloriously alive in Christ.

Remember Dr. Orr's little story about the "whiskey and soda"? What got the boy drunk, the whiskey or the soda? What has transformed these earnest believers? Is it tongues or is it the Holy Spirit? It is the Holy Spirit! With or without tongues, when you begin to walk in utter dependence upon the Spirit's power in you; when you make yourself available to all that God has made available to you; when you step out of the picture, admitting your weakness, and let Him take control; then you too will know the experience of a transformed life.

But Mr. Deception himself has sneaked in along with this new charismatic revival. We can count upon the Devil to be consistent. Wherever there is a victory, he will bring about a counterattack. And perhaps no spiritual gift is more susceptible to Satanic counterfeit and confusion than the gift of tongues. This statement is not made with any attempt to belittle or downgrade the genuine gift, but rather to caution those who have gone overboard with their experience and are not carefully relating it to the Scriptures.

Slips of the Tongues

The first confusion that has slipped in upon the excited but unwary "tongues" enthusiast is that everyone can and should have the experience of speaking in tongues. This is a logical conclusion based on his own experience. Many were either not really born again or may have been Christians who were never taught that the Holy Spirit dwelt in them from the time of their conversion and was there to empower their lives.

Most of them have been taught that if they could get this gift of tongues, then they could have all of the Spirit's fullness and power; this is referred to by them as "the baptism of the Spirit." Naturally, once they got this gift, it turned their focus onto the Holy Spirit and they believed He was filling them—and all that is needed for the Holy Spirit to fill us is for us to believe that He is. If I tell you repeatedly that you can have the Spirit's fullness and power as soon as you can induce goose pimples on your right arm, then the day you get those goose pimples you will begin to believe that the Spirit is filling you. When you believe that, He does fill you. But don't go around trying to get everyone to have goose pimples! Introduce people to the fact that the Holy Spirit lives in them and that His desire is to fill them with the life of Jesus; they will have plenty of goose pimples if that is God's plan for them. If they never get your particular gift, they can still have the Spirit and His power; otherwise, all of the epistles are a mockery on this subject.

In the books of the New Testament called the epistles, Paul, Peter, and John explain the meaning of the historical events chronicled in the gospels and the Book of Acts. To teach that everyone must experience speaking in tongues to gain the full power of the Spirit for living the Christian life is a contradiction of the epistles. In the Book of Romans, for instance, where Paul gives his fullest and most definitive statement about salvation and the central truths of Christianity, tongues are not mentioned once, and yet every other doctrine vital to living in this world as a believer is carefully expounded. Faith in God's promises alone is stressed. Would Paul have left out of this important treatise a truth that was the *key* to receiving power for serving and living for God?

God Does the Choosing

Paul has plenty to say about the gift of tongues, but not what is generally being taught in the charismatic movement today. In First Corinthians 12:28-30 Paul climaxes his argument with three key points: the Holy Spirit decides who gets what spiritual gift; we cannot all have the same gift; and no one is inferior for not having certain gifts that are more spectacular. He says, "And God has appointed in the church, first apostles, second prophets, third teachers, then miracles, then gifts of healings, helps, administrations, various kinds of tongues. All are not teachers, are they? All are not workers of miracles, are they? All do not have gifts of healings, do they? All do not speak with tongues, do they. All do not interpret, do they?"

Each question demands a negative answer. So, when Paul asks the question, "All do not speak with tongues, do they?"—the answer is "no!" All cannot speak with tongues any more than all could be apostles, prophets, evangelists, or teachers.

It should be carefully noted that Paul doesn't say all do not have the "gift" of tongues. Some have taught that there is a gift of tongues and then there is a sign of tongues, which is different from the gift and is given as an evidence of what they call the "baptism in the Holy Spirit." In this teaching, although one may speak in tongues as a sign of having received the Spirit's fullness, one may not have the gift. This is grasping at straws to try to make all of the Scripture's teaching fit experience, and it simply cannot be supported by a careful study of the Word. Even if it could, Paul denied that either kind of tongues must be true of everyone when he said, "All do not *speak* with tongues, do they?"

If the full power of the Holy Spirit is only available to those who experience the "baptism of the Holy Spirit," as it is called, and its sign, tongues, then Paul is saying that there are some who could never have the full power of God for living. For, again, Paul says, "All do not speak with tongues, do they?"

Further Confusion

A second confusion in the tongues movement grows out of the first. It is generally taught by those who emphasize tongues that since you can't really have all of the Spirit's power until you speak in tongues, then naturally all should seek the experience.

I can see the genuine concern for others that would bring them to this conclusion, but I must confess that this particular practice has distressed me greatly. I've seen many seeking the "baptism" with agonizing earnestness, and they have not received it. Their Christian life is in low gear and they feel God simply cannot use them or empower them because they can't speak in tongues. They will not believe the unconditional promises of the Bible about their spiritual assets because they've been taught that those can only be theirs once they've received their "baptism."

Many people go from one "tarrying" meeting to another, somehow hoping that they can get this mysterious "it" they've been seeking.

My spiritual gift happens to be the gift of teaching. I didn't seek it, tarry for it, or even unnecessarily concern myself about what it was. When the Father felt I was ready to handle the gift He had for me, He began to use me and gave great blessing to my first feeble attempts. As I grew in my knowledge of the Word and He continued to bless in a greater way, I realized that He had given me the gift of teaching.

Now, naturally, I'm enthused about the gift which the Lord has chosen for me. I am personally blessed and ministered to as the Spirit of God works through this gift. But what a sorry spectacle it would be—and how completely frustrating for all—if I began to have "after" meetings each time I spoke in which I encouraged people to come forward to tarry for my gift of teaching. It would be frustrating because, let's face it, God just didn't plan that everyone in the Body of Christ should be a teacher. "All are not teachers, are they?"

I have never spoken in tongues, nor do I honestly see any scriptural evidence that I should seek it. I've enjoyed a Spirit-filled walk for many years and have discovered progressively that all God has is available to me when I am available to Him. I don't need to try to get more from God, but to simply claim by faith and enjoy what He has already given me.

Paul wrote to the church at Corinth that "Things which eye has not seen, and ear has not heard, and which have not entered into the heart of man, all that God has prepared for those who love Him. For to us God revealed them through the Spirit . . ." (1 Corinthians 2:9-10). And I have that wonderful Holy Spirit in me doing just that.

In the Scriptures, the order for growth as a believer is *fact, faith, feeling.* The "feelings" should never run the life. Satan can give the most electrifying feelings to an unwary believer who has turned off his understanding of the Scriptures and opened himself up for any experience that will solve his spiritual "blahs." If the end result is to get a believer off into false doctrine and a wrong emphasis, Satan will even help him have some seemingly great personal experiences. He is a master at pulling texts out of context and piecing them together into a patchwork of false doctrine. It is diabolical that most false doctrine has just enough truth in it to make it lethal.

Why Speak in Tongues Today?

Why do people want to speak in tongues today? I think you can see from all I have said that they are sincerely convinced it will give their Christian life a tremendous shot in the arm and cure most of their spiritual problems. Who wouldn't want an easy antidote for the ills of the soul?

The problem is, though, that many dear believers, having had their "baptism in the Spirit," find to their great dismay that all of their problems are not miraculously solved. Day by day they find they still have to cope with the world, the flesh, and the Devil; and for some, great disillusionment sets in. Others live from experience to experience and in this subtle way keep focusing on the gift rather than the Giver, and that is tantamount to walking by sight rather than walking by faith.

Why have I made so much of this point? Because the Scripture says that we are to *walk in the Spirit* and we will not fulfill the lusts of the flesh (Galatians 5:16). Paul pleads with us to allow ourselves to be *continually filled* with and controlled by the Holy Spirit (Ephesians 5:18). Walking in, and being continually filled with, the Holy Spirit are not one shot deals. It's a whole pattern of life God is talking about.

Summing It All Up

I believe there is a genuine gift of tongues which God is giving today. It often quickens a person to believe God for the power of the Spirit to live a godly life. Many people have received this gift without even seeking it, and others who have sought it have been graciously granted it because it was obviously one of the gifts God had already planned for them. The exercise of this gift, both in private and public, has been a personal blessing to them. Some feel that when they pray in tongues they are able to express the inexpressible to God. Others sing in tongues, letting the Spirit compose the music and words as they yield their vocal cords to Him.

I would not in any way want to rob these people of their new love for Christ. It isn't necessary. The exercise of any spiritual gift can greatly bless the life of the one using it, and no one has a right to deny anyone the blessing God has intended for him. As a person walks in the Spirit and exercises his spiritual gift, it can't help but give him a deeper love for Christ and for the lost world.

Here are my only words of caution. It is so easy to become unbalanced in our Christian walk if we are not rightly dividing the Word and walking only in the light of it. The charismatic movement has placed an unbalanced emphasis on the importance of tongues. They have drawn unscriptural conclusions about a genuine and bona fide spiritual gift. The more the Christian world has criticized their movement, the greater the claims they have made for tongues. The more they have sought to validate their emphasis with biblically unsupportable claims, the more conservative biblical scholars and Christians have resisted them.

With a polarization like this, who do you think is the winner? You guessed it! Satan. He goads both sides on in their causes and then stands back and laughs while they battle each other instead of him.

Investigation of Manifestations

If there are certain areas of God's Word where we're a bit shaky, it's important to take them out and examine them occasionally.

In the first century when someone stood up and gave a revelation, or spoke in a tongue, they were to: "Let two or three prophets speak, and let the others pass judgment" (1 Corinthians 14:29).

The words "pass judgment" in Greek mean to "thoroughly discern"—to thoroughly investigate. Deceiving spirits can easily work through people who say they have a prophecy. Someone stands up and says something which has beautiful truth in it while underneath it is deceptive, and he leads others astray by false guidance.

We must depend upon the Holy Spirit and give our renewed mind to the Word of God—to learn and constantly be discerning. I believe Christians could, to some degree, "coast" in times past, but we can't coast now!

We are in a time of the greatest opportunity for service and the greatest possibility of peril. We need to snatch the opportunity and not get caught up in deception. We need to depend upon the Lord and to check out the Word. Only God's truth drives away error.

Paul said that perilous times would come and that "Evil men and impostors will proceed from bad to worse, deceiving and being deceived" (2 Timothy 3:13).

Then he exhorted Timothy, "You, however, continue in the things you have learned and become convinced of, knowing from whom you have learned them" (2 Timothy 3:14).

"All Scripture is inspired by God and profitable for teaching, for reproof, for correction, for training in righteousness" (2 Timothy 3:16).

The antidote for Satan's error is God's truth.

10 ○ Diagnosing Demon Possession

"Behold, I have given you authority to tread upon serpents and scorpions, and over all the power of the enemy, and nothing shall injure you." LUKE 10:19

THE STREETS OF Old Jerusalem are narrow and winding. When two or more are gathered together, it's a crowd. We were pushing our way through the stalls filled with pungent odors, jostling cameras with our American friends on a Holy Land pilgrimage, when we were halted by a traffic jam of eight or ten people listening to a disheveled man making a violent speech.

Jan and I were rather uneasy about the man because he seemed to be looking at us; each time we moved on up the street to get away from him, he followed us. He kept repeating the same short speech in an almost insane frenzy. The only two words we recognized were "Americans" and "Mohammed." He was carrying a large picture of Mohammed.

As a larger crowd began gathering, I quickly snapped a picture of the man and then turned to Jan and said, "Let's get out of here." We headed for the Damascus Gate at a fast pace, and the man, still shouting, followed us right through the gate. Needless to say, we were mighty glad to be out of that potentially explosive situation.

The first time I showed the pictures of our trip after we came home, I was startled as I came across the photograph of that wild character. I remembered what I had been thinking as we watched him in Israel and knew that my original evaluation was correct. His entire facial expression, particularly his eyes, verified to me that he was demon-possessed.

I don't approach this subject flippantly. When you begin to investigate, the tendency is to see everyone as demon-possessed. This is to be avoided as much as pure ignorance.

When we seek to diagnose whether a person is demon-possessed or not, we need discipline and prayer to be able to observe a combination of traits. I don't think any one of the following characteristics applied by itself to someone provides an iron-clad certainty that a person is demon-possessed.

Psychic or Occult Powers

Be wary of those who have psychic powers. This would be the ability to sense things about people, the ability to foretell the future, to have insight into people without having any knowledge of them. It can be a gift of discernment from God, but it can also be a counterfeit from Satan and a symptom of demon possession.

Paul and Silas had an encounter with a girl who had these powers: "And it happened that as we were going to the place of prayer, a certain slave-girl having a spirit of divination met us, who was bringing her masters much profit by fortune-telling" (Acts 16:16).

Divination, as we saw in Chapter Eight, is the ability to foretell future events or discover hidden information. A Bible scholar says that divination is the "Satanic counterfeit of Biblical prophecy."[1]

The fortunetelling slave was a pest. "Following after Paul and us, she kept crying out, saying, 'These men are bond-servants of the Most High God, who are proclaiming to you the way of salvation'" (Acts 16:17).

Two things of importance are noted in this incident. First, the fortuneteller was accurately describing Paul's and Silas's mission. They were "servants of the Most High God." Secondly, she mixed error subtly with the truth. In the original Greek of this passage she literally said, "who are proclaiming to you *a* way of salvation."

The implication was that Jesus Christ was "a way" of salvation, but that there were other ways. The Scripture, however, is explicit on this: "And there is salvation in no one else; for there is no other name under heaven that has been given among men, by which we must be saved" (Acts 4:12).

Notice how demons do things. The slave girl was speaking in the power of a demon, and without knowing Paul and Silas, she was telling the truth about them. Then, as fortunetellers go, error was camouflaged by fact.

Such persistence! "She continued doing this for many days. But Paul was greatly annoyed. . ." (Acts 16:18).

Why was Paul so agitated by this fortuneteller's witnessing as to his mission? He recognized it as Satan's old "if you can't beat 'em join 'em" tactic. To have accepted the witness of a demon-possessed fortuneteller would have done several things. First, in the eyes of the people, it would have been an act of approval of her abilities. This would have exposed many to deceptions, because Satan will inspire much truth only to slip in later with clever lies. Secondly, it would have exposed Paul to demonic attack.

Paul obviously had the gift of discerning spirits, for he settled the problem when he "turned and said to the spirit, 'I command you in the name of Jesus Christ to come out of her!' And it came out at that very moment" (Acts 16:18).

Any complicity with demon activity, whether it be ouija boards, tarot cards, horoscopes, crystal balls, palm readings, or fortunetelling, makes one vulnerable to demonic influences. I have encountered cases where heavy demon influence began in this way.

We are commanded: "resist the devil and he will flee from you" (James 4:7). If we don't resist, we will make an opening in our lives that Satan will be quick to enter.

Playing with any form of the occult is definitely not resisting but assisting the Devil.

As in the case of the demon-controlled slave girl, a fortuneteller may be able to tell you about your past and present and be absolutely accurate. This might give you confidence that this person really has supernatural power and you would accept the possibility of her predictions coming true. Consequently, you could be directed into a self-fulfilling prophecy. We saw how this could happen with the young minister in the last chapter.

When a fortuneteller's prophecy comes true, a person can come under demonic enslavement. A young man in one of my classes told about a fortuneteller who came to the door of his mother's house when she was pregnant with her first child. The fortuneteller told her that she would not have children until she was much older and that she was going to have a tragedy in her family very soon. Since the woman was already pregnant, but not noticeably, she laughed off the fortuneteller as being a fraud.

However, the baby she was carrying did die and her next child also. She became depressed to the extent that she was caught in the demonic snare of the fortuneteller's power.

Don't play with fortunetelling—no matter how innocent it may appear to be!

Magic

Involvement in magic should be suspect when we understand how open a person can be to demon possession. We're not talking about those who do sleight of hand tricks or entertain us with clever showmanship. That's fun and a legitimate form of entertainment. But there is another form of magic which involves mesmerism, black magic, and supernatural powers.

The type of magic we refer to as a sign characteristic of demon posses-sion is a "divinely forbidden art of bringing about results beyond human power by recourse to superhuman spirit agencies."[2]

Sceptics of our time tend to deny the reality of both divine and demonic power, according to Dr. Unger, one of the finest Bible scholars in the world. Combined with this scepticism is a confusion over the nature of magic. For our study, the important point is to understand that many of the phenom-ena which involve the spirit realm and result in spirit-rapping, moving furniture, apparitions, and other weird occurrences are a part of diabolic deceptions.

Some persons may claim to have magic powers which are from God. The Scriptures tell us of one magician who made such false claims: "Now there was a certain man named Simon, who formerly was practicing magic in the city, and astonishing the people of Samaria, claiming to be someone great; and they all, from smallest to greatest, were giving attention to him, say-ing, 'This man is what is called the Great Power of God.' And they were giving him attention because he had for a long time astonished them with his magic arts" (Acts 8:9-11).

The man named Simon was so involved in magic that even though he made a profession of belief, his belief was not genuine. Peter pulled him up by the scruff of his deceiving neck and said: "May your silver perish with you, because you thought you could obtain the gift of God with money! You have no part or portion in this matter, for your heart is not right before God. Therefore repent of this wickedness of yours, and pray the Lord that if possible, the intention of your heart may be forgiven you" (Acts 8:20-22).

The history of magic with devilish works and any involvement with black magic, should be shunned.*

Necromancy

Necromancy means calling up the dead or foretelling the future by com-municating with the dead. Usually when a medium calls up someone from the dead, it is a demonic deception: that is, a demon impersonating some-one who is dead will begin to speak through the medium. Necromancy has been practiced from the beginning of recorded history. The Bible gives a vivid example in the Old Testament.

---

* For a study on this subject, to be read with Christian discernment, see *The History and Practice of Magic* by Paul Christian, The Citadel Press, Inc., New York, 1963.

Saul, the first king of Israel, through repeated disobedience had lost communication with God. God ceased sending him instructions through priests or prophets. Furthermore, the most respected and trusted prophet, Samuel, who had been Saul's friend, was dead.

When the enemies of Israel gathered a great army and threatened to invade, Saul committed his worst sin of all. In an hour of desperation he sent for a medium to call up Samuel from the dead. In other words, he wanted a seance. Saul knew this was forbidden, for he had previously run all the spiritists and mediums out of the land (Deuteronomy 18:10-12; 1 Samuel 28:3).

Saul's men located a medium at a place called Endor. Disguising himself, Saul persuaded the medium to conduct a seance and to call up Samuel.

When Samuel appeared, he rebuked Saul directly for his sin and predicted that Israel would be defeated by the Philistine army and that Saul and his sons would die in battle.

The sin of necromancy was considered by God to be the final straw for Saul. He and his sons did die in battle the next day and Israel was routed.

My young twin daughters have told me of classmates attempting to conduct seances with older students. Seances are considered popular pastimes these days on many junior high, high school, and college campuses, and it should be understood by all that God considers this an extremely serious matter.

Listen again to the warning of God through Moses: "There shall not be found among you anyone . . . who casts a spell, or a medium, or a spiritist, or one who calls up the dead. For whoever does these things is detestable to the Lord" (Deuteronomy 18:10-12).

Any playing with seances may open the door for strong demonic influence in your life, whether you are a Christian or a non-Christian. It may even lead to an early death.

Bishop Pike was deeply involved with mediums and necromancy before he was led to his death.*

Marked Change in Intelligence

When a demon is heavily influencing a life, there may be a sudden or sporadic increase in the person's intelligence. The greatest example of this was Adolf Hitler. This man had incredible intelligence, yet had no formal

* See Dr. Merrill Unger's *The Haunting of Bishop Pike* for a detailed account.

education. After he became involved with the Nazi party, he began to show unusual mental ability and oratorical power. His skill in speaking was obviously demonic.

Hitler mesmerized the German people, and they followed him willingly. His great oratorical ability was the deadly Pied Piper for millions.

The operation of demonic power is strong in an area where people are willing to follow a demonic leader. If ruthless ambition and the desire for prominence take over a man's life, Satan can gain a foothold.

Satan, Give Me Strength

Demons are able to energize people with incredible strength. In the case of the demoniac of Gerasene in Mark 5, it was said that he was bound with heavy chains and he broke them. No one could subdue him.

Since studying about demon possession and encountering its reality, I recall a neighbor who was thought by everyone to be mentally ill. From the characteristics he showed, I believe that he was demon possessed. One night he almost killed his wife with a hammer. The police came to get him and handcuffed him. He was only about 5'6" tall and weighed around 130 pounds, but he was able to break those handcuffs. It took several policemen to drag him down and lock him in a squad car.

I know now that this was something more than human strength.

I saw a demon-possessed man at Berkeley with such superhuman power it took six men to hold him down to keep him from doing physical harm to himself or others.

Depression, Despondency, and Suicidal Tendencies

Another word of caution: we must be careful to weigh any of these symptoms, because they may have been brought about by other causes. However, in combination with other symptoms they could be a strong indication of demon possession or influence.

Some examples from Scripture: after Satan had used Judas for his purpose, he then used the power of guilt to drive Judas to self-destruction (Matthew 27:5-10).

The demon-possessed boy in Matthew 17:14-15 had a strong tendency toward self-destruction. He threw himself into fire and then into water. This was the result of the demon attempting to inflict harm and self-destruction upon the child.

The demoniac of Gerasene continually gashed himself with stones, indicating how demons arouse a tendency toward self-destruction.

Although we probably have no way of telling after the act has been committed, we certainly should admit there is a strong possibility that persons who douse themselves with gasoline and light a match are driven by demons.

In combination with other symptoms, it is possible to observe a person's face and see evidences of demon possession. You recall the story of the Jerusalem orator at the beginning of this chapter. His eyes were wide open and wild, his face a chilling contortion of evil. I have seen the expressions of those who have been demon possessed and the vivid way in which Christ is able to work a miraculous change.

Filthy, Uncontrolled Swearing

A person's almost spontaneous reaction of swearing and cursing when the name of Jesus Christ or God is mentioned can be a symptom of an unclean spirit or demon. Jesus often confronted this.

A continual compulsion to blaspheme the name of God and Christ can, in connection with other symptoms, be a sign of demon possession or influence.

Radical Change in Personality

This characteristic of demon possession was vividly dramatized in one of the letters received from a reader of *The Late Great Planet Earth.*

A woman in the Northwest told how her husband, who was normally a pleasant family man, became fascinated with a ouija board at a party. When the ouija board began to spell out accurate answers to questions about himself and others, he became furious. He determined to prove that it was all a hoax. The next evening he came home from work with a ouija board and urged his wife to participate. Once again the board began to predict that he was to become a great leader and help bring peace to many. To do this, he was told, he would have to abandon his family.

These prophecies continued. His personality began to change radically. He stayed away from home and drank heavily. He moved out, coming home just for short visits.

Whenever he was home, he continued to pressure his wife into sessions with the ouija board. The poor woman became increasingly alarmed about the whole thing and sought help from friends who were believers in Christ, a subject her husband could not stand.

Finally, one evening while they were asking the ouija board questions, it spelled out that they would no longer have to use the board; the spirit would give guidance directly through the husband.

The wife was amazed as her husband immediately fell into a trance and a voice—not her husband's—spoke out of him. The spirit, which was a demon, reiterated all the things previously spelled on the board and told her that it was time for her husband to leave on his mission of destiny.

Shortly afterward a friend told the woman that I was to be in town speaking on the rise of the occult. She persuaded her husband to come with her to the meeting, and they were shocked to find that they were involved with demons through initial contact with the ouija board.

They obtained a copy of *The Late Great Planet Earth*; the wife read it and finally persuaded her husband to read it. As a result he renounced his involvement with demons, asked for forgiveness, and received Jesus Christ as his Savior.

His personality changed immediately for the better. He moved back home, and he and his wife became real witnesses to the saving power of Jesus Christ.

Can a Believer Be Demon Possessed?

Semantics separating demon possession and demon influence seem important to some people. A person who is demon influenced is under the power of evil spirits which may result in anything from mental torment to extreme abnormal behavior. Both believers and non-believers can be subjected to demon influence.

Most Bible scholars and missionaries who have studied or dealt with the problem understand demon possession as the indwelling of one or more evil spirits in a person's body, resulting in the personality of the demon taking dominant control. In a demonized condition the personality of the victim is enslaved and the demon virtually exercises complete control.

Dr. Unger has an excellent study on whether a Christian can be demon possessed.[3] He states that a non-Christian can be totally controlled and manipulated by demonic power, but a Christian rarely has the same degree of complete subjugation. This is my position, also. However, I've talked to many missionaries who have had to deal with these things personally, and I must say that it seems to be possible for a Christian to have a certain degree of demon possession.

An example of a demon-possessed Christian was given me by Dick Hillis of Overseas Crusades. Dick is a man who knows the Scriptures, not just as a theologian, but as a warrior of the faith. A man of careful discernment, not given to sensationalism, he has spent most of his life on the mission field. Hillis told me of one incident which happened while he was in China, before the Communist takeover, when one of the elders of his church, who was unquestionably a believer, became so demon possessed that his personality changed. He became vile and profane in his language and extraordinarily strong. Some of the members of the church locked him up in a room and sent for Hillis.

When Dick walked in the door, this man became violent and a strange voice shouted, "I know who you are."

Hillis said, "And I know who you are," and began to speak to the demon.

This was a case when a believer was actually possessed by a demon who spoke in another voice.

In countries where there is open worship of idols, such as China, a person is much more susceptible to demon influence and possession. As Unger says, "In lands where demon-energized idolatry has flourished unchecked by the Gospel for ages, new believers who were delivered from demon possession have been known to become repossessed when they return to their old idols."[4]

The main argument advanced against a Christian being demon possessed stems from the fact that the Holy Spirit dwells in the Christian. Therefore, a demon cannot dwell in the same place where the Holy Spirit dwells.

However, in Acts 5 two believers named Ananias and Sapphira certainly were controlled by Satan. Peter said, "Ananias, why has Satan *filled* your heart to lie to the Holy Spirit?" (Acts 5:3).

The word translated "filled" is the same one used in Ephesians 5:18 to describe the Holy Spirit's controlling and empowering ministry to the believer. It means the same here, only it is Satan doing the controlling.

For one person to *fill* another person literally means for one to control the other by his consent. Therefore, the one being controlled is responsible because he received the control. This responsibility is brought out clearly when Peter says to Ananias again, "Why is it that *you* have conceived this deed in your heart? *You* have not lied to men, but to God" (Acts 5:4).

The main point is that Ananias was a believer whose heart became controlled by Satan. I believe a serious warning is given us here. Whenever we deliberately turn from depending on the Holy Spirit to resist temptation, and then knowingly plot to commit sin, we open ourselves up for the possibility of Satanic attack and even control.

When Jesus announced to His disciples that He was going to be arrested and put to death, and Peter rebuked Him and said this would never happen, another important statement was made. Jesus said to Peter, "Get behind Me, *Satan!* You are a stumbling-block to Me; for you are not setting your mind on God's interest, but man's" (Matthew 16:23). Jesus addressed Peter as Satan because obviously Satan was influencing him and misleading him at this point. It was Satan who was taking Peter's eyes off God's purpose and turning them to the human viewpoint.

I believe that these and other incidents show how a believer can be possessed to a certain degree, though only temporarily and never as completely as a non-believer. It is certainly an incentive to us to walk in continual dependence upon the Holy Spirit and not try to live by human power.

It should be understood clearly that Satan cannot get control of a believer who is walking by faith and available to the Holy Spirit. Much more will be said about this in Chapter Thirteen.

Exorcists

The ancient subject of exorcism or casting out evil spirits has reentered our streamlined society. *The Exorcist* has become a national best seller. For those in our modern culture who may think all of this is some weird new venture into unreality, we should recall exorcism's pagan origins.

Magic formulas and rituals to expel evil spirits have been practiced for centuries. Many of the methods were painful to the one possessed and involved beating, pinching, burning, and other types of physical abuse. Unger tells us of a shrine in India which is well-known among Hindus and Muslims as a place where demons are exorcised. Violence and the infliction of pain are common, but when the demon that is to be driven out is particularly obstinate, cotton wicks soaked in oil are lighted and stuffed up the nostrils of the possessed. The cruelty of professional exorcists is beyond human understanding.

When we read and hear of the methods of casting out demons used by unbelievers, we understand that it is even possible under the power of Satan to cast out demons, if it furthers his teachings and purpose.

Contrast With Christ

The method which Jesus used to cast out demons was in sharp contrast to the Jewish and pagan exorcists. Matthew 8:16 tells us that when the disciples brought to Him many who were demon possessed, He cast out the spirits with a word. He did not resort to rituals.

His disciples cast out demons "in the name of Jesus Christ." Christ gave them this authority when He spoke to them following His resurrection. He said: "And these signs will accompany those who have believed: in My name they will cast out demons" (Mark 16:17).

The name of Jesus stands for the infinite and omnipotent God behind the name and has no magical power in itself. There is no hocus-pocus about saying, "In the name of Jesus." The warning to the young or immature believer must be emphatic at this point. We need to know what our authority is as believers and learn the truth from God's Word before attempting to "cast out demons" from someone whom we may believe is possessed.

Christ said, "Behold, I have given you authority to tread upon serpents and scorpions, and over all the power of the enemy, and nothing shall injure you. *Nevertheless* do not rejoice in this, that the spirits are subject to you, but rejoice that your names are recorded in heaven" (Luke 10:19-20).

This is a promise given by the Lord which everyone involved in this study needs to grasp. As believers we are given authority over demons, and the only way that demons can get a stranglehold on us is when we deliberately, knowingly, and persistently walk in some sin.

As we walk with Christ, we may be in fearful situations, but nothing can injure us if we claim our authority over the enemy. If we get into this area of the Satanic and do not know our authority, we are going to get into trouble.

Satan will bluff us as far as he can; he will take all the ground we will give him. But if we stand on the promises of God and use our authority from the Scriptures, he will respect that authority and flee. We are not talking about human bravado or the whistle-in-the-dark front; we are talking about the victory of the cross. We must stand behind that victory and have a healthy respect for Satan's power.

One of the dangers of immaturity in the Christian faith is at the point when God begins to show works of power and answers this newly acquired faith. It is easy to become enamored with the power and captured by the gifts instead of the Giver. The great danger in spiritual adolescence is to have a little knowledge and not know it is *a little knowledge.*

Recently I was given an old and priceless book which has some deep perceptions into this subject. The writers were scholars and Christians of great understanding and depth. They said: "For the deliverance of souls under the bondage of evil spirits in possession, much knowledge of God and of spiritual things is needed."[5]

If a believer encounters what he thinks is a true manifestation of demon possession, I believe he should, in most cases, call upon a trusted, mature believer and the two should pray for guidance together as to how to deal with the situation.

What Happened to the Socialite at the Conference?

Before this book was begun, I had never cast a demon out of anyone. It's not something I would seek to do or a ministry I would find particularly enjoyable. But I believe the Lord gave me the experience I described briefly in Chapter One so I would have a better understanding of this entire realm.

When the socialite from the Midwest (see Chapter One) showed me the ring on her finger, the sign of a Satan worshiper, and described the evil spirit which hurled her into periods of great depression and despondency, she also told me that her mother and her grandmother had been fortunetellers. Apparently she had inherited her psychic ability from them.

It wasn't easy telling this woman what her real problem was. With genuine compassion, I told her she was possessed by a spirit of divination, a demon that specializes in fortunetelling. She listened intently while I explained that according to many case histories I had read, this usually occurred in families with a history of occult powers.

I insisted she renounce this psychic power and turn to Jesus Christ, who alone could liberate her, or this demon would destroy her life.

"Would you like to be delivered from this spirit and receive Jesus Christ into your life?"

She didn't hesitate. "If it means finding peace of mind, I sure do."

I then prayed according to the pattern of the Apostle Paul in Acts 16:18. "You evil spirit, I command you in the name of Jesus Christ to come out of this woman and leave her alone."

Never have I experienced such a sense of authority in the name of Jesus Christ as I did at that moment.

The woman shook slightly and began to sob.

"Pray this prayer out loud," I continued. "I believe that Jesus Christ is the Son of God who died for my sins. Jesus, come into my life and make it pleasing to You."

The woman fought to speak for about three minutes. Her throat seemed to be constricted by an unseen hand.

I prayed silently for Jesus to bind the influence of Satan. Finally she prayed the prayer aloud.

As soon as she had finished, her whole countenance changed before my eyes. She became radiant. She exclaimed, "I'm free!" It had a different meaning for her than it does for most people.

She left me abruptly and started toward the final meeting of the conference. The first person she encountered was Jan. She blurted out, "Do you know what your husband just did? He cast a demon out of me."

My wife, who is not easily surprised, immediately saw the startling change in the woman. Sensing her immediate spiritual need, Jan said quietly, "Did Jesus Christ come in?"

"You bet He did," she said jubilantly.

She then found the friends who had brought her and amazed them with the good news.

As the former psychic was about to leave, I instructed her to get rid of all her artifacts of the occult because this is a way demons can keep a foothold in a life. She agreed to do this.

Then I got a real jolt. She pointed to the Scottish kilt she had worn all weekend.

"Do you recognize this plaid?"

I studied it for a moment and said, "I believe it's the Lindsey plaid."

"Right," she answered. "A few weeks ago I was in Scotland. While I was there, I had a premonition that I was going to meet someone named Lindsey and that he would have a profound effect upon my life. That's the reason I bought the plaid kilt."

I was speechless. Later, in reflecting upon the incident, a thrill went through me. The power of Jesus Christ was so real to me!

11 ○ Doctrines
of Demons

"The Devil can cite Scripture for his purpose."

SHAKESPEARE, *The Merchant of Venice*, 1597

"But the Spirit explicitly says that in later times some will fall away from the faith, paying attention to deceitful spirits and doctrines of demons."

I TIMOTHY 4:1

SATAN, IN HIS role as "the god of this age," has conducted a relentless, well-planned strategy to blind men's minds to the truth about God and how to know Him. If you were Satan, out to control men, where would you launch your heaviest attacks?

Against the Bible and those who preach and teach it and against the church, of course!

With the Bible generally accepted as a revelation from God, mankind could not easily be blinded. As long as there were ministers who preached and taught the Bible, the Christian would keep growing in his faith, vitally witnessing to the world, and not easily deceived. While churches were organized and functioning according to the New Testament pattern, they could not be swept away from their real purpose of building disciples and reaching out to the world with the "good news about Christ."

When the apostles realized they were nearing the end of their lives, they warned about the coming attacks upon the truth and the church that would be accelerated in the days just before Christ would return to earth in His Second Coming.

In Paul's last session with the elders of the church at Ephesus, he gave the following exhortation: "Be on guard for yourselves and for all the flock, among which the Holy Spirit has made you overseers, to shepherd the church of God which He purchased with His own blood. I know that after my departure savage wolves will come in among you, not sparing the flock; and from among your own selves men will arise, speaking perverse things, to draw away the disciples after them. Therefore be on the alert, remembering that night and day for a period of three years I did not cease to admonish each one with tears" (Acts 10:28-31).

Paul predicted that there would be ministers from within the church who would teach perverted things while posing as teachers of truth. The antidote to this coming apostasy is given in verse 32. "And now I commend you to God and to *the word of His grace*, which is able to build you up and to give you the inheritance among all those who are sanctified."

Paul exhorted the church leadership to place heavy reliance upon "God and the *Word of His grace*."

When a minister ceases to teach and emphasize a personal faith-walk with God upon the principle of grace instead of law, he has taken the first step down the road to apostasy.

Why Revivals Fizzle

History is strewn with evidence of movements born in the fires of revivals that after a few generations have departed into error and eventual apostasy. Many of the great denominations of today bear little resemblance to the faith and fervor of their original founders.

Christians have been bewildered at this continual trend away from God and have asked "why?" In most instances the trend began in a departure from the grace of God into "legalism."

Legalism—seeking to live for God by the principle of the law—is the first and the worst doctrine of demons. It is the dent in your armor at which Satan will chip away until he has a hole big enough to drive a truck through. I don't know another doctrinal distortion that has been more devastating to believers. The awful thing is that it can sidetrack a mature believer as well as a young one. In fact, this demonic doctrine seems to find especially fertile soil in the life of a growing believer who is intent upon pleasing God in his life.

It was concerning teachers of legalism that Paul wrote, "But I am afraid, lest as the serpent deceived Eve by his craftiness, your minds should be led astray from the simplicity and purity of devotion to Christ. . . . For such men are false apostles, deceitful workers, disguising themselves as apostles of Christ. And no wonder, for even Satan disguises himself as an angel of light. Therefore it is not surprising if his servants (literally ministers) also disguise themselves as servants (ministers) of righteousness, whose end shall be according to their deeds" (2 Corinthians 11:3, 13-15).

According to this warning, Satan has his own corps of dedicated ministers who masquerade as "ministers of righteousness." What could be more effective than a minister, sincere and moral, quoting the Bible, yet missing the emphasis of grace?

Some ministers who truly belong to God's family become tools of Satan by putting their flock "under the law."

If we do not understand the difference between the principle of law and the principle of grace when it comes to relating to God, we will not understand why we sin.

Why Do We Sin?

Sometimes when we sin we like to say, "The Devil made me do it." It helps get us off the hook in our own minds, but we can't blame Satan for all our sinning.

There are two ingredients necessary for a person to sin. In Romans 7:5 Paul says, "For while we were in the flesh (that is, before we became believers), the *sinful passions*, which were *aroused by the Law*, were at work in the members of our body to bear fruit for death."

Paul indicates that there are two things at work within a non-believer to make him sin: his sinful passions or sin nature as it is sometimes called, and the law. When the law stirs up the sinful passions, rebellion against the law occurs and that is what the Bible calls "sin."

Later on in Romans 7:7-8 Paul says that the law works exactly the same way in the life of a believer. ". . . I would not have come to know sin except through the Law; for I would not have known about coveting if the Law had not said, 'You shall not covet.' But sin, taking opportunity through the commandment, produced in me coveting of every kind; for apart from the Law sin is dead."

Paul might just as easily have said, "My sin nature, which used to be aroused by all the laws before I became a Christian, is still getting stirred up by the law even though I'm now God's child. If I could get away from all those laws, then I wouldn't have to be worrying about all this sinning."

Reverse Psychology

Psychology has noticed this same tendency in man to do just the opposite of what he is commanded to do. We call it the "law of reverse psychology." If you want someone to do something, tell him to do just the opposite. Most parents have figured this out before their children get very old.

A classic example of this is a story that appeared in a national publication a few years ago. A new luxury hotel was built out on a pier in Galveston, Texas. As they were about to have their gala opening and the manager was inspecting a room with a Gulf view, it suddenly occurred to him that people were going to be tempted to fish off the balconies. If they did, when they cast out their lines with heavy sinkers on them, the wind might blow them back into the windows below and cause a lot of breakage.

There was a little panic for a while as the management tried to decide what to do. They finally put cards under the glass on each room desk saying that fishing off the balconies was absolutely forbidden!

Opening week came. You guessed it! A number of windows were broken. The management was shaken. Finally one hotel clerk suggested, "Why not throw away the cards and see what happens?"

Immediately the damage stopped. There was no more "law" to stir up the "sinful passions" of all those hotel patrons!

The Law Is Not the Culprit

I know that all of this tends to make the law, whether God's law or man's law, look bad. But the law isn't the real problem. Those sinful passions or sin natures that get stirred up by the law are the problem.

You might wonder why God would give the law if He knew that it would work against us rather than for us. There are four basic reasons why God gave His law.

The first reason is to show man what sin is. The law is a principle which guides our behavior by setting up standards of conduct and threatening certain consequences if the standards are not met.

There are several kinds of law set forth in the Bible. The first *is the law of conscience*. When Adam and Eve ate of the tree of the knowledge of good and evil, they developed a conscious knowledge of what they should and should not do.

The Apostle Paul referred to this law of conscience in Romans 2:14-15. "For when Gentiles who do not have the Law (the Law of Moses) do instinctively the things of the Law, these, not having the Law, are a law to themselves, in that they show the work of the Law written in their hearts, their conscience bearing witness, and their thoughts alternately accusing or else defending themselves."

The only problem with the conscience as a reliable standard of conduct is that it can easily be seared. Within the few hundred years it took to go from Adam to Noah, man had so deadened his conscience that God was sorry He had even made man.

In modern times you can see how effective the searing of the human conscience has been. Jane Russell's seductive film, *The Outlaw*, made in the

1950s, is so tame by present-day standards that it could be shown at a Sunday school picnic.

God rejected the law of conscience as a means for man to know Him. About the time that Moses came along, the people had so little consciousness of what sin was that God saw their need for an objective standard that would forever nail down what He considered to be sin.

The "Big Ten"

When God gave the Ten Commandments and the various other laws to the nation of Israel, for the first time the people knew just how far they could go and still not sin. Before the law was given, if a man had a weakness for sleeping with other men's wives and his conscience didn't bother him, then it wasn't sin. The other husbands may not have liked it, but there was no law to which they could appeal to convict the other man of wrongdoing. There may have been certain tribal laws, but there was no larger moral law which could be invoked against the man.

During the hundreds of years that passed until Jesus came on the scene, the Jews had so stringently interpreted their laws that they had evolved into a mere keeping of outer form and ritual. Jesus' indictment of them was that outside they were like whitewashed tombs, but on the inside they were full of dead men's bones (Matthew 23:27).

Sermon on the Mount

The Sermon on the Mount was the greatest "hellfire and damnation" sermon ever preached. In no uncertain terms, Jesus said that it wasn't just what you did on the outside that was a sin, but even what you were thinking on the inside.

Nothing could have pricked the self-righteous hearts of those religious people more than to hear that "good works" weren't enough to get them to heaven. Over and over again Jesus pulled the rug out from under them by saying, "You have heard it taught," and then quoting one of the Ten Commandments. "But I say to you, it isn't just what you *do* wrong that will convict you, but even your wrong thoughts that will bring you condemnation." Jesus sought to show them what the basic intent of the law of Moses had always been.

So we can see that the teachings of Jesus about man's conduct were a further amplification in the definition to mankind of what sin really was.

New Testament Injunctions

All of the New Testament epistles are filled with words of warning, words of admonition, and words of definition regarding what a Christian should and should not do. This "law of the New Testament" is the most definitive and exacting law given to man. You can see the progression from the easygoing "law of conscience" to the demanding "injunctions of the New Testament."

What if the law hadn't been given?

Suppose Jesus had come and announced to the world, "I'm here. I'm going to die for your sins. I'm the solution to your problem."

If the law hadn't been given, what would they have said? "What problem? We don't have any problem. My conscience doesn't bother me. What problem are you talking about?"

That's the first reason the law was given: to show us what sin is in order to give us a standard against which to compare our lives. When we see that we don't measure up, we're forced to admit we have a problem. Now when Jesus comes and says He is the solution to our problem, we look at the law and we look at our lives and we say, "Man, I need a solution!"

The law is much like pain. If it weren't for pain, we'd be in trouble physically. The most insignificant injury could end up being fatal if we didn't have pain to signal its severity to us.

Man is born into this world with a tremendous injury in his soul, and if it weren't for the "pain" of the law jabbing into his sinful passions and arousing them, he'd go merrily on his way to hell saying, "Problem, what problem?"

That Sin Might Increase

I know it's going to be hard to accept the second reason God gave the law, but it's true. The law was given to provoke man's sin nature to sin more. Paul said in Romans 5:20, "And the Law came in that the transgression might increase. . . ." God wants the unbeliever to get so loaded with sin that there's no way he can fail to see how utterly sinful he is and how much he needs a Savior.

In First Corinthians 15:56, Paul said, ". . . the power of sin is the law." According to this verse, even the sin nature of believers gets a stranglehold on them from the prodding of the law. It seems that God is working against Himself to get us to sin more, but this is God's way of bringing us to total despair of self-effort in living for Him.

And that's the third reason God gave the law: to drive us to despair of self-effort. When we have despaired of self-effort, we're ready for the fourth reason God gave the law: to bring the unbeliever to Christ for salvation and the believer to the Holy Spirit for His empowering.

The Law Is Our Schoolmaster

When Paul wrote his letter to the Galatian believers, he used a terrific illustration of how the law works on unbelievers. In Galatians 3:24-25 he says, "The Law has become our tutor to lead us to Christ, that we may be justified by faith. But now that faith has come, we are no longer under a tutor."

A tutor was a specially chosen slave whose job it was to take a Roman child by the hand every morning and lead him to the school. He would wait there until the lessons were done and then lead the child home again. Once the child's school days were over, he no longer needed his "tutor."

The law takes the unbeliever by the hand and gently leads him to Christ for salvation. Once he has come to Christ, he no longer needs his "tutor," the law.

The law also is designed to do the same thing to a believer.

In Romans 7:14-24, we see a picture of a man who was at the end of himself, and the law had brought him there: ". . . but I am of flesh, sold into bondage to sin. For that which I am doing, I do not understand; for I am not practicing what I would like to do, but I am doing the very thing I hate. . . . For I know that nothing good dwells in me, that is, in my flesh; for the wishing is present in me, but the doing of the good is not. For the good that I wish, I do not do; but I practice the very evil that I do not wish. . . . Wretched man that I am! Who will set me free from the body of this death?"

Do you know who uttered those heartrending words? The Apostle Paul! There he was—right where the law was designed to bring him—at the end of himself. At that point the law tenderly took him by the hand and led him to the Lord Jesus Christ, who set him free as he began to walk in the Spirit.

In Romans 8:3-5 Paul said that what the law couldn't do for him, God had done. God produced in Paul the righteous life which the law demanded of him, and this happened as Paul just walked in the Spirit.

The Law Has Done Its Job

The law has shown us what sin is, and it has actually made us sin more. It has driven us to despair of human effort and it has finally brought us to Christ for salvation and for the moment-by-moment power to live for Him. When this progression is finished, then the law is finally done with the believer.

Because it is so difficult for us to understand and accept this, it is a constant nemesis to the Christian.

The law is through with us, but we won't let go of it. Let's look at what we've done with the law in our Christian lives today. Many say, "Sure, we're free from the law of Moses, but we're under the higher 'Law of Christ,' which means that we have to keep the Sermon on the Mount and all of the laws of the New Testament."

If the law of Moses was impossible to keep, and it was, how on earth do we suppose that we can keep the laws of the New Testament which are a thousand times tougher? The Old Testament laws were external, but most of the New Testament laws are internal, dealing with our emotions and our thought life.

The problem with Judaism was that the Jews thought if they could just be obedient to their laws, then they could obtain righteousness. Paul said that they didn't obtain righteousness because they tried to get it by obedience, rather than by faith (Romans 9:30-32).

One thing you can say for them: they had a zeal for God. But unfortunately, it wasn't in accordance with God's plan (Romans 10:1-3).

We're Guilty Too!

We've done just what the Jews did, with our own refinements, of course. We've had a lot of zeal for God, but much of it has not been according to knowledge. We've made rules about how to be a "good Christian" and we've said, "Okay, here are the things we can do, and here are the things we can't do."

The Jews tried to become righteous by obeying the Ten Commandments, and it didn't work. We've tried to bring righteousness into our lives by obedience to the Sermon on the Mount and all the teachings of Paul plus a few man-made taboos, and that hasn't worked either.

The Solution

What is the answer to a righteous and obedient life?

"Christ is the end of the law *for righteousness* to everyone who believes" (Romans 10:4).

". . . if a law had been given which was able to impart life, then righteousness would indeed have been based on law" (Galatians 3:21).

"Now that no one is justified by the Law before God is evident; for 'The righteous man shall live by faith.' However, the Law is not of faith . . ." (Galatians 3:11-12).

"I do not nullify the grace of God; for if righteousness comes through the Law, then Christ died needlessly" (Galatians 2:21).

"For the law was given through Moses; grace and truth were realized through Jesus Christ" (John 1:17).

The answer to a righteous and obedient life is to walk in the Spirit and walk by faith in His ability to produce God's righteousness and obedience to His laws within you. "In order that the requirement of the Law might be fulfilled in us, who do not walk according to the flesh, but according to the Spirit" (Romans 8:4).

Don't Get the Cart Before the Horse

In the Christian life there is only one *source* of power—the indwelling Holy Spirit. There is only one *means* of releasing that source, and that is faith. There are hundreds of *results* in the life of the Christian who releases the Spirit in him by faith: witnessing, holiness, obedience, good works, power, boldness, praise, faith, etc.

Some of you may still be concerned about how you're going to keep all the commands in the Bible. These commands are simply "*results*" of the Spirit-produced life. We are only to concern ourselves with walking in the Spirit, and He will concern Himself with making all these biblical admonitions a reality in our life. This turns the commands in the Word into promises of what He can be trusted to do in us.

If *we* try to produce the holy life we see expected of us in the Bible, then we are focusing on the "*results*" of the Christian life rather than on its source, Jesus. We are doomed to end up in utter frustration.

We don't get up in the morning and say, "Now I must be obedient today. I must check over all my lists of things that Christians do and don't do. I must do my best to live for God today."

Do you know what happens when you do that? It's like throwing a truckload of fresh meat into a cage of half-starved lions. All your resolve, determination, and good intentions will be torn to shreds before the day is half over. All your sin nature has been waiting for, to turn it into a raging beast, is a "truckload" of law.

If you seek to be made righteous as a believer by obedience to the law, any kind of law, you have cut off the power of Christ in your life. That's what Paul says in Galatians 5:1-5.

Obedience is a *result* of a Spirit-filled relationship with Christ, not the means of producing it.

How Has God Made Us Holy?

We've looked at the law; we've seen what it is. We've examined what its purpose is in both the unbeliever and the believer. We've seen what it has done to us and how we've misused it.

Now then, what has God done about the law and the believer's relationship to it?

He has taken us out from under the jurisdiction of the law and placed us under His grace. The law is still there, but we're not under it.

"But now we have been released from the Law, having died to that by which we were bound, so that we serve in newness of the Spirit and not in oldness of the letter" (Romans 7:6).

The law just doesn't speak to us anymore as a basis of operation in the Christian life. When Christ died, was buried, rose, and ascended, we died with Him to the law and its power over us.

A friend of mine tells a story to illustrate this. You're in a car going twenty in a twenty-five-mile zone. A cop is following you, and you're really watching yourself. Overhead, there's a bird doing forty. You glance at the policeman, but he doesn't move. Why? Because the law of twenty-five-miles-an-hour just doesn't have jurisdiction over that bird.

Law and Grace Are Mutually Exclusive

It is imperative that we realize that law and grace are complete systems in themselves. They are mutually exclusive. To mix these principles robs the law of its bona fide terror and grace of its creative freeness.

What does this mean to us in a practical way?

First of all, it means that there is nothing we have to do to earn favor with God. Under grace, our acceptance with God is based on the fact that we are *in* Christ and God accepts Him completely. Therefore He accepts us the same way. Our acceptance is based on Christ's performance for us.

If we insist on relating to God by the principle of law, then our acceptance with Him is based on our own performance. I don't know a more heartbreaking sight than earnest, well-meaning, but dead-wrong believers plugging away, trying to improve their status with God by all their right-eous deeds. If they could only know that all of that is futile. Their accep-tance is already a settled fact and *in no way* can it be improved upon.

Grace emphasizes love as a motivation for obedience and service, but law uses a fear-threat motive. Satan subtly makes you think, "Something awful will happen to me if I don't shape up in my Christian life. God will take one of my children or let me be in a crippling accident."

There is no way to feel loved by God or loving toward Him under a law-based relationship. Everything depends on your own ingenuity to keep God happy with you, and that's just too heavy a burden of responsibility to bear.

Grace That Is Greater Than All My Sin

Do you know what grace really means and what God's grace has made available to His dearly loved children?

It means that there is not now, nor can there ever be again, for any rea-son, any condemnation of us by anyone, including ourselves and God. It means that we are totally accepted by God in our present, unfinished con-dition. It means that He has set Himself so free to minister in us and to us that He will do it without our even asking Him (Romans 8:1).

Now that's a lot to digest, but it's just a glimpse of what His grace is. It will take all eternity to fathom it.

What Results?

When we come to know and truly believe that we are no longer under law, but under grace, it sets the Holy Spirit free to produce holiness in us. Love, praise, obedience, and performance will all result from the Holy Spirit making this a reality in our lives.

We feel like responding in love to someone who has done so much for us. "We love, because He *first* loved us" (1 John 4:19).

Doctrine of Demons

Perhaps you've wondered why I've taken so much time to show the dev-astating effects of "legalism" on the church. It's because this doctrine is tol-erated in churches today that make an absolute fetish of being doctrinally pure in every area. Satan has completely blinded them to the fact that what they are doing to their people by keeping them under law is guaranteed to wipe out their Christian life.

I know of Christians today who talk about grace, who believe in grace, and who at the same time have almost put grace under the law.

God grant that their eyes will be opened to see the liberty there is in Christ. A true understanding of grace will never produce license, but I have seen plenty of license produced by legalism. Satan is in there pitching all the time.

The Trial of the Truth

Legalism is joined by another "doctrine of demons." This took on steam in Germany in the 1880s when the so-called "Higher Critical" movement (mentioned briefly in Chapter Three) launched its attack against the historicity and authenticity of the Bible.

This biased group brought such convincing arguments to bear upon the Bible that young seminarians became crusaders to spread "the honest truth" about the Bible to other seminaries and from there into the various churches.

These religious liberals, who started with the basic assumption that there can be no real supernatural occurrences, vigorously attacked the accounts of Christ's life in the four gospels. It was dogmatically asserted, with no hard evidence from history or archaeology, that the followers of Jesus had embellished and rewritten the accounts of His life and had inserted the miracles as fanciful myths.

These men, primarily on the basis of speculation, dated the writing of the gospels and other New Testament books, for the most part, in the second century. This permitted them to argue that the writers were so far removed from the actual facts that the original readers had no way to check the accuracy of the books.

Recent archaeological discoveries may explode this "liberal mythology." Perhaps one of the most exciting archaeological finds of this century relating to the New Testament was reported, with little prominence, in the news media. The article by Louis Cassels of United Press was headlined "Bible Accounts Strengthened by Scholar's Finds." These archaeological discoveries concerned the identification of certain pieces of papyrus which were found among the Dead Sea Scrolls in 1947 as possibly being parts of Mark's gospel, written around A.D. 50.

The newspaper account continues: "The date is what matters. Biblical scholars have long assumed that Mark's gospel, based on the recollections of the Apostle Peter, was set down in writing shortly before Peter's death in Rome, which would date it around A.D. 68.

"Since Jesus was crucified about A.D. 33, the previous dating of Mark's gospel—generally regarded to have been the first one written—left a hiatus of 35 years in which the historical details of the life of Jesus either were transmitted by word of mouth or by now lost records. . . .

"German biblical scholarship, sometimes called 'form criticism' has been predicated since the 19th Century on the assumption that during this lapse of 35 years the actual facts of Jesus' life became heavily intermixed with myth and legend."[1]

The papyrus fragments identified by Professor Jose O'Callaghan, a scholar at the Pontifical Biblical Institute in Rome, have been dated by scientific methods as possibly having been in existence from about A.D. 50, which indicates that Mark's gospel might have been in circulation within a dozen years of the time of Jesus' death.

As Louis Cassels points out, if this early date for the gospel is correct, it "means Mark's record had to survive the test of any journalistic or historical writing—being published at a time when it could be read, criticized, and, if inauthentic, denounced by thousands of Jews, Christians, Romans, and Greeks who were living in Palestine at the time of Jesus' ministry.

"That the early church chose Mark as one of only four gospels out of dozens once in circulation to be preserved for posterity in the New Testament also indicates the people closest to the events—Jesus' original followers—found Mark's report accurate and trustworthy, not myth but true history."[2]

Scholars may be working to prove or disprove this and other finds for years to come, but as each day we live becomes history, we will see more evidence of the authenticity of the Bible unfold before the unbelieving world.

For centuries Satan has delighted in making biblical Christianity appear non-intellectual in the eyes of the world. But how great it is to know that we do not have to put our intellect on the shelf to believe the message of God's transforming power through Christ.

12 ∘ The Guilt Trip

"I, even I, am the one who wipes out your transgressions for My own sake; And I will not remember your sins."

THE LORD, ISAIAH 43:25

IF YOU WERE the captain of an invading army, you would find the weakest spot in your opponent's defenses and go in for the kill.

Satan, the archenemy of the saints, has a way of wiping Christians out—over and over again. He moves in on our blind side and steers us in the direction he wants.

When a person becomes a true believer in Christ, he is born into the family of God and out of the family of Satan. Satan does everything he can to keep us blinded to the offer of forgiveness in Christ, but millions have thrown off his shackles and gone from death to life. This has absolutely infuriated Satan, and each time someone responds to the Gospel, it's a slap in his face.

C. S. Lewis, in his amusing book *The Screwtape Letters*, satirizes the daily routine in hell and the foibles and headaches of hardworking demons who just try to put in an honest day's work fouling up Christians.

One of the most successful tactics the demons used in neutralizing their enemies (the Christians) was to get them to dwell on all of their failures. Once they began feeling guilty about their performance in the Christian life, they were no longer any threat to Satan's program.

Things haven't changed much in Satan's tactics. Why should they? He's got a winner.

There's nothing Satan likes better than to get a believer started on the guilt trip.

As I look back over my own life, I realize that guilt is a handle that the Devil constantly tries to grab to steer me. One classic illustration that comes to mind happened to me my third year in seminary. One fellow was a real close buddy of mine. We had had three years of great times together. Then I borrowed some money from him. I told him I would be able to pay him back in about two weeks.

After a week went by, I began to be concerned a little about where the money was going to come from to pay him. But I had another week to work on it, so I wasn't too worried.

The second week went by, and I just couldn't raise the money anywhere. I felt kind of strained around my friend, but I didn't bring the subject up because I'd hoped he'd forgotten what the date was.

As the days went by, it seemed to me as though he was looking at me with an accusing expression every time I saw him, and I did the best I could to stay out of his way. After the deadline had passed by two weeks, I began planning my day so I wouldn't run into him. It was awful. I felt terrible to have lost such a good friend, but on the other hand, I couldn't see why he wasn't more understanding of my problem. Mind you, not a word had passed between us regarding the money, but I felt so guilty that I was sure he had written me off as a friend.

Finally one day, to my horror, I saw him coming toward me in the hall. There was no place to hide! He cornered me and said, "Okay, Hal, what's the matter with you?"

"Well, it's about that money I owe you," I answered defensively.

He laughed and put his big hand on my shoulder and said, "Brother, I thought that was it. Look, Hal, I haven't changed. I don't feel any different toward you than I did a few weeks ago. If you had the money, I know you'd pay me. But money doesn't mean that much to me. Your friendship means a lot more, and I'm still your buddy."

For three weeks I had been going around thinking he was condemning me. But that wasn't true at all—he was still my best friend.

That taught me an unforgettable lesson. If we think someone is holding something against us, we become alienated and hostile toward them. It's simply an inevitable reaction, a defense mechanism.

I believe this is the number one reason why Christians fail in their relationship with God. Because we're always aware that in many ways we fall short of what we should be as Christians, it's only natural to assume that God must be displeased with our performance. The more we let God down, the more we assume His anger, until such alienation sets into our minds that it is virtually impossible for us to enjoy a vital fellowship with God.

And the pitiful tragedy is that all this is just in our minds. God isn't mad at us!

I know what some of you are thinking. You can hardly believe that what I'm saying is true. On the human level if we let people down or offend them, it does produce alienation on their part. And besides, if you've been riddled with guilt, then you have a gnawing suspicion that you really deserve God's hostility.

I want to say something loud and clear, in no uncertain terms: "He has now reconciled you in His fleshly body, through death, in order to present you before Him holy and blameless and beyond reproach—" (Colossians 1:22).

When do you become "holy and blameless and beyond reproach"? The minute He reconciles you to the Father, and that happens the moment you believe in Christ's substitutionary death on your behalf.

Let's substantiate this from the Scripture.

There are several words in the original Greek New Testament for reconciliation. One is found in Matthew 5:24: "*diallasso,*" which means that two parties are at enmity with each other and need to be reconciled by removing the cause of the enmity. This word is used strictly of human relationships in the Bible.

There is another word, however, which is always used in connection with God and man: "*apokatallasso,*" meaning that only one party has enmity in his heart and needs to have the barriers separating fellowship removed, while the other party has no enmity. You see, God has no hostility toward us. He has always loved man. This is why He became a man, so that as our substitute He could bear the judgment due us and in so doing remove every barrier that our sin had erected between Himself and us. God never needed to be reconciled; man is the one who needs it.

As the Scripture puts it, ". . . God was in Christ reconciling the world to Himself, not counting their trespasses against them . . . ," for "He made Him who knew no sin to be sin on our behalf, that we might become the righteousness of God in Him" (2 Corinthians 5:19, 21).

It doesn't seem like an even exchange; He gets our sin and we get His righteousness. But there you have it. It was God's incomparable plan to reconcile man back into fellowship with Him.

This is why God can say in effect to all who receive Christ, "You are *now* holy and blameless *in my sight*" (Colossians 1:22; Ephesians 1:4).

Can you think of another human being, including yourself, who views you as totally holy and blameless? I can't! Yet, in God's eyes we are already perfect; not will be, but *are!*

This is not a status which is given on a temporary basis while we try to become worthy of it as Christians. Once God puts us into union with His Son, we become clothed with His righteousness and God sees us as holy and blameless because that's the way He views Jesus. Experientially we may be quite imperfect, but our acceptance in God's eyes is never based on how we perform, but rather on the fact that we are *in* Christ and God accepts Him perfectly.

Knowing these liberating facts and counting them true on a moment-by-moment basis is the most important factor in living a life pleasing to God.

You can't help but respond with love and obedience to someone who loves and accepts you.

Now Satan is dedicated to keeping Christians from finding out what I've just told you, and he's done a pretty good job in the Christian world today. He lets them have a little taste of victorious living and then he moves in on them with his heavy artillery. He'll get them to fail God and get their eyes on themselves. After a series of failures, Satan gets them into a pattern that I have called "the sin syndrome."

The Sin Syndrome

First, we knowingly *sin*. The inevitable result, if we don't relate the sin to the Cross, is that we develop *guilt*. And guilt always leads to *estrangement*. There's the syndrome: *sin, guilt, estrangement*.

Now man can't live with guilt. So he tries to deal with guilt in one of two ways—both of them wrong.

If he is the type who doesn't have a particularly sensitive conscience, he tries to *justify* himself. He makes excuses and offers valid reasons why he did something:

"It was only a little lie, and it was easier on everyone involved."

"After all, the government spends my tax money on things I don't agree with anyway."

"But we really love each other, and everyone is doing it."

When we justify our actions, the result will be a feeling of loss of fellowship with God, because deep down inside we know that we haven't been honest with ourselves or God. We sense we've offended God by our deviousness. And when we feel that God has been offended, then we will also feel estranged from God. Remember, God isn't mad, but we think He is.

Another way man deals with guilt, and it's equally wrong, is to *condemn* himself. He sins over and over in the same area, guilt sets in, and then he begins the self-condemnation trip.

Satan loves to get his hands on one of these "sensitive" Christians. With no trouble at all, he can get them to feel like no-good worms before God. He'll convince them they couldn't possibly expect God to hear them when they pray, and surely He wouldn't answer their prayers even if He did hear. He gets their eyes so focused on their shabby Christian lives that they're sure God couldn't possibly use them.

Satan just sits back and relaxes when he gets us going on self-condemnation. We're out of the ball game as far as he's concerned.

At this point you may ask, is there any kind of bona fide guilt in the life of a believer in Christ?

There is what I call *"legal"* guilt. This is every man's curse as he comes into the world. It is his inherited culpability for sin, and this is what Christ removed as a barrier between God and man when He went to the cross for us. I have a lot more to say about this a little later.

Then there is the *"emotion"* of guilt. This is what Satan delights in heaping upon believers who feel they have failed God. This kind of guilt is Satan's tool and has no place in the life of a child of God.

Finally, there is a convicting ministry of the Holy Spirit described by the Apostle Paul in Second Corinthians 7:8-9 as *"sorrow"* which leads to repentance. If the "godly sorrow" caused by the Spirit's conviction doesn't lead to a repentance, or a turning around, then it well may go into the second kind of guilt, the *emotion of guilt*, which is deadly to a Christian's walk with God.

There is a need to acknowledge to God when we are guilty of sinning, and we freely can if we know for sure that God will keep on loving and accepting us. When we continue to feel unforgiven after we have acknowledged or confessed our sin, it's an indication that we have turned our focus away from God's forgiveness to ourselves. Then we're saying that our sinful weaknesses are more powerful than God's forgiving power. Either He isn't big enough to forgive us or He doesn't want to forgive us.

In either case, when there is unresolved guilt in the life of a person, he will feel estranged from God. He will not trust God to work in his life through the Holy Spirit and deliver him from the temptations of the flesh and the cunning wiles of Satan. He just won't come to God for help if he believes He is angry with him.

A Christian caught in the guilt trip will begin to seek to do things for God in the energy of the flesh to appease Him for his sense of guilt. This results in more frustration because, as the Bible says, ". . . the mind set on the flesh is hostile toward God; for it does not subject itself to the Law of God, for it is not even able to do so" (Romans 8:7).

King David of Israel certainly understood this progression. He knew quite a bit about sinning and its repercussions. Not only was he guilty of adultery with another man's wife, Bathsheba, but later he plotted her husband's death to cover up his sin.

In his later life David wrote Psalm 130, which shows us what he had learned from his rugged experiences. Listen to this particularly: "If Thou, Lord, shouldst mark iniquities, O Lord, who could stand? But there is forgiveness with Thee, that Thou mayest be feared" (Psalm 130:3-4).

In the original Hebrew the word "mark" meant to keep an itemized account of something—to write it out. David is saying here, "Lord, if You were a celestial bookkeeper keeping an itemized account of my sins, I'd be in big trouble!"

What did David learn from God's dealings with him? He learned that "there is forgiveness with (God) that (He) may be feared." That word "fear" in Hebrew means to be able to *reverently trust* someone.

David put his finger on a fantastic truth here, one of the most important things we can ever know about God. If we think God is keeping an itemized account of our sins and holding them against us, we can't really trust Him; it's impossible to have a dynamic, bold faith in Him. Why? Because you can only trust someone whom you believe really loves and accepts you *completely* in spite of all your faults.

Learning what Christ accomplished at the cross is the most important truth you will ever absorb in your lifetime. It should saturate your mind every day.

Counting as true the absolute forgiveness which Christ accomplished at the cross is the foundation of having a power-packed faith. You can't really respond to God in faith unless you know He has accepted you just as you are, unless you know what it means to be accepted in the Beloved (Ephesians 1:6). *The Beloved* is the title for God's dear Son, Jesus. God sees us all wrapped up in Jesus. The acceptance He has for Him, the Son of His love, the Beloved One, is the acceptance He keeps on having for us.

To fail to be accepted completely by God for even one second would mean that somehow we had gotten out of Christ, and that just isn't possible. He won't let go of us! Isn't that great news?

Satan Blinds Us to the Cross

Satan would like to blind us to all this wonderful truth. In fact, he keeps trying to blind us every day. We may not even realize it, but the number one reason the power of God is short-circuited in our lives is that we have never really learned what the cross of Christ means on a day-by-day basis. The cross is the continuing basis of God accepting and forgiving us.

We've all had experiences that we consider "mountaintoppers"—times when we experienced the Holy Spirit's working in our lives in a fresh way. For a while everything was going great and then, without even really knowing why, things began to drag. Spiritual flabbiness began to weaken us, and we wondered what was wrong.

I've gone down this painful road before, and each time I've discovered the real problem: I've started off on a "guilt trip." I've failed to believe that from God's perspective I'm already forgiven for disappointing Him; I only need to claim a forgiveness that is already a fact, not beg God as if forgiveness were in doubt.

The Believer's Defense Attorney

It's the Lord's desire that His children live godly lives and not sin, but our omniscient Father, knowing our nature, made provision for His erring children.

The Apostle John, in writing to the new believers of his day, said, "My little children, I am writing these things to you that you may not sin. And if any one sins, we have an Advocate with the Father, Jesus Christ the righteous; and He Himself is the propitiation for our sins; and not for ours only, but also for those of the whole world" (1 John 2:1-2).

An advocate means a defense attorney. Why would we need a defense attorney in the presence of God, our Father? Most of us think that it means Jesus defends us against the Father so that He won't judge us. Is that true? Absolutely not. Because of what Jesus did at the cross, the Father will never condemn us again.

The word "propitiation" means to turn away deserved wrath by the satisfaction of justice. What Christ did on the cross was to bear the compounded wrath of a Holy God on every sin that would ever be committed by every man who would ever live. The big theological word "propitiation" simply means, "God isn't mad at me anymore."

He poured out all His anger that He would have against our sins onto Jesus as He hung on the cross. Now He has set Himself free on a perfectly just basis to keep on dealing with us in love, even when He disciplines us.

God Doesn't Get Even

Are you ready for this?

God does not punish. Punishment means to "get even," and God doesn't do that. He's already "gotten even" with Jesus for all our sins. God "disciplines" His children, but it's always in love—never in anger. The words "discipline" and "training" are interchangeable words. God's disciplining always has a forward look to it (Hebrews 12:5-13).

When God sees a child of His who continually refuses to depend upon the Holy Spirit to deliver him from his temptations, then out of deep concern for that child's well-being and happiness God will begin to train him so that he will come to depend upon Him in the future. God knows we are only happy when we are living holy lives. This is true discipline and it has no resemblance to punishment.

Sometimes this discipline may seem grievous, but if we are learning to see everything that comes our way as being permitted by the loving hand of our Heavenly Father, then we can give thanks even for the discipline.

Unfortunately, at this point Satan has taken his toll with many believers. They live in constant fear of punishment for their sins.

Most of us have a few especially gross sins we committed in our past that spook us like the proverbial skeleton in the closet. Whenever some difficulty or calamity hits our lives, we trot the skeleton out and say, "Oh yes, God is getting even with me for 'that sin'."

Some live with the gnawing fear that lightning is going to strike them or God is going to kill one of their children to get even with them for some sin they committed long ago or are involved in at the moment.

God does not deal with us that way. To be sure, adversities are permitted in the believer's life, but they are designed to teach us to trust God, not to destroy us with vengeance.

But What About . . .

Now some of you may be saying, "All right, Hal, if God never punishes us for our sins, what about Galatians 6:7 which says, 'Do not be deceived, God is not mocked; for whatever a man sows, this he will also reap'?"

This verse is jerked out of context by so many Christians that it's incredible. The verse just before this one says, "And let the one who is taught the Word share all good things with him who teaches" (Galatians 6:6). This context is talking about supporting financially the one who gives himself to studying and teaching the Bible.

This same idea of sowing money for God's work is contained in Second Corinthians 9:6, "Now this I say, he who *sows* sparingly shall also reap sparingly; and he who sows bountifully shall also reap bountifully."

This concept of "whatsoever a man sows, he shall also reap" is concerned with investing our money in God's work and the reward or lack of reward for our stewardship.

To apply this passage to God's method of discipline is to contradict the whole principle of grace with which God now deals with His children.

Satan, the Old Guilt Tripper

If you still feel guilty after you acknowledge your sin and have remembered that you are forgiven, guess who is laying it on you. It's the old guilt-tripper himself, Satan.

Satan does not want you to remember that God did away with your sin at the cross. That's why you need a defense attorney before the Father. Satan's name means "The Accuser."

Christ doesn't have to defend you against the Father; He defends you against Satan, before the Father.

Here's a scene which has probably taken place in heaven in the presence of God today. We can thank Job for this bit of insight into Satan's tactics.

Satan's been up there today with a portfolio on each one of God's children. He brought a dossier on Buzz and Tom and Karin and an especially large file on Hal. He charges in and points, "Ah ha! There's Hal. He's one of Your children, huh? Did you see what he just did?"

And Satan begins to accuse.

Then Jesus steps up and says, "Father, Hal believed in Me in 1956. The forgiveness I paid for at the cross was then applied to him. This is our only plea."

And the Father says, "Case dismissed!"

God will not let anyone discipline His children but Himself. He'll do it in love because He has set Himself free to deal with us in grace. God, on the basis of His indwelling Spirit whom He trusts and has put into the life of every believer, is conforming us daily into the image of Jesus.

Old Testament Pictures

There's a wonderful picture in the Old Testament of Christ's intercessory work for believers. He bears our names upon His heart as He continually represents us before the Father.

We're taught this in the Old Testament from the practice of the high priest. He would go into the Tabernacle before the Presence of the Lord, before the Ark, as it was called, and he would burn incense, which was a picture of prayer.

Bound over his heart was a special vest with precious stones upon it, and on each stone were the names of the children of Israel.

God said, "And Aaron shall carry the names of the sons of Israel . . . over his heart when he enters the holy place, for a memorial before the Lord continually" (Exodus 28:29).

This is a beautiful picture of how Jesus Christ continually is before the throne of God with your name on His heart.

That's why in Hebrews 7:24-25 we have these encouraging words: "but He, on the other hand, because He abides forever, holds His priesthood permanently. Hence also He is able to save forever those who draw near to God through Him, since He always lives to make intercession for them."

According to this fantastic promise of assurance, once we have believed in Christ as Savior, it is impossible to be lost again or unforgiven. For a child of God to become lost, Christ would have to stop interceding for him. The promise is that "He is able to save *forever* those who draw near to God through Him." "Forever" is a very long time.

Jesus Himself promised, "I will never desert you, nor will I ever forsake you" (Hebrews 13:5). Thank God that "He always lives to make intercession for us," and because of that we can "draw near with confidence to the throne of grace, that we may receive mercy and find grace to help in time of need" (Hebrews 4:16).

Satan: Accuser Before God and Conscience

After Satan accuses us before God and doesn't make any headway there, he begins to accuse our consciences. He'll get us into a hopeless treadmill: sinning, vowing we won't do it again, trying not to sin, and then sinning again.

Here's the way it works:

First, he'll start working on an area of weakness. Every Christian has at least one area where he is especially vulnerable. We still have the old sin nature in us which can tempt us, and when we don't depend upon the indwelling Holy Spirit to overcome temptations, we will sin.

Seeking to be a good Christian we might say, "God, I know I've been wrong: thank You for forgiving me." Our burden is lifted and everything goes along fine for awhile. Then Satan gets us to fall down again in the same area. We hate ourselves for being such an awful Christian, but we accept His forgiveness and keep moving—only we're feeling a little guilty about having so little will power to live for God.

Pretty soon Satan will get us to sin again in the same area, and this time we're feeling so unworthy that we promise, "Oh God, if You'll just forgive me one more time, I vow I won't do this again."

At this piece of news, Satan and his demon hordes let out a rousing cheer of victory. He has us right where he wants us—on the sin treadmill.

We try so hard to please God, only we do it in the power of the flesh. The harder we try, the more we fail. The more we fail, the more we vow not to do it again.

Then Satan steps in and says accusingly, "Too bad! God won't forgive you this time. You've had it. There's no more grace for you." Or if he sees that we're too smart to fall for that extreme line of reasoning, he'll say, "God may forgive you, but He can't forget how unreliable you are. You'll never be able to be used by God as fully as before."

It's that old "bird with the broken wing will never fly so high again" routine.

Wham! You're wiped out! You forget that the issue is not *will* God forgive you, but will you believe that He *has* forgiven you and trust Him for the inner strengthening to turn from sin.

I'm not trying to teach that we can go out and sin and have no conscience about it, so don't get all uptight about that. The Holy Spirit will faithfully convict a believer of sin, not so he can confess in order to get forgiven, but so that he can claim forgiveness and believe Him again.

God does not want us to dwell on our sins, but rather on our forgiveness. If your focus is continually on yourself, then you cannot be "Looking away [from all that will distract] to Jesus" (Hebrews 12:2, *Amplified Bible*).

When you finally understand what Jesus Christ accomplished at the cross, you realize that God never stops forgiving you, even while you're in the process of sinning, although you yourself cannot appreciate the comfort of the forgiveness while you're sinning.

When Christ died on the cross, how many of your sins were future? Every last one of them.

I used to think that when I accepted Christ it meant that Christ had died for my sins up to that point, but from that point on I'd just have to confess them as I did them or else I wasn't forgiven. That's a perilous position to be in because you're never quite sure if you've confessed all your sins, and there just might be one or two that God is holding against you.

One day I realized what the *all* in Colossians 2:13 meant: "And when you were dead in your transgressions and the uncircumcision of your flesh, He made you alive together with Him, having forgiven us *all* our transgressions."

We were dead before we accepted Jesus, dead spiritually, unable to know God as a living reality, as a Person.

Then the Bible says, "He made you *alive* together with Him." This is talking about the new birth, the experience of being given spiritual life the moment you believe in Christ. Why is this possible? "Having forgiven us *all* our transgressions."

The verb translated "having forgiven" means something which happens at a point of time that doesn't have to be repeated. A final act. In God's mind, how many does that *all* mean? How many of our sins did God see when He judged them in Jesus on the cross?

The answer is *all!*

God Sees the Whole Parade of Life

God is looking at our lives as a helicopter pilot would look down at a parade. If we're standing on a corner watching a parade, we see the beginning of the parade, each segment passing by, and then we see the end of it. We see consecutively. But God, like the pilot, sees the whole parade at one time. That's the way God sees your life: your past, present, and future is all in the *now* with Him.

When you place faith in Jesus as your Savior, God has already seen (back in A.D. 33) your life go by like a parade. He took your whole life and the sin and guilt of it and put it all on Jesus Christ.

So when you believe in Christ as Savior, how many sins has God forgiven you? Not just those you have committed up to that point, but those from your whole lifetime. He couldn't accept you into a relationship with Himself at all unless He could forgive you for the whole thing.

This doesn't mean that God condones sinning in the life of a believer—far from it. It means He has set Himself free to be ready to work in us the moment we see that we've sinned and acknowledge it and accept His forgiveness.

First John 1:9 says, "If we keep on confessing our sins, He is faithful and righteous, to have forgiven us our sins and to have cleansed us from all unrighteousness" (literal translation of the Greek verb tenses). The Word never tells a believer *after the cross* to ask forgiveness. It's already a settled fact with God, and He just wants us to claim what is already true.

In First John 1:9 the word "confess" means to agree with someone about something; in this case to agree with God about our sins. But I can't agree with God about His attitude toward my sins until I see clearly what His attitude is.

Agree With God

First of all, God wants us to see our sin as He sees it—it is sin. But He doesn't want us to stop there. If we really agree with God about our sin, then we also have to see it as already forgiven. That's the way God sees it.

Finally, He wants us to turn from the sin and begin to trust Him to empower us to have victory over it in the future.

If we don't judge our sin in this way, accepting His forgiveness and turning from the sin in His power, Satan is going to come in and grab hold of that handle of guilt. He will get us to try to make up for our sins, and we'll end up punishing ourselves or someone else to try to relieve the guilt.

Someone Has to Pay

Every time we sin, we instinctively know someone has to pay for it. We don't have to be taught that; it's part of our very make-up. When I sin, either I've got to pay for it, or I make someone else pay (usually those dearest to me), or I look to Jesus as already having paid for it.

In the years I have been a believer I have had many counseling experiences in this area. I remember a beautiful young girl whose husband had to go on a long trip abroad. While he was gone, she committed adultery. That was a sin, no question about it.

After this happened she realized it was a sin and acknowledged this to God. But she didn't believe what God said, that it was already forgiven. She did not count His forgiveness as being true in her case. She was in much worse shape than she realized, because unresolved guilt is one of the most destructive forces on earth.

Her husband returned. Deeply implanted in that girl's mind was the sin and the unresolved guilt from it—not because God still held her guilty, but because she didn't believe what God said and therefore she didn't forgive herself.

A few years after her husband returned, they had their first child. Satan began to put his hand into her subconscious mind and grab hold of that guilt. Pretty soon she was having serious mental problems. She told her husband what had happened, thinking that maybe this would clear her conscience. He forgave her, but she still couldn't forgive herself.

Do you know what she wound up doing? One day her husband came in and found her trying to strangle their child. Why? Because she loved that child more than anything in the world. Killing him was a way of inflicting maximum punishment upon herself for the sense of guilt. What a needless tragedy!

She didn't understand all this at first until it was unraveled in counseling. Deep down inside was this unresolved guilt. Instead of relating this to the cross of Jesus Christ and saying, "Thank You for forgiving me," she had tried to punish herself for what she had done. She instinctively knew that someone had to pay, and she was making herself pay.

Guilt is the most crippling disease in the world today!

A friend of mine was in a doctor's office when he looked across the street at a hotel and saw a woman about ready to jump from the tenth floor. He rushed across the street, went up in the elevator, and got there just in time to say, "Wait, don't jump. Let me just talk to you."

Slowly and distinctly he said, "God loves you."

The girl turned and looked at him with a horrible expression of guilt and despair, then turned and jumped. She was killed immediately.

Psychiatrists and doctors say that unresolved guilt is the number one cause of mental illness and suicide. Over half of all hospital beds are filled with people who have emotional illnesses. The greatest therapy they could possibly have would be to find out that God loves them and has made an all-encompassing forgiveness available to them in Christ.

God didn't have to wait until Freud came along to have an answer for mental illness. We don't have to go to a psychiatrist to get the answer for guilt. Jesus provided the only real answer to guilt some two thousand years ago. If we believe what God has said, there's an answer that cleanses us in our conscience and sets us free from dead works to serve the living God.

I don't want you to suffer from crippling guilt like this. I want you to be able to release the power of God in your life day by day, moment by moment—to be set free from a guilt complex and be able to acknowledge to God, "Yes, Lord, I'm guilty, but I thank You that I've been forgiven."

Then turn and believe that the Spirit of God will work in your life right now. You don't have to wait until you are worthy for it or earn it.

Here's a passage that thrills me every time I read it—it never gets old. "Having canceled out the certificate of debt, consisting of decrees against us and which was hostile to us; and He has taken it out of the way, having nailed it to the cross" (Colossians 2:14).

Out of Debt

This is a powerful word picture. In the day in which this was written the word translated as "certificate of debt" was widely known. Whenever a person would be convicted in a Roman court, a "certificate of debt" or bond would be prepared. The scribe of the court would itemize and write down every crime for which the person had been convicted. This certificate meant that the prisoner owed Caesar a prescribed payment for those crimes. It would then be taken with the prisoner to wherever he would be imprisoned and nailed to the door of his cell.

What an illustration the Apostle Paul used to show how God has dealt with our sins. When Jesus hung on the cross nineteen centuries ago, the "certificate of debt" of every man who would ever live was nailed to the cross with Him.

Our certificate of debt lists every time that we fall short of God's perfect law in thought, word, or deed. Just as that certificate would have been nailed to the cell of the criminal, Jesus took our certificate of debt and nailed it to the cross.

Why? Because He intended to pay for it.

According to Roman law, when a person was put in prison and the certificate of debt was nailed to the door, it would remain there until the sentence was carried out. Then they would take this certificate and write across it the word meaning "It is finished." They would roll it up, give it to the prisoner, and he could never be punished for those crimes again.

Did you know that was one of the last things Jesus shouted from the cross?

Just before He bowed His head and said, "Father, into Your hands I commit my spirit," He gave a cry of victory. He called from the cross "It is finished." The Greek word for this is "tetelestai," meaning "paid in full" (John 19:30).

Paid in Full

Jesus took our certificate of debt and wrote across it in His own blood, "Paid in full." We can never be tried for our sins again after we receive the pardon. It's settled forever in heaven by the blood of the only begotten Son of God.

That's why it says in Colossians 2:14, "He has taken it (our certificate of debt) out of the way, having nailed it to the cross." I owe God perfect obedience to His law, but God will never grade my law-keeping on the curve. It's perfection or nothing—and I can't pay.

That's what the word "redemption" means: to purchase out of slavery and set free by paying the price of a ransom. The ransom that Christ had to pay to set us free was the price of our owing God perfect obedience to His law, and Christ paid the sentence of debt in full. ". . . knowing that you were not redeemed with perishable things like silver or gold from your futile way of life inherited from your forefathers, but with precious blood, as of a lamb unblemished and spotless, the blood of Christ" (1 Peter 1:18-19).

That's why it says in Colossians 2:15: "When He had disarmed the rulers and authorities, He made a public display of them, having triumphed over them through Him."

The "rulers and authorities" are Satan and all his armies.

And Christ disarmed them! They have no legal basis to put their hands on a child of God any more. *Satan has no legal grounds to work in a Christian's life.* We can give him the legal ground, if we don't want to believe in God, but we certainly don't have to. God wants us to take our Magna Charta of freedom, which is the perfect forgiveness of Jesus Christ, and to realize that when we sin we should come to Him immediately with the heart attitude, "Oh, Lord, I agree with You that I have sinned." This is not in order to be forgiven, however. It's just to realize a forgiveness which is already a fact.

When Christ died on the cross, He took care of the sin problem forever. Another sacrifice will never be necessary. Why? Because of the value of the life of the One who was sacrificed. It's not like the blood of the goats and the bulls in the Old Testament, which merely covered sin. When Christ died for sin, He took it away as an issue.

"And not through the blood of goats and calves, but through His own blood, He entered the holy place once for all, *having obtained eternal redemption*" (Hebrews 9:12).

How long is eternal? God doesn't offer anything less. It is based upon the value of the sacrifice of Jesus Christ.

"For if the blood of goats and bulls and the ashes of a heifer sprinkling those who have been defiled, sanctify for the cleansing of the flesh, how much more will the blood of Christ, who through the eternal Spirit offered Himself without blemish to God, *cleanse your conscience from dead works to serve the living God?*" (Hebrews 9:13-14).

License to Serve

This is the most powerful message the Holy Spirit ever brought home to me. It was a license to serve, not to sin. The motivation which comes from knowing a perfect acceptance with God is so much greater than walking in fear that you're going to lose the relationship that there's just no comparison.

God wants us to serve not out of duty, but out of thanksgiving for what He has done in Jesus Christ.

"Cleanse your conscience"—that's where guilt becomes imbedded—"from dead works to serve the living God."

A "dead work" is anything which you and I do to try to help God forgive us for our sin. It is trying to add to what Christ has fully accomplished on the cross.

A dead work is when we don't believe we're really forgiven and we try to do something to make up for what we've done.

What does God want us to do when we sin?

We need Him at that moment more than at any other time in our lives. It's not a time for running from God, as Adam did. When Adam sinned, God appeared in the Garden and said, "Adam, where are you?" Did God really need to ask? Don't you think He knew where Adam was?

Adam hid himself because he was afraid. He should have known that God still loved him or He wouldn't have been looking for him. Then Adam committed the first dead work of history! He tried to hide his sense of guilt with fig leaves. He tried to cover his sin and guilt by the work of his own hands, and in doing that he committed the first "religious" act. That's really what "religion" is, if you understand it correctly.

Christianity isn't a religion; Christianity is a personal relationship with God through Jesus Christ and His finished work. It's not our trying to gain God's approbation by what we do.

In God's Family

Think of it!

We have an access into the presence of God. "Let us draw near with a sincere heart in full assurance of faith, having our hearts sprinkled clean from an evil conscience and our body washed with pure water" (Hebrews 10:22).

When we knowingly sin, God wants us to draw near to Him "with a sincere heart," to be honest "in full assurance of faith" (i.e., in what Christ has done). "By this will we have been sanctified through the offering of the body of Jesus Christ once for all" (Hebrews 10:10).

God loves us and accepts us. We're forgiven. He wants us to own up to what we've done and thank Him for His forgiveness. If we don't do this, we will have an evil conscience.

I know one heart-breaking story after another of people who have gone into mental illness because of unresolved guilt; others remain reasonably sane but have no power in their lives. They try to draw upon some experience they have had in their past and wonder why they don't have the same power any more.

How absolutely fantastic to know there is a forgiveness which is guaranteed to us through the once-and-for-all offering of Jesus Christ on our behalf. That's why it says, "Therefore He is able also to save to the uttermost—completely, perfectly, finally and for all time and eternity—those who come to God through Him, since He is always living to make petition to God *and* intercede with Him *and* intervene for them" (Hebrews 7:25, *Amplified Bible*).

I'm sure that some of you reading this have allowed guilt to tie you in knots for years. You've just been waiting for God to lower the boom on you for some secret sin or for a life lived in open rebellion against His will for you. That very guilt has produced an estrangement from the one Person you need to be closest to right now—your loving Heavenly Father. Can't you see how wonderful it would be to have Him fold His great, strong arms of love around you and comfort and reassure you of His love and acceptance?

Let Him do it now. He isn't angry with you—no matter how much you've let Him down. He has utterly forgiven you for any offenses toward Him. The only thing that grieves God now is for His children to feel alienated toward Him when He cares for them so much.

13 ∘ Weapons of Warfare

> *"Finally, be strong in the Lord, and in the strength of His might. Put on the full armor of God, that you may be able to stand firm against the schemes of the devil. For our struggle is not against flesh and blood, but against the rulers, against the powers, against the world-forces of this darkness, against the spiritual forces of wickedness in the heavenly places. Therefore take up the full armor of God, that you may be able to resist in the evil day, and having done everything, to stand firm."*
>
> EPHESIANS 6:10-13

WHENEVER NATIONS HAVE fought wars, covering the battlefields of history with broken lives, there have been some countries which have remained neutral in spite of the conflict surrounding them.

In this book we have seen that we are in a war where we can't be neutral! The battle lines are clearly drawn. There are no conscientious objectors in this war, no draft dodgers, no armchair generals, no advocates of peace at any price.

This is a time when every Christian must stand for Christ, covered to the hilt with the full armor of God. It doesn't make any difference if you are old or weak physically; the Lord Jesus will be your strength. It doesn't make any difference if you are young and don't understand all the battle strategy of your adversary, the Devil; God's armor will protect you.

But you can't be a do-it-yourself expert. You cannot assemble a self-made armor from bits and pieces of determination, grit, resolve, intelligence, or basic goodness. Satan can and will find every hole in a suit with a hand-made label in it.

Our only defense against the "prince of darkness" who works in the world system, distorting for his own purposes everything that is good and beautiful, is to put on the full armor of God. It is our only protection against the temptations that bombard the body, soul, and spirit.

Be Strong in the Lord

We cannot live the Christian life in our own strength. You've probably already discovered that. It is imperative that we allow the Lord to give us His strength. Without it, we don't stand a chance against the incredible power of Satan. Human strength is totally useless against the attacks of the Devil and his ingenious "schemes."

Paul's command to "be strong in the Lord" is even more powerful in the original text. The command is in the passive voice, which means that we receive the action that the verb is describing. It is actually saying that we are to be "constantly allowing ourselves to be strengthened by the Lord." In other words, He does the strengthening and we enjoy the results in our lives.

What does it mean to be strengthened with "His might"? Luke gives us the answer to that question: "And Jesus, *full of the Holy Spirit*, returned from the Jordan and was led about by the Spirit in the wilderness" (Luke 4:1).

Perhaps you're thinking, "Of course Jesus was full of the Holy Spirit, but how does that affect me?"

The writer of Hebrews tells us that Jesus was the author and the perfecter of our faith. That means that Jesus thought up the whole plan of the Holy Spirit living through man, but He didn't just sit up in heaven and say, "Now you guys, go live it." He came down into the arena and lived by faith Himself and showed that the whole plan worked beautifully.

He Laid Aside the Use of His Deity

In the second chapter of Philippians we're told that when Jesus came into this world, He chose to temporarily leave the *use* of His divine powers behind and live here on this planet just as any other man would have to do. Had He chosen to do otherwise, He would not have been a true man and would not have qualified as a substitute to bear the penalty for our sins in our place.

Also, if He had met and handled life's problems using part human and part divine strength, He wouldn't have set any kind of example we could follow. We would have been licked before we got started because we aren't part divine.

The great truth that Jesus wants us to know is that He chose to live His life as He expects us to live, in a moment-by-moment reliance upon the Father who worked through Him by the Holy Spirit. That fantastic life that the world knew as the life of Jesus was actually lived not *by* Jesus, but *in* Him by the Holy Spirit.

I remember one day when a friend asked me who I thought was the only person who had ever lived the Christian life just the way God wanted it lived. After thinking for a minute I replied, "Well, Jesus, of course."

I was shocked when he said, "No, Jesus didn't live the Christian life; it was lived in Him by the Holy Spirit."

After I thought about that for awhile, it really made sense and shed some light on a few Bible verses—one in particular, John 14:12, where Jesus said, ". . . the works that I do shall he do also; and greater works than these shall he do; because I go to the Father."

While Jesus was here on earth, the specific residence of the Holy Spirit was in Him. When He went to the Father, He sent the Holy Spirit back to fill His followers, just as He had been filled. The life which had been produced in Jesus by the Holy Spirit was produced in His followers as they relied upon the Spirit as Jesus had.

This makes the Christian life an exciting possibility. If I thought I had to duplicate a life like Jesus lived with my own strength or even with some of the Holy Spirit's strength mixed in, I would be discouraged before I started. But it's great to know that is not God's plan for doing His work on earth.

Jesus' Temptation

Jesus gave us a tremendous pattern for walking in the Spirit. In Luke 4:23, we read that the Holy Spirit *led* Jesus out into the desert to be tempted by the Devil.

"And He ate nothing during those days; and when they had ended, He became hungry. And the Devil said to Him, 'If You are the Son of God, tell this stone to become bread.'"

Here you see one of Satan's clever tactics: how he capitalizes on situations in our lives trying to get us to sin. Satan is a master strategist; he knows our pattern of weakness. Jesus had not eaten for forty days, and He was hungry. The Devil said sarcastically, "If you are the Son of God, tell this stone to become bread."

Don't you think Satan knew this was the Son of God? Of course he did. Satan isn't stupid. He wouldn't have been wasting all that time on Jesus if he hadn't believed that He was the Son of God.

In reality he was saying, "Now look, Jesus, *since* You're the all-powerful Son of God, why don't You fix Yourself a little lunch here; make these stones into bread."

As a matter of fact, this temptation is a great proof of the deity of Christ. If we hadn't eaten for forty days and forty nights and the Devil came to us and said, "Since you're a child of God, why don't you make these stones become bread?" it wouldn't be a temptation to us—because we couldn't do it!

Jesus could have snapped His fingers and there would have been a bagel on every bush!

Satan's Real Purpose

Do you see Satan's sinister plan? Jesus was being tempted to stop living in total dependence upon the Holy Spirit to provide His needs, as any man would have to do, and to use His own deity to meet those needs. Satan knew that Jesus was both God and man and that He had chosen never to use His own divine power while here on earth. Satan would have done anything to get Jesus to step outside the Father's will and use His own divinity to meet His needs.

Jesus flatly rejected Satan's offer and allowed the Father to sustain Him through the Holy Spirit. One reason He did this was so that you and I might have a pattern to follow and might know what a great and powerful God we have available to meet our every need.

He took all the guff this world and Satan had to offer, and He did it all as a man, depending upon the inner strengthening and power of the same Holy Spirit who lives in us.

Christ's Walk, Our Example

Christ's whole life was lived in dependence upon the Father who worked in Him by the Spirit. He related every circumstance He faced to the Father's ability to handle it through His humanity. He could have handled any one of them in His own divine strength, but for the sake of the example He wanted to leave us, He didn't.

John said of Jesus, "The one who says he abides in Him ought himself to walk in the same manner as He (Jesus) walked" (1 John 2:6).

Jesus Christ walked with His focus on the Father, and the Father worked through Him by the indwelling Holy Spirit.

We are to walk with our focus on Jesus, and He will work through us by the same Holy Spirit who indwells us.

Be Filled With the Spirit

This pattern of living is called "the filling of the Spirit" in Ephesians 5:18, where it says, "And do not get drunk with wine, for that is dissipation, but be filled with the Spirit."

The command to every Christian, "be filled with the Spirit," is in a verb tense in the original Greek which means to be *continually* filled with the Spirit. It is to be a moment-by-moment experience in the life of the believer.

Many people have the idea that being filled with the Spirit is like screwing the lid off one's head and pouring Holy Spirit in until one is full.

This is not what it means. You don't get more of Him; He gets more of you.

What exactly does it mean, then, to be filled with the Spirit?

Paul uses a good illustration in Ephesians 5:18 when he compares the filling of the Spirit with the experience of being drunk. When you are drunk, it means that another force has taken over your mind and dominates your personality. You have voluntarily yielded control of your life to the stimulant alcohol.

When Paul commands all Christians to be filled with the Spirit, he means to voluntarily yield control of yourself to another person, the Holy Spirit. Let Him empower your personality.

How Can We Do This?

We must first know that the Holy Spirit has taken up permanent residence in us the moment we received Christ. Romans 8:9 says that not to have the Holy Spirit in you is tantamount to not being a Christian. The Holy Spirit who indwells us is a person who is co-equal and co-eternal with the Father and the Son.

Secondly, we should know that sin grieves the Holy Spirit but doesn't cause Him to leave us (Ephesians 4:30). Jesus promised, "I will never desert you, nor will I ever forsake you" (Hebrews 13:5).

The third thing we should know is that it is one thing for the Holy Spirit to dwell in us, but quite another thing for Him to fill or control us.

God wants us to be continually *filled* with the Spirit. The only way we can have this happen is to decide who runs the show in our lives. We need to make a once-and-for-all decision to give the title deed of our lives to God. This does not mean that we are always going to do what God wants us to do. It does mean that we have come to a point in life where we have soberly assessed what God has done for us in Christ. We reason that if He has given us eternal life, put us into His forever family, given us an inheritance with His Son, and made us kings and priests forever, then we can say with confidence, "I can trust a God like that. If I give my life totally into His keeping, He will know how to handle it and do the best with it that can be done."

Present Your Body to Him

When we get to that point—and for some of us it's after we've hit bottom spiritually—then we can really appreciate the Apostle Paul's words: "I urge you therefore, brethren, by the mercies of God, to present your bodies a living and holy sacrifice, acceptable to God, which is your spiritual service of worship" (Romans 12:1).

When Paul uses the word "present" in this verse, it is in the aorist tense in the original language, and it means to do it once and for all time. It's something which doesn't need to be done over and over again.

Maybe you've come to a place in your Christian life when you think, "I've had it. So much is stacked against me; I can't run my life the way it ought to go. I'm worn out trying. I give up."

Believe me, that's a great place to get as a Christian. When you hit bottom spiritually, there's no place to go but up. God lets us exhaust every trick we have for living a victorious life. When we're finally hanging on the ropes, He steps in and says, "Will you throw in the towel now and let Me take over?"

I remember when I made the decision to do this myself. I'd been a believer for several years and had enthusiastically worked for God. What had been easy at first began to get to be work after awhile. I found myself on a spiritual roller coaster, and the Christian life was getting to be a drag.

In an effort to get myself back in shape, I began following various people's advice on how to be a victorious Christian. I tried giving up all my bad habits and found that some of them had a tight grip on me. One friend urged me to begin memorizing Bible verses. I did, but that didn't produce the consistency for which I was looking.

I went through one gimmick after another, most of them good things in themselves such as witnessing, Bible study, prayer, and confession, but none of these helped for long.

Finally one day as I was driving around in my car, desperately asking God for the solution to my problem, He seemed to say, "Stop struggling, child. Just give Me your life right now, and you won't have the headache of running yourself from this point on."

I don't really know what happened, except that I stopped struggling and gave myself to Him unreservedly. The peace of God flooded my soul. I felt a tremendous burden lift from me and John 7:38-39 became a living reality. "'. . . From his innermost being shall flow rivers of living water.' Now this He said about the Spirit. . . ."

Starting that day, I began to experience what it meant to walk in the Spirit. I saw God remake me emotionally and psychologically. He took some impossible situations in my life and worked them out fantastically to His glory and my good.

I Know Who Holds the Future

Since that time I've had this attitude: I don't know what the future holds, but I know who holds the future.

This is the attitude that God wants of us if we are going to have a life continually filled with the Spirit. However, let me warn you: Be sure that you mean it when you give your life to God this way, because He will be serious about taking it. You will be saying, "Lord, I want Your will, even though I don't know now what it will be."

As you get to know God in this intimate way, you'll discover you haven't made a risky deal. His will for your life will go far beyond your wildest dreams. All He's been waiting for is a blank check from you so He could begin to fill in His marvelous plan and purpose.

There have been times when I've said, "Okay, Lord, things have been going all right, but I'd like to try running my life for awhile." I was in the process of running it into the ground when suddenly I was reined up short and the Lord said, "You're not going that way, pal."

There have been times when I have had tears in my eyes from the Lord pulling me away from the direction I was going, but I have never regretted the fact that I gave Him the right to hold those reins.

God wants you to decide who is master of your life. When you accept Jesus Christ, you receive eternal life and become a member of God's family. After that He urges you to present Him the title deed to your life, although He will not force you. But it does make sense to do it. After all, who really would know better how to run you than the One who put you together, atom by atom, molecule by molecule?

"Do Not Be Conformed to This World" (Romans 12:2)

What did Paul mean by "this world"? He meant the world system of thinking and doing which excludes God. I like the way J. B. Phillips puts it in his modern translation of the New Testament: "Don't let the world around you squeeze you into its own mold, but let God remold your minds from within . . ." (Romans 12:2).

The only way we can escape conformity to the world's mold is to come to that place where we present ourselves to God and say, "Here is my life. You run it, God. Make me over from the inside by giving me a new mind, a new outlook on You, on myself, and on the world."

If we by faith depend upon Him to do this and simply live our lives daily expecting Him to control and fill us with the Holy Spirit, He will do it.

You don't have to have any ecstatic emotional experience to be filled with the Spirit. You don't get zapped by some mysterious force which indicates that you've arrived in the Christian life. Sorry, it just doesn't work that way.

God has a plan that's even better. He has promised to meet the circumstances of life which we encounter moment by moment and handle them for us if we let Him. He can overcome fear, timidity, hostility, anxiety, pride, lust, jealousy, and any other emotions we can't handle. All He wants us to do is back away from the problem and let Him at it.

And He doesn't want *any* help from us. Either He does it all for us and through us, or He lets us tackle it alone. Don't patronize God by asking for His help. *He doesn't help those who help themselves. On the contrary, He helps those who admit they are helpless.* That really goes against the grain of the world's thinking, but that is God's plan of action.

I remember the first time I ever tried to give a speech in public. It was in a college speech course, and as I stood there in front of the class I became more and more flustered. Finally I said, "Oh phooey! I quit," and turned around and walked out. That was the end of my speech-making days.

A few years later I became a Christian. One Sunday at church I was asked to teach an adult Sunday school class. I nearly fainted when they asked me, but I had been learning the principle of walking in the Spirit, so I decided to see if it would work in this needy area of my life. I stood up in front of the class that morning and literally let the Holy Spirit pour His message through my yielded vocal cords. It went quite well, too, but I can't take any credit for it. It was God's show all the way.

Walking in the Spirit

Sometimes it gets a bit confusing as to just how we're to live the Christian life. First you read that you're to be *filled* with the Spirit and that will give you the power you need. Then someone comes along and speaks of *walking* in the Spirit and tells you that will keep you from sinning. Someone else has found that walking by *faith* is the secret of victorious Christian living. Currently, many are claiming that we must be *baptized* with the Spirit to overcome the temptations of life.

Just what is the formula anyway? Is there some point in our Christian lives where we must have a special encounter with the Holy Spirit which will alter the course of our lives and the way we live?

Let me share with you what I feel the Word teaches about this. Paul's exhortations to the believers to be *filled with the Spirit* (Ephesians 5:18), to *walk in the Spirit* (Galatians 5:16), and to *walk by faith* (2 Corinthians 5:7; Hebrews 11) all refer to the same principle of the believer coming to the conclusion that he can't live *for* God. He must trust the Holy Spirit to live the Christian life in and through him.

For many Christians the realization that the Holy Spirit wants to and is able to live the Christian life through them is such welcome news that when they begin to experience victory instead of defeat, they are literally overwhelmed.

For many, this entering into the Spirit-filled life is a crisis experience. If for years you've been wallowing in defeat in your Christian life and suddenly the indwelling Christ becomes magnificently alive to you, you may feel like you've been zapped!

God doesn't want to give us a one-shot exposure to His power, however. He wants to give us a new pattern of living where He fills us moment by moment with new life and spiritual energy. Any encounter with the Holy Spirit which doesn't produce a whole new life isn't the walk in the Spirit or filling of the Spirit that the New Testament teaches.

Baptism of the Spirit

The baptism of the Spirit is mentioned many times in the New Testament, but it is only defined in one place, 1 Corinthians 12:13: "For by one Spirit we were all baptized into one body, whether Jews or Greeks, whether slaves or free, and we were all made to drink of one Spirit."

This verse simply tells us that the baptism of the Spirit is that particular ministry of the Holy Spirit which joins us into a living union with Christ and His body, the Church. This happens to each person the moment he places faith in Jesus Christ as Savior.

The baptism of the Spirit is *not* the ministry of the Holy Spirit which is designed to give the believer power in his daily life. That is the *filling* ministry of the Spirit. *Walking* in the Spirit, being *filled* with the Spirit, and walking by *faith* are synonymous terms.

Nowhere in the New Testament epistles are we commanded to be baptized with the Spirit. If that were the means of power in the Christian life, Paul's teachings would be full of it.

The baptism of the Spirit is a valid biblical teaching, but it must be carefully related to all the New Testament scriptures. (For a more complete treatment of this subject, see the appendix to this chapter.)

Satan's Domain

Naturally Satan is livid with rage when a believer finds out about the Spirit-filled life and begins to walk in the Spirit. A Christian who begins to live in this new realm will find himself exposed to such open hostility from Satan that sometimes it's overwhelming. Areas of our old sinful life that have laid dormant for years begin to give us trouble.

Why? Because the Holy Spirit is not the only one who dwells in the realm of the spirit. Satan lives there too, and when we begin to traverse his home base, we're in enemy territory.

To go into this battlefield without being filled with the Spirit and clothed with His armor is utter folly. Satan will make mincemeat out of us. Don't forget, he's had thousands of years of practice fouling up God's children. We're no match for him.

But praise God, Jesus is! As we walk in the Spirit, we will not fulfill the lusts of the flesh. That's what Paul promised in Galatians 5:16.

As he states in another passage, ". . . we are more than conquerors *and* gain a surpassing victory through Him Who loved us" (Romans 8:37, *Amplified Bible*).

If the filling of the Spirit sounds like just what you've been needing in your Christian life, why not make a decision right now to begin to let the Holy Spirit control your life? He is more than willing, and He's certainly able to answer your faith, however small, and begin to duplicate Jesus' life in and through you.

Short-Circuiting God's Power

What happens to us if we don't walk by faith? Paul says, "Whatever is not from faith is sin" (Romans 14:23).

If we don't walk in the Spirit, then we are walking according to the flesh, and that is sin (Romans 8:4-5). That means that we are seeking to handle our lives and problems with our own human wisdom. We are living in the realm of the five senses and concluding that what we feel, see, and think is what is really true, instead of relating the problem to God's wisdom and ability to handle it.

If we walk in the energy of the flesh, we are prime candidates to end up on a class-A guilt trip or get caught in the sin syndrome. We cannot knowingly be walking in the flesh and walking in dependence upon the Holy Spirit at the same time.

When we stop trusting the Holy Spirit to deliver us from temptations and seek to handle them ourselves, we are guaranteeing a spiritual nose dive. The inevitable result of the activity of the flesh is sin, and sin will short-circuit the power of God in the life of a believer.

It isn't that God stops loving us and accepting us. It's simply that we've stopped believing in that love and acceptance, and our focus is off the problem-solver and onto the problem—us!

The moment a child of God recognizes the futility of living this way and acknowledges to God that he's walking in the flesh, he is restored into God's fellowship in his own mind. God never stopped "fellowshiping" with him, but he stopped fellowshiping with God.

Don't let the world, the flesh, or the Devil spook you. We are the victors in all three of these areas as we walk in the Spirit and wear the full armor of God.

Let's Take a Look at the Armor

"Put on the full armor of God, that you may be able to stand firm against the schemes of the devil" (Ephesians 6:11).

The Devil exploits our personality quirks, the lusts of the flesh, and our natural physical drives to conspire against us.

There are times when I have a message to prepare or studying to do. I gather my materials and settle down in my study. Then they hit me—hunger pains! Now I know I shouldn't be hungry—I probably had breakfast less than an hour before—but a built-in excuse has been offered me to get away from the Word of God.

I wish I always said, "Satan, be gone," but I don't. I begin prowling around, getting something to eat, and before I know it I've killed an hour—an hour of valuable time. I didn't really need that food, but Satan can use any natural drives we have if they are not being controlled by the Holy Spirit.

Another drive which Satan uses is our natural need for sex. Once you are married, that need has the potential of being met, but even in marriage it can get out of control. Satan can use that normal drive to break up a marriage or produce such hostility that there's no communication at all. He can get a man too intense in his desire at the expense of not meeting his wife's emotional needs.

Satan uses another natural drive in his campaign on young people: the need for a mate. This is an area where the girls are especially vulnerable. If they think they need a mate, and if they don't trust the Lord with this area of their lives, Satan can come in and get them so anxious about finding the right man that he has them in a tailspin.

I have seen so many great Christians get fouled up because they don't trust the Lord to provide them with a mate. Satan gets a grip on them, and in some cases they become involved sexually because they feel this is the only way they can hold their boyfriend or girlfriend. Others don't trust the Lord to provide them with a mate, and they marry the wrong person. Perhaps they marry a non-Christian or a Christian who is really out of it spiritually.

Satan uses these natural needs when they are not under the Spirit's control. This is why we need the armor of God.

"For our struggle is not against flesh and blood. . . ."

What is really behind these drives when they get out of control? Our own flesh or sin nature starts rumbling in us for satisfaction, and then along come the "rulers . . . the powers . . . the world-forces of this darkness . . . the spiritual forces of wickedness in the heavenly places" who energize our flesh with unnatural cravings (Ephesians 6:12).

Satan is on constant guard, watching every believer and waiting for his armor to slip, even slightly, so he can fling in his fiery darts.

"Therefore take up the full armor of God, that you may be able to resist in the evil day, and having done everything, to stand firm" (Ephesians 6:13).

The Belt

When the Apostle Paul wrote this letter to the Ephesians, he had been closely guarded by a Roman soldier for several months. He must have had a good opportunity to observe pieces of the soldier's armor at close range.

"Stand firm therefore, having girded your loins with truth, and having put on the breastplate of righteousness" (Ephesians 6:14).

The Roman army had the finest armor of the ancient world, and Paul used it as an illustration of the armor God has for the Christian to use against Satan.

In the Roman's armor the girdle was the belt, six to eight inches wide, which went around his waist. It was one of his most important pieces of equipment because everything else was fastened to his belt. If the belt wasn't in place, then the armor wouldn't be secure.

Paul says that the Christian's foundation piece of armor is *the truth*: a growing knowledge and understanding of the Scriptures and how they apply to life. God wants us to have defensive armor against the wiles of Satan. A soldier does not put on his armor after going *into* battle, but in preparation *for* battle. The belt of truth must be secure or everything else will fall off!

Breastplate

In the Roman armor there was a breastplate which was made of bronze backed with tough pieces of hide. This protected one of the most vital areas of the body, the heart.

The breastplate of our armor which protects our heart from attacks of Satan is *righteousness*. This refers to the righteousness of Christ. In his second letter to the Corinthians Paul describes what Christ has done for us: "He made Him who knew no sin to be sin on our behalf, that we might become the righteousness of God in Him" (2 Corinthians 5:21).

This is not talking about *our* righteousness; when we believe in Jesus Christ, *His* righteousness is given to us. We are not only forgiven for all our sins, but we are clothed with the very righteousness of Christ. From that point on, as far as our relationship with God is concerned, He sees us as righteous as Christ.

What Satan likes to do is to come in when we have failed God and say, "Aha, you are not going to be acceptable to God now. Look what you did!" At that time, if we have on the breastplate of righteousness, we can say, "Phase out, Satan. I don't appear to God in my own righteousness, and I never did. It's Christ's righteousness which has always made me acceptable, and it hasn't changed."

Boots

"And having shod your feet with the preparation of the gospel of peace" (Ephesians 6:15).

Anyone who has ever fought in any kind of hand-to-hand combat knows that sure footing is most important. I used to box, and I remember how we put resin on the bottom of our shoes. More than once I was floored because I lost my footing just at the time I was throwing a punch. In fighting with a sword as they did at the time of the Roman legions, losing your footing could mean death. So the G.I. issue in footgear at that time was the hobnail sandal. When they were fighting in face-to-face combat, their feet were planted solid; their footing was sure.

In the Christian life we need solid footing, too, if we are going to walk and resist Satan. That solid footing is provided by the *gospel of peace*. This is not the same as the Gospel of salvation. "Gospel" means "good news," and it is certainly great news that we have forgiveness through believing in Jesus Christ, but there is some more good news for us. There is a place of rest and peace of mind for every Christian; it is God's hiding place for every believer in Jesus Christ. Hebrews 4 tells us about entering God's rest. It is a rest for here and now, not the "sweet by and by." That is good news!

God has peace of mind and a resting place available to every believer in Jesus Christ. If we do not learn how to depend upon the *promises* of God for peace, then we will not have the sure footing to be able to stand against the wiles of Satan. He will knock us off balance and have us on the ground before we know it.

Satan uses worry, anxiety, and tension to really keep us off balance. The gospel of peace is concerned with meeting worry with the promises of God.

Are you afraid? Then claim this promise: "Do not fear, for I am with you; Do not anxiously look about you, for I am your God. I will strengthen you, surely I will help you, surely, I will uphold you with My righteous right hand" (Isaiah 41:10).

Are you worried about your needs? Bills stacking up? Pressures of business closing in? Children or parents presenting problems which seem impossible to handle? Look at these promises and claim them: "Be anxious for nothing, but in everything by prayer and supplication with thanksgiving let your requests be made known to God. And the peace of God, which surpasses all comprehension, shall guard your hearts and your minds in Christ Jesus" (Philippians 4:6-7).

These promises are real. One of the few things God tells us to fear is that we will fail to claim His promises (Hebrews 4:1).

When we get up in the morning, we should check out our armor. Do we have on the belt of truth? Do we have on the breastplate of righteousness? Are we beginning to slip into a performance-based relationship with God? Are we collecting merit badges for our good deeds, church work, and charitable contributions? If Satan gets us on that trip, we are in for a lethal blow.

Make sure you are resting on the promises of God.

Shield

"In addition to all, taking up the shield of faith with which you will be able to extinguish all the flaming missiles of the evil one" (Ephesians 6:16).

A Roman soldier's shield was about two feet wide by four feet long. He used it to ward off the blows of the enemy and also to hide behind when the enemy archers would let go a volley of arrows. The Romans could kneel down on the ground and erect a wall of shields around them to block out the flaming missiles.

Satan is always firing his hot darts at us; he is always trying to get inside of us with guilt or with some accusation. If you have the shield of *faith* protecting you, that simple, implicit faith in the fact that Christ is more than able to meet your needs, you have adequate protection right there.

Helmet

"And take the helmet of salvation . . ." (Ephesians 6:17).

The helmet, of course, protected the head, another area which needed to be guarded from a fatal blow. This was a vital piece in the Roman armor, just as it is in ours.

Satan loves to pervert the Word of God. This is what he did with Jesus. When Jesus was tempted in the wilderness, He repeated to Satan, "It is written" and "It is said." In the last temptation that Satan fired at Jesus, he quoted the Word to Jesus. Satan knows the Bible by heart; the Word is no stranger to him. If he finds a Christian who is standing on the Word, he will try to distort it. That is when we need the helmet of *salvation*.

I have met too many people who are virtually on the brink of mental illness because they think they have lost their salvation—that eternal life is no longer theirs. They believe they have committed some terrible sin, and the enemy comes in and says, "You have committed the unpardonable sin." Or, "You've committed some sin that God won't forgive you for this time." Back on the old guilt trip!

The helmet of salvation is knowing that your salvation is absolutely secure and complete. Once you believe in Jesus Christ you are forgiven for your sins—past, present, and future. Once you have believed in Him you can never be taken out of His family. "And I give eternal life to them; and they shall never perish, and no one shall snatch them out of My hand. My Father, who has given them to Me, is greater than all; and no one is able to snatch them out of the Father's hand. I and the Father are one (essence)" (John 10:28-30).

However, Satan will take some obscure verse and try to undo all of the clear teaching in the rest of the Bible and have you thinking you have lost your salvation. He will take some of these verses and twist them to undo the teaching of the entire Book of Romans which clearly declares that salvation is a once-and-for-all matter through faith alone.

Salvation does not depend upon performance; it never has and never will. It depends upon what Christ did for us. If you do not have that helmet or assurance of salvation, you cannot have a vitally strong faith.

Sword

"And the sword of the Spirit, which is the word of God" (Ephesians 6:17).

The sword is an offensive weapon; the Roman sword was the atomic bomb of ancient warfare. It had a blade about twenty-four inches long which was sharp on both edges and pointed on the end.

The design of this sword was important. A trained legionnaire could thrust and cut from any position so that he was never caught off balance. Opposing soldiers with larger swords had to get into a certain position to swing. The Roman soldier would duck, catch his opponent off balance, and finish him off before he could crawl back for another swing.

The Word of God is like that. It is "living and active, and sharper than any two-edged sword . . ." (Hebrews 4:12).

When we are trusting the Holy Spirit to teach us the Bible and help us use it against Satan's temptations, we are never out of position or knocked off balance by the attacks of Satan.

When Satan tempted Jesus (Luke 4), Jesus quoted verses of Scripture to him that expressed God's viewpoint regarding each temptation. There is no greater example from whom we can learn than Jesus, is there? This is why whenever I sense I am being attacked by Satan I begin to quote *out loud* verses of Scripture addressed to him.

I'll never forget the thrill of the first time I tried this. I had been plagued with a certain temptation for hours. Nothing made it subside. I had claimed promises, depended on the Holy Spirit, prayed and asked the Lord to take it away—nothing worked.

Then I recalled what Jesus had done in His hour of trial, so I found a verse of Scripture which directly expressed God's viewpoint about the temptation. Then, feeling a little silly, I said, "Satan, leave me alone, for it is written . . ." and I quoted the verse out loud. Pow! The temptation was gone—and so was Satan.

I believe this is how we are to "resist the Devil." When we do, God's promise is, "he (Satan) will flee from you" (James 4:7).

The believer needs a combat knowledge of the Word of God.

Prayer

"With all prayer and petition pray at all times in the Spirit, and with this in view, be on the alert with all perseverance and petition for all the saints" (Ephesians 6:18).

The sword of the Spirit and prayer are the Christian's offensive weapons. Once we have Satan on the run, we can keep him from a counterattack by using these weapons. But remember, God answers prayer because we believe Him, not because we bombard Him with profound and lengthy phrases.

Check List

In view of the deluge of Satan's attacks today, we need to check out our armor, keeping it polished and oiled at all times, ready for active duty. If our sword is getting rusty because we haven't been studying the Word, we'd better sharpen it. If our breastplate is slipping out of place because we are getting on the performance-kick, we'd better adjust it. If our helmet is off because we are not sure about our salvation, then we'd better get into the Word of God or go to someone who knows the Word and make sure it is in place.

We cannot afford to be tin soldiers: we do not dare play games with Satan. He is capturing men right and left, using all his arsenal of weapons to do it.

"For our struggle is not against flesh and blood, but against the rulers, against the powers, against the world-forces of this darkness, against the spiritual forces of wickedness in the heavenly places" (Ephesians 6:12).

Real spiritual beings are beginning to come out in the open to such an extent that people are willing to worship Satan, and he is still practicing his subtle ways on the people who do not believe he exists—in fact, he is having a field day with them!

Whistle a happy tune, if you wish, but be sure your armor is in place while you are whistling.

To the armory, troops!

14 ○ On a Note
of Triumph

DID YOU BEGIN this book with a feeling of apprehension? Was the subject matter intriguing but frightening?

The magnitude of forces arrayed against us may overwhelm some; the reality and power of Satan and his hordes, the steady pull of the flesh, and the subtle attractiveness of the world system could easily get our focus off Christ's super provisions for victory.

Nothing would delight Satan more!

Satan's strategy has always been to blind men's minds to the truth of God's forgiveness in Christ. When that doesn't succeed and a person is rescued from the kingdom of darkness and born into the kingdom of light, then Satan commands all of his efforts to keep the believer unaware of the miraculous provisions God has made for his daily victory.

Satan will use every clever and insidious device of the world and the flesh to focus attention on ourselves and our problems instead of on Christ.

Satan will magnify our natural human weaknesses in our own minds, causing us to feel inferior with God and with man. He will stir up our pride to make us think that we're not getting the recognition from other believers that we feel we deserve. He will let jealousy bring division between brothers in Christ. He loves to get Christians so off-balance on doctrinal issues that we forget to love and accept those real brothers who differ with us.

If we spend much time dwelling on our weaknesses and sins, it won't be long before we become discouraged and defeated.

Spiritual Myopia

God knew that this "spiritual myopia" would be our biggest problem. I think that's why Jesus went to all the trouble to give us a classic example of the folly of focusing on ourselves and our circumstances rather than on Him.

In Matthew 14:22-33 we read how Jesus deliberately sent his disciples out in their boats on the Sea of Galilee, even though He knew that a storm was coming. He knew that they had more confidence in their seamanship than they did in anything else because of their long years of being fishermen.

When the storm hit, it was more violent than anything they had experienced, and the disciples were terrified. For the first time in their lives they could not rely on their own abilities to handle a problem.

God will test His children in areas where they are most confident of their human ability in order to show them their complete need to depend upon Him.

When the disciples began to despair, Jesus came to them walking upon the water. Peter said boldly, "Lord, if it is really You, command me to come to You on the water." He had enough faith to believe that if Jesus commanded him to come to Him on the water, He would also enable him, somehow, to do it.

At this point Peter had no confidence in his own ability to walk on water, but he did have confidence in Jesus. He took what little faith he had and put it on the right object.

This is an important principle to remember. Christ will *empower* us to do whatever He *commands* us to do. "For it is God who is at work in you, both to will and to work for His good pleasure" (Philippians 2:13).

Peter gingerly stepped out of the boat onto the stormy sea. He was actually walking on the water and moving toward Jesus with his trusting eye fixed on Him and His ability to miraculously support him.

Everything was going fine until we read, ". . . but *seeing* the wind, he became afraid, and beginning to sink he cried out, saying, 'Lord, save me!'"

Peter's Lesson Learned

What happened? Peter was doing great until he did what you and I do frequently. He got his eyes onto the problem, in his case the stormy seas, and off of the Problem-Solver, Jesus. When he did, down he went.

Praise the Lord for His faithfulness in spite of our lack of it. He caught Peter just before he went under; just in time for him to have learned his lesson, but not be overwhelmed by it.

Peter isn't the only one this lesson was designed for. As you and I walk through our particular storms, we must keep our eye of faith focused on Jesus and His ability to handle us in the midst of the storm.

What is your "storm" right now? Are you out of a job and getting desperate financially? As the bills pile up, do your spirits go down? You're no fool. You know you've got to have food and a roof. And there's Satan, always around to take advantage of the situation, saying, "Look at the condition things are in. Can't you see what a failure you are in providing for your family? Where do you think the money is coming from to get you out of this mess?" On and on he accuses, with the purpose of taking your eyes off your loving, powerful, all-providing Heavenly Father and onto yourself and your problems.

Remember what happened to Peter when he did that? The same thing will happen to us unless we sink our teeth into His promises to meet our needs.

"And my God shall supply all your needs according to His riches in glory in Christ Jesus" (Philippians 4:19).

"Behold, I am the Lord, the God of all flesh; is anything too difficult for Me?" (Jeremiah 32:27).

If we take our eye of trust off Christ and put our focus onto the problems, even with the good intention of trying to deal with them ourselves, we will begin to sink into despair and defeat.

Faith, the Key

You may be saying to yourself, "That sounds great, Hal—now all I need is enough faith to believe it would work for me."

You're right! Faith is really the key to appropriating everything the Lord has already provided for us. For this reason, Satan will try to confuse us about what faith is and how it works.

When we begin to learn about all our spiritual assets and armor with which to live for God, Satan will come in and whisper what you were just thinking: "All of God's provisions are wonderful! Wouldn't it be great if I just had enough faith to use them!"

How Much Is Enough?

Once Satan gets us thinking about faith in a quantitative way, we're sunk. To say, "I wish I had more faith" is to reflect a basic misconception of what faith is.

Faith is responsibility: *my response to God's ability*. It's just that simple!

In biblical faith, it's the *object* of faith that gives it its power. Jesus said that if we have as little as a mustard seed of faith, if it's placed in Him, we can move mountains. There is *no* power in faith. The power is in Jesus.

Faith is similar to eyesight. There must be an object in order for sight to occur. Faith must have an object in order for power to occur, and that object is Christ and what He provided for us at the Cross.

It's so sad to hear Christians begging God for more faith. Every believer already has 20/20 faith. To be sure, some see God more clearly than others, but that is because some have moved closer to Him, the object of their faith.

If you're standing a hundred miles away from a mountain, it will be obscure and indistinct to you. You may know a lot of facts about that mountain, but it will never grow in size until you move closer to it.

We just can't respond to God's great ability to meet our needs until we get to know Him in a closer way and find out about all the provisions He's made for His children to live in this world today.

The Leap of Faith

Suppose you are on the fifth floor of a burning building. There is no way to escape, and you are trapped out on a ledge. You can't see the ground because of the smoke, but suddenly you hear a voice cry out, "Jump, we have a net ready to catch you!"

Fear grips your heart. You find yourself thinking of all the sadistic people in the world; it might be some splatter-happy lunatic down below hollering at you. You don't have any confidence in that person because you don't know anything about him.

Suddenly you hear another voice. This one is familiar to you. It calls, "Son, it's Dad. Jump, there's a net down here." On the strength of your confidence in your dad and your knowledge of his love for you, you commit yourself to him and jump. And what do you find as you fall through the darkness? "Underneath are the everlasting arms" (Deuteronomy 33:27).

Keep Your Eyes on Christ

Have you ever had anyone tell you that all you need to do is just look to Jesus when you have a problem and that will solve it? I remember the first time someone told me that. I was having a problem in my life, so I tried to conjure up a mental image of Jesus in my mind, picturing my favorite painting of Him. I just kept thinking about this picture. You know, that didn't seem to help me at all with my problem.

I decided right then that there must be something else I was supposed to focus on about Jesus other than His physical image. I'm glad that situation happened to me because it forced me to sit down and think through just what it is that I'm supposed to look at when I focus on Jesus.

First, I must see that God loves me unconditionally. Second, I must believe that God's forgiveness of my sins covers *all* of them, past, present, and future, and He is not holding any of them against me. Third, I must realize that God has a plan for my life and He will take everything that happens to me, whether seemingly good or evil, and work it all together for my good (Romans 8:28). And last, I must see that God is utterly faithful and able to keep every promise He has made to me in the Bible.

Triumph in Trials

When you know and count upon these facts, then you can properly relate to the trials that God permits to come into your life. You can see that they are all planned as a means of blessing, not cursing, in your life. When a trial hits, you can say, "I know that God loves me so much that He could not allow one thing to touch my life that is not consistent with that great love."

Because you have come to know that God judged Christ for all your sins, you know that this testing is not to get even with you for some secret sin or to punish you for any reason. God has already punished Christ for all your sins.

Whenever a trial or a real tragedy should enter your life, if you know that God has an overall plan and He is fitting this situation into a pattern of good for you, then you can praise Him for the trial. You may not see one ounce of good in the difficulty itself, and there may be none, but God has unalterably committed Himself to work it into the greatest possible blessing in your life. For it not to have happened to you would have cheated you of a rare privilege of God's special blessing.

Is Your God Too Small?

As we grow in our understanding of all these marvelous provisions God has made for our needs, we begin to see God as being bigger than our problems. If the difficulties in our lives still seem too much for God to handle, then our God is too small for us.

Once we see that the issue is not how much faith we have, but rather how faithful, trustworthy, and powerful Jesus is, then we are ready for the major leagues in the Christian life. When we take whatever faith we have at the moment, whether little or great, and put it in the Lord Jesus Christ, it releases His power to work through us and in our behalf.

If God's provisions for me were always just a little bit beyond the grasp of my faith, what good would all these spiritual assets be to me? How could I ever grow? It would be like dangling a carrot in front of a donkey to make him move. It might result in some semblance of progress, but at the expense of utter frustration.

Far from God's rich blessings always being just beyond our faith, the
Scripture says, "Blessed be the God and Father of our Lord Jesus Christ,
who *has blessed us* with every spiritual blessing in the heavenly places in
Christ . . ." (Ephesians 1:3). Victory over the flesh, the world, and the Devil
is ours—*now*.

Power Versus Authority

Much has been said in this book about the *power* that works within the
believer through the Holy Spirit. But until now, nothing has really been set
forth about the *authority* that is available to us. In fact, little seems to be
said anywhere in the Christian world about this critical truth. Yet when it
comes to dealing with attacks from demons and Satan, no other spiritual
asset is more important to understand and appropriate.

You may be saying, "What's the difference between power and authority in the Christian life?"

There is a great deal of difference. In the Greek of the New Testament
two words are consistently used for the two concepts. The word "dunamis"
is used to describe the power of the Holy Spirit which operates within the
Christian. The word "exousia" is used to describe authority. Unfortunately
the translators are not always consistent in translating "exousia" into the
English word, authority.

"Exousia," or authority, means delegated power.

Dr. F. Huegel, a great Christian theologian and friend, told me a story
that illustrates the difference in these two concepts. We were sitting near
the great boulevard of Mexico City, the Avenue Reforma, and discussing the believer's authority over the demonic world when he related this
story.

He told of a group of young Mexican boy scouts who were trying to cross
the Avenue Reforma during the wild rush-hour traffic. They made it half-
way across the broad street and took refuge on the esplanade in the street's
center. At the corner of the esplanade there was a special pedestal where
the traffic officer stood to direct traffic. The boys watched as the traffic officer
would raise his right arm and all the powerful speeding automobiles would
screech to a halt.

In Mexico City that pedestal is a place of authority, and all the motorists
know it.

About this time a slight accident occurred nearby and the officer left his
place to investigate. While the officer was arguing with the motorists, one

of the boy scouts stepped up on the pedestal and raised his right hand. Instantly cars began to grind to a halt. You see, the motorists recognized that the boy was standing in the place of authority and that all the power of the Mexican government backed up the one who stood upon the pedestal.

Suppose the boy had tried to physically stop one of those powerful automobiles. That would have been a case of pitting his power against the car's power, and you can guess who would be the loser. This is what happens when we try to deal with the Devil in our own power. We get steam-rolled!

But the motorists had to stop, even when a small boy stood in the place of authority because all of the power of the government of Mexico was invoked with just the wave of his right hand.

The same principle applies to us when we realize our place of authority and step into it. Only in our case, all of the power of God is behind us, and even Satan has to respect that and back off.

To exercise authority is to operate in the realm of delegated power. The greatness of the authority is proportionate to the greatness of the power of the one who delegated it.

In the case of the believer's authority, there is the greatest power in the universe standing behind it, Jesus Christ Himself. He said, "All authority has been given to Me in heaven and on earth" (Matthew 28:18).

Christ's Authority

Most Christians have some vague concept of the power and authority that are Christ's, but most cannot put their finger on just how He got His authority or how it relates to them.

I can't think of another truth that has been more foundational to my whole understanding of God's working in my life than the truth of Christ's victorious defeat of Satan. It's impossible to appreciate your position of victory in Christ until you know how He won His victory over your three great enemies, the world, the flesh, and the Devil.

In numerous places in the New Testament Paul makes crystal clear God's plan for subjecting all hostile powers to Christ and those who believe in Him.

There are three words that summarize Christ's acquisition of authority for Himself and us: *crucified, resurrected,* and *ascended.*

If you understood no other concepts of the Bible than these three words, you would know enough to live a victorious Christian life daily.

Crucified

When Christ hung on the cross with our sins on Him, He was not only bearing our sin and its consequence of death, but we were actually hanging there on the cross with Him. This complete union with Christ is the incredible truth Paul wants us to fathom in the sixth chapter of Romans.

When God poured out His unleashed wrath and judgment upon our sins, He not only judged *Christ* with the guilt of our sins, but He judged us too. When Christ experienced the final sting of sin, *death*, we died too.

I have often imagined the hysterical joy that must have swept across hell as news of the death of the Son of God was spread. Not realizing that Christ's death was the final nail in his coffin, Satan mistakenly cheered His crucifixion.

You see, many times in Jesus' life Satan tried to get Jesus to sin so He would be vulnerable to sin's consequence, death. When he saw Jesus assume the sins of mankind and then voluntarily die because of those sins, Satan thought he had finally won in his conflict with God. He had cleverly gotten God's first perfect man, Adam, to sin and now God's second "Adam," Jesus Christ, the Perfect One, was also bearing sin and death.

There must have been a wild celebration among Satan and his demon hordes for those three days and nights—a real lost weekend. But then a sobering and deadly hush fell over Satan's forces as these astonished beings observed the greatest display of power ever unleashed from the hand of Almighty God.

The Son of God was resurrected from the dead!

And so were we!

Resurrection Power

"O death, where is thy sting? O grave, where is thy victory?" (1 Corinthians 15:55, KJV).

The defeat of Satan was sealed! With the resurrection of Jesus, Satan forever lost his authority over the humanity of Jesus and over everyone who claims union with Him.

Just picture the chagrin that Satan must have had before his rebel followers. Far from being the victor, he became the vanquished; he and his hordes were the captives in the victory train of the triumphant Jesus.

Paul tells us that "He (Christ) had disarmed the *rulers* and *authorities*, He made a public display of them, having triumphed over them through Him" (Colossians 2:15).

When Jesus stripped Satan and his demons of their authority, that victory was ours. In Satan's mind, not only is Jesus his conqueror, but so are those who are *in* Christ.

Satan knows that he has no legal right to any ground in the life of a believer, but if he can keep us from finding out this truth, he will have a field day in our lives.

We are told that Jesus "disarmed" those hostile powers. That's just exactly what it means. Satan is like a toothless bulldog. He can growl and intimidate, but he has no authority to back up his threats in the life of a believer. If we don't know this or believe it, though, we will allow him to intimidate us, and he is a master at that. He loves to get Christians to cower or run from him in fear.

Many people think that God and Satan are opposites, but equal in power and authority. Nothing could be farther from the truth. Satan is a vanquished enemy. But he is alive and well and a master of bluff, threat, intimidation, accusation, and temptation.

The believer who does not know and count upon his complete identification with Christ in His crucifixion and resurrection is a prime target for these clever attacks of Satan.

Ascended With Christ

I said that there are three words that comprise Christ's position of authority over Satan. We've briefly seen what Jesus' crucifixion and resurrection have done to the hosts of hell.

The culmination of God's whole redemptive plan was to place Christ on the throne at His right hand, forever putting Christ's enemies under His feet. Any enemy of Christ's is an enemy of ours, and anyone put under Christ's feet is put under ours also because "we are members of His body" (Ephesians 5:30).

Because of my total identification with Christ in the mind of God, whatever is true of Christ is true of me.

Christ is now seated on His throne in heaven at the right hand of God, the center of the greatest power and authority in the whole universe. And we are seated there with Him. He has delegated to us the use of the same authority He has and the power to use it over our mutual enemies while we are here on earth.

Isn't that fantastic? God has so completely dealt with me, the sinner, and my sins that He has *already* seated me in the heavenlies with Christ. I may be standing in the state of California right now, but I am also seated in the heavenlies. I don't have to wait until I die and go to heaven before this becomes true of me.

Claiming Our Legal Rights

These truths that I have set forth here are the "legal" rights of every child of God. These legal facts were forever settled in the "Divine Courtroom of the Godhead" in ages past. Nothing can annul them, and the only thing that can keep a believer from exercising his power and authority in Christ is his ignorance of these truths or his refusal to believe them.

In Ephesians 1:18-23 and 2:4-7 Paul earnestly pleads with us to see what our tremendous inheritance is as a child of God. God isn't offering us "pie in the sky, by and by" either. Every tense of every verb that Paul uses emphasizes our divine position *now*.

"I pray that the eyes of your heart may be enlightened, so that you may know what is the hope of His calling, what are the riches of the glory of His inheritance in the saints, and what is the surpassing greatness of His power toward us who believe. These are in accordance with the working of the strength of His might which He brought about in Christ, when He raised Him from the dead, and seated Him at His right hand in the heavenly places, far above all *rule* and *authority* and *power* and *dominion* (these refer to Satan's powers), and every name that is named, not only in this age, but also in the one to come. And He put all things in subjection under His feet, and gave Him as head over all things to the church, which is His body. . . .

"But God, being rich in mercy, because of His great love with which He loved us, even when we were dead in our transgressions, made us alive together with Christ (by grace you have been saved), and raised us up with Him, and seated us with Him in the heavenly places, in Christ Jesus, in order that in the ages to come He might show the surpassing riches of His grace in kindness toward us in Christ Jesus."

The Wonderful Name of Jesus

"Therefore also God highly exalted Him, and bestowed on Him the name which is above every name, that at the name of Jesus every knee should bow, of those who are in heaven, and on earth, and under the earth, and that every tongue should confess that Jesus Christ is Lord, to the glory of God the Father" (Philippians 2:9-11).

There is more power in the name "Jesus" than in any other word ever uttered from the lips of God or man.

When we use His name in prayer, God the Father knows all that that name encompasses and the riches it has made available to the one who uses it in faith.

When we declare that wonderful name in telling the good news of salvation to people today, and when they come to believe what that name has done for them, they are turned from darkness to light.

But there is a realm of spiritual existence that is more aware of the power in that name than any other sphere, and that is Satan's domain.

When a believer, knowing he is seated in the position of authority in Christ in the heavenlies, uses that name on Satan or demons, they *must* back off. They are terrified of His name because it represents to them their humiliating defeat at Jesus' resurrection.

A Word to the Wise

Using Jesus' name also reminds the believer that the conquest of Satan was Christ's victory; we are only conquerors *because of Him*. If we dare to step out from behind the cross of Christ and try to battle Satan in our own strength, we've had it.

I've seen zealous believers get hold of this new authority in Christ and go along great for awhile. Then they begin to get heady with power, and before long they are ordering Satan around and naively dismissing demons from Christians' lives. Satan will "roll over and play dead" the first few times we try this just to get us overwhelmed with *our* great new power. But he'll lay in wait for us, and once we've become convinced that *we're* his conquerors, it's just a matter of time before we're flat on our backs looking up and wondering what hit us.

Jesus is the victor, and as we abide in Him and draw upon *His* power and count upon *His* victory, He delegates it to us. If we dare to draw upon our own power and authority, we'll be no match for Satan.

The only place of safety is the heavenly throne itself. It is located "far above" the enemy camp, and as long as we are mentally abiding there, we can't be touched.

Satan will employ every possible trick to get us to step down from the heavenlies and deal with him ourselves. But if we are walking in the Spirit, our normal daily lives will be lived with the awareness that we are seated with Christ in His position of authority and power.

Alive and Well

The world is groaning with its problems. Hearts are crying with their needs. How can anyone bear to live today without Christ?

If you know Him, does your very being ache for those who do not? If you know Him, are you living on a note of triumph?

Each morning as we awaken to the new day which God has given to us, we need to put on our armor and take our seat with Christ. We need to remind ourselves that we have victory over the world, the flesh, and the Devil through the work of Christ on our behalf. Personally, I reaffirm my life commitment to Jesus and authorize the Holy Spirit to control me moment by moment.

As the day progresses and the world begins to press in, if I blow it spiritually I talk it over with my understanding Heavenly Father, admitting freely what I've done. He then reassures me of His love and acceptance of me. If I've harmed someone else, I seek to set it right with them.

One of the greatest blessings I've continually experienced is to allow Jesus to carry my burden of "self-condemnation" and guilt. This truth alone has done more to free me from Satan's grasp than any other concept God has taught me.

What a time for *us* to be alive! We can see the "rulers, the powers, the world-forces of this darkness" engulfing Planet Earth, but we can have Christ's authority, Christ's power to bring about victory.

Tell it to the world!

May God use these liberating truths to bring new freedom to your life, new hope for the future. Remember our victory cry which Jesus shouted from the cross—"It is finished!"

Tetelestai!

BAPTISM OF THE HOLY SPIRIT

Appendix (To Chapter 13)

WE HEAR MANY believers talking about the "baptism of the Spirit," and its proponents make many claims for it. Some are seeking to show, mostly from the Book of Acts, that this experience ushers a Christian into a dynamic, power-packed life. Some say it is the actual point at which the Holy Spirit indwells one who is already a believer.

Most adherents, however, believe that this is a crisis point in a Christian's life when he initially comes into contact with the Spirit's filling power. In fact, they often use the phrase "filling of the Spirit" and "baptism of the Spirit" interchangeably. The charismatic and Pentecostal brethren believe this "baptism" will be evidenced by speaking in tongues.

The question we must raise is: was the baptism of the Spirit the means designed by God to give power to impotent believers?

Without emotional bias, let's look at what the Word teaches on this subject. I'm going to limit myself to two aspects of this question: what the baptism of the Spirit is and the transitional nature of the Book of Acts.

The baptism of the Spirit is defined in only one place in the Word, First Corinthians 12:13. "For by one Spirit we were all baptized into one body, whether Jews or Greeks, whether slaves or free, and we were all made to drink of one Spirit."

The word "baptism" is from the Greek word "baptizo," and it means *to totally identify one thing with another*. When a person is baptized in water, it is a public testimony of his faith that he was taken by the Holy Spirit at salvation and joined into living union with Jesus. This identifies him with Christ in His death, burial, and resurrection (Romans 6).

In the baptism of the Spirit, each believer, at the moment of his conversion, is totally identified with Christ in His death, burial, and resurrection and with that one body which is Christ's body here on earth, of which He is the head (1 Corinthians 12). The ritual of water baptism is a symbol of the inner baptism of the Spirit which has already taken place at the moment the person was born again.

The Transitional Nature of Acts

The Book of Acts is a book which shows us the transitional problems of believers who were living under the law of Moses. With the giving of the Holy Spirit they were taken from under that law and placed under grace.

The first Jewish believers had been raised under the Mosaic system of worship and teaching. In that teaching the Holy Spirit only came upon certain people for special ministries. Before the Cross, not all believers had the Holy Spirit dwelling in them. Also, they had no teachings of a union with each other and with God that would make them into one body. This was the mystery, hidden from the world, which Paul revealed in Ephesians 3. This was part of the New Covenant which Christ was instituting.

In the Book of Acts an unusual situation is present. Hundreds of Jesus' followers and believers were not even aware that He was going to change their way of relating to God by joining them into union with His own body. This He was going to do by baptizing and indwelling *each* believer with the Holy Spirit.

God first revealed this new truth on the day of Pentecost when the Holy Spirit was poured out on the 120 Jewish believers who were present in the upper room in Jerusalem (Acts 2). After this initial giving of the Spirit to the Jewish nation, whenever a Jew believed in Christ, he simultaneously received the Holy Spirit and was baptized by Him into living union with the body of Christ.

In Acts 8, the half-Jew, half-Gentile Samaritan believers were introduced into this new indwelling and empowering ministry of the Holy Spirit. They were brought into union with the Jewish believers through their new union with Christ. After that, whenever Samaritans became believers, they were baptized with the Holy Spirit at the same time.

In Acts 10 the Roman centurion, Cornelius, and his friends were Gentiles who experienced the initiation into the body of Christ, the Church. The Jewish believers who were present were astonished to realize that this new relationship to the Holy Spirit was the privilege of Gentile believers, too.

In Acts 19 there was a group of devout believers who had been converted through John the Baptist's ministry. Although they were already true believers in all that he had taught them about Jesus, they hadn't heard that there was a Holy Spirit. When Paul got to Ephesus, he asked them, "Did you receive the Holy Spirit *when* you believed?" If they said "yes," then he would have known that they had become believers *since* Pentecost (all new believers received the Holy Spirit simultaneously with conversion after the transition took place at Pentecost—Acts 2, 8, 10).

When he found out that they did not have the Holy Spirit yet, but had been true believers before Pentecost, then he knew they were in need of an initial giving of the Holy Spirit. So Paul laid hands on them and they received the Holy Spirit the same as the 120 *Jews* in Acts 2, the *Samaritans* in Acts 8, and the *Gentiles* in Acts 10.

All the different ethnic groups of believers were now initiated into the New Testament way of relating to God through His indwelling Spirit and through union with Him. From that point on, all believers have been baptized with the Spirit *at the moment of their conversion*. This is the pattern set forth in the Epistles. They assume the *transition* as complete.

Union With Christ

The clear teaching of the Word is that the baptism of the Spirit is that ministry whereby a new believer is joined into a living union with Christ and His body, the Church, here on earth.

This happens to every person the moment he believes in Christ for personal salvation. You don't need to ask for it or seek it; it is done *to* you by the Holy Spirit as a part of salvation.

It does not need to be evidenced by speaking in tongues because there is no biblical or historical evidence that tongues were the *required* manifestation of this baptism.

I believe that confusion has arisen regarding this term "baptism of the Spirit" because in the Book of Acts each time a group was initially introduced into the new relationship with the Holy Spirit there was a manifestation of new power, and in several, *but not all*, cases they spoke in tongues.

However, we cannot use the pattern of the baptism of the Spirit in the Book of Acts as the pattern for our relating to the Holy Spirit today unless we understand the fact that the whole book is dealing with a transition from the Old Covenant to the New Covenant, from law to grace.

It is in the epistles of the New Testament that we find our pattern for relating to the Holy Spirit today. Over and over again we are given the imperative of being *filled* with the Spirit, of *walking* in the Spirit, and of walking by *faith*. We are NEVER told to be baptized with the Spirit because Paul knew that all true believers had already been baptized by the Spirit at the moment of their conversion.

Let me say it again. The *filling* of the Spirit is the means God has given for living the Christian life with power. It isn't optional. It is a command.

"And do not get drunk with wine, for that is dissipation, *but be filled with the Spirit*" (Ephesians 5:18).

I know that the people who urge others to be baptized with the Spirit are sincerely seeking to meet a legitimate need for power in the church today. The church has become weakened through the centuries, and there is a great need for revitalization.

However, we must be doctrinally correct in what we teach. Many Christians who are desperately in need of the Spirit's power won't buy the *message* intended by the term "baptism of the Spirit" because they know that term is a misapplication of a valid biblical doctrine.

Unfortunately, the whole concept of being filled with the Spirit has been brought into disrepute and confusion for some because of those who have applied excessive and unscriptural claims to what they term the "baptism of the Spirit." This has closed the minds of many who critically need to be *filled* with the Spirit and experience what it is to walk in Him moment by moment.

There is only one person who wins in this kind of confusion—Satan!

NOTES

CHAPTER 1

1. Arthur Lyons, *The Second Coming: Satanism in America* (New York: Dodd, Mead & Co., 1970).

2. Robert Somerlott, *Here, Mr. Splitfoot* (New York: Viking Press, 1971).

3. Lyons, *The Second Coming*.

4. *Santa Monica Evening Outlook*, 24 June 1971.

5. *Life*, 11 November 1964.

6. *Los Angeles Times*, 7 March 1971.

7. *Commonweal*, 6 November 1970.

8. *Los Angeles Times*, 7 March 1971.

9. *Los Angeles Times*, 21 April 1972.

10. *Los Angeles Times*, 28 January 1972.

11. Somerlott, *Splitfoot*.

12. *Life*, 9 January 1970.

13. *Los Angeles Times*, 4 May 1970.

14. *Los Angeles Times*, 5 May 1970.

15. *Los Angeles Times*, 10 May 1970.

16. *Life*, 11 November 1964.

17. *Ibid*.

18. *New York Times*, 1 June 1969.

19. *Los Angeles Times*, 22 March 1971.

20. *Time*, 19 June 1972.

CHAPTER 2

1. *Los Angeles Times*, 18 April 1972.

2. Merrill Unger, *The Haunting of Bishop Pike* (Wheaton, Ill.: Tyndale House, 1968).

3. *Chicago Tribune*, 17 April 1972.

4. *Saturday Review of Literature*, 7 February 1970.

5. *Los Angeles Times*, 8 November 1970.

6. Eden Gray, *The Tarot Revealed* (New York: Crown Publishers, Inc., 1970).

7. Eden Gray, *A Complete Guide to the Tarot* (New York: Crown Publishers, Inc., 1970).

8. *Los Angeles Times*, 31 October 1971.

9. *Los Angeles Times*, 25 April 1972.

10. *Life*, 9 January 1970.

11. *Los Angeles Times*, 31 October 1971.

12. McCandlish Phillips, *The Bible, The Supernatural and The Jews* (New York: World Publishing Co., 1970).

13. Advanced Organization of Los Angeles, *Advance*, Issue 4, Volume 1.

14. The Church of Scientology of California, *The Auditor*, No. 61.

15. *Ibid.*

16. *Life*, 15 November 1969.

17. *Ibid.*

18. *West*, supplement of *Los Angeles Times*, 25 April 1971.

19. Raphael Gasson, *The Challenging Counterfeit* (Plainfield, N.J.: Logos International, 1966).

20. Ostrander and Schroeder, *Psychic Discoveries Behind the Iron Curtain* (Englewood Cliffs, N.J.: Prentice-Hall, 1971).

21. *Ibid.*

22. *Today's Health*, November 1970.

CHAPTER 3

1. Merrill F. Unger, *Introductory Guide to the Old Testament* (Grand Rapids, Mich.: Zondervan Publishing House, 1956).

2. *New York Times Magazine*, 1 June 1969.

3. Hal Lindsey with C. C. Carlson, *The Late Great Planet Earth* (Grand Rapids, Mich.: Zondervan Publishing House, 1970).

CHAPTER 4

1. Donald Barnhouse, *The Invisible War* (Grand Rapids, Mich.: Zondervan Publishing House, 1965).

2. *Ibid.*

CHAPTER 5

1. Albert C. Wedemeyer, *Wedemeyer Reports* (Henry Holt and Co., 1958).

2. William Arndt and F. Wilbur Gingrich, *A Greek-English Lexicon of the New Testament* (Chicago: University of Chicago Press, 1959).

3. Barnhouse, *The Invisible War*.

4. Francis Schaeffer, *The God Who Is There* (Chicago: Inter-Varsity Press, 1968).

CHAPTER 6

1. *Los Angeles Times*, 8 November 1971.

2. Maurice Merleau-Ponty, *The Structure of Behavior* (Boston: Beacon Press, 1963).

3. *Lincoln Library* (The Frontier Press Co., 1970).

4. Soren Kierkegaard, *Fear and Trembling* (1843).

5. Cleon Skousen, *The Naked Communist* (Salt Lake City, Utah: Ensign Publishing Co., 1961).

6. J. Edgar Hoover, *Masters of Deceit* (New York: Holt, Rinehart and Winston, Inc., 1958).

7. *Lincoln Library*.

8. Desmond Morris, *The Naked Ape* (New York: McGraw-Hill, 1969).

9. Dr. A. A. Brill, *The Basic Writings of Sigmund Freud* (New York: Random House, 1938).

10. Franz Alexander, *Fundamentals of Psychoanalysis* (New York: W. W. Norton & Co., 1948).

11. Sigmund Freud, *A General Introduction to Psychoanalysis* (Garden City, N.Y.: Garden City Publishing Co., 1943).

12. Boris Sokoloff, *The Permissive Society* (New Rochelle, N.Y.: Arlington House, 1971).

13. *Ibid*.

14. *Time*, 24 April 1972.

15. *U.S. News and World Report*, 24 April 1972.

16. *Ibid*.

17. James Kilpatrick, *Los Angeles Times*, 21 April 1972.

18. William L. Shirer, *The Rise and Fall of the Third Reich* (New York: Simon and Schuster, 1960).

19. *Ibid*.

CHAPTER 7

1. *Time*, 30 September 1971.

2. *Ibid*.

3. Prof. Dennis L. Meadows, *A Report for the Club of Rome Project on the Predicament of Mankind* (New York: Universe Books, 1972).

4. Sokoloff, *The Permissive Society*.

5. Lewis Alesen, *Mental Robots* (Carton Printers, Ltd., 1957).

6. *International Socialist Review*, Winter, 1960.

7. Erich Fromm, from the foreword to A. S. Neill's *Summerhill* (New York: Hart Publishing Co., 1960).

8. *Ibid.*

9. *Ibid.*

10. Bertrand Russell, *New Hopes for a Changing World* (New York: Simon and Schuster, 1951).

11. H. G. Wells, *The New World Order* (New York: Alfred Knopf, 1940).

12. D. Talbot Rice, *Teach Yourself to Study Art* (London: The English Universities, Ltd.).

13. Calvin Tomkins, *The Bride and the Bachelors* (New York: Viking Press, 1965) .

14. H. R. Rookmaaker, *Modern Art and the Death of Culture* (London: Intervarsity Press, 1970).

15. *Los Angeles Times*, 7 January 1972.

16. *Time*, 20 September 1971.

17. *Santa Ana Register*, 27 March 1968.

18. *U.S. News and World Report*, 22 May 1967.

19. *U.S. News and World Report*, 3 February 1969.

20. H. G. Wells, *New World Order.*

CHAPTER 8

1. Jeane Dixon, *The Call to Glory* (New York: William Morrow & Company, 1972), p. 42.

2. *Ibid.*, p. 43.

3. *Ibid.*, p. 175.

4. *Ibid.*, p. 24.

5. *Ibid.*, p. 23.

6. Jeane Dixon, *My Life and Prophecies* (New York: William Morrow & Company, 1969), p. 10.

7. *Ibid.*, p. 54.

8. *Ibid.*, p. 62.

9. Kurt Koch, *Between Christ and Satan* (Grand Rapids, Mich.: Kregel Publications, 1970).

10. Dixon, *My Life and Prophecies*, p. 26.

CHAPTER 9

1. Delphine Lyons, *Everyday Witchcraft* (New York: Dell Publishing Co., 1972).

2. Koch, *Between Christ and Satan.*

3. Jesse Penn Lewis, *War on the Saints* (Bournemouth, England: The Overcomer Book Room, 1912).

CHAPTER 10

1. Merrill F. Unger, *Demons in the World Today* (Wheaton, Ill.: Tyndale House, 1971).
2. *Ibid.*
3. *Ibid.*
4. *Ibid.*
5. Jesse Penn Lewis, *War on the Saints.*

CHAPTER 11

1. *Los Angeles Times,* 14 April 1972.
2. *Ibid.*

CHAPTER 14

References: 1 Corinthians 12:13; Romans 6; Colossians 3:1-15; Ephesians 1:15; 2:10; 3:14-21; Galatians 2:20; 3:26-27.